Human Resource Practice

7th edition

Malcolm Martin and Fiona Whiting

The Chartered Institute of Personnel and Development is the leading publisher of books and reports for personnel and training professionals, students, and all those concerned with the effective management and development of people at work. For details of all our titles, please contact the publishing department:

tel: 020 8612 6204

email: publish@cipd.co.uk

The catalogue of all CIPD titles can be viewed on the CIPD website:

www.cipd.co.uk/bookstore

An e-book version is also available for purchase from:

www.ebooks.cipd.co.uk

Human Resource Practice

7th edition

Malcolm Martin and Fiona Whiting

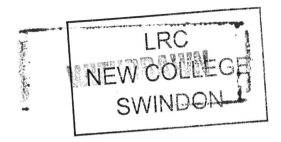

Chartered Institute of Personnel and Development

2014004025

Published by the Chartered Institute of Personnel and Development
151 The Broadway, London SW19 1JQ

This edition first published 2016

Designed and typeset by Exeter Premedia Services, India
Printed in Great Britain by Ashford Colour Press Ltd, Gosport, Hampshire

British Library Cataloguing in Publication Data
A catalogue of this publication is available from the British Library

ISBN 9781843984061
eBook ISBN 9781843984481

Chartered Institute of Personnel and Development

151 The Broadway, London SW19 1JQ
Tel: 020 8612 6200
Email: cipd@cipd.co.uk
Website: www.cipd.co.uk
Incorporated by Royal Charter.
Registered Charity No. 1079797

Shelfie

A **bundled** eBook edition is available with the purchase of this print book.

CLEARLY PRINT YOUR NAME ABOVE IN UPPER CASE
Instructions to claim your eBook edition:
1. Download the Shelfie app for Android or iOS
2. Write your name in **UPPER CASE** above
3. Use the Shelfie app to submit a photo
4. Download your eBook to any device

Contents

List of figures and tables

Authors' biographies

Malcolm Martin, BSc, MCMI, Chartered FCIPD, has been involved in the design and delivery of Certificate in Personnel Practice programmes for over ten years, primarily at the training provider MOL. His experience covers a range of sectors from care, education and manufacturing, to polymers, chemicals and steel. He has held middle management positions in industrial relations, project management and HR. Malcolm is also managing director of Employer Solutions Ltd, specialising in the preparation of employee handbooks for small and medium-sized organisations and delivering training and consultancy services in employment practices. He lives in Lancaster.

Fiona Whiting, LLB, MSc, Chartered FCIPD, is a freelance HR and organisational development consultant. She has over 20 years' experience as a generalist HR practitioner, including a number of HR executive board-level posts, working predominantly in the NHS. She also has experience of working with local authorities and academic institutions and with a variety of private and third-sector organisations, including social enterprises, community interest companies, charities and organisations working in the recruitment, new technology, retail, media and utility services fields. Fiona is co-founder and director of The People Effect Ltd.

Acknowledgements

We recognise that directly or indirectly those with whom we work, and have worked, help create such practical knowledge and skill as we have. Preparation of the revised material in this seventh edition has been greatly helped by comments, informed suggestions and contributions from students, delegates, business clients, tutors, associates and publisher. These have been invaluable in providing insights into current trends and organisational procedures and practices. We would like to thank them all for their assistance.

Finally, Malcolm and Fiona would like to thank their respective partners, Christina and Derek, for their continuing understanding and support during the preparation of this seventh edition of the book.

Walkthrough of textbook features and online resources

LEARNING OUTCOMES

At the beginning of each chapter a bulleted set of key learning outcomes summarises what you expect to learn from the chapter, helping you to track your progress.

CASE STUDY 3.1

A 2012 study of science faculties in higher education institutions in the US (Moss-Racusin et al 2012) asked staff to review a number of job applications. The applications reviewed were identical, apart from the gender of the name of the applicant.

It was discovered that science faculties were more likely to:

- rate male candidates as better qualified than female candidates
- want to hire the male candidates rather than the female candidates

- give the male candidate a higher starting salary than the female candidate
- be willing to invest more in the development of the male candidate than the female candidate.

Here, unconscious bias impacts not only on the recruitment decision, but the salary of the individual and the amount of development that is invested in their ongoing progression.

CASE STUDIES

A range of case studies from different countries illustrate how key ideas and theories are operating in practice around the globe, with accompanying questions or activities.

? REFLECTIVE ACTIVITY 2.4

Think about other departments in your organisation, such as purchasing, finance, research and development, marketing, and data processing, as well as the HR department. What characterises people in those departments in terms of attitudes to, and concern with, the following issues: deadlines; accuracy; documentation; cost; profit; status; ethics; and personal financial reward?

REFLECTIVE ACTIVITY

In each chapter, a number of questions and activities will get you to reflect on what you have just read and encourage you to explore important concepts and issues in greater depth.

EXPLORE FURTHER

References and further reading

BERGGREN, C. (1992) *Alternatives to Lean Production: Work Organisation in the Swedish Auto Industry.* Ithaca, NY: ILR Press/London: Macmillan.

CRESSEY, P. and TAYLOR, S. (2011) *Contemporary Issues in Human Resource Management.* London: CIPD.

LIEBERMAN, M.D. (2013) *Social: Why Our Brains Are Wired to Connect.* New York: Crown Publishers.

TAYLOR, S. (2008) *People Resourcing.* London: CIPD.

See also Factsheets on the CIPD website, available at www.cipd.co.uk/hr-resources/factsheets:

EXPLORE FURTHER

Explore Further boxes contain suggestions for further reading and useful websites, encouraging you to delve further into areas of particular interest.

ACTIVITIES FEEDBACK

At the end of each chapter, feedback on a selection of activities allows you to reflect on your understanding, highlighting any areas of development.

ONLINE RESOURCES FOR TUTORS

- PowerPoint slides – design your programme around these ready-made lectures.
- Lecturer's guide – including guidance on the activities and questions in the text.

ONLINE RESOURCES FOR STUDENTS

- Annotated web links – access a wealth of useful sources of information in order to develop your understanding of the issues in the text.
- Author blog – keep up-to-date with the latest developments in HR through our author's blog.

EBOOK BUNDLING

CIPD have partnered with BitLit to offer print and eBook bundling. BitLit has built a free eBook bundling app called Shelfie for iOS and Android that allows you to get a highly discounted eBook if you own a print edition of one of our titles.

Visit **www.bitlit.com/how-it-works/**

CHAPTER 1

Introduction and Overview

1.1 OUR PURPOSE

Our purpose is to set out a practical approach to HR practices. We hope that anyone wanting a good working understanding of HR practices will find that this book meets their needs. Students on a variety of HND, undergraduate and certificate programmes should find it valuable as an introduction and as a supporting text that provides a practical perspective to the issues that they are studying. The structure of the book follows the rationale set down in the CIPD Professional Standards for the Certificate in HR Practice (CHRP). This programme is self-standing but also provides an access route to the Professional Development Scheme (PDS). CHRP students, enrolled at a CIPD-approved centre, will find that this book provides essential background reading to reinforce their learning.

The central purpose of the CHRP is to develop competence in a range of core HR and development skills together with the acquisition of underpinning knowledge and understanding. Many line managers also need these skills, knowledge and understanding. This book has been written to provide a variety of readers with a grounding in the basics of HR activities. It therefore considers the breadth of knowledge and range of skills necessary for the effective performance of HR work, while taking into account the organisational culture and environment. Whether you are a line manager with responsibility for HR or an HR practitioner, you will be concerned with the many different aspects of employing and managing people in your organisation. You will be interested in not only ensuring compliance with the law but also in good practice; in the quality of relationships at work; in how to improve people's engagement with their work and the organisation; and in how to ensure both employer and employee get a good deal. We also consider ethics at work throughout the book, including, amongst other things, behaviours, fairness, justice, values and culture. We see high-profile cases of lapses in ethics making the news on a regular basis – for example, insider trading, sexual harassment, fraud, conflicts of interest, whistleblowing, pay and matters of work–life balance. We have tried to address relevant ethical issues throughout the book – you'll see references to good practice and see ethical dimensions in case studies. We would encourage you all to think about the ethical dimension of what you do – to think about the impact and consequences of your actions and to seek support and advice from colleagues and managers if you find yourself in a situation where you feel compromised or concerned.

A summary of the book's structure and an overview of its contents follow. But first we consider the type of reader most likely to benefit from the book and the learning sources you should use.

1.1.1 YOU, THE READER

This book's focus on the core skills required in managing and working effectively with people makes it suitable for a large range of potential readers. The CHRP programme is widely regarded as an ideal course for all newcomers to the profession, but we expect that readers will belong to one or more of the following groups:

- HR officers and managers who are newly appointed to the role and who lack previous generalist experience (you may be the sole HR practitioner within your organisation, or your post may be a newly established one)
- HR assistants, administrators and PAs who support more senior HR staff
- students on the Certificate in HR Practice programme
- students on any of a variety of management, business and supervisory programmes with an HR unit or module
- employees working for new but rapidly expanding organisations who acquire responsibility for establishing and formalising HR policies, procedures and practices
- staff who work in HR-related areas – for example, a personal assistant to a managing director or a payroll supervisor
- staff who work in specialist areas of HR practice, such as training, employee relations or job evaluation, who wish to progress into or have more knowledge of generalist roles
- line managers or supervisors who have responsibility for HR activities
- owners or managers of small businesses who have overall responsibility for the 'people element' within them.

We've sought to achieve an easy and informal personal writing style that we hope will encourage readers to engage in the subject.

The text includes case studies, activities and reference material, updated for this edition.

Please note: We use the title 'HR practitioners' throughout this book as a generic term to cover all the above types of job and all levels of HR work, including those for whom the activities may be only part of wider responsibilities.

If you are tutoring, we trust that the text will offer useful material for you. We hope you will find many opportunities that will encourage discussion and provide course work.

1.1.2 LEARNING SOURCES

This book has been written by two authors, both experienced in the field of HR but with very different experiences, styles and, sometimes, perspectives. In order to understand each of the issues tackled within your own organisational circumstances, you will need to draw upon your own experience and perspective. Much of what we offer is considered good practice. We also provide coverage of relevant legal issues.

Further components are the culture and the commercial or political reality of your organisation that you will confront on a regular basis. Cultures and commercial and political realities vary in their effect enormously from organisation to organisation. While we touch on these where we can, you will need to use your experience of working in your organisation to fully understand the culture and the commercial and political reality.

Striking a balance between good practice, the law, the organisational culture and commercial/political realities will be important if you are to be effective.

To gain the maximum benefit from the book you will find it valuable to discuss the issues raised with appropriate people, particularly if you are relatively inexperienced in the areas under consideration.

These people, or 'learning sources', may include:

- senior colleagues, such as HR specialists and line managers, peers and subordinates who have knowledge and experience of the organisation and how it operates
- HR managers and officers from sister/parent companies and outside organisations
- specialists within your organisation such as company solicitors, health and safety officers, computer programmers/analysts, medical personnel and occupational health advisers
- members of your local CIPD branch and other networking bodies

- college tutors and fellow students
- other contacts that you have made through networking activities
- appropriate contacts that you might make through social networking
- employees of advisory bodies such as the Advisory, Conciliation and Arbitration Service (Acas; see Chapter 3), the Health and Safety Executive (HSE) and the Equality and Human Rights Commission (EHRC), and representatives of employers' organisations and trade union bodies.

You should establish contacts with these learning sources and make use of them to facilitate your learning experience. We shall be making periodic reference to your 'learning sources' throughout this book, so – bearing in mind the above list – choose those sources that are going to be of most benefit to you in terms of their knowledge, availability and willingness to help.

In addition to these 'people resources' there is also a range of publications available that provide general guidance and practical help. If you are a member of the CIPD you should already have information on the following:

- the CIPD Professional Standards
- the CIPD Profession Map
- continuing professional development (CPD)
- the CIPD Code of Professional Conduct
- any relevant CIPD resources – for example, survey reports.

We also make reference to CIPD factsheets, which are an invaluable source of further detail on the topics we cover.

You will find all this information, and much more, on the CIPD website: cipd.co.uk

Acas has also produced a series of advisory booklets that provide invaluable assistance in a wide range of people management activities. We recommend that you acquire, or download, copies of these booklets either for your personal use or for the whole of the HR department.

It is also worthwhile becoming familiar with a number of useful websites, such as Acas, GOV.UK, and various government departments, such as the Department for Business, Innovation and Skills (BIS). If you add the most useful sites to your favourites list, you will be able to discover up-to-date information on almost any topic of interest. There are also bookmarking services such as Delicious.com that you might use. Other suggestions are made in Chapter 10.

In order to keep up to date with changes in the world of HR management, employment legislation and case law, you might also want to encourage your organisation to subscribe to a reputable information service such as those provided by the CIPD (for example, HR-inform), Croner or XpertHR. Subscriptions provide online reference material which is kept regularly up to date.

1.2 THE STRUCTURE

We have designed this book to make it easy for you to dip in to chapters and sections that are of particular interest. It is divided into 12 Chapters (including this one). The subject areas represent the major activities associated with HR work, and we highlight the links between these activities throughout. We also provide brief details of the contents of each chapter in 1.2.1 'Overview' below, including the changes that have been made in writing the seventh edition of this book.

The next two chapters set the scene for what follows. We examine the internal and external factors that exert an influence on an organisation along with their effect on the work of HR practitioners, and we look at the legal background to employment. While we see these two as setting the scene, each chapter can be read independently, and cross-references between chapters are intended to assist this and to minimise duplication of material.

Each chapter contains the following features, where appropriate:

- learning objectives
- an introduction
- an explanation of why the topics covered are important to HR practitioners
- the main body of information
- case study material to reinforce key issues and demonstrate points of good and poor practice
- the many and varied roles played by HR practitioners
- a summary
- activities to encourage the acquisition and application of knowledge in an organisational setting and the planning of work experiences aimed at skills development
- a section covering references, legislation and codes of practice, further reading and recommended websites.

The last two features highlight our desire to change your learning experience from a passive to an active one. You are recommended to tackle at least two activities from each chapter.

In this new edition we have incorporated recent and forthcoming legislative changes throughout the book (but particularly in Chapter 3). Recent trends in HR-related matters have been noted and commentary provided on the changing nature of employment and the changing organisational context of HR. Within the text, many examples have been revised to illustrate points in a current context. The impact of the rapid growth in the use of social media is examined and recognised throughout the book. We have also updated the suggested further reading and the references, including extended lists of relevant CIPD factsheets and surveys. Most of the latter material is also available to non-CIPD members by registering on the CIPD website. These and other changes are highlighted in 1.2.1 'Overview'.

The chapters and content of the book reflect the units of the Foundation Award in Human Resources in the Qualifications and Credit Framework (QCF).

Table 1.1 How to find relevant material for each unit

Units	The most relevant material
Developing Yourself as an Effective Human Resources Practitioner	Personal Effectiveness (Chapter 12) (There are suggested activities in each chapter, except this one.)
Understanding Organisations and the Role of Human Resources	The Organisational Context (Chapter 2) The Legal Background to Employment (Chapter 3) Learning and Development (Chapter 9) (The practitioner's role is indicated at the end of every relevant chapter of the book.)
Recording, Analysing and Using Human Resources Information	Information and Communication Technology in HR (Chapter 10)
Resourcing Talent	Recruitment and Selection (Chapter 5)

Units	The most relevant material
Supporting Good Practice in Managing Employment Relations	Employee Relations (Chapter 8) The Legal Background to Employment (Chapter 3)
Supporting Good Practice in Performance and Reward Management	Performance Management (Chapter 6) Reward (Chapter 7)
Contributing to the Process of Job Analysis	Job Analysis (Chapter 4)
Supporting Change within Organisations	Change in Organisations (Chapter 11)

1.2.1 OVERVIEW

Chapter 1   Introduction and Overview

As you will have seen, here we cover our purpose and the types of reader borne in mind when compiling this book, the wide range of learning sources available to you, the book's structure, an overview of its contents and an indication of the main changes in content from previous editions.

Chapter 2   The Organisational Context

We consider the broader aspects surrounding the HR function, as well as the wide range of activities involved in its execution. We pay attention to the different types of organisation and organisational structures in which practitioners may work, as well as including the concepts of customer care and stakeholders. The effects of the internal corporate culture and the external corporate environment are summarised, noting the types of action that practitioners can take. In this latest edition the chapter takes a fresh look at corporate culture and considers current models for the organisation of the HR function, including the challenges faced by business partners.

Chapter 3   The Legal Background to Employment

Building on the external influences on organisations that we examined in Chapter 2, in this chapter we address the complex area of legislation. Concentrating on aspects of employment law, we look at where employment legislation comes from and provide a summary of the relevant legislation at different stages of employment under three main headings:

- pre-employment and starting work with a new employer and in particular employment checks, contracts of employment and employment status
- rights and responsibilities during employment, concentrating on the important issues of equality and diversity, family-related rights and working time
- ending employment, concentrating on dismissal and redundancy resolving disputes and dealing with claims.

In this latest edition, we look at the impact of the Children and Families Act 2014 (and the introduction of shared parental leave) and the latest developments around zero-hours contracts. Opportunity has also been taken to update many minor but important changes throughout the chapter. Now we start the process of homing in on specific groups of HR activities.

Chapter 4   Job Analysis

We examine the importance of good job analysis in relation to HR activities before considering jobs in three categories. We look at the most commonly used approaches to job analysis and job design. Job evaluation is covered in detail including the process for, and some of the implications of, using job evaluation. In this seventh edition we also examine the changing nature of occupations, and the challenge this presents to HR practitioners in job design.

Chapter 5   Recruitment and Selection

Taking into account and updating the legal context, we consider the processes of:

- recruitment – job analysis (job descriptions, person specifications and competency frameworks) and advertising, particularly advertising using the Internet and social media
- selection – collecting information on candidates via application forms, various types of interviews, aptitude and personality tests and assessment centre performances, and assessing and comparing candidates (with specific guidance on good interviewing practice)
- making an offer – conditional offers and employment checks
- induction – of new starters
- evaluation – of the whole process.

We have provided current information on the changing nature of the workforce. We draw attention to the presence of older workers in the workforce, immigration, the increase in flexible forms of working and the changing nature of work itself. Suggestions on the use of online recruitment are provided.

Chapter 6   Performance Management

First we consider what performance management is and examine the differences between performance appraisal and the broader concept of performance management. In this latest edition we introduce a major new case study and have updated the references to recent trends in performance management practices in UK organisations, including the emergence of ongoing feedback as an alternative to appraisal and the growing importance of behaviours as well as skills and competencies. We use the case study to demonstrate the need for all performance management systems to be closely integrated and directed towards achieving business goals. Performance appraisal is looked at in some detail: its purposes, motivational effects, trends, and the various components requiring consideration when designing a new scheme. We also address various theories of motivation and how appraisal can impact on motivation. We continue to emphasise the importance of giving and receiving feedback. Although we touch on payment systems, including financial and non-financial rewards, more information on this is contained in Chapter 7. The legal references have also been updated.

Chapter 7   Reward

In this chapter we look at definitions of reward and why it is such an important issue. We consider the different types of pay systems and structures in some detail, and explore the use of flexible benefits. We also look at non-pay reward. In this new edition we touch on the introduction of the National Living Wage, the changing pensions scene, and how collective bargaining can now affect jobs that are transferred between businesses. We examine the link between pay and performance and motivation. We take a detailed look at the legal aspects of reward, including equal pay concerns. Finally we consider the different things that impact on decisions about pay in organisations and where supporting information can be found.

Chapter 8   Employee Relations

In this chapter we survey the changing nature of employee relations and changing focus of activity and examine individual conflicts, looking at disciplinary rules and grievance procedures against the backdrop of relevant employment legislation. We provide tips on good practice in carrying out disciplinary, capability and grievance interviews, and highlight the need for an organisation to follow the correct procedures at all times. We stress that poor handling of conduct or capability cases increases the risk of claims to employment tribunals of unfair dismissal, and that employee relations problems may result from the mismanagement of formal grievances. A section on absence management tools is also featured. We also include a section on bullying and harassment. We consider the area of preventing and managing conflict, the importance of partnership and collaboration, and the role and practice of mediation as an alternative approach to managing conflict.

In this revised edition we take a more detailed look at employee voice and employee engagement. The importance of employee involvement is emphasised when considering triggers for potential collective conflicts, in both unionised and non-unionised environments. As in Chapter 3, we cover the impact of the Information and Consultation Regulations, and provide further information on the role of the psychological contract in employee relations.

Chapter 9   Learning and Development

In this chapter we look at definitions of learning and development (L&D) and then work through the stages of the training cycle, starting with the identification of learning needs and proceeding through the stages of planning, implementing and evaluating. We consider important issues such as the range of available L&D techniques and individuals' preferred learning styles. In addition, we consider national initiatives such as Investors in People and National Vocational Qualifications. Other sections reflect the relevance of competencies, changing technology and e-learning. This latest edition touches on globalisation and the implications for L&D.

Chapter 10   Information and Communication Technology in HR

The legal background to information and communication is included here. This includes the implications of the data protection code, which are spelled out in stressing the importance of keeping accurate HR records (manual and/or computerised). A section on job references is now included. In response to earlier feedback, we look at issues to consider if you are implementing or replacing a computerised HR system. We take account of the increasing value (and risks) of social media for HR practitioners. Also, in this new edition we continue the emphasis on data, including big data, and its relevance to HR responsibilities.

Chapter 11   Change in Organisations

In this chapter we look at why change is important and why organisations need to change. We reflect that change has become almost a constant state for many organisations in a fast-moving world and as such will be something all HR practitioners will become experienced in dealing with. We consider different tools, techniques and approaches for managing change, building capability and confidence in handling change, and then move on to consider in some detail the impact of change on individuals. We also look at individual responses to change and consider the different behaviours that those affected by change might display. We examine the impact of change on the psychological contract and look at different approaches to supporting employees through change. In this current edition, we give some recent examples of change in organisations with which all readers will be familiar.

Chapter 12   Personal Effectiveness

The final chapter seeks to provide further guidance on the variety of skills necessary for effective performance in an HR role, along with consideration of the increasingly important area of behaviour. We introduce the CIPD Profession Map in detail. We examine the broad issue of self-development before covering the following skills areas:

- communication – report-writing, making presentations and making a business case for introducing change
- negotiating, influencing and persuading – in formal and informal situations
- handling difficult conversations (including the use of counselling techniques)
- assertiveness – in work-related and personal situations.

We include additional material in this new edition on influencing styles. We also look at the important characteristics of empathy and emotional intelligence. We have added a new section on resilience. Finally, we refer to the emphasis placed by a large number of professional associations, such as the CIPD, on the concept of CPD. The main focus of this concept is the proposition that learning (and the acquisition of knowledge and skills) is not a one-off process, but one that should carry on throughout your working life. We have tried to reinforce this message and hope that it is one you take to heart at this, the beginning of a new learning experience. May it open doors for you.

CHAPTER 2

The Organisational Context

LEARNING OUTCOMES

After reading this chapter you will:

- appreciate the type of activities in which HR practitioners may be involved
- recognise the type of organisation for which you work and the main implications for you as a practitioner
- have a better understanding of culture in the context of your employing organisation.
- recognise how the HR function is structured in your organisation and be aware of the Ulrich model for the HR function
- grasp the main principles of the customer care and the stakeholder concepts
- know the behaviours involved in good customer care
- be able to distinguish administrative, advisory and executive tasks as carried out in the HR function
- be able to develop links with your management team, your employees and the community
- have a broad understanding of the role of trade unions and be aware of the services of Acas
- be able to understand the key roles and tasks of the HR function and its contribution to organisational success
- understand the concept of outsourcing functions and services.

2.1 INTRODUCTION

Because the HR function operates within an organisational context, we shall be considering the nature of organisations and the relationships that HR practitioners need to establish with managers, trade unions and employees. The corporate environment is also important, and this includes the effect of changes that occur in that wider environment.

We believe that the HR role is the most interesting and exciting one in any organisation. It may be a cliché that people are an organisation's greatest asset, but no organisation exists without people and nothing is achieved except through their efforts. HR practices, therefore, go to the heart of the organisation and potentially have a part to play in every facet of its activities. As an HR practitioner, you could conceivably be called on to help solve very personal individual problems. Equally, you could be asked to contribute to significant strategic policy decisions in the boardroom. Quite possibly, both could happen on the same day.

Organisations of different sizes and in different sectors organise and structure HR in various ways and use different models of service delivery. We will touch on some of this throughout the chapter, including the concept of HR shared services and also the importance of customer care within the context of HR services. Because we consider it important for you to understand your role, each chapter will comment on the HR practitioner's role in the context of the material covered by that chapter. Here we are taking an overview of HR practice within the context of the organisation.

We will start by looking at the environment in which your organisation exists.

2.2 EXTERNAL ENVIRONMENT

We do not need to look far to see tremendous change in our society. Indeed, change is the third great certainty – the other two being death and taxes! Look back over the last ten years and consider the increase in the number of smaller businesses created in that period. Reflect on the implications that the Internet and social networking have had for your employer, for society and for yourself. Look at the impact of European legislation where the regulation of equality and of health and safety are just two effects in the employment area alone. How are migrants from Europe and elsewhere changing the labour market? To what extent have green issues and climate change come to the fore?

The environment in which organisations operate is broad, and change originates from six areas which may be summarised with the mnemonic PESTLE. The areas are:

- **P**olitical – changes brought about by powerful bodies such as governments, the European Union (EU), the trade union movement and regulatory bodies.
- **E**conomic – economic climate, interest rates (which affect the cost of borrowing and, potentially, company profitability), skills shortages, the housing crisis, consumer debt, demand for goods, import tariffs, troubles in the Eurozone and austerity.
- **S**ocial – changing boundaries between work and non-work time, changing family structures, an ageing population, consumer expectations, demographic changes (changes in the structure of the population), immigrant workers, lifestyles, consumer attitudes to social, environmental and other issues.
- **T**echnological – developments in medicine, smart phone technology, energy sources, nanotechnology.
- **L**egal – new laws originating from acts of Parliament, interpretations of the law by the courts (both domestic and European), international laws (for example, covering disposal of waste at sea).
- **E**nvironmental – climatic change, melting ice caps, pollution.

The sources of change are often interrelated. Shared parental leave (a legal change), for example, was spurred on by social change (men taking an increasing role in child upbringing). Organisations need to embrace change to survive. Managers must anticipate and respond to the effects that such changes have on their organisations if they are to embrace that change.

Some serious implications are arising from the changing environment for employees. Smaller organisations mean fewer opportunities for promotion from one level to another. But rapid growth in the size of an organisation may compensate for this, offering other opportunities. To be effective in this changing world, you as HR practitioners must keep in close touch with changes in the external environment, with employees, and with the community as a whole. Doing so will help you to anticipate and respond effectively to people issues. You will find that change is a recurring theme throughout this book and sufficiently important to have a chapter dedicated to it. Reading professional magazines, a quality newspaper and keeping in touch with current affairs, for example by following appropriate sources on Twitter, is an important part of this process.

We will look more closely at how you might keep in touch with employees and the community in 'Building bridges' in 2.4.7. Here, though, we will first examine the corporate environment in which an HR function operates.

2.3 CHARACTERISTICS OF ORGANISATIONS

Organisations exist for different purposes and in a broad range of sectors. Thus there exist organisations of very different types. The activities and functions to be seen in a manufacturing company differ markedly from those in a recruitment agency, for example.

An organisation of any size will be subdivided into different functions. In a traditional manufacturing company, these might include groups of people responsible for purchasing, manufacturing, sales, finance, design and HR. Raw materials are purchased, products are manufactured and they are sold.

Manufacturing activities form a line from supplier to customer. The people working in these functions are often referred to as being 'in the line' and their managers as 'line managers'. Costs associated with these functions are referred to as 'direct' costs.

People working in other functions such as finance, design and HR are not part of the line because the product does not pass through their responsibilities on the route from suppliers to customers. Often they are referred to as 'overhead' functions. In a recruitment agency, however, some HR activities such as selection could be regarded as 'line' activities. Indeed, a large recruitment agency may have HR practitioners in both line and support functions.

Support functions are those such as accountants, maintenance and HR that assist the primary task or purpose of the business. One disadvantage for support workers is that they may be seen as less important because they are a fixed cost (independent of the volume of product or amount of service provided) and do not bring in business directly. An advantage is that they can often be nearer the heart of the company strategy and are impartial when it comes to a conflict between line functions. For example, an HR practitioner (who is a support rather than a line manager) should be involved in discussions about how to attract talented candidates. This is close to the business strategy because it can affect business decisions, such as where the organisation locates its operations geographically.

Not all organisations are commercial, and one way of distinguishing some characteristics that are important to the HR practitioner is to look and see to whom the body is accountable – for example, to shareholders, to trustees or to a government department. These characteristics will, in part, determine how practitioners should seek to influence others in the organisation.

It has been said that organisations do not have objectives – it is people who have objectives. Because of this it is also important for you to look at those people who have the greatest influence over the direction of your organisation. The circumstances surrounding them, their motivations and their accountability will exert a marked effect on what is regarded as important within any organisation.

We will now look at some examples of different organisations and the accountability of their senior people.

2.3.1 THE SMALL PRIVATE LIMITED COMPANY

The owners of a small private company may well have much of their personal capital invested in the business. Although their liability is limited (to the capital they have invested in the business), they may find themselves in considerable financial difficulty if the enterprise fails. In taking such risks they are usually seeking significant financial gain. Inevitably, this will affect how they view activities that may be desirable but which do not produce income. But it does not necessarily mean that wealth creation is the only or even the prime motivation. In such a company, the chief executive is likely to have a clear vision of where he or she wants the company to go and to be totally committed to the success of the enterprise.

You need to try to recognise this vision and relate your responsibilities towards achieving it. It will invariably help if you can also relate your activities to profit, productivity, risk reduction and the assistance of business growth.

2.3.2 THE PARTNERSHIP

Partners who have equity in the business (who in effect have invested their own capital) may be of comparable standing with each other, especially in a small partnership. This often means that all the partners must be prepared to go along with proposals that you may make, otherwise there is little chance of progress. In large partnerships, many matters will be delegated to a managing partner, a managing team or similar body. The influence that any individual partner has will be determined by the structure of each particular firm and his or her position in it.

Partnerships are common in the professions such as law and accountancy. Professional firms seek to maximise fee-earning activities and minimise activities that do not attract fees. Recognising this will be important. Reducing the time that partners spend on problems associated with people management will be seen as a valuable contribution.

Many professional firms are limited liability partnerships (LLP), a form of partnership which protects the individual partners in the event that the partnership becomes bankrupt.

2.3.3 THE PUBLIC LIMITED COMPANY (PLC)

The shares in a PLC are usually traded on the stock exchange. This can have a number of effects – for example, the senior members of the company may from time to time be heavily engrossed with how the shares are trading and with all the figures that influence how company performance is viewed. One knock-on effect of this is that you could be under pressure to keep very accurate records of employee numbers. PLCs are hugely varied in character and range in size from small to multinational, but they are all strongly commercial because they have to provide a return for their investors.

You may work for a small subsidiary company of a large PLC, or even for a small site within such a company. How much independence smaller units of that kind have depends on the approach of the parent company.

In some cases, the chief executive of a subsidiary may have his or her own vision and be able to manage the business with a moderate level of independence, treating the parent company almost as if it were a banker. Such chief executives are not usually at as much financial risk as private owners. Although the chief executives may have shares in the organisation, they are unlikely to be rendered bankrupt personally if the business were to fail. Nevertheless, failure might bring serious consequences for their careers.

In other cases, subsidiary companies may be subject to a strong corporate identity and firm control from the parent company. If this is the case, your chief executive is likely to be concerned with how his or her performance is viewed by the parent company, and this may influence how you or your senior managers relate to the chief executive.

Many factors influence the attitudes in any large commercial company: where the company's product might be in its life cycle, its position in its marketplace, the nature of its marketplace (whether it is growing or declining) and its edge (or otherwise) over competitors. In general, the more prosperous and secure the company, the more it is likely to invest in good people management. In companies that are less prosperous or suffering declining sales, you will have to work harder to get new ideas adopted and there may be a need to consider more challenging issues such as redundancy.

2.3.4 PUBLIC SECTOR ORGANISATIONS

Organisations in the public sector can be very different from those described above. Public sector organisations are likely to have a hierarchical structure (see 2.3.8 below) with more clearly defined jobs and positions than are generally found in the private sector.

The emphasis in the public sector is on service delivery and is underpinned by the public service ethos and the specific requirements placed on public servants. These organisations are significantly affected by government policy and changes in government at election time. For many organisations in the public sector, change and large-scale reorganisation prompted by political decisions have become a constant. In most public sector organisations there will be employed executives at a senior level in day-to-day control of the organisation, plus some 'lay' involvement through, for example, local councillors and non-executive directors. In some public sector organisations – for example, the NHS – a strong influence will also be exerted by professional bodies who regulate, register and train professional groups – for example, the medical Royal Colleges. Government organisations exist to implement government policies either locally or nationally. In addition, all spending is subject to the scrutiny of the Audit Office, which is independent of government and reports to Parliament directly on the efficient use of public money.

Public sector organisations have to comply with European Directives, as well as with UK legislation, because failure to do so can render them liable to action in European courts. There are also various statutory duties placed on them by legislation. For example, within HR there are statutory duty codes of practice relating to equality issues. On the other hand, private sector organisations have to comply with UK legislation and must be aware of the obligations of public organisations (such as employment tribunals). However, they do not have to comply directly with European Directives until those Directives have been translated into UK law.

Government organisations, therefore, exist in a precise environment in which policies, procedures, and actions are generally well documented.

It is important to be mindful of this as an HR practitioner. Those to whom you might report are likely to be very conscious of risks, accountability, governance and compliance.

Some public sector organisations are centrally funded but relatively independent of direct accountability to an electorate, although there will still be accountability to government ministers and, increasingly, representatives of the local community, through such organisations as NHS Foundation Trusts. Universities, the NHS, academy and free schools, local education authorities and various government agencies such as Jobcentre Plus all account to the government and Parliament to a greater or lesser degree. Independence is provided by various funding arrangements, but when funds are granted, the grant is invariably subject to conditions that can restrict the level of independence.

Government control is also exercised in a variety of other ways. For example, league tables are used to monitor the performance of schools and universities, among others. Inspection authorities are used to assess standards, share best practice and assist continuous improvement; for example, the Office for Standards in Education (OFSTED) monitors performance in schools and colleges, while the Care Quality Commission inspects and reviews performance in the NHS, social services, and the private care sector. The National Audit Office monitors an organisation's activities, and tendering processes are used to ensure that services provided by public bodies and agencies are at a competitive level.

In such organisations it is inevitable that there will be a preoccupation with the measures used to determine performance and thus access to funds. Inspection processes require a focus on quality, good governance arrangements and proper documentation. HR practitioners must familiarise themselves with the funding arrangements and control processes that exist in their own organisation if they are to contribute appropriately to meeting objectives.

2.3.5 THE THIRD SECTOR

There is an increasing level of employment in what is often called 'the third sector'. This includes charities, employers of volunteers, and social enterprise organisations.

Broadly, we define a social enterprise as a business with primarily social objectives. Surpluses are reinvested for the purpose in the business or in the community, rather than distributed as dividends to shareholders ... Social enterprises can encompass everything from mutuals, employee-owned businesses, private companies limited by guarantee or cooperatives.

Douglas Alexander, formerly of the DTI

Funding for these organisations can come from donations of various kinds but also from bodies in the public sector such as social services or the NHS. Charities can tap into public funds by providing services that might otherwise have been provided from within the public sector. The hospice movement is a good example.

Sometimes these organisations report to boards of voluntary trustees who appoint managers to administer day-to-day operations. There can be some important stakeholders in social enterprise companies (we expand on the term 'stakeholder' under 2.5.2 below) depending on the type of activity in which a company is engaged; for example, the public sector bodies already mentioned, the Charities Commission and various regulatory agencies such as the Care Quality Commission can be stakeholders.

In many cases, those in the third sector are motivated by altruistic rather than by hard commercial interests. Nonetheless, to have profits to reinvest they need to be reasonably astute and realistic about business.

2.3.6 REGULATED ORGANISATIONS/SECTORS

Some organisations operating in certain parts of the private sector do so under significant regulatory control. An example of this is the care sector where residential homes (in England) are subject to the Health and Social Care Act. Homes can be inspected and there are specific expectations about such matters as induction, employment policies and procedures, health and safety and many operational matters. Meeting inspection standards can be a major responsibility for managers in regulated sectors, in addition to the commercial pressures mentioned above.

2.3.7 OTHER ORGANISATIONS

It is important to realise that we have only scratched the surface here in terms of the types of organisations and the issues they may regard as important. We have not mentioned mutual societies (owned by their members), the armed forces, the police, nationalised industries or public-private partnerships – and even this list is not exhaustive.

?   REFLECTIVE ACTIVITY 2.1

Look carefully at your own organisation. What is specific to your organisation that distinguishes it from other organisations? To whom is it ultimately accountable? What is regarded as important? Are there regulations or inspections that affect how the business should operate? Discuss your conclusions with appropriate learning sources within and, for comparison, outside your organisation.

2.3.8 ORGANISATION STRUCTURES

Hierarchical

In a typical hierarchical structure, each member of staff reports to an immediate superior and there are several layers between the most junior and the most senior individuals. As a general rule, each person has a relatively small span of control with no more than five or six people reporting to him or her.

If the organisation is large, each job is likely to be specialised and may be closely defined. For example, within the HR function alone there may be separate departments for employee relations, learning and development (L&D), recruitment, and compensation and benefits. Such subdivisions will be reflected in other parts of the organisation.

Typically, each person reports to only one immediate superior to whom he or she is accountable for all job responsibilities. In practice, there can be some reporting to another person, often referred to as a 'dotted-line' responsibility (because it may be shown by means of a dotted line on the organisation chart) or matrix management. For example, a store HR manager might report to a head office HR director, but have a dotted-line relationship to the store manager (or vice-versa).

Hierarchies are characterised by protocol to varying degrees from the very informal to the strict. Conventions place restrictions on who talks to whom about what. Accountants do not often venture onto the shop floor, nor do sales people always talk to operatives. When one of the authors organised a works open day, it was the first time most of the office staff (some of whom had been there for decades) had seen the company's products being made. In a hierarchical organisation with very established protocols, there can be little sideways communication between departments, all disagreements being reported upwards. These protocols arise for a variety of reasons – practical geography, communication channels, social interaction, personal background, professional pride and sometimes prejudices – but they can also help senior individuals maintain political power bases for security and reward.

It should be said that these very traditional approaches are under threat simply because they are ineffective. For example, in the NHS and associated bodies, great efforts are put into breaking down such barriers and getting people to work in multi-disciplinary/multi-agency ways.

For the purposes of looking more closely at organisation structures, we shall now use the example of a typical manufacturing company.

Figure 2.1 represents an illustration of this hierarchical structure. A salesperson may become aware of a customer need. In many cases, he or she will have little or no contact with a product designer, perhaps partly due to geography, but often because salespeople do not talk to designers. So the great idea has to travel up the organisation, through the regional manager to the sales director, who might talk to his or her colleague, the design and development director. When the idea finally reaches the designer, there may be an unforeseen problem.

Does the designer then talk to the salesperson? The answer is 'It depends. . .' on many relationships, on protocol and on other organisational matters (such as geography). We touch on this in Chapter 4 when we describe the 'elevator structure' and the importance of inter-relationships across an organisation.

? REFLECTIVE ACTIVITY 2.2

How many layers are there in your employer's organisation? Look for the most junior member and count the links between him or her and the CEO (or other most senior post). You are likely to find that the number varies for different functions in your organisation.

If you are familiar with another organisation (a partner's or relative's employer, for example), count the number of levels there. What does this information tell you about that organisation?

Figure 2.1 A hierarchical organisation

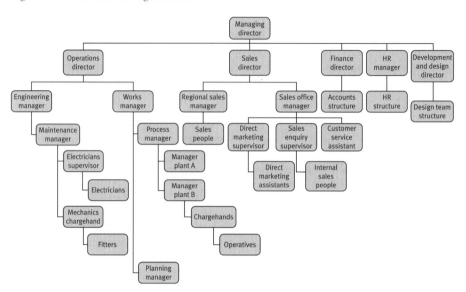

The need to reduce costs in order to meet international competition has led many companies to reduce the size of their workforce and to 'de-layer' their organisational structure. That is, to decrease the number of levels of reporting relationships. As well as reducing both costs and bureaucracy, de-layering can often lead to much more effective internal communications. However, companies have to be careful to avoid downsizing to such an extent that the remaining staff only have time to deal with day-to-day operational activities and strategic thinking is driven out of the organisation altogether. The concept of 'shared services', which we shall explain later, often separates day-to-day activities from more strategic thinking.

Flatter organisations

This trend towards smaller organisations and flatter structures reduces the likelihood of protracted decision-making. With fewer organisational layers, individuals have easier access to senior decision-makers. However, each person is likely to be in greater demand, with many people reporting to him or her, and people at all levels need to have a wider range of skills. Flatter structures encourage, even require, collaborative working across the organisation. This is illustrated in Figure 2.2.

In a small company, the HR practitioner may need to handle a range of HR activities. In larger but flat-structured companies, HR staff may still have a narrower responsibility (say, recruitment) but could find that they have to balance the needs of all the other functions in the organisation (sales and production, for example) rather than relying on one boss to set the priorities. This demands a greater understanding of the organisation's wider operations and its priorities.

In flat organisations, individuals sometimes report to more than one boss, in what can be called a matrix structure. For example, the HR manager may be responsible to the factory manager, the sales manager, the distribution manager and the head office head of HR, all in approximately equal measures.

Figure 2.2 A flatter structure

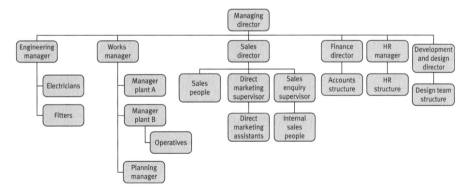

In this flatter type of organisation, HR practitioners who want to introduce a new application form can talk to all their colleagues directly. When everyone is convinced of the benefits of the change, the practitioners can introduce the new form. By contrast, practitioners in a strict hierarchical structure would have to convince their immediate boss and (if they are lucky) the boss would then convince his or her own boss. Eventually, a decision will be taken at a level sufficiently high for all the practitioners' colleagues to fall in line, and the new application form may be imposed from above.

Here we have looked at two important and relatively common forms of organisation structure. There are other forms – and even these two cannot be precisely defined since they exist to varying degrees in different organisations.

If you want to influence decision-making, you need to understand how your organisation is structured and how decision-making takes place.

? REFLECTIVE ACTIVITY 2.3

If you wanted to introduce a new recruitment application form (to reflect changes in legislation, perhaps), how would you go about getting a decision made? Which of the above scenarios most closely represents what ought to happen in your organisation? Is there another scenario that would apply? Discuss your conclusions with an appropriate learning source.

2.3.9 CORPORATE CULTURE

As we stated above, HR activities take place within an organisation. This means that your role – what you do, and how you do it – is inevitably influenced, or even constrained, by the organisation's nature or corporate culture, not just by its formal structure.

It is valuable to understand your organisation: it will help you decide how to earn some 'brownie points'. It may be that you do not want to advance your career in terms of responsibility. But identifying and performing well in those activities that are valued will increase your professional credibility, enhance the esteem in which you are held, your influence and, perhaps, your salary. If you are an employee of a shared services or an outsourced services provider, then knowing your client(s) may be important too, depending on your level of engagement with them. A drawback for companies that undertake outsourced activities is that they may be unfamiliar with the culture of their client organisation, especially if they are located on a separate site.

If you have changed employers during your working life, you will appreciate how they differ even within the same industrial sector. The differences between large and small organisations, between the various industrial sectors, and between public and private are even more marked.

Don't assume that the ways in which tasks are carried out in your organisation – say, the way in which job descriptions are prepared – is the only approach or, indeed, a necessary approach. Many companies, for example, survive profitably without job descriptions.

Within your organisation, observe the characteristics or 'culture' of different departments. In our experience, sales teams are often characterised by positive, open attitudes and a preoccupation with status, targets, performance and reward (for example, the commission scheme).

Production teams are more likely to evince a 'no-nonsense' attitude, be driven by meeting deadlines, and reject what they see as 'time-wasting' activities (such as writing job descriptions, perhaps).

There are many ways of identifying and describing corporate culture.

Attitudes

Table 2.1 sets out a few typical attitudes that might form important aspects of culture.

Table 2.1 Corporate attitudes

Openness	Ask yourself how much do you (or perhaps employees generally) know about the management of the organisation. Do you know what the current issues facing the organisation might be? Do you know how well the organisation is performing? Do senior levels of the organisation talk with you, or with employees generally? Answers to these questions will help you gauge the degree of openness and inform how open you yourself will be expected to be.
Initiative or empowerment	How much initiative is encouraged in people's jobs? Are they allowed to make mistakes (even if only the same mistake once) or are they likely to be castigated for any mistakes? Indeed, does everyone scatter when something goes wrong, fearing the blame being placed on them?
Internal regulation	There will always be a degree of this in every organisation as there needs to be a sense of direction, control, and co-ordination. Jobs can be deskilled by creating very prescriptive courses of action (thus saving costs). This can happen in call centres, and you may have experienced frustration as a customer when the person at the other end of the phone seems unable to help you. In these cases what you are asking may fall outside what they are authorised to do and they have to give the answers they are told to give.

External regulation	Many services are highly regulated meaning that very specific courses of action need to be followed, especially where things might go seriously wrong. The health sector is one specific example, but tight regulations apply in other sectors too, such as aircraft manufacture. All businesses work with some degree of external regulation and it affects the amount of individual initiative or empowerment that can be allowed.
Honesty and ethics	This is a significant subject area in its own right. There are many ethical issues to consider in organisations – workers' conditions in supplier organisations, transparency of pay levels, the ingredients used by food manufacturers and corporate travel arrangements. How does your own organisation deal with these issues? Are they open for discussion with employees?
Fun	Is it fun and exciting to work in the organisation, or is it characterised by earnest seriousness or drudgery? For most of us our experiences fall somewhere in between.
Commitment	Are employees actually committed to the organisation and its purpose or are they there just to earn their daily bread?
Management style	How are individuals motivated? Is the approach positive or is it negative with a predominance of bullying, even harassment? Do employees work out of love or out of fear?
Training	Does the organisation 'grow its own' or tend to poach trained people from elsewhere? Are employees expected to grow in their jobs or just to do their jobs?
Diversity	Attitudes to women, racial groups, age or disability, among other groups, can be very revealing.
Well-being	Does its interest in its employees extend beyond the 'wages for labour' concept? How far does it extend to looking after employees' physical and emotional welfare? How much consideration does it give to issues such as job design, the quality of leadership, flexible working and employee engagement?

Drivers

It is worth considering the 'drivers' in the organisation. Again, the following list is not exhaustive:

- Altruism – we might expect to find this in most charities.
- Sales – in most retail and trading businesses this will be the driver.
- Finance – a major driver in all private sector businesses, it assumes higher presence, understandably, in the financial services sector and where businesses are run by accountants or, perhaps, venture capitalists.
- Excitement – likely to be the driver in many entrepreneurial companies.
- Making a difference – the driver for public sector organisations.

Culture affects every aspect of the organisation from what people talk about in the loos, to risk-taking in the boardroom.

Understanding culture in the context of your own employer will inform everything that you do as an employee and HR practitioner. Your opportunities to influence it may be limited, but your role will enable you to help to communicate and embed it, whether it is via recruitment, induction, training, performance management, communication or the manner in which you approach problems involving individual employees.

? REFLECTIVE ACTIVITY 2.4

Think about other departments in your organisation, such as purchasing, finance, research and development, marketing, and data processing, as well as the HR department. What characterises people in those departments in terms of attitudes to, and concern with, the following issues: deadlines; accuracy; documentation; cost; profit; status; ethics; and personal financial reward?

? REFLECTIVE ACTIVITY 2.5

Next time you are in a restaurant (perhaps one that is part of a chain) and you are asked if everything is 'all right', find some reason for deciding why it is not and say so. The reaction you get will tell you a great deal about the culture of the organisation.

Next time try a different restaurant chain and see if the reaction is any different.

If you send the food back, you may want to be able to see the kitchen from where you are sitting!

? REFLECTIVE ACTIVITY 2.6

Explore your employer's culture further.

Seek out (if you haven't already) the stories that surround the organisation. Who are the heroes and the villains, and why has their respect or dislike developed? What noteworthy events have there been in the history of the organisation? How do other employees generally view those events?

2.4 WHAT SHOULD AN HR PRACTITIONER ACHIEVE?

This very much depends on your employer's expectations. Unless you work for a sole trader (someone who is self-employed – see Chapter 3), your employer will be an organisation.

You may notice that in this book we refer to 'organisations' frequently, although we may from time to time use related terms such as 'employer', 'business' or 'company' where it is more appropriate. 'Organisation', though, is a convenient term because the points being made will generally apply whether the 'organisation' is a small private enterprise or a multinational, a small charity or a government department.

We've looked at organisation structures above and given some general guidelines on the different types and some implications for practitioners.

Nevertheless, each organisation is unique and the concepts described in this book will vary in their applicability to a greater or lesser extent with those different organisations. This is one of the reasons why we stress the importance of using learning sources in the first chapter.

It is, therefore, wise to think through the fundamental nature of the organisation for which you work in order to understand what your employer may expect of you.

? REFLECTIVE ACTIVITY 2.7

If you are an HR practitioner, prepare a 30-word statement describing the purpose of your job. (If you are not yet in the function, speculate on the purpose of someone who is in such a position in your organisation.) Ask yourself:

● Why do I have a job?
● What would happen if the tasks I do were not completed?
● How might my contribution be measured?

Human resources management in the UK can trace its origins back to the early part of the twentieth century when welfare workers were appointed in ammunitions factories to exercise care towards female employees. Personnel management, as a business function, assumed prominence in the latter half of that century. Further development saw the term 'personnel' being widely replaced by the term 'human resources' or HR. Originally, a more strategic perception was associated with HR – a view that it was a tougher, less people-sensitive function, and closer to the decision-makers. Today the terms are, arguably, indistinguishable and in practice they are used interchangeably. There is also a more current trend to move on from the term 'human resources', with some arguing that humans are not resources at all, but are people who should be treated as individuals, with compassion and humanity and not as resources. We can see this trend visibly with job titles and HR functions in some organisations being changed to things like 'People Director' and 'People Function'. Watch this space – this is an ever evolving debate!

Many HR practitioners are generalists and administrators engaged in: finding employees; looking after employee administration such as contracts of employment; ensuring employees are paid properly; organising learning opportunities; maintaining policies and procedures; meeting legal requirements; monitoring attendance; assisting managers in disciplinary action; and responding to employees' needs and problems (such as grievances). They may also be involved in organisation restructuring and redundancy programmes.

More experienced practitioners are likely to take a lead in the relationships within the organisation. This may mean involvement in job design, selection processes, employee communication, performance management, and reward. It can also include participating in a change in culture, promoting diversity and facilitating performance management.

This is a brief snapshot of the role and of topics covered in this book.

Involvement in strategic decision-making, setting the direction of the HR function and structural change, is likely to rest with experienced HR professionals who will often also have acquired know-how, such as commercial experience, outside the HR function. We can only touch on these topics.

Below we outline some of the activities in which you are most likely to become involved or where there may be expectations of you.

2.4.1 FINDING EMPLOYEES

This is not just a question of advertising and recruiting, although that may be a major part of the task. Effective practitioners build relationships with relevant local bodies such as schools, colleges, job centres, employment agencies and the community as a whole. A positive profile in the community helps to attract the best candidates. Finding employees is covered in detail in Chapter 5.

2.4.2 HELPING EMPLOYEES TO LEARN

Occasionally this is a separate, or sister, function, but HR is professionally linked with L&D. The activity does not mean only arranging training courses and other learning opportunities. As we shall see later, it can include diverse activities such as identifying needs, planning appropriate learning opportunities and evaluating the success of these activities. Employees joining an organisation need to learn about how things are done in the particular environment. Sound learning helps an organisation to respond effectively to change (see Chapter 11).

2.4.3 ARRANGING PAYMENTS

For many administrators in small organisations, administering the payroll is the entry route into HR practice. Paying employees regularly, correctly and on time is a contractual obligation backed up by legislation (the Employment Rights Act 1996, for example). Proper authority, accuracy and absolute meeting of deadlines are vital issues for payroll staff. Because of this, a payroll officer should be allowed to work to a regular routine and not be interrupted by other priorities. The demands of working in an HR office can be slightly different – a point of which those who are making the transition from payroll to HR need to be aware.

HR aspects of paying employees can, at one extreme, involve clarification of entitlement to individual pay items and, at the other, negotiating pay rates.

It is good practice (to reduce the possibility of fraud) for those who authorise payments (such as HR practitioners) to have separate reporting relationships from those who pay employees (the payroll staff).

2.4.4 FACILITATING COMMUNICATION WITH EMPLOYEES

Where you need to do this, we hope you will have been able to make a contribution to the decisions themselves. Justifying actions that you may not have chosen yourself is one of the greatest challenges for the HR practitioner. It is a central aspect of managerial responsibility that once you have put forward all your arguments, you accept and implement whatever is decided. That may be stressful, particularly if you have not been able to put those arguments at the right level. Typical actions that HR practitioners might be called on to justify are restructuring and redundancy, reductions in fringe benefits, changes within the place of work, and relocation. An example is provided in Case Study 2.1 below.

CASE STUDY 2.1

A company providing services for the public carried out market research and found that it was losing valuable business by not opening on a Saturday. The board decided that it was in the interests of the company to move to Saturday opening – indeed, if it did not, there was a risk of losing market share, with consequential risks to job security.

In this highly unionised company, the trade union representatives were informed of the need to open on a Saturday and the HR manager took the time to explain the reasons.

The objective – of opening on a Saturday – was defined and a consultation process was begun with the purpose of finding the most acceptable approach. The HR manager chaired several meetings with both line managers and representatives present.

The outcome was an agreed rota system, which meant that each staff member would work on alternate Saturdays for an agreed premium.

The union representatives felt unable to agree on all aspects. Several employees did not wish to work on Saturdays and one, in particular, objected strongly. The HR manager then became involved in individual consultations. A conclusion was reached that if an exception was made (there was no legitimate reason for one), the whole agreement would 'unravel'.

Together with the general manager, the HR manager held a meeting with all employees, re-emphasised the reasons and gave notice that Saturday opening would go ahead after the summer break (which was adequate notice for ending the contracts). The single employee realised he was on notice and, without compromise to the agreement, the HR manager continued to work with him to try to find a solution. Suitable alternative employment was not possible because Saturday working was a requirement for all jobs. When the notice expired, the employee left, claiming that he had been dismissed (which was correct, of course). However, all other employees accepted the new terms and Saturday opening was achieved without further disruption.

The important good practice points here are the time taken to consult, a statement of the problem, consultation on a solution, an agreement that could be justified, proper notice to end one contract, consideration of reasonable alternatives, and the role played by the HR manager. Incidentally, the case on which this is based was judged to be fair at tribunal.

2.4.5 RESPONDING TO EMPLOYEES' WORK-RELATED NEEDS AND PROBLEMS

These are needs such as health and safety, fringe benefits (company vehicles, for example), welfare matters and long-term protection such as life assurance and pensions. In large companies some of these issues may be dealt with by a separate department.

Grievances are raised on a huge range of issues. Many of these will be settled by line managers. Those matters that are not will invariably require a relatively neutral broker – an HR practitioner. We look at this in detail in Chapter 8.

Other employee matters for which you may need to be prepared include redundancy consultations, debts and bereavement.

These can be stressful matters for employees who may look to their employer to treat them with fairness and understanding – concepts which they may view differently to the employer. HR is invariably the channel for fairness and understanding between the employer and the employee.

But HR practitioners can be vulnerable to stress themselves, particularly when they fail to modify those management actions that conflict with their own values.

A career in HR, as may have already been pointed out to you, is not a 'soft' option. Confidence, credibility, assertiveness, judgement and emotional resilience are qualities needed by effective practitioners. They are particularly important for those who take on the role of 'business partner', which we shall describe later. Given these qualities, practitioners are more likely to find that senior managers listen to HR practitioners.

We shall also look at how you can develop your personal skills in Chapter 12.

2.4.6 UNDERSTANDING AND ARTICULATING EMPLOYEES' ASPIRATIONS AND VIEWS

HR practitioners' capacity to influence management actions depends on their ability to judge the outcomes of those actions. Judging outcomes means understanding the language of the employees; influencing managers means using the language managers understand. Understanding and communicating well with both employees and managers is an important skill for practitioners. You can foster both languages by spending time with each group.

Walking the floor is better than opening the door. Stay in your own office and you will meet only the more confident employees or those with specific issues to resolve, however wide your door may be open. Senior managers have their own language – that of the chief executive, for example, may be different from that of the board members. Management courses and finance for non-financial managers' courses provide some of the vocabulary. You may be able to learn from social opportunities (talking to senior managers at in-company award ceremonies, for example). There may be external opportunities to learn the decision-makers' language by taking on a responsible community role (for instance, by becoming a school governor or a magistrate).

Employees at your establishment may be represented by trade unions. If so, that is another group with which to develop a good relationship. Our experience has been that those who become involved in trade unions are genuine and articulate people. Their influence can be valuable in resolving differences between employees and management. It is usually easier to resolve a matter with a few representatives than with a whole workforce. Nonetheless, in our view, managers must always reserve the right to communicate directly with their own employees.

2.4.7 OTHER CHALLENGES

Broad though this examination of HR work may be, it does not include every activity an HR practitioner may be asked to do. You will probably identify activities with which you are involved that are only touched upon here, or even omitted altogether. Managing the company car fleet, editing the company newsletter or carrying out health and safety audits are just three examples. Much of the work that falls to HR departments may not be viewed as strictly HR-related work. Indeed, a prominent twentieth-century management guru, the late Peter Drucker, described the HR department as the 'trash can' department that takes on almost any activity no one else wants!

It is important to find the balance on the one hand between customer care activities when you try to 'delight' customers, and on the other taking on 'trash-can' activities. The latter are activities that often don't add any value to the organisation, waste your time and do not gain any credit from the people who have influence over your career. Identifying which is which is not always easy; priorities have to be set. You may want to keep an eye on what activities influential people regard as being most important. It is easy to find yourself bogged down in marginal activities.

For marginal activities, ask yourself some questions:

- What would happen if this were not done?
- If it needs doing, what is the opportunity cost of me doing it? That is, could my time be better spent on other activities that would add more value to my employer?

- Would it be more effectively done by someone else? Perhaps someone is seeking to avoid doing it.
- Am I, or perhaps *how* am I, going to challenge the person who is seeking to marginalise me?
- Or is it that I prefer this marginal, low risk, activity to doing more challenging work?

You might like to take a look at the 'Courage to challenge' part of the CIPD Profession Map.

There is a view that many marginal HR activities should be done by line managers, leaving time for HR practitioners to concentrate on the medium- to long-term strategic issues. At one of our Certificate in HR Practice courses a guest speaker put it succinctly: 'We must avoid becoming embroiled in detailed reactive issues; in essence, more day-to-day HR activities must be the responsibility of line management'. Other approaches to dealing with activities associated with day-to-day issues are to outsource the work or to use a shared services centre.

But first we will look at the types of actions an HR practitioner can take in order to carry out the tasks that may be expected.

2.5 WHAT TYPE OF ACTIONS CAN PRACTITIONERS TAKE?

We describe several types of action below. In practice, the types of things that you can do arise from a complex mix of the authority vested in you, your persuasive abilities, your credibility with decision-makers, your responsibilities and the norms of your organisation. To these you should add your own capabilities, risk tolerance, emotional resilience and assertiveness.

Generally, you will have to discover for yourself most of the organisational factors in the mix, but we hope that the section on the characteristics and structure of organisations has given you some pointers. Observing and taking counsel from your boss, others in your department and others in the organisation is the way in which you should consolidate this. Personal effectiveness can be increased through self-development, as we outline later.

However, if you are a newly established 'HR person' within your organisation, you will have less advice to draw upon. If you have grown to the position from within the organisation, you will already have some idea of the authority you have and your own credibility. If newly appointed, then your manager will probably indicate the boundaries within which you can act. All being well, you will have a job description setting out your primary responsibilities and accountabilities (we look at job descriptions in Chapter 5). This job description may indicate your 'authority' – perhaps it specifies a budget – but it is unlikely to be specific about every activity that you will undertake.

One approach is to examine each activity and in each case ask, 'Should I be taking administrative action, advisory action or executive action?' The answer will lie in the factors we discussed above. Let's have a look at each type of action.

Administrative action

This consists of maintaining procedures and operating systems. For example, an HR practitioner may be advised of the outcome of salary negotiations and then be expected to calculate new salaries and notify the payroll department. Other examples are the headcount (regularly establishing the number of employees), recruitment activities, maternity leave and issuing letters of appointment. In the case of administrative activities you will usually be given some specific instructions initially and, if supervised, details of how to carry out the task. This type of work is often assigned to a shared services centre because it is straightforward to delegate.

Advisory action

This assumes that you have some specialist knowledge or information and can provide guidelines for managerial decisions. Areas in which HR practitioners typically advise are disciplinary procedures and employment law. Clear knowledge and understanding here will enhance your credibility considerably. Keep in mind, though, that this is a difficult area – if in any doubt, seek advice from more senior colleagues or Acas. There are more details of the legal background that you need in Chapter 3.

In salary negotiations, HR practitioners frequently brief the negotiating team on current remuneration packages or on market rates. They may also be members of the negotiating team.

Advisory actions can also be centralised as shared services utilising a central team to advise local line managers of disciplinary actions they can take. Advisory actions can sometimes be determined by 'expert systems' – essentially a computer providing a question-and-answer process. The questions and answers can be managed by an individual in a call centre or even provided as an e-HR resource for managers to access the advice for themselves. These processes are relatively new and no doubt some will work well and others prove to be unwise, at least initially. Incorporating 'experience' into a computer algorithm (decision-making process) takes time.

The development of policies and procedures may be seen as another form of advisory action. In creating these an HR department is partly providing documented advice and partly engaged with senior members of the organisation to arrive at decisions that will guide managers and others.

Executive action

This means taking full responsibility for certain tasks, making decisions and taking appropriate action. For example, in some organisations an HR practitioner may be sufficiently senior, and authorised, to make the decision to dismiss an employee. Similarly, some practitioners can assume full responsibility for salary negotiations – that is, for reaching an agreement and implementing it. You will not, of course, be taking such decisions unless you have been very clearly authorised to do so. These types of action are quite likely ones that will be taken by an HR business partner working in partnership with the line management.

?   REFLECTIVE ACTIVITY 2.8

Study Table 2.2. Identify activities and tasks that take place in your HR department.

Now select the types of action that your department takes, placing a tick in the appropriate column(s).

Circle those actions that you might take yourself.

Discuss the results with others in a similar position in different organisations.

How do the activities of your department differ from theirs?

This brings us to how you build strong links between yourself, your management team, employees and the community. This is an important task, representing a whole group of actions that you can take. They will enable you to relate effectively to others in the organisation.

Table 2.2 Activities and tasks of HR departments

Activity	Task	Executive	Advisory	Admin
Recruitment and selection	Determining methods			
	Defining requirements			
	Advertising			
	Processing applications			
	Interviewing			
	Taking part in decisions			
	Organising programmes			
	Offering jobs			
	Taking up references			
Industrial relations	Attending meetings			
	Applying agreements			
	Acting as a specialist			
	Advising on law			
Direction and policy	Participating in procedures			
	Developing policy			
Health, safety and welfare	External relations			
	Counselling			
	Occupational health			
Pay administration	Pensions			
	Instructions to pay			
	Initiating transactions			
Workforce – planning and control	Dealing with complaints			
	Maintaining records			
	Controlling numbers			
Learning and development	Identifying needs			
	Providing learning			
Employee communications	Planning			
	Operating			
Organisation design	Job descriptions			
Information and records	Determining needs			
	Providing information			

Source: Adapted from Farnham (1999, p 114)

Building bridges

Spend some time considering the questions below and the discussion that follows each. They should give you some clues as to how you can develop the links we have just mentioned.

- **What are your methods of communication?**

In face-to-face spoken communication, only a small proportion of the communication is conveyed by the words used. Estimates vary, but it is somewhere in the region of 6–10%. The remainder depends on body language, eye contact, pitch, speed, volume, and tone of voice. So when we use the telephone, body language and eye contact are lost, and volume and tone can be altered by the phone line to some extent. When we use email, what is left? We see this as a particular problem for shared services because emails can easily sound blunt. It is worth taking care in composing emails. We suggest that it is important to be able to respond using normal language. Responses abbreviated because a full grammatical sentence takes too long to type are too easily open to misinterpretation. It is good practice to use a grammar checker because that can help ensure your meaning is not misunderstood. Compose, read, amend, re-read, amend, and re-read is one way of improving the written tone of your correspondence whether it is by letter, email or on social media.

- **How do employees make contact with you?**

Interruptions are a serious source of inefficiency, but at the same time you cannot afford to be remote. Is your department close to where most employees work? Is your department found easily? An open door encourages contact, whereas a formal appointment system may discourage it. For a larger department, a front desk helps avoid the whole department being interrupted by an enquiry. Accessibility via email is helpful too. Emails reduce interruptions by allowing a choice over when a response is sent. Intranets, perhaps with a 'Frequently Asked Questions' page or a dedicated e-HR page, may be an effective way of reducing interruptions while also answering employees' questions. Placing HR policies and procedures on an intranet or online also enables employees to answer questions (such as about maternity leave) for themselves.

- **How do you make contact with employees?**

Making time to 'walk the floor' can ensure that employees know who you are, foster contact and help you to assess the general mood and spot any changes in mood. It takes time, of course, on your part and on that of employees. Furthermore, not all management teams will welcome direct contacts between you and (their) employees in this way. Another approach is to make a habit of going to see employees directly to deal with matters that arise, rather than telephoning, calling them to your office, or issuing an email. You can inform the employee's manager first if protocol requires it.

- **How healthy are your relationships with trade union representatives?**

Keeping representatives in touch with issues that concern their members helps build good relationships. You need to be careful what you do discuss, consulting senior management members first if you have any doubts. Nevertheless, making time to talk with the representatives and taking an interest in their viewpoint can be revealing, and you may very probably see your organisation in a different light. Often you will pick up minor issues that you can remedy, or more serious ones in which you can still have an influence. We provide some background on trade unions in 2.6.

- **Are you in touch with your management team?**

Whilst email is efficient and promotes good time management, using the telephone or visiting individuals may be more effective and, crucially, builds relationships. Face to face is even more effective in communication, as we discussed above. Be mindful of people's time and the pressures on them. Nonetheless, most managers enjoy discussing issues face to face. A useful tip is to stand up for informal meetings, thus encouraging contact to be short. The tip also works for telephone calls, because your voice changes when you stand up – it conveys more urgency. Make sure you attend at least some relevant formal meetings. Some organisations have a meetings culture, in which case you will probably want to attend as few as possible. Whatever the culture, try to be present at important meetings and go along prepared to make a positive contribution.

- **Does the community regard your organisation as a good employer?**

The manner in which you recruit, respond to unsolicited applications and reject unsuccessful job applicants is often commented upon, especially if you are in a small community. Contact between the community and an important local employer invariably increases the regard in which that employer is held. It may also provide you with valuable information – and liaison between HR practitioners and local bodies, such as schools or societies, is usually welcomed. If community activities interest you, you may be able to foster links with the community by being active in, for example, the Chambers of Commerce, or in the various clubs for executive, professional and business people. Your employer may welcome your involvement in activities that contribute to improving the social environment and you may be able to gain support from them for suitable endeavours.

Many organisations take social responsibility seriously, perhaps yours does, and have a specific corporate social responsibility (CSR) policy.

- **What is the department's profile?**

The quality of communications can help set the scene. Here we are thinking of examples such as induction information and the employee handbook, company intranet, Facebook or other social media, notices on the noticeboards, clarity of payslips, notification of pay increases, web pages and contributions to the company newsletter. The tone of communications, even the tone of the employee handbook, sends messages. We see many such handbooks that refer to 'the employee' as if that is somebody completely different from the person who will be reading the handbook. How you deal with personal issues will go deeper. Learning good counselling skills helps here. Actions always speak louder than words.

- **How will you react to a redundancy programme?**

Redundancy-handling is one of the most emotive issues with which you are likely to come into contact. Whether you are involved in handling the issues directly or not, you will probably be identified with such programmes by other employees, and you should think through the implications of this. More information on handling redundancies is contained in Chapter 3.

- **What else may you have to face?**

Other personal issues such as bereavement, maternity, illness/disability, debts or bankruptcy may well demand your attention. The sympathetic, consistent and practical way in which you handle these will reflect strongly on your department's reputation. As with redundancy, it helps in these cases if you think through in advance how you will handle the issues. You will find guidance in Chapter 12 on developing the necessary skills.

We had a look at organisation structures earlier and examined the tasks required of an HR function and the types of action you as an HR practitioner may be able to take. But you will, in many cases, be working within an HR department. Organisations differ in how the role of HR is structured within an organisation.

2.6 ORGANISING THE HR FUNCTION

In a small organisation – say, up to 50 employees – there is unlikely to be an HR department. Essential HR activities are likely to be undertaken by the owner or managing director and activities that are more administrative in nature carried out by a PA. Employment advice (which we look at in Chapter 3) is often provided by insurance firms (who protect small employers from employment tribunal claims), law firms, accountants, employer associations or HR consultants. Unfortunately, when it comes to selection decisions, disciplinary hearings or attendance problems, the owner or managing director is often left to handle the difficult situation on their own.

Once an organisation employs more than this number, it is typical to assign someone to, or even appoint them to, the HR role. The role may be delegated to the PA, who has been handling the administrative functions, or it might be assigned to the accountant or one of his or her staff. Ideally, a dedicated, qualified and experienced HR officer would be appointed – but this is more likely only as the number of employees increases beyond the 100 mark. Even organisations of 250 employees do not always have a dedicated HR person.

As the size of an organisation increases beyond this size, so it is increasingly likely that there will be not only a dedicated HR person, but most probably an HR department. Such a department is likely to be generalist, handling a broad range of HR activities as we discussed earlier.

HR departments are structured in many different ways, often dependent on the role and size of HR and on the type of organisation. Some will encompass health and safety, training, facilities management and employee relations. In other organisations these functions may be elsewhere in the organisation structure, outsourced or even not present at all. Job titles and terms vary too. The terms 'HR', 'personnel', 'director', 'executive officer', 'head of...', 'manager', 'adviser', 'officer', 'assistant', 'secretary', 'trainer', and 'instructor' are just a sample of those you may come across. The significance of each title will also vary from one organisation to another. The term 'HR business partner' tends to have a particular meaning, which we address below.

Figure 2.3 shows an HR structure that might be found in a manufacturing organisation.

Of course, some organisations employ thousands of people, often with several sites, and most of our largest organisations operate internationally too. In these organisations there is likely to be significant differentiation even within the HR department. Further functions such as employee relations, talent management, training, policy, strategic advice, and employment law may each have independent specialists or even separate departments.

Figure 2.3 An HR structure

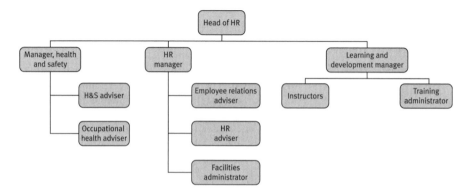

In these latter circumstances the structure of the HR function itself becomes an important decision for the organisation. Should each location have its own team (decentralisation)?

Should the main functions and particularly policy be centrally located at the head office, or should there be some combination, with some aspects centralised and some distributed? Indeed, should the function be outsourced, in whole or in part, by using an external company to provide the service?

2.6.1 SHARED SERVICES, BUSINESS PARTNERS AND CENTRES OF EXPERTISE

In the 1990s David Ulrich in the USA developed a model for the HR function that came to be described as the three-legged approach. In this model HR can be seen as having three separate legs, as follows:

- a shared services component
- business partnering
- centres of expertise.

Shared services

These are primarily administrative functions, dealing with transactional activities, that may be centralised and then shared across different divisions of the organisation, or even in some cases, across different organisations, for example different NHS Trusts. Payroll, typically, has been a shared service in many organisations, but this concept may be extended to a wide range of administrative tasks. Recruitment administration, contracts of employment, employee records or an employment law helpline are examples of business processes that may be shared by many divisions in a large organisation. The use of information and communication technology facilitates such an approach.

There are many examples of shared services in government organisations and the public sector generally. Larger private sector organisations also adopt shared services, sometimes across international boundaries. In larger organisations, particularly, they offer the benefit of economies of scale and they provide the opportunity for outsourcing services. Indeed, many small organisations already outsource such services as payroll, recruitment, and employee relations support. Outsourced providers are often a form of shared service in themselves, supporting a number of businesses rather than divisions of a single business.

Business partnering

This concept rests on HR professionals working closely with senior managers or business owners at a strategic level rather than an administrative level. By focusing on the needs of the organisation and its senior managers, the HR function has the opportunity to make a greater contribution. An often valid criticism of the HR function is that it does not understand the business from the perspective of those charged with running it. By partnering with managers, rather than getting bogged down in heavy administrative tasks, there is an opportunity for a better understanding. HR practitioners who are business partners need to focus on understanding the organisation from the business perspective. To step up to the role, HR practitioners need commercial savvy as well as HR savvy.

Typical challenges for business partners (based on *HR Outlook* Winter 2014–15) are:

- understanding exactly how your organisation delivers its objectives
- being able to use data and evidence to persuade others
- being curious, recognising business objectives, and being able to demonstrate the impact on the business
- partners need to have integrity and consideration for senior managers, but also the courage to challenge those managers.

Despite business partnering being popular and widespread there are differing views on the precise role of business partnering across organisations and therefore of its success.

Centres of expertise

As this book shows, HR has a wide remit covering everything from recruitment to dismissal and beyond. Performance management, L&D, reward and trade union relationships are just a few of the specialist areas within HR that in a large organisation might be separate functions in themselves. In centres of expertise, small teams of HR practitioners focus on particular areas, providing specific specialist advice. A specialist in learning and development might know virtually nothing about reward and vice versa.

Context

This three-legged approach relates mainly to larger organisations.

The Ulrich model has also come in for criticism, notably for being divisive within the HR function and for its ability to handle issues that might span two or three of the 'legs'.

The most popular model in the UK is a single HR team with a mixture of expertise, which is used by around four in ten businesses. Just over a quarter of organisations surveyed use the Ulrich model and this is more prominent amongst larger organisations. The survey also showed that the private sector favours the single HR team structure whereas the public sector is more likely to adopt the Ulrich model'.

(*HR Outlook* Winter 2014–15)

HR practitioners in small and medium-sized enterprises (SMEs) and other small organisations such as charities usually need to be generalists able to deal with administration, strategy and delivery of specialist expertise. Often all these roles are vested in one person. At the start of 2015 SMEs accounted for 99.9% of all private sector businesses in the UK and just under 60% of private sector employment (source: Federation of Small Businesses).

2.6.2 OTHER CONCEPTS

The customer care concept

This concept originated outside the HR function. It is based on the idea that all functions have a responsibility to serve customers. Those functions that do not deal directly with the organisation's customers, but nevertheless have 'internal' customers. This concept applies a sound discipline to which it is easy to relate: we all experience the customer relationship when we are customers ourselves. In that position we expect to be treated with respect.

In a shared services centre you are providing more than one part of your organisation, perhaps at different geographical sites, with HR services. Customer care concepts are particularly important because there is often some geographical distance between the service centre and the units served.

Reflective Activity 2.9 encourages you to look at what customer care might mean and how it might relate to the work you do.

?   REFLECTIVE ACTIVITY 2.9

Good customer service is most in evidence when things go wrong!

Think back over recent weeks and months when something did go wrong. Choose an occasion when you felt, despite the problem, that you had some excellent customer service. Make a list of what it was that led you to that feeling – how did the other person or organisation behave?

This activity works well in a small group because not all behaviours in excellent service occur on every occasion. At the end of this chapter we have provided some thoughts of our own – but look at those only after you've made your own list and had at least an initial run through the rest of this exercise.

Now, considering each experience in turn, review how much behaviour is in evidence in the department or central service where you work.

Finally, draw up an action plan of steps you could take to improve the customer service delivery of your department or service.

However HR is organised within your organisation you need to give thought to how you will be judged by your internal customers, and more often than not, that judgement will be on the service you are perceived to give to them.

Service-level agreements are an extension of the customer care concept so that it can operate within an organisation. A typical agreement might be one in which the HR department agrees to fill all staff vacancies within, say, ten weeks of recruitment being authorised. As practitioners, we have found that setting some standards of service goes down well with other functions and motivates us strongly to achieve them. For HR departments (as with other functions and many professions) the question still arises: 'Who are our customers?' Are they other departments, prospective employees, current employees, senior managers, or all of these? Since the last option is essentially correct, how can we balance conflict between different customers? Who will have priority?

One way of understanding the dilemma this poses is to look at the notion of stakeholders.

The stakeholder concept

In the stakeholder concept these other parties or customers are seen as having a stake in our department's time. Although balancing conflicting interests may be regarded as a managerial function, we all have to mediate between the various people who make demands on our time at and away from work.

As an example, consider others who have a stake in your personal time: your partner, your family, your source of income, and any voluntary leisure commitments. You need continually to balance the demands of each of these on your time and energy and against each other.

Looking again at the work situation, the stakeholder concept is not restricted to internal departments. The organisation itself needs to consider a whole range of groups that have a stake in its activities. These are likely to include employees, shareholders, trade unions, the Government and local communities, as well as customers and suppliers.

> **?   REFLECTIVE ACTIVITY 2.10**
>
> Taking your organisation, or the site within it where you work, identify the main stakeholders. Which groups or organisations benefit from the existence of your employer? Who would lose out if your organisation became less successful or reduced its presence? What implications do these stakeholders have for your work? (As an example, in a small community the local school may be a major supplier of new employees. The implications for you could be that you would wish to foster good relations with the school.)

Balancing the differing needs of stakeholders demands good communication, understanding, assertiveness and judgement. It is a crucial challenge for all managers.

Now have a look at Reflective Activity 2.11. You will find feedback on this activity at the end of the chapter.

> ### ? REFLECTIVE ACTIVITY 2.11
>
> Think carefully of the service you or your HR department give to line managers or other internal customers in your organisation.
>
> How might you measure the level of service that you provide?
>
> Make a list of appropriate measures and appropriate levels of service that you might provide. At the end of this chapter we give some examples, but ones from your own experience are most valuable.

Up to now we have focused on the nature of organisations themselves, expectations of the HR function, how it might be organised and some underlying concepts behind service delivery. There is one particularly significant stakeholder in most larger organisations: the relevant trade union or trade unions.

2.7 TRADE UNIONS

For many HR practitioners, trade unions are part of the organisational context within which they work. We will, therefore, provide some background to trade unions and the issues that surround working in a unionised environment.

2.7.1 WHAT IS A TRADE UNION?

A trade union is an association of members – in which respect it is different from, say, a private company, which has a distinct legal identity. To be a trade union an organisation has to be recognised by a certification officer (appointed by the Government) and is usually a member of the Trades Union Congress (TUC).

Each trade union has its own rules for membership and its own administration and operation. However, there are significant restrictions on union activities brought in by legislation, much of it aimed at 'increasing democracy' within trade unions. Legislation outlaws discrimination in employment on the basis of membership or non-membership of a trade union, which effectively prevents closed shops. It also outlaws blacklists (where a list is kept, and shared, of so-called 'troublemakers' who then find it difficult to get employment) that have been held by some less scrupulous employers' groups, even recently.

2.7.2 RECOGNITION AND COLLECTIVE AGREEMENTS

Not all employers, of course, welcome unions. Others pride themselves in having such good communications with employees that unionisation has not been desired by those employees. But the employers who recognise a trade union give that union the right to make collective agreements with them on behalf of its members (and other employees). In order for a trade union to form and enter into collective bargaining, there are two requirements: the ability to organise; and recognition by an employer.

If groups of workers feel sufficient mutual interest for them to wish to negotiate jointly, they would normally join an appropriate existing trade union. 'Organisation', in this context, implies the ability of these workers to meet in one place and formulate some common objectives. This has always been easier in large establishments, or where there is a lot of commonality in jobs, such as education and teaching or BAE Systems. Industries in which workers are scattered in smaller groups (such as retail shops, hotels and farming) find organisation less practical, and they tend to be less unionised and, therefore, less likely to have collective agreements.

Where a union has a substantial number of members within a particular group of workers, it may apply to the employer for recognition. Employers may then draw up agreements with a union branch to recognise the right of the trade union and its shop stewards to represent its members with the employer. Shop stewards are employees who are also representatives of the trade union at the place of work. Where recognised by the employer, they have legal rights to go about a variety of duties related to their trade union responsibilities.

Where employers do not reach agreement on recognition voluntarily, there is a legal procedure under which a trade union may apply to a Central Arbitration Committee (set up by the Government) to have a ballot for recognition. Recognised trade unions have the right to negotiate on behalf of their members in relation to pay, hours and holidays as well as any other matter that may form part of the recognition agreement.

In addition, they have a statutory right to be consulted by the employers on a number of matters. This includes consultation on occupational pensions, on health and safety issues, on redundancy, on any transfer of ownership of the business, and on training policies and plans.

A key part of trade union philosophy, enshrined in the word 'union', is that by joining together, employees can counter employers' powers to 'exploit' them. Traditionally, it was manual workers that most strongly felt this need, then in the latter part of the twentieth century, many white-collar workers became unionised. A 2015 BIS survey reports that union membership is now higher among graduates, people in professional jobs, women, middle-income earners and those working in the public sector. The process of negotiating as part of a union is usually referred to as 'collective bargaining', and the outcomes of such bargaining as 'collective agreements'.

In negotiating agreements, trade unions have a statutory right of access to the information necessary for the bargaining process. If they are denied access to particular information, they may apply to the Central Arbitration Committee for adjudication on whether they are entitled to access the information. Collective agreements can cover almost any part of the employer-employee relationship. They may be divided into *substantive* and *procedural*.

CASE STUDY 2.2

A residential home for older people found it needed to respond to new employment legislation. The Employment Rights Act, Working Time Regulations and the Employment Relations Act (see Chapter 3), among others, had all created the need for more formal working relationships than had been the case in the past. Written particulars (see Chapter 3) had been prepared and annual leave arrangements had been made. Employees were concerned about these changes and had joined a trade union that then sought and was granted recognition. Even so, members of staff were still concerned about the need for written particulars and the management

team was uncertain how to deal with this new trade union relationship.

In consultation with an HR practitioner, the managers drew up an agreement that recognised appropriate rights for the trade union and confirmed the trade union's respect for the charitable status of the home and the aims of the management team. In particular, it determined how collective bargaining would be conducted and how any disputes would be resolved.

The approval of the agreement at a meeting with the trade union has provided a framework for tackling employment matters jointly. Importantly it has created a co-operative approach to the annual pay review. Although other essential changes have been taking place in the home; nevertheless, it is acknowledged that a trade union environment has contributed to better working relationships.

Substantive agreements relate to aspects of the contract between employer and employee – for example, the terms and conditions of employment, the rate of pay or the hours of work. They are sometimes subject to annual negotiation – the annual pay round.

Procedural agreements cover the procedures for regulating the relationship, including the method by which the parties will conduct collective bargaining. An overall procedural agreement is usually made in order to define the areas in which trade union representation is acknowledged. The procedures themselves provide a means of dealing with issues and resolving conflict in fair and consistent ways. Making procedures a part of collective agreements effectively means that as long as the procedures are followed, unions and management will be in agreement on issues. At the least they will have clear steps to follow in resolving them. Areas covered by procedures may include:

- how trade union representatives are appointed
- disputes, and the arbitration procedure if they are not resolved
- discipline and grievance handling
- redundancy.

Procedures also enable the organisation to indicate the flexibility that it will allow individual managers in order to ensure that they do not make decisions that counter organisational objectives.

Procedures usually provide for disputes and disagreements to rise through levels of management if they cannot be resolved at a lower level. Generally, they would require matters to be raised at the lowest appropriate level first, and then at other levels later. So, for example, under a disciplinary procedure a supervisor may be empowered to warn an employee about his or her behaviour, but not to dismiss. Where such action is necessary, the supervisor will raise the matter to the next level.

Employers often see the principle of collective agreements as beneficial to them. It is necessary, for example, to consult workers at a branch of the company that is closing. Where employees are unionised, employers can usually negotiate with a few representative individuals and form an agreement that covers all, or at least a whole category of, employees. Without a recognised trade union, an employer is dependent on workers' electing employee representatives or on 'information and consultation' arrangements. Unless some arrangements are in place, the employer would have to consult every single employee on an individual basis. In our example, that means all the workers in the branch that is closing. Those covered by collective agreements will have many, if not most, of their employment terms determined by such agreements. Where these terms are not to their liking, their first port of call is then their trade union shop steward – a practice which, in effect, filters out many minor issues.

Despite the advantages that collective agreements can offer, the consequences of strikes lead the public, who are often inconvenienced by such action, to question collective bargaining. It is to such action that we now turn.

2.7.3 INDUSTRIAL ACTION

The term 'industrial action' is still widely used, although such action now frequently takes place outside traditional industries. Strikes are the most prominent form of action but other options exist, such as the refusal to do overtime.

It can be argued that power implies the capacity to hurt another party (and the willingness to do so), even though exercising such power may involve a cost to both parties. The desire to avoid that cost means that much can be achieved by the knowledge that such power exists and the fact that it is in the interests of both parties to avoid the costs of a breakdown. Don't be deceived by media treatment that likes to emphasise the conflict between 'trade unions and management'. Conflict is more newsworthy, hence the emphasis. More often than not, the two parties work together very positively. Nevertheless, the fact that employees may decide to take industrial action is a source of power in coming to collective agreements. The power balance, of course, shifts continuously with many factors, such as the changing legal background, the level of unemployment and the market position of an individual employer.

Where employers and employees (represented, usually, by a union) cannot negotiate satisfactory agreements, either party may resort to industrial action. For example, in recent years many strikes have taken place, or been threatened, in the public sector where pay packets have fallen in real terms, pension contributions have been increased and new contracts proposed for junior doctors. In each case both sides seek to use skilful manipulation to distort the picture of who is responsible for the breakdown of talks.

It, therefore, follows that great skill and care is required and that sensitive industrial relations issues will probably be handled by the most senior and the most experienced people in your organisation. You must be aware, too, that complex legislation regulates industrial action, that there is a need for a union to hold secret ballots, and that employees can exercise a right not to strike.

Sometimes trade unions try to achieve their aims across society, or with particular organisations, by means of marches, protests, national days of action and the use of social media to generate bad publicity.

If circumstances mean that you cannot avoid involvement in a dispute, always seek appropriate advice. In a large organisation this will be from more senior members of the HR department. In a small organisation, Acas (see below) or a consultant practitioner may be your most important source.

? REFLECTIVE ACTIVITY 2.12

Subject to consultation as appropriate with a senior member of your management team, initiate a discussion with a trade unionist, shop steward or convenor. Seek their views about the employment relationship, about trade unionism and about your organisation's corporate culture and objectives. Do they see themselves as partners seeking to work with management for the greater prosperity of the organisation, or as workforce representatives whose sole responsibilities are to represent the interests of their members?

2.8 ADVISORY, CONCILIATION AND ARBITRATION SERVICE (ACAS)

Acas is a body set up by the Government, but which is required to act impartially in seeking to promote good industrial relations. Its services are available both to employers and individuals, and it receives enquiries from both sources in comparable proportions. It can be called in by parties that are failing to agree on employment matters. It will endeavour to conciliate (essentially getting the parties to talk their problems through), appoint mediators (to suggest solutions to the parties) or appoint an arbitrator, who must have the full consent of both sides. In this latter case the parties agree to accept the arbitrator's decision in advance of the decision being made. The result is that Acas officials have a huge bank of experience in industrial conflict and are therefore excellently placed to assist in industrial relations.

Acas also has a valuable role in mediating disputes with individuals who have brought employment tribunal claims, which is explored in Chapter 8.

2.9 SUMMARY

- HR practice and management offer an interesting and exciting career. Potentially, the function encompasses any issue in which the employer, as a corporate body, relates to the employee. You should, therefore, have a good relationship both with employees (and their representatives – usually a trade union – where applicable) and with managers at all levels, as well as with relevant outside bodies.
- Practitioners must be mindful of the type of organisation within which they work so that they can direct their contribution and influence others appropriately.
- HR can be organised in different ways depending partly on the size and complexity of the organisation. Division of the function into a shared services centre with HR business partners and centres of expertise replaces the traditional department in some larger organisations in the UK.
- The HR function provides a service for the operational functions. It is not in itself profit-earning or a direct contributor to the operational purpose. What it does is to assist others in that role. To be effective it has to be mindful of caring for its 'customers' and of the various stakeholders, who may have conflicting interests.
- The actions that HR practitioners can take invariably include administrative actions, and frequently they include advisory actions. In many cases, particularly at senior levels, practitioners may have the authority to make executive decisions as well. For practitioners to be well regarded, they must be in tune with the corporate culture in which they work: they need to identify what is valued.
- Practitioners cannot ignore the pace of change and the effects that that has on employers and employees. Anticipating these effects will greatly enhance your performance.
- To be well informed, practitioners must build and maintain healthy relationships with a variety of stakeholders, particularly managers, trade unions, employees and the community from which their employees come.
- Trade unions are relevant for many practitioners, and you will have seen that a union is a different entity from a private company, for example. You should now understand the concepts of recognition, collective agreements, and industrial action.

EXPLORE FURTHER

References and further reading

BEARDWELL, J. and THOMPSON, A. (2014) *Human Resource Management: A contemporary approach.* London: Pearson.

DRUCKER, P. (2007) *The Effective Executive.* Revised edition. Oxford: Butterworth-Heinemann.

HANDY, C. (1993) *Understanding Organizations.* 4th ed. London: Penguin.

FARNHAM, D. (2015) *Human Resource Management in Context: Insights, Strategy and Solutions.* London: CIPD.

TORRINGTON, D., HALL, L., TAYLOR, S. and ATKINSON, C. (2009) *Fundamentals of Human Resource Management.* Essex: Financial Times/Prentice Hall.

Web references

Courage to Challenge: www.cipd.co.uk/binaries/Courage%20to%20Challenge.pdf

HR Outlook Winter 2014–15: www.cipd.co.uk/binaries/hr-outlook_2015-winter-2014-15-views-of-our-profession.pdf

Lucy Adams and the school of hard knocks: www.hrmagazine.co.uk/article-details/lucy-adams-and-the-school-of-hard-knocks

The Emperor Ulrich's new clothes: re-evaluating the role of HR Business Partners: www.hrzone.com/lead/strategy/the-emperor-ulrichs-new-clothes-re-evaluating-the-role-of-hr-business-partners

Social enterprise: www.socialenterprise.org.uk/uploads/files/2012/04/what_makes_a_social_enterprise_a_social_enterprise_april_2012.pdf

See also the following CIPD factsheets, available at www.cipd.co.uk/hr-resources/factsheets:

- Change management (October 2015)
- Employee voice (September 2014)
- HR business partnering (September 2015)
- HR outsourcing (September 2015)
- HR shared services (September 2015)
- Strategic human resource management (September 2015)
- The role of line managers in HR (June 2015)
- Understanding the economy and labour market (August 2015)

Websites

Advisory, Conciliation and Arbitration Service (Acas): www.acas.org.uk

Chartered Institute of Personnel and Development: www.cipd.co.uk

Department for Business, Innovation and Skills: www.gov.uk/bis

People Management: www.peoplemanagement.co.uk

Trades Union Congress: www.tuc.org.uk

REFLECTIVE ACTIVITIES FEEDBACK

Reflective Activity 2.9

You may have points of your own that are not listed below – your points are still valid. Equally, you might not agree with everything on our list, but these points are valid for us.

- I was able to speak to someone quickly.
- My call was returned.
- When I explained the problem, I knew I was understood because the problem was acknowledged by the other person. Perhaps they repeated it back to me in their own words.
- My complaint was treated as legitimate.
- The person spoke in language that I understood. For example, they did not use their jargon, but understood and used mine.
- There were delays but I was kept informed.
- I was treated with respect.
- The person took responsibility for solving the problem. ('Responsible' is an interesting word – think of it as 'response-able', that is, able to respond.)
- The commitment to find out the answer was kept.
- The apology was genuine.
- The person was not able to help, but I understood why.

- The person was not able to help, but escalated it to his or her manager, without my having to explain the problem again.

Note how many of these behaviours are about communication and understanding.

1   What is on your list of actions that you can take?

2   Are there responses that you'd like to make but are not able to do so?

3   Are you changing the things that you can?

4   Can you accept and live with what you cannot change?

5   Do you know the difference?

Reflective Activity 2.11

Examples of service levels:

- response times to provide information on employees such as current salary or disciplinary record or attendance record
- response times for information on collective information, such as attendance levels for a department
- time to fill a vacancy
- time to resolve a job-grading query
- number of disputes
- number of employment tribunal claims.

CHAPTER 3

The Legal Background to Employment

LEARNING OUTCOMES

After reading this chapter you will:

- know which legislation is likely to apply in the main areas of HR activity
- be able to discuss relevant legislation and requirements in discussions with managers and legal specialists
- be able to respond to the fundamental legal expectations placed on employers
- recognise the limitations of your knowledge and know where to find further information
- have an understanding of the basic employment legislation affecting HR practice, including employment contracts, individual employment rights, equality and diversity and ending the employment relationship.

3.1 INTRODUCTION

In this chapter we'll be considering the legal framework that underpins and regulates the formal employment relationship between employers and their employees and workers. First we'll consider why employment legislation is important for HR practitioners, how employment legislation is made and where it comes from. Next we'll use the concept of the employee life cycle as a framework to consider what legislation is relevant whilst recruiting, selecting and appointing employees (pre-employment and starting work), then how employment legislation impacts during employment, with a particular focus on individual employee rights and finally what legislation is relevant as the employment relationship comes to an end (ending employment). We will then end by looking at how disputes about employment rights and legislation are dealt with and the role of HR practitioners.

Whilst considering the impact of employment legislation on the formal employment relationship it is also important to be aware that legislation and other statutory regulation (areas that you may come across later in your HR career) also plays a much wider role in the employment field. This is often influenced by political, social and economic changes in society more widely – think about the cap on bankers' bonuses with its consequent impact on reward policies and the rules relating to driving time for drivers of goods vehicles and passenger-carrying vehicles with the impact this has on working practices. Consider the free movement of people around the EU with its impact on recruitment practice and cultural equality and diversity.

3.2 WHY IS LEGISLATION IMPORTANT?

In the employment relationship there is usually an imbalance of power – in favour of the employer. Having employment legislation in place ensures this imbalance is not exploited. It affords rights to employees that, in some organisations, may not otherwise exist. Employment law also serves to reinforce values in society and create workplace cultures that support the direction of travel in the wider world – think, for example, of the evolution of equality law from a narrow focus on sex and race discrimination to a much wider focus now, mirroring societal changes. For example, equality now applies regardless of sexual orientation and gender reassignment. Many employers view employment legislation as a helpful framework to refer to when managing employees, although some feel that bringing the law into employment relationships creates rigidity and sometimes makes it difficult for the business to be agile and respond to opportunities. Employees often feel that the law provides a degree of protection from poor management and exploitation, such as in the recent debates about zero-hours contracts. Many other feelings surround the question of law and employment. Some may arise from political beliefs, others from personal experience.

In recent years there have been attempts by successive governments, not entirely successful, to reduce the burden of legislation on employers. However, after the US, employment in the UK is one of the most lightly regulated regimes in the developed world. The extent to which strong feelings exist, and their relevance to HR practice, varies from organisation to organisation. Government organisations necessarily attach great importance to legal matters, whereas some entrepreneurial businesspeople may seek to minimise, or even disregard, the impact of the law on their employment practices. Other employers adopt employment practices that go over and above any minimum provided by the law. They aspire to practices that are the best that can be found, embracing the spirit as well as the letter of the law. One example, common in many larger employers, is having more generous maternity leave and pay than required by law.

Knowledge and understanding of employment legislation, and its impact, is a key competence for HR practitioners and business-owners/managers alike. The law has a bearing across many areas of HR practice – recruitment, reward, employee relations, change management, well-being, and performance management, to name a few. It is a huge area that changes rapidly and can, at times, be very specialised and complex. So, in this chapter, although we shall explain the main principles that you need to know, you are likely also to need advice from more senior colleagues, the Advisory, Conciliation and Arbitration Service (Acas), or legal and other specialists. A note on Acas: look for the logo as shown here if you use an Internet search engine. There are more details about Acas in Chapter 2.

? REFLECTIVE ACTIVITY 3.1

Think about your own organisation. How do managers and workers view the effect of law on employment? Do managers use it to control or manage people? If so, how? Do employment rights reassure employees? What do you think of the attitudes in your organisation? Write down your thoughts and discuss them with one of your learning sources, as described in Chapter 1.

3.2.1 A NOTE ON EMPLOYEES AND WORKERS

You will notice that we have already used the terms 'employees' and 'workers' and have mentioned the 'employment relationship' many times. The definition of 'employee' and 'worker' is not always consistent in different pieces of legislation, but in general, the rights we are going to talk about in this chapter only apply to either employees or workers – and not, for example, to self-employed people. The majority of people in work will be employees, but the distinction between employees and workers is important because different rights apply to each. In broad terms, employees have more rights than workers, and legislation that applies to workers will normally also apply to employees, but not necessarily vice versa. The intention behind the distinction is to ensure that some rights, although not all, will apply to less typical employment arrangements such as casual workers, zero-hours workers, 'as and when required' workers, freelance workers and some other types of subcontractors. There is more on this below.

3.3 WHERE DOES EMPLOYMENT LEGISLATION COME FROM?

In the UK, employment law comes from three different places:

- the UK Parliament – primary legislation (Acts of Parliament, for example the Equality Act 2010) and secondary legislation (Regulations, for example the Working Time Regulations 1998)
- tribunals and courts through case law – for example, the Employment Appeal Tribunal or the Supreme Court
- European bodies – for example, the European Parliament and the European Court of Justice.

Acts of Parliament generally start out as White (broad statements of policy) or Green (specific proposals and options) Papers and Bills. They will be subject to consultation with interested parties and debate in Parliament. At the early stages of new employment legislation, consultation will often be conducted by the Department for Business, Innovation and Skills (BIS). Once the full Parliamentary process has taken place, then new legislation will appear in the form of an Act. Often for Acts relating to employment matters, there will be a phased introduction of different clauses or parts of the Act, although they will also have a formal enactment date – in the case of employment legislation usually April or October. Some of the key Acts of Parliament that apply in the employment relationship include the:

- Trade Union and Labour Relations (Consolidation) Act 1992
- Employment Rights Act 1996
- Employment Act 2002
- Work and Families Act 2006
- Employment Act 2008
- Equality Act 2010
- Children and Families Act 2014.

The situation is somewhat different in relation to law that originates from the tribunals and courts – properly termed 'common law'. This common law evolves over time as cases are brought to tribunals and courts and judges make decisions or are asked to interpret a particular piece of primary or secondary legislation. Decisions by judges in higher courts must be applied by judges in lower courts. So, for instance, if an employee takes an unfair dismissal case to an employment tribunal and wins, but the employer then appeals and the case is heard by the Employment Appeal Tribunal, which overturns the decision, then in future cases of the same nature, all employment tribunals must apply the ruling/ interpretation as set out by the Employment Appeal Tribunal. Common law can be overturned by a subsequent Act of Parliament. Common law is particularly important in the field of employment legislation and decisions from employment courts lead to an almost constant evolution in employment law that anyone involved in HR must be aware of.

In relation to laws coming from the European Union, there are three main sources, which to some extent reflect the two UK based sources outlined above. These are:

- 'Treaties' which are directly enforceable in member states (for example, the Treaty of Rome 1957, which contained the principle of equal pay for equal work).
- 'Directives' which require further relevant national laws to be passed by member states – in the UK by an Act of Parliament (for example, the European Working Time Directive was enacted as the Working Time Regulations in the UK).
- Rulings of the European Court of Justice, which are binding on all member states (which, for example, led to the definition of discrimination on the grounds of pregnancy as 'direct discrimination').

It is possible to see the interaction of laws from these different sources by considering the area of working time – maximum allowable working hours per week, rest breaks, paid holidays and so on.

The European Commission introduced the Working Time Directive (WTD) in 1993. The stated aim of the WTD was to ensure the health and safety of workers and safeguard workers' rights. As a European Union (EU) *Directive*, it required member states, including the UK, to enact or pass it into national law. After some reluctance in the UK, the WTD was enacted as the Working Time Regulations (WTR) 1998. These Regulations have subsequently been amended a number of times by the UK Parliament. As indicated above, as this originated in the EU and was then enacted in the UK via *Regulations*, this is a piece of secondary legislation. Since 1998, the WTD and WTR have been subject to a number of challenges through both UK courts and tribunals and through employment courts in other EU member states and, ultimately, through the European Court of Justice. As challenges have been made through UK courts and tribunals and judges in these institutions have interpreted the WTR they have made decisions which must be followed in lower courts, thus *common law* about working time has been created. So, now, employers must be aware of legislation from each of the three sources identified above, and be aware of which takes precedence, when considering matters relating to working time. A complex and complicated area of HR practice we're sure you'll agree!

? REFLECTIVE ACTIVITY 3.2

Consider the question of paid holiday entitlement for workers. Do some research and try to find out:

- how much paid holiday workers in the UK are entitled to
- how bank holidays are treated
- what is included in the calculation of 'pay' when working out holiday pay
- what happens to holiday entitlement during sick leave and other types of leave (for example, maternity leave or shared parental leave).

Can you work out where the current rules on each of these matters come from – EU legislation, UK legislation or common law? Discuss what you have found out with one of your learning sources.

Compare your responses with the feedback given at the end of this chapter.

In considering where employment legislation comes from, it is important to also mention, briefly, Statutory Codes of Practice and the European Convention on Human Rights. Statutory Codes of Practice are issued by certain statutory agencies in the UK. They are documents that have been approved by Parliament and, in many instances, have to be taken into account by courts and tribunals when hearing complaints from workers and employers. The bodies that issue Statutory Codes of Practice include Acas, the Health and Safety Executive and the Equality and Human Rights Commission (EHRC). As seen in Chapter 8 on employee relations, it is advisable for employers to be aware of relevant statutory codes (for example, the Acas Code of Practice 1: Disciplinary and Grievance Procedures) both when writing their policies and procedures and when implementing them. The European Convention on Human Rights was incorporated into UK law in 2000, through the Human Rights Act 1998. The impact has been that common law must be compatible with human rights and previous decisions can be challenged on that basis. It means that all UK Acts of Parliament must be implemented and interpreted in line with the principles of the Convention and all public bodies (Local Government, hospitals, police, schools, etc.) must act in accordance with the Convention. This covers all their activities – policy-making, HR matters, decision making and so on. So it can be seen that when considering the impact of employment legislation from the three primary sources, it is also important to have one eye on both relevant Codes of Practice and human rights issues.

Having looked at why employment legislation is important and where it comes from, we will now look at the key components of the legislative framework that apply over the course of the employee life cycle: pre-employment/starting work; during employment; and ending employment.

3.4 PRE-EMPLOYMENT AND STARTING WORK WITH A NEW EMPLOYER

In terms of employment legislation, the most significant issues prior to employing someone are to ensure all recruitment and selection activity promotes and upholds the principles and legal requirements around equality and diversity and to address the requirements for pre-employment checks. As any new starter joins the organisation and moves through their first few weeks of employment, the critical issues concern the offer of employment, the contract of employment, the type of contract and employment status.

3.4.1 EQUALITY AND DIVERSITY IN RECRUITMENT AND SELECTION

It is important to consider equality and diversity at all stages and in all activities undertaken as part of any recruitment and selection process, including attracting a pool of applicants and making decisions about who to offer a job to. It is critical to ensure that any bias (including hidden bias) that might creep into the process is removed and that no unnecessary obstacles are placed in the way of the widest possible range of applicants getting involved. Issues such as clarifying the requirements of the job, drafting job descriptions and person specifications, deciding where to advertise and designing the selection process, including interview questions, must be considered carefully to ensure no breach of the relevant legislation and no discrimination or stereotyping. Further details of this legislation and its specific impact can be found in Chapter 5.

3.4.2 PRE-EMPLOYMENT CHECKS

Before making any offer of employment following a successful recruitment campaign, employers must ensure they undertake any necessary pre-employment checks. This is sometimes referred to as 'vetting' or seen as part of organisations' due diligence processes – in other words, ensuring that the organisation doesn't commit an offence. The areas where there are legal requirements are:

- Right to work in the UK – it is illegal for an organisation to employ foreign nationals who do not have the right to work in the UK and they could be subject to fines (at the time of writing of up to £10,000) for doing so. Employers are required to inspect and copy specified official documents that confirm identity and status – for example, a passport. There is a Code of Practice which sets out which documents are acceptable and situations where more than one document is required. Undertaking these checks in line with the Code will give an organisation a defence unless they knowingly employ an illegal worker. Knowingly employing a foreign national who does not have the right to work in the UK is a criminal offence. Employers must conduct a three-stage process to comply with the requirement to check right to work: request and review original copies of one or two specified documents; check as far as possible that the document(s) is genuine, relates to the worker and allows him or her to do that kind of work; and take and keep a copy of the document that cannot then be altered. This three-stage process must be completed before the individual starts work. In order to avoid falling into the trap of potential discrimination, employers should take a consistent approach to all applicants and avoid any assumptions, using the prescribed checks as the sole determinant of right to work. (The relevant legislation is the Immigration, Asylum and Nationality Act 2006.)
- Criminal records checks – in certain circumstances employers have the right to ask for a criminal records check, which is processed through the Disclosure and Barring Service (DBS). Under the Rehabilitation of Offenders Act 1974, people who have been convicted of a criminal offence can have their sentences treated as 'spent' after a certain period of time. This depends on age at the time of conviction (18 and over or not) and length of custodial sentence or other type of penalty. This means that, except in limited circumstances, the individual does not have to disclose a previous, and now 'spent', conviction to a prospective employer. There are, however, certain situations where a conviction never becomes spent and must always be disclosed. This relates to the type of job an individual is applying for and includes jobs in certain professions, those employed to uphold the law, those who work with children and vulnerable adults, and those whose work means they could pose a risk to national security (for example health professionals, care workers, lawyers, accountants, teachers and other workers in schools, childminders and anyone who works in a prison or similar institution). Full details can be found on the DBS website.
- Health checks – the Equality Act 2010 generally prevents employers from asking questions about health until after a job offer is made. The aim of this is to ensure recruitment decisions are made on the basis of merit and someone's ability to do the job and to ensure no conscious or unconscious bias against, for example, people with disabilities. Once a job offer is made, it can be subject to necessary health checks and questions. There are some limited exceptions to this general rule – for example, where health issues are relevant to decide whether an applicant can do a function that is intrinsic to the job (such as asking applicants for a job as a scaffolder whether they have a disability or condition that affects their ability to climb ladders), or for the purposes of monitoring and promoting equality and diversity.

In addition to these general legislative requirements in recruitment, there are also certain sector-specific requirements that go over and above the legal requirements on most employers. These include The NHS Employment Checks Standards, The Code of Practice on the Security Screening of Individuals Employed in a Security Environment, and particular checks in the financial services industry, to name three. Readers would be well advised to check whether any types of staff in their own organisations are subject to any wider checks.

?   REFLECTIVE ACTIVITY 3.3

Consider the pre-employment checks carried out in your organisation. Are the required checks always undertaken? Who is responsible for doing them? Are there any jobs in your organisation that might require a criminal records check? (You can check this on the DBS website.) Do you know whether the general requirement not to ask health questions until after a job offer has been made, for example by ensuring there are no health questions on your job application form, is applied? If you find any aspects of your organisation's recruitment process that are not legally compliant prepare a report on what needs to change and how, and share it with your manager.

3.4.3 OFFER OF EMPLOYMENT

Once a recruitment process has reached a successful conclusion, and all the necessary pre-employment checks have been done, a job offer will be made. It is advisable that all offers of employment are made in writing; however, readers should be aware that a verbal offer, made at interview or afterwards, is as legally binding as a written job offer. In employment, offers are often subject to issues such as the required employment checks outlined above, but also to references or verification of qualifications. In such cases, agreement is not reached until all the 'subject to' issues have been resolved.

The person making the offer on behalf of an organisation must be properly authorised to do so. This is very important for you as an HR practitioner. If you offer an employment contract without proper authority, your organisation could disown the decision. This would place you in a most invidious position and almost certainly leave you liable to disciplinary action. If the rejected employee had already accepted your offer, and handed in notice in his or her current employment, he or she may seek damages.

Notice that contracts do not have to be in writing. Many offers are made and accepted over the phone. If it can be established that a formal offer has been made and accepted, then an enforceable contract exists. Telephone offers are quicker and therefore reduce the danger of losing a good candidate while a written contract is being prepared. They can make negotiations easier so long as both parties are prepared for them and you have clear authority to reach an agreement. In the longer term, written offers and acceptance have the advantage that both parties know exactly what has been agreed. There is therefore less room for confusion (if references prove to be unsatisfactory, for example). Care has to be taken to be sure that an interview candidate is not led to believe an offer exists (by agreeing a pay rate, for example) when that is not the intention. Words such as 'If we were to offer you. . .' are important to help avoid confusion.

You need to find out whether your organisation has a policy on how offers should be made, or whether you are expected to use your best judgement.

Offers may be made and accepted by email. Offers can also be accepted by a person's behaviour: for example, arriving for work would indicate acceptance. It may be helpful to place a time limit on an offer, or formally to withdraw it if it is not accepted within a satisfactory timescale. As soon as an offer of employment is accepted, then an employment contract starts. An employment contract is an agreement between an employer and employee, is legally binding and is the basis of any employment relationship. It is in many ways no different from any other contract that two parties might enter into. It is governed by contract law, and requires the elements that make any contract legally binding:

- an *offer* (of employment by the employer)
- *acceptance* (of that offer by the employee)

- *consideration* (something of value the parties agree to exchange to make the contract valid, for example, the work done by the employee in return for the wages paid by the employer)
- *intention* (to create a legally binding arrangement).

We will now look at employment contracts in more detail.

3.4.4 CONTRACTS OF EMPLOYMENT

The contract sets out the legal basis of the employment relationship. It should therefore include those matters on which you wish your employee to be legally bound and matters on which you, as an employer, will be legally bound. For example, you may want to legally bind an employee to your office hours. If there is a clear written agreement specifying this as part of the contract, the hours become contractual.

On the other hand, there will be matters that you do not wish to be legally binding. Typically, disciplinary and grievance procedures are not part of the contract and it is advisable for only the minimum details required to be referred to in the written particulars (described below). You may have good reason to use judgement in operating disciplinary and grievance procedures. If such procedures are contractual, a failure to follow them to the letter can result in a breach of contract claim. For example, if grievance procedures are part of the contract, and you refuse to use them when an employee raises a grievance, the employee might claim that you have dismissed him or her by breaching the contract (known as constructive dismissal). In this case the employee could sue for damages such as entitlement to notice pay. He or she would be claiming wrongful dismissal – that is, dismissal in breach of the contract. The employee might also claim unfair dismissal, if he or she is entitled to do so. We will look at constructive and unfair dismissal again later. It is also important to remember that contracts cannot be changed unilaterally. To vary a contract, both parties have to agree to the change.

It is impossible to predict every possible employment situation that can arise. In some areas judgement or discretion is needed, therefore some matters should as far as possible not be contractual. Typical examples might be bonus scheme rules, job descriptions and policies and procedures. For the employer, gauging the degree of flexibility that should exist in the employment relationship is an important decision and requires careful judgement, although the final decision as to whether a particular term is contractual or not may rest with the courts.

Just to clarify the issue further, let's take the example of job descriptions. If you include a job description in an employment contract, every variation in the duties of the job can, potentially, become a legal issue. For this reason it is advisable to specify only the job title when making a contract. (Indeed, technically, even this could be left for the written particulars – see below.) Similarly, there is no requirement to include a job description in the written particulars. There is actually no legal need to have a job description at all, although, as discussed in Chapter 5, it may be good practice to do so.

The degree of formality involved in job descriptions affects an employer's flexibility to a significant degree. At one extreme, a lot of formality (job descriptions signed, or included in the contract) tends to encourage disputes over duties. Such disputes can focus on wording rather than the purpose of the job or the interests of the parties concerned. At the other extreme, complete informality (no job descriptions) may aid early resolution but can make it much more difficult if relationships do eventually break down. In informal situations it is easy for the employer to have one expectation about the employee's responsibilities and for the employee to have another.

This brings us to the distinction between statutory, implied and express terms in employment contracts. Statutory matters are not usually written into the employment contract but override other terms. This also means that they apply whether the parties specifically agree to include them or not. They include the requirements of the Health and Safety at Work Act 1974 (HASWA), the right to maternity leave, to statutory sick pay, to itemised pay statements and a wide range of matters, many of which are covered elsewhere in this chapter and this book. Other terms that may be implied in the contract include:

- common-law duties (such as the duty of care and co-operation with the employer and the duty of mutual trust and confidence between employer and employee)
- custom and practice (such as tea breaks, in cases where they are established).

Tribunals may imply terms into a contract where there is a dispute; they might consider the customs in the workplace and industry, or even the essential needs of the business, in reaching a decision. For example, in the residential care sector, where 24-hour cover is needed, it might be implied that employees can be required to work on Christmas Day even if there is no express term to that effect.

What do we mean by 'express terms'? These are matters that are clearly agreed between the two parties, either verbally or in writing. They normally take precedence over implied terms. Typically, express terms include matters such as hours of work, pay and holidays, and a range of other employment details. If you want a matter to be contractual, make it an express term – but you must be very careful in drawing up the contract because it will not be easy to vary it later. For example, if you want the place of work to be part of the contract, state it clearly and accurately.

However, you can put into the contract reasonable rights to vary aspects of the contract. So in the case of the place of work, you might include a mobility clause. Indeed, you can put into the contract (and written particulars) variation clauses for any right that you may wish to vary, so long as the variation is justifiable and reasonable; but if you are providing for something that might happen sometime in the future, you should still consult the employee(s) concerned when the variation is required.

It is important to include the notice period for termination of the contract by either party. Alternatively, the statutory minimum notice periods (based on length of service) may be stated.

Where a trade union is recognised, there may be collective terms included in the contract. These are terms that are agreed with a trade union and are applied to a 'collection' of employees. Employees need not be members of the trade union for collective terms to apply to them. This is because there should be no discrimination on the basis that an employee is, or is not, a trade union member.

As we discussed earlier, employment procedures such as disciplinary and grievance procedures may be incorporated into the contract. This means that if such procedures are not followed (in carrying out a dismissal, for example), there may be additional compensation awarded at a tribunal because the contract has been breached. Many employers specifically exclude employment policies and procedures from the contract to avoid this complication.

Both procedures and rules can be open to interpretation, and this may be a further case for not making them contractual. Nonetheless, contractual or not, they have significance because a tribunal will take their content, and the extent to which they may have been followed, into account when deciding whether an employer has acted fairly.

3.4.5 COMPONENTS OF THE CONTRACT

As has been seen, an employment contract does not just comprise one neat written document. There can be a number of sources that are considered when determining the totality of the contractual terms between an employer and employee – including but not limited to any job offer (written or verbal), the written particulars document, custom and practice in the workplace, employment legislation and so on. So a contract has many components and inevitably they interact. Their relative importance is summarised here, but the order should be taken as general guidance only.

Unwritten offers that may have been made and accepted form a contract, even though the fact may be difficult to prove in some circumstances. Matters discussed and agreed at a selection interview could be deemed part of the contract. Interviewers should be aware of this.

Statutory rights (and statutory terms such as the right to notice) apply to a contract once that contract has been made, even if that contract is only verbal. Furthermore, they apply even if the employee (or the employer) does not know about them! So, for example, if a worker agrees to work for a figure below the national minimum wage, because he does not know about it, he still has the right to that minimum wage.

Express contractual terms (made part of the contract, usually by the employer) do not override statutory terms but they can enhance such terms – by providing for more generous notice, for example. Express terms provide the opportunity for the employer (and, potentially at least, the employee) to determine how they wish the employment relationship to be structured.

Those terms that are determined by collective agreement must be specified in the contract (or written particulars, which we shall examine shortly), thus avoiding conflict between the main contractual terms and the collective terms.

Where there is no express contractual term, there could be terms implied into the contract if there are particular customs in an industry.

Lastly, rules, policies and procedures may be best kept out of the contract itself, but instead provided as guidance as to how the employer will act, what it expects of its employees and what it might regard as a breach of contract. Furthermore, they are invariably important in determining whether an organisation has acted fairly – a matter we return to in Chapter 8.

3.4.6 WRITTEN PARTICULARS

Throughout this book we use the term 'written particulars' to describe the terms and conditions of a person's employment. You may often hear reference to a 'written contract of employment' or just 'contract of employment'. Usually what is meant by this is the written particulars of the employment. However, as we saw earlier, a contract does not need to be written. Furthermore, even when it is written there will be other components of the contract that are not written, such as common-law duties. So, technically, the contract of employment is not a written document. Instead we have 'written particulars' that describe the main components of the contract. 'Statement of terms and conditions' is also an alternative term for the written particulars. Technically such particulars are provided for information only and represent the employer's view of the terms of the relationship; where they conflict with any contractual terms, the contract will prevail. Remember, the contract does not need to be written; it can be enforced even if there are no written particulars. It follows, therefore, that it can also be broken (leading to a possible breach of contract claim) even if nothing is in writing. However, new employees, employed to work for one month or more, have the right to receive written particulars of their employment within two months of starting employment. These rights are provided for in the Employment Rights Act 1996.

Look at the boxed text below that describes the required content of written particulars. Think through why the law provides these rights and what benefits they confer.

1   Is it fair and reasonable for employees to know where they stand?

2   Do written particulars protect employees from maltreatment? If so, how?

3   Is a better understanding between employer and employee likely to arise as a result of putting particulars in writing?

4   Why do you think many employers still do not provide written particulars? Is it:

  – through lack of knowledge of the law?
  – to save administration costs?
  – for power, gained by keeping employees ignorant of their rights?

WRITTEN PARTICULARS

The following are required in one document, termed 'the principal statement':

- names of employer and employee
- date when employment began
- date when continuous employment began
- scale or rate of remuneration or method of calculation
- intervals at which remuneration is paid
- terms and conditions relating to hours of work (including normal working hours)
- holiday entitlement (including entitlement to accrue holiday pay)
- job title or brief job description
- place of work.

The following may be provided in separate documents:

- terms relating to injury, sickness and sick pay
- pensions and pension schemes
- period of notice each party must give to terminate the contract
- where the employment is temporary, how long it is likely to last, or the termination date for a fixed-term contract
- collective agreements which directly affect terms and conditions
- disciplinary rules and steps in the disciplinary and grievance procedures, specifying the people with whom, and how, an employee can raise a grievance or appeal if dissatisfied with a disciplinary decision.

Certain additional details are also required for employees sent to work outside the UK for more than one month.

Compiling written particulars demands care.

There are many guides available for preparing particulars – for example, the Government website (see References and Further Reading at the end of this chapter).

You might like to know what the consequences of not providing written particulars are likely to be. Bear in mind that government officials will not arrive at your door to check their existence, and neither you nor your employer is going to be prosecuted for such failures. However, if you fail to provide written particulars within the time limit, an employee can apply to an employment tribunal, which may then determine particulars of employment as it sees fit.

More seriously, if a tribunal claim is made and you have failed to provide adequate written particulars, tribunals must award two or four weeks' pay to the employee as compensation. You may feel this is unlikely to happen. Although it is clearly not good practice to neglect written particulars, so long as relationships with employees remain fair, you might be right. However, redundancies, dismissals or even resignations increase the chances of aggrieved employees making employment tribunal claims. Furthermore, a complaint that you have failed to provide written particulars will substantially weaken your case at tribunal. So you would be wise to encourage the managers in your organisation to accept good practice. Indeed, most managers like to be thought of as good employers.

> **?   REFLECTIVE ACTIVITY 3.5**
>
> Look into how contracts are made and written particulars are prepared in your organisation. Compare the written particulars for a typical appointment with the details here. Discuss any differences with a suitable learning source.

3.4.7 TYPES OF CONTRACT

When deciding to recruit a new member of staff, and certainly at the point of negotiating contract terms with the successful candidate, you will give consideration to the type of contract that is required and most appropriate. The different types of contract that you might consider include:

- permanent (full- or part-time)
- fixed-term
- zero-hours/casual
- freelance/agency/sub-contractor.

Let's take a look at these in a bit more detail.

Permanent contracts

These are probably the most common type of employment contract and can be full- or part-time. Holders of these types of contracts will usually be classed as employees when it comes to the important question of employment status (see 3.4.8 Employment status). Employees on permanent contracts are often the cornerstone of any organisation's workforce. Permanent employees can be paid hourly, weekly or monthly and contracts can be straightforward or more complicated depending on the level of seniority. For part-timers, there is likely to be a greater focus on contractual terms such as hours and holidays to ensure accuracy in calculation. The law (The Part-time Workers (Prevention of Less Favourable Treatment) Regulations 2000) prohibits less favourable treatment on the basis of being part-time and therefore it is important to ensure that the terms and conditions of full-timers and part-timers are the same, except for any pro rata calculation for pay and holidays.

Fixed-term contracts

These are generally used for temporary employees and last for a certain length of time, ending when a specific task is finished (for example, a work project or a seasonal activity) or a specific event takes place (for example, the return to work of someone who has been on maternity leave). Fixed-term employees are entitled to the same rights as permanent staff by virtue of the Fixed-term Employees (Prevention of Less Favourable Treatment) Regulations 2002 in relation to terms and conditions of employment. The Regulations also provide additional rights in relation to the ending of the contract or conversion to a permanent contract.

Zero-hours/casual contracts

'Zero-hours' is not a legal term and there is no legal definition of a zero-hours contract. However, these types of contract have received a lot of attention and press coverage and so it is important to understand what they are. So-called zero-hours contracts (also sometimes known as 'casual' or 'as and when required' contracts) come in a number of forms and cover a number of different arrangements – the worst of which are the ones that have received a bad press. In essence, this is an arrangement whereby one party (the individual) can be asked by the other party (the employer) to work but without a set minimum number of contracted hours. Unlike the contract types described above, with a zero-hours arrangement there is not usually an ongoing mutuality of obligation under which an employer agrees to provide a set amount of work and an employee agrees to do it. In most instances, the individual has the right to turn down any offer of particular shifts. However, there has been a lot of case law on this and in some instances there has been found to be a mutuality of obligation during specific periods of work or particular assignment, although not in gaps between work and assignments. A lot of the bad press focused on so-called 'exclusivity' clauses, where working for other employers was not allowed, although this practice was outlawed in July 2015. Individuals working under a zero-hours arrangement may be termed 'workers' or 'employees' (see 3.4.8 Employment status) and the terms and conditions may differ to those offered to permanent employees. This is a complex and potentially confusing area and will surely be subject to further change and development.

Freelance/agency/sub-contractor

In these types of arrangements the individual is not employed by the organisation and is therefore neither an employee nor a worker. There may be a written agreement between the parties (such as a consultancy agreement) that is known, legally, as a 'contract for service'. These types of contracts often involve an employer contracting with a self-employed individual to provide particular services or to undertake a particular piece of work – for example, engaging the services of a freelance self-employed photographer to take photos for the company's marketing brochure or website. Agency workers are slightly different in that an organisation will usually contract with an agency to hire temporary staff to meet particular needs or workload demands – for example, a nursing home going to an agency for additional care workers during a sickness outbreak amongst their permanent staff, or a school hiring a specialist accountant through an agency to help the bursar produce year-end accounts. Agency workers will usually, but not always, be employees or workers of the agency and are specifically covered by The Agency Workers Regulations 2010. Agency workers are afforded greater employment rights under the Regulations than self-employed people in that after 12 weeks in the same role they get the same terms and conditions as permanent employees. The 'Swedish derogation' provides an exemption from these regulations so far as pay is concerned. Even so, it does not affect agency workers' entitlements to other provisions such as annual leave after 12 weeks, 'day-one' rights and rest breaks. There are certain requirements to be met if the derogation is to be used; see the Acas website for more details.

We have now mentioned employment status a number of times. It is an important concept which we will now look at in more detail.

3.4.8 EMPLOYMENT STATUS

It is important to understand whether someone who is doing work for you is an employee, a worker or self-employed. These are the main categories of employment status and different rights and responsibilities apply to each. But this is a very complicated area and we can look only at broad principles, which may be subject to change. The correct category is determined by looking both at what the contract says and how the working arrangements work in practice. You may wish to offer work to a person who claims to be self-employed. One difficulty, if you reach an agreement on that basis, is that Her Majesty's Revenue and Customs (HMRC) may not be willing to treat that person as self-employed if how things work in practice differ from or contradict what you may have agreed. In that case you, the employer, will probably have to pay tax and National Insurance contributions to HMRC for the person (even if he or she has already been paid without deductions). A link to the HMRC website for an Employment Status Indicator is provided at the end of this chapter.

Indeed, if a person is an employee rather than self-employed, then he or she has a wide range of employment rights, including the right not to be unfairly dismissed. The claim to be an employee could come after a contract has ended, in order to assert employment rights. So let's have a look at the distinctions.

If you have your house decorated, you do not, usually, employ a decorator; what you do is make a contract for service. Your decorator is likely to be a self-employed contractor or business – it may possibly be the decorator's own business or he/she may work for somebody else. The person you meet may be an employee of the business, but he or she will not be an employee of yours. However, if your organisation retains an individual person as a decorator to decorate its premises, that person could be an employee or a worker.

Employees have a contract of employment. They will receive other benefits such as sick pay and redundancy rights. Employees are obliged to provide personal service (*they* must do the work you have employed them to do; they cannot send along somebody else) and employers are obliged to provide work (mutuality of obligation again) and how employees undertake their work is largely controlled by the employer (the employer decides what the job is and designs the work processes and systems). On the other hand, self-employed people do not have that mutuality of obligation, they do not have to perform work personally and they will determine for themselves how to undertake the work.

It is perhaps the hardest to understand what constitutes a 'worker'. Workers are people who do the work for you, or your organisation, personally (that is, they cannot sub-contract the work to others); there is sometimes a mutuality of obligation, particularly during work periods/assignments, usually they are supervised, and work specified hours, but crucially, in other ways do not meet the test for being an employee. It is a category that has evolved over time to ensure those who are simply called 'self-employed' in order for employers to avoid their legal obligations but in practice have some of the characteristics of employees (for example, being told how to do their work) have some legal rights. Employees are workers, but workers can also include freelance people and those from agencies. So all employees are workers, but workers are not necessarily employees. Workers are usually paid on a scale that is determined by the employer and may pay tax by PAYE.

Workers have some employment rights, such as protection from discrimination and the right to the national minimum wage. However, employees have additional rights, including entitlement to written particulars of employment (see 3.4.6 above) and protection from unfair dismissal. Whether or not agency workers (see under 3.4.7 above) have the status of an employee is a particularly fluid area and case law on this subject has served to complicate rather than to simplify matters. Table 3.1 outlines in greater detail the tests used to determine employment status.

An agency worker, if they are an employee of the agency (with a contract of employment confirmed by written particulars), has a clear position. However, it is often not so clear-cut, and case law does not determine whose employee an agency worker might be, or indeed whether they are an employee at all. As already mentioned, The Agency Workers Regulations give temporary agency workers the same basic rights as your permanent workers after 12 weeks' employment. This means comparable pay and conditions including, for example, sick pay and holiday leave, but not necessarily other employment rights such as the right to not be dismissed unfairly or the right to redundancy payments. So the Agency Workers Regulations do not determine employment status. Unless it is quite clear who is employing an agency worker, this is an area where you should seek advice. Meanwhile, even if they are not employees of the organisation that provides the work, agency workers have certain worker rights – under the Working Time Regulations, for example.

Genuinely self-employed people usually provide their own equipment (such as paint brushes in the case of decorators) and will almost certainly work for others as well as your organisation. They submit invoices and will probably be VAT-registered and may even be limited companies. They may contract to do a particular task (as opposed to working set daily hours), and any profit or loss in doing the work accrues to them rather than your organisation. So as not to be held liable for any tax or National Insurance contributions, anyone contracting work from the self-employed may be wise to see a supporting letter from HMRC, a contractor's certificate or check limited company status. If you contract with a limited company, you may also need a contract to ensure the work is done by the person by whom you wish it to be done.

Finally, there are also employee shareholders, who have a contract of employment and own at least £2,000 worth of shares in the employer's company. They have most of the same rights as workers and employees but don't have protection against unfair dismissal, aren't eligible for statutory redundancy pay and don't have the right to request flexible working.

Table 3.1 The employment status of 'employees', 'workers' and others

Employee	Worker	Genuinely self-employed
He or she has a contract of service (that is, to serve)	He or she does the work personally	He or she contracts for services; you are the customer
You pay by PAYE	You pay by PAYE or on invoice	You pay on invoice
He or she is not VAT registered	He or she is not VAT registered	He or she prepares business accounts, is probably VAT registered and may even be a limited company
You set the working hours	Either party may set the working hours	He or she sets hours of work
He or she can't decline work	He or she can decline work	He or she can assign work to others

Employee	Worker	Genuinely self-employed
You can expect work to be done and you are expected to provide it	You cannot expect work to be accepted and you are not obliged to provide it	He or she has no right to expect work from you or to accept it from you
You provide written employment particulars	The contract may not be in writing	Contracts for each piece of work; could be written
He or she would be subject to disciplinary procedures	He or she may need to respond to complaints or may be subject to procedures in some cases	He or she must be prepared to respond to complaints, but is not subject to disciplinary procedures
He or she uses company equipment	He or she uses company equipment	He or she uses own equipment
He or she is employed for an indefinite time	He or she works as and when required or for a particular assignment	The contract is by service, not time

The table above provides a broad guide to help you understand the employment status of different people. The genuinely self-employed are included in this table for completeness, but this group has no employment rights, unlike workers, who are protected by the National Minimum Wage Regulations, the Working Time Regulations, and equality rights. Note that the table is drawn up from the viewpoint of an employer (who is therefore 'you'). Not included here specifically are agency workers because of the uncertainties surrounding their status.

So despite the differences explained here, it is very important to realise that the distinction is not always clear-cut and that you may need to seek advice. Courts and tribunals can come to differing conclusions on seemingly similar situations and are not bound by decisions made by other bodies such as HMRC. You will find frequently asked questions on employment status under that heading on the CIPD website and further guidance in a reference under Further Reading at the end of this chapter. Remember that if a contract of employment is made, a statement of written particulars should be provided within two months.

?   REFLECTIVE ACTIVITY 3.6

Consider the people who help accomplish your organisation's objectives. Are they all employees? If not, how would you categorise them? Carry out some appropriate research into the nature of their relationship with the HR function. For example, you might want to investigate what records are kept for them and what employment rights they have, and reflect on how the responsibilities of the HR department differ for these people and your employees. Discuss the issues with your learning sources.

3.5 DURING EMPLOYMENT – RIGHTS AND RESPONSIBILITIES

We could probably devote a whole book to the employment legislation that is relevant during the employment relationship. As this section is only part of one chapter, we will necessarily be taking a broad overview of the relevant legislation and will focus on the key individual rights that an employee has under the law during the employment relationship.

3.5.1 DISCRIMINATION AND EQUALITY RIGHTS

Here we shall be looking at a wide range of areas of potential discrimination; first we examine some broad principles.

Although it may be argued that it makes sound business sense to recruit people solely on their ability to do the job, that judgement is easily influenced by beliefs that are not relevant or by conscious or unconscious bias. Even those committed to recruiting on ability can find themselves victims to prejudice that they did not realise they had. More disturbingly, there are still managers who will admit, privately, to unlawful discrimination. For example, they may have prejudices about women who 'might go off on maternity leave' or feel unable to relate to people of a different culture from their own. Unfortunately, in bringing such prejudices to the workplace, they mistakenly believe they serve themselves and their employer better because of it.

As an HR practitioner you may need to examine your beliefs carefully. It is helpful to read relevant articles in *People Management* which show how HR practitioners are positively tackling equality and diversity issues. Make sure you understand your own organisation's policy and practices towards women, ethnic minorities and other groups.

These policies should be designed to encourage equality and diversity by raising awareness, challenging and educating workers and decision-makers. The spirit or intention of equality legislation, as well as the letter of the law, is important.

CASE STUDY 3.1

A 2012 study of science faculties in higher education institutions in the US (Moss-Racusin et al 2012) asked staff to review a number of job applications. The applications reviewed were identical, apart from the gender of the name of the applicant.

It was discovered that science faculties were more likely to:

- rate male candidates as better qualified than female candidates
- want to hire the male candidates rather than the female candidates

- give the male candidate a higher starting salary than the female candidate
- be willing to invest more in the development of the male candidate than the female candidate.

Here, unconscious bias impacts not only on the recruitment decision, but the salary of the individual and the amount of development that is invested in their ongoing progression.

Notwithstanding the merits of your employer's policies, men and women, people of different ethnic or racial groups, people with disabilities and many ex-offenders (those with spent convictions) and others (see below) have protection against discrimination. So you must be aware of the legislation.

Keep in mind that applicants as well as workers can be discriminated against. Everyone who is applying for or undertaking work personally is eligible for these rights: there is no length of (employment) service requirement. There are no limits to the amount of compensation that an employment tribunal can award in cases of discrimination.

The EHRC promotes equality and human rights and challenges discrimination. It provides advice and guidance, works to implement an effective legislative framework, and raises awareness of rights amongst employees and others.

As part of this work, the EHRC publishes Codes of Practice that represent authoritative guidance on the requirements that must be met by public authorities to make sure they are complying with the law.

The EHRC has responsibilities in relation to sex, race, disability, religion or belief, sexual orientation, pregnancy and maternity, age, gender reassignment, and marriage and civil partnerships – nine 'protected characteristics' in all (see 3.5.5 below).

There are several other areas where discrimination can be unlawful: fixed-term and part-time workers; trade union membership (or non-membership); and ex-offenders.

Fixed-term workers

Fixed-terms workers are those who have a contract that terminates on a specific date, on completion of a specific task or on the occurrence of a specific event. They are protected under regulations from less favourable treatment by comparison with a permanent worker.

The relevant legislation is the Fixed-term Employees (Prevention of Less Favourable Treatment) Regulations 2002.

Part-time workers

Part-timers also have the right to equal treatment with full-timers. The relevant legislation is in the Part-time Workers (Prevention of Less Favourable Treatment) Regulations 2000.

Trade union membership

Employees cannot be dismissed on grounds relating to union membership or non-membership. In addition, a worker (not just an employee) should not be subject to any detriment (such as being passed over for promotion), victimisation or discrimination.

This is only a summary. Relevant legislation is in:

- Trade Union and Labour Relations (Consolidation) Act 1992
- Employment Relations Act 1999
- Employment Relations Act 2004.

What equal treatment means

It means acquiring unfair dismissal or redundancy pay rights after the same periods of service as permanent employees or full-timers. Equal treatment covers a range of pay elements such as pensions, severance pay, access to promotion and training opportunities and sickness benefits. This equal treatment is now provided for in the above legislation, and failure to recognise the right to equal treatment can give rise, at an employment tribunal, to claims of discrimination or to claims for equal pay.

Employing ex-offenders

Unless people who have served prison terms can be rehabilitated into employment, it logically follows that they are likely to resort to crime again. So there is some legal protection for those who have received sentences of up to four years (in England and Wales). They have the chance to 'wipe the slate clean' after a certain time. The time required varies according to the original sentence. 'Spent' convictions do not have to be disclosed, and even if disclosed, cannot be taken into account in employment decisions. There are, however, exemptions where the work involves access to vulnerable groups such as young people or those with disabilities. The relevant legislation is the Rehabilitation of Offenders Act 1974, the Rehabilitation of Offenders Act 1974 (Exceptions) Order 1975 and the Legal Aid, Sentencing and Punishment of Offenders Act 2012. If you employ people in an exempted occupation, you will need to familiarise yourself with the services provided by the DBS (formerly the Criminal Records Bureau), which provides facilities for criminal record checks or DBS checks (formerly CRB checks).

3.5.2 EQUAL PAY

Men and women are entitled to claim equal treatment in respect of pay and conditions. In practice, the operation of equal pay is complicated by measurements. Equal treatment requires determination of like work, of work rated as equivalent, and of work of equal value. And of course, what constitutes equal treatment itself is not easy to measure.

Tribunal cases arising under the Equal Pay Act 1970 have frequently led to appeals, proving very expensive for employers. Despite the complications, therefore, every endeavour should be made to ensure equal treatment of men and women. There is now an Equal Pay Code and employers are being encouraged to adopt equal pay policies and carry out equal pay audits (see Chapter 7 for more information). Legislation is now forcing more transparency in pay policies so that inequalities are brought into the open. The Equality Act (of which other aspects are discussed below) specifically forbids 'secrecy clauses' where employees would break their contract if they discussed their pay with others.

3.5.3 EQUALITY ACT 2010

This replaced the Sex Discrimination Act, Race Relations Act, Disability Discrimination Act and other legislation relating to most forms of discrimination. These Acts were on the statute books for some years, so you may hear references to them from time to time. As well as defining those characteristics that are protected from discrimination (see below), the Act also defined a number of types of discrimination. Not all types of discrimination are unlawful in relation to every protected characteristic.

To understand what may be lawful or otherwise, we will first look at each type of discrimination and relate each to the characteristics that might be protected from them.

3.5.4 TYPES OF DISCRIMINATION

Direct discrimination

Direct discrimination means allowing one of the protected characteristics to influence employment decisions; for example, in passing over a woman for promotion in favour of a less-qualified man or selecting a white person in favour of a black person. Direct discrimination is often clear and consequently may be difficult to defend. However, if the discrimination is a 'proportionate means of achieving a legitimate aim', a defence may be possible. This can be quite an uncertain concept, meaning any discrimination may have to be judged on its merits. For example, in 2010 a question as to whether a business partnership had legitimate aims in retiring a partner at age 65 reached the Supreme Court for a decision. In the particular circumstances the Supreme Court decided the specific aims were legitimate.

Indirect discrimination

Indirect discrimination occurs if conditions that effectively create discrimination are applied. These could be certain criteria on job specifications or advertisements if they tend to preclude particular people. For example, a job specification that determines a minimum height would be indirectly discriminatory and unlawful unless objectively justified. Since men tend to be taller than women, this would discriminate indirectly against women. So care has to be taken when choosing selection criteria; these have to be job-requirement-related. An example of objective justification, in this instance, would be if there were safety implications to being below the minimum height.

Discrimination by association

This is where an employer might discriminate directly against an employee because that employee has an association with someone who has a protected characteristic. An example might be where the employee's partner has a reassigned gender. A more common of association application is where an employee is caring for a disabled partner or relative. To refuse an employee promotion for that reason would be discrimination by association.

Discrimination by perception

This is discrimination against a person because the discriminator thinks the person possesses that characteristic, even if they do not. This form of discrimination is well illustrated by a case prior to the Equality Act where a heterosexual man was subject to ridicule for being homosexual, even though he was not. This was ruled to be discrimination and is now enshrined in the Equality Act as 'perception discrimination'. The particular form of discrimination here was harassment, our next type of discrimination.

Harassment

Harassment is defined by the Equality Act as 'unwanted conduct related to a relevant protected characteristic, which has the purpose or effect of violating an individual's dignity or creating an intimidating, hostile, degrading, humiliating or offensive environment for that individual'. It is also possible for colleagues to complain of harassment even if ridicule or offensive behaviour is not directed at them. The employer is responsible for the behaviour of its employees.

Victimisation

If an employee makes a claim of discrimination (or any other claim) to a tribunal and is then treated by the employer less favourably as a result, that is victimisation. Victimisation also applies where an employee supports another employee and is then treated less favourably themselves. Victimisation is a word often used loosely, but in employment terms it applies only to behaviour directed at an employee who has sought to assert their statutory rights.

3.5.5 PROTECTED CHARACTERISTICS

There are currently nine protected characteristics in relation to which discrimination can be unlawful, as defined in the Equality Act 2010. These are:

- age
- disability
- gender reassignment
- race
- religion or belief
- sex
- sexual orientation
- marriage and civil partnerships
- pregnancy and maternity.

Age

Broadly, it is unlawful to make an employment decision using a person's age either as the reason for or as a factor in the decision. But there are a few exceptions, particularly at the younger end of the scale. There are lower minimum wage rates for young people, for example.

Making decisions on any basis that could be age-related (such as on a person's length of service) or providing service-related benefits could be discriminatory. However, if you have a 'legitimate aim' and the decision is 'proportionate to achieving that aim', discrimination may be lawful. This may leave HR practitioners with frequent dilemmas. Is it legitimate (and proportionate) to prefer to recruit a 40-year-old over a 60-year-old because you are seeking future potential? We cannot answer this question because it may depend on many factors specific to the situation, and on developing case law. Case law may have to be considered in many specific instances.

Disability

It is often the case that a disability has no practical implications for job performance, and yet conscious and unconscious bias continues to persist.

Accomplished blind and deaf musicians are one reminder that disability need not be a barrier to achievement. We have to be very wary of mindsets that lead us to make unjustified assumptions about others.

The Equality Act protects people who have disabilities. It is unlawful to treat a person less favourably, on account of their disability, than you would treat someone in a similar position who does not have that disability. Employers are required to make reasonable adjustments to premises, interview arrangements, work stations and so on, so that applicants, or workers, with a disability are not put at any substantial disadvantage.

Be aware, too, that there are also restrictions on health questionnaires being used prior to recruitment decisions (see 3.4.2 'Pre-employment checks').

Gender reassignment

There is protection against unfavourable treatment for people who intend to undergo, have undergone or are undergoing gender reassignment.

Race

Most larger and progressive organisations in both the public and private sectors have provided good examples of good practice in equality for many years. But there are still big issues to tackle and progress to be made; for example, people from minority ethnic or racial groups still tend to be over-represented in low-pay occupations.

Whether diversity is driven by a desire to be morally right, by commercial pragmatism, or by the law, the Equality Act underpins racial equality in employment and other areas.

However, if you have a 'legitimate aim' and the decision is 'proportionate to achieving that aim', discrimination may be lawful. Reasons of authenticity (possibly in theatrical productions) or welfare (for different ethnic communities) are likely to prove legitimate aims (they have been allowed in earlier legislation), but actions will need to be proportionate to achieving those aims.

Religion or belief

What amounts to a religion or a belief is not specified in statutory legislation, but is interpreted by tribunals. Some decisions make interesting reading. For example, a fervent belief in climate change has, in a particular set of circumstances, been deemed to be a belief for the purposes of the Act. Therefore, in some cases, you may need to take further advice. Following this Act, Acas has issued helpful guidance to deal with putting appropriate practices in place.

Sex

Originally the social unacceptability of sex discrimination encouraged appropriate legislation, but much of it has since been driven further by membership of the EU, in which the Treaty of Rome 1957 provides for equal treatment of men and women. Consequently sex discrimination has been unlawful in the UK for several decades.

Certain legitimate aims may justify discrimination if the decisions are proportionate; for example, aims such as privacy, decency, welfare and authenticity (for example, modelling clothes), certain accommodation needs, or staffing certain single-sex establishments (for example, prisons).

?   REFLECTIVE ACTIVITY 3.7

In your capacity as an HR practitioner, assume you are invited to assist a manager at an interview. You fear that the manager has no intention of accepting a woman for the vacancy although two of the five interviewees are women. Write down what you would do.

Discuss your intentions with one of your learning sources.

Sexual orientation

Originally unprotected, this became a protected characteristic along with religion and belief in 2003.

Marriage and civil partnerships

It is often a point of interest that while married couples (including civil partnerships) are protected from discrimination, single people are not. However, the amount of protection here is limited to direct and indirect discrimination.

Pregnancy and maternity

Women have the right not to be unfairly dismissed because of pregnancy, the right to maternity pay and the right to return to work following maternity leave. Over the years, legislation and case law have strengthened and enhanced these rights. Dismissal on maternity-related grounds is now automatically unfair, irrespective of length of service or hours of work. It is also important to recognise that the contract of employment now continues through the maternity leave period. This has a number of effects. For example, annual leave accumulates during the period of maternity leave and may have to be paid in lieu if the woman does not return to work. Pregnant women and those on maternity leave are also protected from direct discrimination, such as not being offered training.

You can nevertheless lawfully dismiss a pregnant woman or one on maternity leave so long as the reason is not related to the pregnancy. Theft, for example, would be a potentially safe reason whereas unreliable attendance might not.

CASE STUDY 3.2

John is a small businessman employing five people. Emma returned from maternity leave recently, having been his administrator prior to that.

While Emma was away John employed Ling as a temporary replacement. It was at this point that he realised how inefficient Emma had been in the three years she had worked for him. Ling introduced new computer software, reorganised the filing system and took on a range of valuable duties in the resulting free time that she herself had created.

On Emma's return John decided to make Emma redundant, maintaining that the work she was employed to do no longer existed, and to retain Ling.

He now faces an employment tribunal claim for unfair dismissal and sex discrimination. If the tribunal concludes (as it seems it must) that the work is suitable and appropriate for Emma or that Emma has been dismissed for a reason related to her pregnancy or maternity, then John will lose this case.

The right to return from maternity leave is heavily protected in law and employers cannot safely 'construct' situations that suit their ends.

3.5.6 THE BURDEN OF PROOF

In the event that an applicant or employee can provide evidence of probable discrimination, it is the employer's responsibility to prove that it has not discriminated against a person with any protected characteristic. This means that you need to keep good records of all employment decisions so you can show that such decisions did not discriminate by reason of any protected characteristic, as illustrated in Case Study 3.2.

The main legislation relating to discrimination is now in:

- Equal Pay Act 1970
- Employment Rights Act 1996
- Employment Act 2002
- Equality Act 2010.

There is also a code of practice: Equality Act 2010: Employment – Statutory Code of Practice.

3.5.7 FAMILY-RELATED RIGHTS

As society has changed over recent years, so we have seen an increase in the amount of what we can loosely term family-friendly employment legislation. In addition to maternity leave and pay there are a number of other parental and family-related rights including paternity pay and leave, parental leave and adoption leave, as well as time off for emergencies involving dependants. We can also see this continues to be an evolving area of employment law with announcements in 2015 about the Government's intention to bring in increased rights for grandparents too.

These family-friendly rights have developed in response not only to societal changes but also to increased pressure in the workplace and demands from employees, such as:

- increasing numbers of women in the workplace
- increasing numbers of older people requiring care
- parenting being increasingly a shared activity
- calls for greater flexibility in when work is done and the degree of control individual employees have over this
- the need for increasing numbers of people in work to balance work with caring responsibilities
- a backlash against a long-hours culture
- increasing diversity in family structures, requiring greater rights for same-sex couples, for instance.

Let's now take a look at the rights employees have in a bit more detail.

Maternity leave and pay

All female employees have the right to 52 weeks' statutory maternity leave (SML) regardless of length of service with their employer. In addition, women who have 26 weeks' service are likely to qualify for 39 weeks' statutory maternity pay (SMP). Within the 52-week period of leave there is a period of two weeks' compulsory leave, immediately after the birth, when women are not allowed to work. Some employers, particularly larger organisations and those in the public sector, often also offer what is known as occupational maternity leave and pay, which may, in some cases be a contractual right, and is usually more generous than the statutory provisions. A woman also has the right to return either to the same job or a job with no less favourable terms and conditions (depending on when she returns) at the end of maternity leave and has additional rights in relation to health and safety, keeping in touch and matters such as how sickness absence related to pregnancy is treated.

Paternity leave and pay

Paternity leave applies where the man (or partner) has been in employment for 26 weeks and entitles him to two weeks' paid leave. The basic right is to statutory paternity pay, but again, some employers offer more generous pay and leave.

Adoption leave and pay

For children adopted on or after 5 April 2015, the rights the adoptive mother has to adoption leave and pay mirror maternity leave and pay rights.

Shared parental leave

For babies born on or after 5 April 2015, shared parental leave may be available to both biological parents and adoptive parents. This works by mothers in employment opting to turn part of their SML and SMP into shared parental leave and shared parental pay. There are eligibility criteria that must be met, including both parents having worked for their employers continuously for at least 26 weeks. There are also very complicated notification criteria and you would be advised to seek advice should you get a request for this type of leave.

It is important to note that all of the above rights also apply to same-sex parents.

The relevant legislation is:

- Employment Rights Act 1996
- Employment Relations Act 1999
- Employment Act 2002
- Work and Families Act 2006
- Children and Families Act 2014.

Emergency leave

Employees also have rights in relation to time off from work for certain needs to do with their dependants. An employer must allow an employee to take reasonable time off during working hours to deal with particular unexpected emergencies concerning their dependants, such as a dependant falling ill or a breakdown in usual care arrangements. The key is for both employers and employees to take a commonsense approach when dealing with requests for emergency leave – the matter does not have to be a sudden and unexpected emergency as the name might imply, but does need to be an unusual disruption in normal arrangements.

CASE STUDY 3.3

An employee of a utility company had seven days' absence over the period of a year to look after her child when he was too ill to attend nursery. On each occasion, she used the employer's policy on time off for dependants and was granted the emergency absence.

She was then invited to a formal capability meeting due to her levels of non-medical absence. She was given a 'first written notification of concern' and threatened with dismissal if she had 'further unsatisfactory attendance due to time off for dependants'.

The employee brought a tribunal claim stating that she had been subject to a detriment for exercising her right to time off to care for her son.

The employment tribunal held that the first written notification was a detriment because it threatened the employee with further disciplinary action if she took more time off to care for dependants.

It should be noted that in finding that the employee had taken a reasonable amount of dependants leave in this case, the tribunal took into account that:

- she had followed the employer's procedure on each occasion (telephoning on the morning of each day's absence)
- the reason for her absence was due entirely to her son being ill
- there was no other parent or relative nearby to look after the child.

Parental leave

Unpaid parental leave is available to employees (men and women), with one year's employment, to take time off to look after a child's welfare. It applies to all parents of children under the age of 18. The period of leave is a maximum of 18 weeks, although no more than four weeks can be taken in any one year, and applies separately to each child.

Flexible working

All employees with 26 weeks' employment, regardless of caring or parental responsibilities, now have the right to request flexible working. Employers must consider the request 'reasonably' and can only refuse if certain conditions apply, such as an inability to reorganise the work amongst other employees or recruit replacement staff. There are also particular requirements around the process that should be used by employers for dealing with flexible working requests. There is an Acas Code of Practice that you would be well advised to follow.

3.5.8 THE WORKING TIME REGULATIONS

These introduced a maximum working week of 48 hours as averaged over one of three possible periods: 17 weeks, 26 weeks (certain special cases) or 52 weeks by workforce agreement. They provide restrictions on the maximum length of night shifts, and provide for rest periods, work breaks and statutory annual leave of 5.6 weeks.

Workers can opt out of the 48 hours voluntarily, but leave must be taken: it cannot be paid in lieu. The Regulations place specific requirements on records that are kept in relation to the 48-hour week and night shifts, and records will, of course, be needed if there are disputes over any of the other provisions.

The Working Time Regulations are complicated, so you would be wise to take advice, or at least read them carefully, if they have implications for decisions you have to make.

The legislation is:

- Working Time Regulations 1998
- Health and Safety (Young Persons) Regulations 1997, providing additional protection for young workers.

3.5.9 THE NATIONAL MINIMUM WAGE

The way in which the wage has to be calculated (with particular pay and hours elements) is quite specific, and employers have to be able to show that they are complying.

It is necessary to calculate a wage for all workers and to be able to provide the necessary information for HMRC. Individuals are also entitled to statements on request. Failing to keep records is a criminal offence.

The relevant legislation is the National Minimum Wage Act 1998.

The National Living Wage was introduced in April 2016 and will act as a top up for workers aged 25 and over. In future years, the Government will ask the Low Pay Commission to recommend any increases.

If you are called on, as well you might be, to administer any of the rights and the corresponding pay outlined above, there are government publications and online resources which you can use for guidance. See 'References and Further Reading' at the end of this chapter.

?   REFLECTIVE ACTIVITY 3.8

Choose a piece of legislation that has been enacted or changed in the last few years. Investigate what practices have changed in your organisation as a result. You could look at application forms, staff handbooks, induction and other training documents, disciplinary procedures and other staff records and could also talk to other staff (especially if there are any other HR staff in your organisation) who have been in the organisation a long time.

Is there anything that should have changed in response to the legislation but still needs attention?

3.5.10 HR INFORMATION AND COMMUNICATION

In addition to the above legislation, which has direct relevance to employing people, there is also much legislation relating to the information employers may hold on an employee and on how you must protect it or, in some circumstances, communicate it. Details are provided in Chapter 10, which makes reference to:

- data protection
- freedom of information
- investigatory powers
- criminal justice
- information and consultation.

We will now look at relevant employment legislation at the end of the employment relationship.

3.6 ENDING EMPLOYMENT

3.6.1 DISMISSAL – THE RIGHT NOT TO BE UNFAIRLY DISMISSED

Although this is a right that exists throughout the duration of the employment relationship, it becomes particularly relevant, in terms of the information contained in this chapter, at the end of the employment relationship. As an employee you will be investing a good proportion of your life in the work of your employer. Most probably you will feel that you make a valuable contribution and represent a good investment, not least because of your ongoing desire to learn and improve your performance. All being well, your employer will be of the same opinion.

Unfortunately, it is not always the case that employers and employees share the same views: what the employee may see as conscientiousness, the employer may see as being exceedingly pedantic; singlemindedness may be praised or seen as tunnel vision; and so on. So employers and employees do not always measure performance in the same way.

Let's take another example. An employee may need an emergency doctor's appointment early in the morning. If the employee forgets to call the employer to say he or she will be late because of being preoccupied with concern over the appointment, he or she may see this as a simple oversight. The employer may see the same action as unauthorised absence or even an attempt to defraud the company.

These conflicting views bring us to an important point: it is not acceptable, at least in the case of an employee who has been with the employer for some time and has a record of good conduct and performance, for the employee to be dismissed without some serious attempt to resolve conflict or improve matters, without a fair reason and without a reasonable procedure.

Chapter 8 provides more information about potential disciplinary situations and the requirements around reasonable disciplinary procedures. Here we will look specifically at the right not to be unfairly dismissed and the potentially fair reasons for an employer doing so.

This is a right that applies to employees and, in most instances, requires a qualifying period of two years' continuous service with the employer. For an employee to be dismissed fairly there must first be a fair reason for the dismissal and the employer must act reasonably (follow a reasonable procedure) in arriving at the decision to dismiss.

A fair reason

There are five potentially fair reasons for dismissal (although the fifth is quite broad):

1 Capability – the inability to perform the type of work for which the employee was employed. This can include health factors such as ill-health absence.

2 Conduct – failure to meet reasonable expectations. This can include failure to carry out reasonable instructions, bad time-keeping and attendance, as well as gross misconduct, such as theft from the employer.

3 Redundancy – the work for which the employee was employed has ceased or diminished or is expected to do so. Here the selection of a particular individual has to be shown to be fair.

4 Legal restrictions – this may apply, for example, when the employee becomes disqualified from driving and the only work available requires the employee to drive.

5 'Some other substantial reason' – this area is established by precedents in case law. Many cases in this category involve a loss of trust and confidence in the employee.

Whenever a decision to dismiss is taken, it is wise to determine which of the above reasons the true one is. Dismissed employees (subject to two years' service) have the right to ask for a written statement giving particulars of the reasons for dismissal, and the reason, or reasons, chosen may have to be defended in a tribunal. Employees dismissed while pregnant or on maternity leave or adoption leave must be given a statement of the particulars of the reasons for dismissal irrespective of whether they request it.

Acting reasonably

Employers also have to show that they acted reasonably, and the best way to do this is to follow a fair procedure. Even when the procedure has been followed, the employer has to show that he or she has acted reasonably in reaching the decision to dismiss. Various Acas publications cover these procedures in detail, and you should consult the Acas Code of Practice on Disciplinary and Grievance Procedures (see 'References and Further Reading' at the end of this chapter). More information on how such fair and reasonable procedures operate can be found in Chapter 8.

Different procedures are appropriate in different circumstances. Having disciplinary and grievance procedures makes sense for all employers because they provide a framework for resolving conflict fairly. Ill-health issues are more effectively tackled by a specific ill-health or capability procedure. What is a reasonable course of action when behaviour is within an employee's control may no longer be reasonable when illness is involved (see Chapter 8 for more information).

Reasonableness is the key to fairness. What may be seen as reasonable procedures for a small employer may be considered to be inadequate procedures for a larger employer. Case Studies 3.4 and 3.5 below represent illustrations of this.

Workers also have the right to be accompanied by a fellow worker or trade union representative at disciplinary hearings. For the purpose of this right, any hearing at which you contemplate taking some action on behalf of the employer is a disciplinary hearing.

So, for example, if you are discussing the employee's ill-health (and a demotion or transfer could be potential outcomes), the employee has the right to be accompanied – and you must inform him or her of that right.

It is worth noting that fairness will be judged in the light of information available at the time the decision is made. An employer must carry out a thorough investigation to gather as much relevant information as is reasonable. He or she needs to have grounds for his or her beliefs – for example, for believing that an employee is stealing. However, in most cases employers may make the decision on the balance of probabilities; they do not need proof beyond reasonable doubt. Subsequent, more conclusive, evidence of guilt or innocence is not relevant to the fairness of the decision.

CASE STUDY 3.4

After establishing grounds for believing an employee to be guilty, a sole proprietor with ten employees decides to dismiss the employee in question for fiddling his bonus. The proprietor may have been the only person to have investigated the allegation, may have been the only person to assess all the evidence, and may have taken the decision to dismiss without consulting anyone else. He might be expected to consider questions such as: were other employees fiddling their bonuses too?

Did the employee know, or was it reasonable to expect him to know, that bonus fraud was gross misconduct that could result in dismissal without warning? Although the employer can be expected to have asked and answered such questions, he may nonetheless have to make the final decision without being

able to consult anyone else. He should, however, still have followed the Acas Code of Practice in arriving at the decision. He must also have allowed the employee to be accompanied at the disciplinary hearing, and at any appeal, having previously informed the employee of that right.

In an organisation of 2,000 employees, such a course of action could not rest with one person. More would be expected in terms of the degree of thoroughness. Were the questions posed above properly answered? Was the accusation thoroughly investigated by appropriate people? Was the decision to dismiss taken at a senior level in the organisation by someone other than the investigating officer? Was the appeal heard by a more senior person who had not been involved in the original decision?

The guidelines contained in the Acas Code of Practice are crucial. This comes in two parts (separate documents): a brief statutory code and more prescriptive guidance. The extent to which both are followed, or not followed, will not only be taken into account when a tribunal judges fairness, but may affect any compensation.

Dismissal

Dismissal takes place when the employer terminates the contract with notice, without notice, or because of actions that effectively breach the contract. Fixed-term contracts that expire without renewal are also dismissals.

In many instances the fact that there has been a dismissal will be clear; for example, there has been a disciplinary hearing and the employee has been notified of the decision to dismiss or an employee has been made redundant. However, there are times when a dismissal is disputed. For example, a supervisor may 'blow up' at an employee, perhaps humiliating the employee in front of his or her colleagues. The employee decides 'enough is enough', goes home, and does not return to work. Has the employee been dismissed, or has he or she resigned?

On the face of it you might conclude that the employee has resigned. But these are circumstances in which the employee might be entitled to terminate his or her employment by reason of the employer's conduct. So let's look at some of the arguments that might be put either way.

The employer might argue that the supervisor carried out a reprimand, that it was justified, and that it was carried out respectfully – although it may be conceded that colleagues should not have witnessed it. The employer could maintain that the employee has simply resigned. There is therefore no question of dismissal, fair or unfair. Conversely, the ex-employee may produce evidence of previous mistreatment and seek to show that the reprimand was clearly humiliating and very public. It could have been 'the last straw'.

He or she might contend that it would be quite intolerable to continue to work in such circumstances. Because of the actions taken, therefore, the employee may argue that the employer has dismissed him or her *constructively* – and unfairly at that. Before the employee takes the case to a tribunal, he or she should raise the grievance with the employer, and well-established and respected procedures facilitate this. But there is no guarantee that a grievance will be raised, and the employer may not get the chance to provide a resolution before an employment tribunal claim is made.

Were the case to come before an employment tribunal, the question of dismissal or resignation would be examined very thoroughly. For example, the words used in the reprimand (or emotional outburst), evidence of previous mistreatment and any protests the employee may have made in the past could all be taken into account. The employer's response to any grievance, or especially any lack of it, would be important. In some cases a tribunal may decide that the employee resigned. In others, it may feel that the employer's treatment of the employee meant that trust and confidence had broken down and that, in effect, the employment contract had been broken. This would be 'constructive dismissal', entitling the employee to presume, from the employer's actions, that he or she had been dismissed. That is, that the employer had broken the contract.

Whether such a dismissal would be unfair might depend on the reason for the reprimand, on whether there had been a thorough investigation, on whether the employee had been formally warned beforehand and on a range of other factors.

From the employer's viewpoint, sets of circumstances that could lead to an employee claiming constructive dismissal are to be avoided. A dismissal may be claimed even if it was not intended. The issue then becomes the employer's misconduct and the employer will have to listen carefully to any grievance. The employer will, in effect, have been 'wrong-footed' and will have given power to the employee. Rescuing the situation may require disciplining of the supervisor (not a very satisfactory situation), providing the supervisor with training or even changing reporting relationships.

Once again, the main relevant legislation here is the Employment Rights Act 1996. The Employment Relations Act 1999 has relevance to accompaniment at disciplinary hearings.

CASE STUDY 3.5

A distribution division of a large national clothing company employs 80 people either as drivers or on the warehouse floor. There are two drivers who work only locally, one of whom is Ravi, who has worked for the company for 12 years. These drivers' responsibilities are to distribute smaller loads in the highly built-up area in the immediate vicinity of the warehouse. They are not HGV-licensed.

Ravi was driving home from a private social function one night, was stopped by the police and subsequently lost his driving licence for 12 months. The distribution division should not dismiss him without first considering all the circumstances. For example, can Ravi be employed in the warehouse? It is very likely that there will be some suitable

unskilled work that he could do. Could someone else drive the van, perhaps someone from the warehouse, even though he or she might need some training? Has Ravi any solutions to offer? Such options should be formally investigated, and if no solution is possible, the reasons carefully documented with evidence as to why they have been rejected. If Ravi is dismissed and makes a claim, a tribunal will want to be satisfied that, taking into account the size and resources of the organisation, dismissal was the type of response that a reasonable employer might have made. If the employer cannot convince the tribunal of this, the dismissal will be unfair. Following procedures alone is not sufficient to establish fairness.

? REFLECTIVE ACTIVITY 3.9

Many tribunal cases are reported in the media. Look through a newspaper or a paper's website, TV news company website or search on the Internet for a report on a dismissal case. Make sure you use a reputable source, such as the BBC, *The Guardian* or *The Times*. Review the case in conjunction with the text here. What was the reason for dismissal? Can you see, from the newspaper report, whether the employer acted fairly? While it is useful to complete this exercise, remember that newspaper reporting is not necessarily precise or particularly comprehensive – a whole week in a tribunal might be described in a few hundred words.

3.6.2 REDUNDANCY

When an organisation has more employees than it needs for its activities, it invariably has to look to reducing the total number. Employees are a major cost and an organisation whose income is depleted (by the loss of a major order, for example) may not be able to continue to afford to pay all its employees. The process of reducing the number of employees when they are dismissed for this reason is known as redundancy. In legal terms there are two slightly different definitions of redundancy. The Employment Rights Act 1996 s 139 refers to:

- a reduction or cessation of work of a particular kind, or
- a reduction or cessation of work of a particular kind at the place where the employee is employed.

The Trade Union and Labour Relations (Consolidation) Act 1992 (TULR(C)A) s 195 refers to redundancy as being dismissals where the reason(s) for dismissal are not related to the people being dismissed. Although it may seem inconvenient to have two meanings, in practice one refers to the employees' rights and the other to the need to consult.

There is a duty under TULR(C)A s 193 to give 30 days' notice to the Secretary of State (a form is available from the Employment Service) where there are 20 or more employees who may be made redundant at one establishment. If 100 or more may be made redundant, the notice period is 45 days.

The law protects redundant employees in a number of ways, discussed below.

Consultation

Firstly, there has to be consultation, and there are precise rules on the length of consultation required according to the numbers to be made redundant (see References and Further Reading at the end of this chapter). Consultation has to be with a trade union or with employee representatives (if there is no recognised trade union) and with the individuals themselves.

The consultation has to seek to avoid redundancies. Where the reduction in work could be temporary, it should be possible to reduce the labour cost by means of reductions in overtime, by short-time working (working less than normal hours) or by lay-offs (periods of time in which employees do not work and might not be paid).

In circumstances where the reduction is not expected to be temporary, one of the most popular alternatives to declaring redundancies is to use 'natural wastage'. This refers to the fact that in any organisation people tend to leave 'naturally'. They may choose to retire, find other jobs or leave for personal reasons such as a partner moving his or her job location. Indeed, organisations facing redundancies may seek to encourage wastage by offering voluntary early retirement packages, reduced promotions or steady wage levels.

During the consultation process there may be requests to allow natural wastage to take its course or for any early retirement packages to be enhanced. Allied to natural wastage is a recruitment freeze. In these circumstances the organisation places a ban on recruiting more employees. Trade unions may call for a recruitment freeze partly because it puts pressure on the organisation.

This pressure encourages consideration of other alternatives such as redeployment (to alternative work) and retraining. It is not unusual for an organisation to be recruiting in one area of its activities and making redundancies in another. Organisations have a high level of investment in employees in terms of their experience of the organisation's culture.

Redundancy is also expensive in terms of payments to individuals as well as the disruption it causes to the day-to-day activities and the senior management time that is invariably involved, so redeployment and retraining may be a cost-effective option. Other options include offering employees sabbaticals, seconding them to other organisations, or asking for voluntary reductions in hours or even pay.

Relocation to another place of work, a form of redeployment, can also be an option in some cases. While redundancy may be a cessation at a place of work, it may be reasonable to offer alternative work some short distance away. How far is reasonable is best based on advice. There are several past cases that give guidance.

Retaining specialist skills and experience is important so that an organisation is better placed when its economic situation improves. But this is not always possible.

Voluntary redundancy may be an alternative to compulsory redundancy. Here employees who might have been considering leaving or retiring are offered a financial package (usually a favourable one) to encourage them to leave voluntarily. During a consultation process there may be requests to improve the package to encourage volunteers.

Outplacement, career assistance or other means of assisting employees to find other work is often provided. Because the employer is seen as a party with a vested interest, these services are often provided, at the employer's expense, by outside consultancies.

They may be provided before an employee has been declared redundant, to assist natural wastage, or afterwards. Because demand for employees can fluctuate, some employers keep employees on after they no longer need them – that is, they keep a surplus pool of employees. An opportunity may arise later and the employee is there, ready to take the position. In addition, natural wastage can take effect over a longer period. Surplus employees are sometimes seconded to charities. This can keep their skills up to speed, give the charity some benefit and avoid a demotivated employee remaining on site. It is an expensive option, though, generally taken up by large employers with substantial resources only.

When all else fails, an organisation will be forced to declare compulsory redundancies.

Fair redundancy

For the employees, their next line of protection is that their selection for redundancy has to be shown to be fair. One of the most popular means of establishing fairness has been a simple rule such as 'last in, first out'. Here the employees most recently recruited are the first ones on the list if redundancies are declared. This does not always serve the employer's interests. For example, recent recruiting may have been a response to a skills shortage. Employers therefore often use alternative procedures to determine who is to go first.

Furthermore, the 'last in, first out' selection process can be considered indirectly discriminatory on age grounds. This is because it is more likely that those recruited most recently will be younger than those who have been employed for some time. As a last resort, however, it is generally considered acceptable (although that may change).

The essential point of any procedure is that it must be demonstrably fair. Dismissing those who lack essential skills may be fair. Dismissing on the basis of a performance rating may also be fair. However, if the rating is a subjective one, perhaps involving ratings where different employees have been rated by different people, then that would be very questionable.

Ideally, the rules for determining fairness will have been laid down at an earlier (less emotional) time – that is, a redundancy policy and procedure will have been agreed.

Consultation is therefore likely to centre on application of the rules ensuring that they are indeed applied fairly.

Unfortunately, this is not always the case. The rules, formulated at an earlier time, may no longer be appropriate. Or there may be no rules at all. In these circumstances there is little option but for the determination of the rules to form part of the consultation process.

Redundancy pay

Finally, a redundant employee aged over 18 with two years' service or more has a statutory right to redundancy pay. The precise details are available on the Acas website, among others. The amount ranges from one week's pay to 30 weeks' pay depending on the employee's age and length of service.

The main relevant legislation is the Trade Union and Labour Relations (Consolidation) Act 1992 and Employment Rights Act 1996.

3.6.3 TRADE UNIONS

The sections above covering individual employee rights before, during and at the end of employment are inextricably linked to trade unions. In some cases the rights exist, at least in part, due to campaigns and lobbying by trade unions. Others, for example the right to a fair and reasonable process if being dismissed, require employees to be given the right to be accompanied by a trade union representative. It would be remiss therefore, not to briefly mention in this chapter the legislation that regulates the activities of trade unions, which is complex. But understanding how trade unions fit into the employment framework is important for HR practitioners. They have to know what a trade union is, what trade union representatives do, the significance of trade union recognition and of collective agreements, and the power of trade unions as manifested in the threat of industrial action. Awareness of Acas and the services it offers is also important. All these matters are covered in Chapter 2.

The legislation that regulates trade unions and their activities is the Trade Union and Labour Relations (Consolidation) Act 1992 as amended, and the Employment Relations Act 1999.

3.7 RESOLVING DISPUTES AND DEALING WITH CLAIMS

Whatever an employer's intentions are, it is likely that there will be times when an employee feels that he or she has been unfairly treated. If disputes about employment rights, or one party feeling that the other party has broken the contract, cannot be settled 'in house' – for example, through grievance or appeals procedures, or through alternative approaches such as mediation (see Chapter 8 for further information), then either the employer or, more frequently, the employee may resort to taking action through the legal system. Most employment law in the UK is what is known as civil law (as opposed to, say, criminal law), where disputes are resolved by one party suing the other. Usually this involves a claim to an employment tribunal.

A tribunal may consist of three people – a legally qualified chairperson (an employment judge) and two lay people, one from an employer list (for example, managers or HR practitioners) and one from an employee list (for example, trade union representatives). Often, though, an employment judge will sit alone.

If the tribunal upholds the claim it will, in most cases, award compensation. Although in most instances compensation is relatively small, it may be thousands of pounds or, in some types of claim for example discrimination cases, an unlimited amount. Whether the claim is upheld or not, substantial preparation work is involved if the employer decides to fight the claim. Such work makes no direct contribution to business objectives, and adverse publicity may even damage achievement of those objectives.

In some cases, trade unions can challenge the employing organisation by taking actions that disrupt its activities, damage its relationship with customers and threaten its profitability. Knowledge of employment law is therefore a key requirement for HR practitioners.

However, employment law is not an area where issues are necessarily clear-cut. Indeed, even at an employment tribunal with an employment judge, one party may not agree that the law has been correctly interpreted and may appeal against the decision reached. The matter will then be referred to a higher court for it to advise on interpretation of the law. In some cases it falls to the Supreme Court or to the European Court of Justice to decide this. One consequence is that, quite frequently, the precise way in which the law is interpreted changes.

Since 2013, claimants at employment tribunals (usually employees) are charged a fee. The amount of the fee depends on the complexity of the case – for example, whether it is a straightforward breach of contract claim or a multifaceted discrimination claim. In complex cases, the fee amounts to over £1,000. Unsurprisingly, this has resulted in a significant reduction in employment tribunal claims – some claim that this is appropriate because of the previous high number of weak or vexatious claims, whilst others feel it undermines natural justice and puts justice beyond the reach of many ordinary people. The fees have been subject to, as yet unsuccessful, challenge through the courts by trade unions.

3.8 THE ROLE OF HR PRACTITIONERS

As an HR practitioner, your organisation will be looking to you and your colleagues to help keep its activities in line with legislative requirements, if not to go further and help it to adopt best practices. But don't be surprised if, from time to time, colleagues outside the function do not seem as committed to such practices as you might expect. Let's have a look at your likely roles.

3.8.1 AN ADVISORY ROLE TO LINE MANAGERS

To be effective, you need to know and understand the basics of employment law and to know where to go to find more detailed information in specific instances. This chapter has outlined the main aspects of employment law, but it can only provide general guidance.

Minor details of law can become very important in specific instances, so always check the detail if you have decisions to make. Follow the law, not your intuition. Remember that the legal situation changes continually, both in response to legislation and in the way in which it is interpreted. You will also find a great deal of helpful information and guidance on the Acas website, perhaps your first port of call. Posting questions on appropriate websites (for example the CIPD) or simply googling a short question can provide invaluable guidance. Take care to check the authority of answers. Answers by individuals may be mere matters of opinion – check out the background of those giving the advice.

Answers from prominent law firms such as www.out-law.com (part of Pinsent Masons) should be trustworthy.

You will also find Acts and Regulations available at the OPSI website (see References and Further Reading). However, it is crucially important that you do not overestimate your understanding of the law, so if you are in any doubt, always seek further advice. This would normally be from senior colleagues or from bodies such as Acas. Acas has offices in all regions of the UK except Northern Ireland, where similar services are available from the Labour Relations Agency.

3.8.2 A DECISION-MAKING ROLE

From time to time you may be called on to make decisions that require an understanding of employment law. As an example, you might be involved in the decision to move employees from one place of work to another. While you must act within a legally defensible position, be wary of invoking the law with employees in a direct fashion. It would be inappropriate, for example, simply to demand that an employee moved his place of work just because, five years ago, he signed a contract which included such a clause.

However, much can be achieved by consultation and negotiation. Remember that you are expected to act fairly and reasonably, and in this context that would mean consulting with the employee about the issue. So acting fairly and reasonably is not just a moral requirement but also a legal necessity. As an HR practitioner, therefore, you may often find the law supporting you in your desire to 'do the right thing'.

3.8.3 AN OVERSEEING ROLE

If you maintain regular contact with your colleagues by 'walking the floor' in workshops and offices or through other network activities, you will often become aware of potential legal problems or potential disputes that can be 'nipped in the bud'. Some overseeing roles may have to be more formalised, such as equality monitoring, which is essential for public sector employers.

3.8.4 AN ADMINISTRATIVE ROLE

This may be your key role, ensuring good accessible records of contracts, and keeping equal opportunities records, health and safety records and disciplinary records. Your diligence in this area may attract scant attention, and even a little resistance. But when problems arise, these good records can afford real protection for employers and managers who may need to defend their actions at a tribunal or in other courts.

3.8.5 A TRAINING OR EDUCATIONAL ROLE

If line managers are to take true responsibility for HR matters – a direction in which many organisations are progressing – they too will need an understanding of employment law.

The very process of passing on your own understanding will force you to become more familiar with the subject and should reinforce your own role as 'the expert' in your organisation.

3.9 SUMMARY

In this chapter we have outlined the main areas of legislation that have relevance to HR activity. We have looked at the different provisions that apply before the employment relationship starts, during the employment relationship and when the relationship comes to an end. Within this we have discussed the essential components of contracts and described the main characteristics of contracts of employment, written particulars, employees as opposed to workers and the nature of business relationships.

In looking at individual employment rights, we have looked at the laws that give employees rights to support them in balancing work and life outside work, laws protecting employees and potential employees from discrimination and other issues such as the national minimum wage.

In looking at the end of the employment relationship we examined the question of unfair dismissal and looked at the need for a fair reason and a fair procedure and the requirement to establish dismissal in alleged constructive dismissal cases. We also looked at redundancy.

Finally, we considered how disputes are addressed and resolved and the HR practitioner's main responsibilities in this area.

You will by now be familiar with the terms used and know which legislation is likely to apply in the main areas of HR activity. References, further reading and website addresses are provided at the end of this chapter for your information, and activities have been suggested throughout. You are encouraged to complete some, if not all, of these activities in order to reinforce and apply your learning.

? REFLECTIVE ACTIVITY 3.10

Visit an employment tribunal as an observer. You will find observing a tribunal case puts much of the practice discussed in this book into a real context. Find your local regional office on the Internet and phone up the clerk in charge of observers to book a visit. A list of cases will be available on the day and you should select one that interests you but which is likely to conclude in a day (so you see the whole process). Alternatively, your college may arrange a visit or numerous other organisations offer accompanied visits. With a little guidance on the day you will learn even more.

EXPLORE FURTHER

References and further reading

BARNETT, D. and GORE, K. (2014) *Employment Law Handbook*. 6th edition. London: The Law Society.

DANIELS, K. (2006) *Employee Relations in an Organisational Context*. London: CIPD.

DANIELS, K. (2012) *Employment Law: An Introduction for HR and Business Students*. 3rd edition. London: CIPD.

LEWIS, D. and SARGEANT, M. (2015) *Employment Law: The Essentials*. 13th edition. London: CIPD.

MOSS-RACUSIN, C.A., DOVIDIO, J.F., BRESCOLL, V.L., GRAHAM, M. and HANDELSMAN, J. (2012) Science faculty's subtle gender biases favor male students. *Proceedings of the National Academy of Sciences for the United States of America*. Vol 109, No 41. pp 16474–16479.

SMITH, I. and BAKER, A. (2015) *Smith and Wood's Employment Law*. 12th edition. Oxford: OUP.

TAYLOR, S. and EMIR, A. (2015) *Employment Law: an introduction*. 4th edition. Oxford: OUP.

TORRINGTON, D., HALL, L., TAYLOR, S. and ATKINSON. C. (2014) *Human Resource Management*. Hemel Hempstead: Financial Times/Prentice Hall.

Codes of practice and other guides

The following codes and guides are available online, or by telephone/email from Acas Publications: website: www.acas.org.uk; tel: 0300 123 1150; email: events@acas.org.uk

- Code of Practice 1 – Disciplinary and grievance procedures (2015)
- Discipline and grievances at work: The Acas guide (2015)
- Equality and discrimination: understand the basics (2015)
- Religion or belief and the workplace (2014)
- Age and the workplace – a guide for employers and employees (2014)
- Shared Parental Leave: a good practice guide for employers and employees (2015)
- Code of Practice 5 – Handling in a reasonable manner requests to work flexibly (2014)

The following codes of practice are available for online download from the Equality and Human Rights Commission: www.equalityhumanrights.com. There are also other codes of practice on the website including statutory duty codes of practice that place specific duties on employers in the public sector.

- Code of Practice on Equal Pay
- Equality Act 2010 Statutory Code of Practice – Employment
- Fair Employment (Northern Ireland): details from the enquiry line of the Equality Commission for Northern Ireland: 028 90 500 600

Subscription advisory services

CIPD HR-inform: a practical online employment law resource providing up-to-date employment legislation and HR best practice guidance: tel: 020 8612 6200; www.cipd.co.uk/hr-inform

XpertHR: tel: 020 8652 4653; www.xperthr.co.uk

Cronersolutions: tel: 0800 634 1700 www.cronersolutions.co.uk

See also survey reports on the CIPD website (www.cipd.co.uk/hr-resources/survey-reports), such as:

- Diversity and Inclusion – Fringe or Fundamental? (December 2012)

See also factsheets on the CIPD website (www.cipd.co.uk/hr-resources/factsheets):

- Age and employment (2015)
- Contracts of Employment (October 2015)
- Disability and employment (2015)
- Dismissal (June 2015)
- Employment Tribunals (2015)
- Equal Pay (2015)
- Maternity, paternity and adoption rights (2015)
- Pre-employment checks (2015)
- Race, religion and employment (2015)
- Redundancy (2015)
- Sex Discrimination, Sexual Orientation, Gender Reassignment and Employment (2015)
- Working Hours and Time off Work (2015)
- Zero-hours contracts (2015)

Websites

Arbitration, Conciliation and Advisory Service (Acas): www.acas.org.uk (be cautious about sites that may appear to be Acas)

Business in the Community (Opportunity Now): www.bitc.org.uk

Department for Business, Innovation and Skills: www.gov.uk/government/organisations/department-for-business-innovation-skills

Disclosure and Barring Service: www.gov.uk/government/organisations/disclosure-and-barring-service

Health and Safety Executive: www.hse.gov.uk

HMRC Employment Status: https://www.gov.uk/guidance/employment-status-indicator

Incomes Data Services: www.incomesdata.co.uk

Law Society: www.lawsociety.org.uk/advice/practice-notes

The Office of Public Sector Information: www.opsi.gov.uk

People Management: www.peoplemanagement.co.uk

The Stationery Office: www.tso-online.co.uk

TUC: www.tuc.org.uk

UK Government site (includes Business Link and BIS): www.gov.uk

Working Families: www.workingfamilies.org.uk

Squire Sanders Employment Law Cloud –provides push notifications for employment law updates (available from iTunes).

REFLECTIVE ACTIVITIES FEEDBACK

Reflective Activity 3.2

How much paid holiday are workers in the UK entitled to receive?

In the UK workers are entitled to 5.6 weeks' (28 days') paid holiday per year. This may include the eight bank and public holidays. Four weeks (or 20 days) of this entitlement are known as statutory leave and come from the European Working Time Directive (WTD) 1993, whilst the remaining eight days come from the UK's implementation of that European Directive, the Working Time Regulations (WTR) 1998 – so a combination of EU and UK legislation.

How are bank holidays treated?

Bank and public holidays can be included in the 28 days'/5.6 weeks' entitlement or can be in addition – it depends on what is agreed in the contract. There is no statutory right to paid leave on a bank holiday, any right to time off or extra pay depends on the contract. This is a complex area with many different legislative sources – the Banking and Financial Dealings Act 1971 (UK legislation), the WTD (EU law) and the WTR (UK law). Bank holidays can also be declared by Royal Proclamation (think of the additional bank holidays occasionally awarded for celebratory occasions) and there is a significant amount of case law affecting this area. It can be a challenge to stay on top of!

What is included in the calculation of 'pay' when working out holiday pay?

Again, this is a complex and changing area. There have been many developments and changes over recent months as a result of both UK and EU case law. For many people holiday pay will be calculated using the normal weekly pay – this is the case if normal weekly pay doesn't vary. If normal weekly pay does vary – for example because different shifts are worked each week, some of which may attract a pay premium (for example, time and a half for working on a Sunday) – then holiday pay is based on a 12-week average. Both of these come from the WTR 1998. The Employment Rights Act 1996 ensures that contractual overtime, bonuses and commission payments are taken into account in determining holiday pay, whilst most recently EU case law has determined that all overtime, bonuses and other allowances – contractual and non-contractual – should be included to reflect the reality of what a worker actually earns. Watch this space.

What happens to holiday entitlement during sick leave and other types of leave (maternity leave, shared parental leave, etc.)?

A worker is entitled to holiday pay during any period of sickness absence. Workers on sick leave accrue the WTD (EU legislation) 20 days' holiday. This can be taken at a later date, even if sickness is long-term and continues into the next holiday year. Workers can carry over holiday if they're unable to take it in one year because of sickness – EU case law suggests a period of 15 months to take carried-over leave, whilst the European Court of Justice has said that the carry-over period must be 'substantially longer than the leave year'. The WTR 1998 (UK law) currently states that leave must be taken in the year it is due and is therefore inconsistent with EU case law and will have to be changed.

For most employees, paid holiday builds up (accrues) during the whole of maternity leave/shared parental leave. For employees taking shared parental leave the amount of leave that will accrue during each parents 'share' of the parental leave will be based on their contractual leave entitlement and the proportion of the shared parental leave they are taking – potentially a confusing calculation. Relevant UK law includes the Employment Rights Act 1996, the Children and Families Act 2014 and the WTD 1998. Relevant EU law includes the WTR 1993. UK and EU case law is also relevant here. The ECJ has held that a woman must be able to take at least her statutory minimum holiday entitlement under the WTD during a period other than her maternity leave, which will impact on arrangements for carry over of leave.

Whilst these are answers are correct at the time of writing, readers will have picked up that this is an evolving area of employment law and would be advised to seek advice and do further research to determine the most up-to-date position.

CHAPTER 4

Job Analysis

LEARNING OUTCOMES

After reading this chapter you will:

- be aware of the relevance, to HR responsibilities, of job analysis and design
- be alert to opportunities to design jobs that have both meaning and efficiency
- have an outline of approaches to job analysis that you can develop for your own use
- recognise that there can be a number of obstacles in implementing job design
- know the main techniques for job evaluation and be able to discuss the practicalities.

4.1 WHAT IS JOB ANALYSIS AND FOR WHAT IS IT USED?

Job analysis should determine what a job-holder is expected to do and how the job should best be performed. It will also help decide what skills and qualities are required of the person who is to perform the job. Questions of how the task and work should be organised, how the job interrelates with other jobs, how many people are required to meet the demand of the workload and how the work itself might flow from one job to the next are all among those answered by job analysis.

Job analysis and design play a major role in organisations – indeed, you could say that organisations are made up of jobs rather than people since many 'jobs' are performed by machines, both mechanically and electronically. In small organisations the analysis and design may be very informal, perhaps only in the mind of the business owner. Even in medium-sized enterprises there is often no formal process.

But in looking at a job we should be able to assess for that job, for example:

- day-to-day tasks that will be involved
- the skills or competencies required
- the qualifications or the body of knowledge required
- physical requirements
- specific interpersonal skills, such as the ability to sell
- the degree of interpersonal skill required – say, in balancing conflicting interests
- key performance indicators (KPIs).

A knowledge of the content, demands and authority to use discretion in jobs impacts on all aspects of an organisation, from recruitment to redundancy selection. These include:

- staffing levels
- recruitment
- selection

- productivity and performance
- performance appraisal
- job evaluation
- reasonable adjustments (for disability)
- business process management
- redundancy selection pools.

Staffing levels are determined using information from job analysis, even if that is only a manager recognising that there is a job to be done that could add value, or needs to be done to fulfil another criterion such as absence cover. When you queue at a supermarket checkout, you might reflect that the number of till operators has to be determined by job analysis. Without analysing how long it takes to carry out the transactions (and the arrival rate of customers), determining the required number of checkout operators would be a guess, at best.

Recruitment, as we shall see in Chapter 5, should be done to a person specification, which flows from a job description, which in turn flows from job analysis and design. Even if these documents are not created formally, this process takes place even if only in the head of the person carrying out the recruitment.

Selection decisions also rest heavily on the quality of the job analysis. Unless we know clearly what the job requires, we are not going to be able to make an informed judgement as to whether the person in front of us can do the job. Where assessment centres and/or psychometric testing are used (Chapter 5), the design of the job is crucial to deciding for what you will be testing. Selection tests and processes need to stand up to scrutiny and be based on an accurate analysis of the job requirements. Where the process of selection is automated – for example, using psychometric tests – you may need to demonstrate the logic of the selection process to an applicant. It is your responsibility to do this (not that of the testing agency), so it is important to know that this information would be available if you use an agency. Job analysis is necessary so as to be able to demonstrate that the selection criteria are related to the job (and are not unlawfully discriminatory).

Job design can help the organisation to improve its *productivity and performance.* The speed and efficiency, with which tasks can be performed, directly affect an organisation's competitive edge or the cost of providing its services. This is particularly so in repetitive work such as assembling products, checking out groceries or data entry. Using everyday tasks as examples, Table 4.1 shows how careful attention to the components in repetitive tasks can increase productivity.

Table 4.1 Analysing by splitting into component parts

Where a job is analysed by splitting it into its component parts, many opportunities for productivity improvements come to light.	
Eliminating repeated actions	If you iron a shirt, how many times do you run the iron over each area: once – or several times? If once is enough, you save time by not doing it again.
Identifying the critical path – the sequence of actions that will take the least time to complete a task	In making a cup of tea, the critical path would be: filling the kettle, boiling the water, brewing the tea, pouring it out. Other tasks – such as getting the cups out, putting milk into cups or even warming the pot – can be carried out in parallel and so are not critical. Reducing the time means that you need to address critical path actions. An example would be boiling no more water than is needed, so that the kettle boils more quickly.

Symmetrical actions	Often two or more actions can be made at the same time. These work better if they are symmetrical – for example, lifting a clean pan onto the draining board with the right hand while picking up a dirty pan with the left and putting it in the sink.
Eliminating unnecessary steps in an operation	Next time you make breakfast, study how many times you walk around the kitchen. With a little planning, could you reduce backtracking? Some people eat breakfast standing up: that may be unwise, but it eliminates one step –sitting down!
Save four minutes a day on routine chores and you have another day in the year – in every year.	

Performance appraisal should not be done in isolation but against a job description, performance targets and skill needs.

The demands of the job, the experience required, qualifications and other aspects of the job design are crucial to effective *job evaluation*, which we shall look at later in this chapter. Again, even when job evaluation is not done formally, a subjective assessment of these factors is usually carried out, perhaps in conjunction with a knowledge of labour market rates, before determining a salary.

Job evaluation also has a major role to play in equal opportunities by helping to ensure that work of equal value is determined as such without any gender or disability bias. Work that is of equal value should receive equal pay.

In the case of disability, job analysis can help identify *reasonable adjustments*. Be careful here, though, because reasonable adjustments are not determined simply by reference to the job. Reasonable adjustments must be considered in relation to the person doing the job and relate to the particular disability in question.

Businesses consist of processes. If you think of a supermarket, there are ordering processes, supplier payment processes, stock control processes, point-of-sale processes – to name just a few. It is part of the effectiveness of a supermarket to have efficient processes. For example, when you buy a product, the point-of-sale equipment can update the stock list, and as the stock list falls, more stock can be ordered from the supplier, and the cost put into the cash flow for future payment. In businesses these processes are carried out by people but, increasingly, by computer processes.

Designing the workflow round the organisation is known as *business process management*. As a business develops and grows, more and more of these processes become standard and need to be managed, often to integrate them with computer processes. Job analysis assists integration of work with new processes. Business process management had a forerunner: business process *re-engineering*. This usually led to a reduced need for staff and, often, redundancies. It did not, therefore, have a very popular reputation.

And so, finally, job analysis can be relevant to redundancy in a wider context.

Redundancy selection must be made from a pool of employees, and these should be ones who are doing similar types of work – work that has either ceased or diminished perhaps because of a recession or on account of business process re-engineering. Determining the pool on a basis that can be defended is crucial to fair selection in redundancy situations, and job descriptions can be helpful in determining the pool and often in the selection itself. For example, a job will often demand a range of skills or a level of skill. Where these skills have been defined by job analysis those who have the skills, or the level of skill, that the company needs to retain will be less at risk of being selected. In redundancy situations, this can often justify, and hence enable, the selection of those who are less skilled.

4.1.2 DIFFERENT APPROACHES FOR DIFFERENT JOBS

It is useful to distinguish between three very broad categories of jobs: those with repetitive activities; technical/administrative positions (including service delivery); and managerial/professional posts. These are discussed in turn below.

4.2 JOBS WITH REPETITIVE ACTIVITIES

Many jobs require measurable, determinable activities that are repetitive. Examples are:

- assembling parts on a production line
- checking out groceries at a supermarket
- security checks at an airport.

These activities may be repeated many times, perhaps hundreds of times, a day. The length of time that each task takes is therefore critical to the level of staffing required to make a car, collect cash or to avoid queues at check-in. And shaving a few seconds off each repetition saves labour costs for an organisation and increases its competitiveness. We saw in Table 4.1 how this can be achieved.

I keep six honest serving men

(They taught me all I knew);

Their names are What and Why and When

And How and Where and Who.

Rudyard Kipling, *Just So Stories*: 'The Elephant's Child.'

Kipling's six honest men provide the basis for the method study approach to analysing jobs and improving productivity. Table 4.2 presents examples of how they may be used. We are going to consider 'evaluating a job' as the task in question. We've picked this because it is relevant to the chapter, but you could test the process out yourself with any activity with which you might be familiar, such as making breakfast or a work activity.

Table 4.2 The method study approach

WHAT?	The job is being evaluated to assess the value of the work to the organisation.
WHY?	There are many reasons, the most common of which is to determine a salary level for the organisation. This answer can be tested by asking if other, alternative approaches could satisfy the reason why this activity is being carried out.
	Questioning the reason for an activity opens up other options and alternatives.
WHEN?	This activity has to be performed after a job analysis has been carried out and a job description has been prepared – but before the job is assigned to a salary band or level. In asking this question we can consider whether this is the best time in the sequence of events. For example, job analysis and job evaluation might be combined in one operation, saving significant work.
	The purpose of method study is to examine alternatives such as this – to challenge the status quo.
HOW?	We've already looked at some approaches to job evaluation, but we might broaden this question in many ways. For example, could the evaluation be carried out by a software application or even by the job-holder themselves completing an online questionnaire? Remember the customer checking their own groceries?
	Again, the purpose of method study is to learn to 'think outside the box'.

WHERE?	It may be best to carry out this activity on site or in a remote office. Asking the question encourages consideration of the pros and cons. On-site may make it easier to check out any queries. Conversely, a remote office removes the evaluator from the pressure that could arise from individuals on site who may wish to influence the evaluator. The key point of a question like this is to discourage assumptions.
WHO?	We can assume we want an 'honest broker' to carry out the activity. That could be someone in HR, but then their knowledge of the jobs may be biased. Perhaps the task could be conducted by an external consultant or a computer program. Again, the key point of a question like this is to discourage assumptions.

Analysis of these jobs is founded on scientific management, which originated in the early twentieth century. Its principle is that by applying scientific methods to managing work, productivity can be improved. It led to a range of techniques to improve productivity of which the most famous (or infamous) is 'time and motion', in which each component of a task is timed with a stopwatch. More formally, this is known as work measurement, and it forms the basis on which work can be examined and on which improved methods can be developed.

Aligned, therefore, to work measurement is method study, where the work itself is examined and methods evaluated using the questions shown in Table 4.2.

4.2.1 APPLYING WORK MEASUREMENT TO STAFFING LEVELS

Using information from work measurement and method study, it is practical to build up a database of times for tasks and, therefore, assess the staffing levels required for any new operation.

In an assembly line each operation along the line is carefully planned so that the step can be completed in a specified time, before the product moves to the next operation. In a motor vehicle assembly line the planning is detailed and complex, and just watching the process is impressive.

At a supermarket checkout the number of checkout operators is determined by both the time taken to serve a customer and the rate at which customers arrive. Statistical methodology (known as operational research) is applied to ensure that staffing does not allow over-lengthy queues to build up.

Work measurement is routinely applied to call centres, in hamburger outlets and in cleaning firms to determine optimal staffing levels.

4.2.2 ASSESSING JOBS WITH MULTIPLE ACTIVITIES

Often it is more relevant to know how a job is made up – that is, how much time is spent on the various activities involved in performing the job. Continuous observation of a job is very time-consuming and for much of the time a job-holder will be engaged in one activity before moving to another. To render observation cost-effective, 'activity sampling' is employed. This involves observing the job at regular intervals and noting what activity is being undertaken at that time. In this way several jobs can be seen in the same time period.

An example would be carrying out a sampling observation in a steel stockholding warehouse and regularly noting the activity of the crane driver, the slingers, the forklift truck driver and the warehouse operative. This enables a job profile to be completed for each employee over a period of a few shifts. Statistical techniques are used to determine how frequently to make observations and over how many shifts.

Observation, whether by work measurement or activity sampling, can distort the actual picture of a job because job-holders may alter their behaviour when they are being observed. Many employees find it intrusive and some find it stressful to be observed at work.

4.2.3 IMPROVING JOB CONTENT AND MEANING

Often the design of repetitive jobs is very prescriptive and detailed instructions for carrying out each repetitive task are provided. Quality assurance processes and standard operating practices seek to eliminate discretion on the part of individual operators who may be trained to follow these practices precisely. This approach has been widely criticised for designing jobs that are devoid of meaning. To address this issue three concepts evolved in the twentieth century:

- job rotation
- job enlargement
- job enrichment.

In *job rotation* the workers move from one job to another on a periodic basis. For a worker in a shoe factory, for instance, this might mean cutting leather in one period, skiving (shaving the edges of the leather so it can overlap) in the next period, and gluing components in the third period.

In *job enlargement* workers still work at the same level but do a wider variety of tasks at that same level. For example, instead of each worker carrying out one task in making a shoe, he or she might make a whole shoe.

In *job enrichment* the work should include tasks at different levels. So the worker may be asked to plan his or her workload, take responsibility for recording his or her work and deal with unexpected problems arising, such as components not arriving when they should – as well as making a shoe.

The cynics describe rotation as combining one boring task with another, enlargement as doing more boring tasks, and enrichment as doing someone else's boring tasks as well!

Overall, this understandably creates a lack of commitment on the part of workers.

There is a continuing trend away from this type of low-skill work, and many of these jobs are disappearing. In 2000 one job in five was a low-skill job. By 2015 it was one job in six. Mechanical robots on assembly lines take some jobs, customers on websites do their own enquiries and order without human intervention, and it is increasingly recognised that employees are more productive when they are trusted and can use their brains.

4.2.4 CONTINUOUS IMPROVEMENT

There are a number of approaches to improving business processes, many of which acknowledge intelligent qualities in employees. These go under a variety of names and the popularity of particular names changes from decade to decade. Essentially, these are all about bringing improvement to the methods by which an organisation's objectives are achieved.

A number of approaches, notably *Kaizen*, *Kanban* and quality circles, were seen as very successful in Japan. The spectacular rise of the Japanese motor industry in the twentieth century was largely attributed to these techniques. They meant that the employees who carried out the work had an increased say in how the work was done.

This compared to a traditional approach where production and assembly processes had been designed by industrial engineers who specified, sometimes in great detail, how work was to be done.

Japanese shop workers were viewed differently. When Toyota set up its UK plant, UK manufacturers began to take note. Toyota's lean manufacturing approach focused on what added value for the customer.

The term 'lean' derives from eliminating any part of the product or process that does not add value. It has been widely adopted, well beyond manufacturing. Take, for example, a doctor's prescription. There is no value for the patient in a piece of paper that has to be taken to the pharmacy, so now prescriptions are sent electronically to the pharmacy – that is a 'lean' process: it cuts out an unnecessary step in the process.

One outcome in manufacturing has been greater responsibility placed on to employees and a significant reduction in the number of inspection jobs in manufacturing. The adage 'you cannot inspect quality into a product' became popular. Employees have to produce quality products in the first place. The focus is on quality at the point of manufacture or service delivery. Where it is successful, inspectors are not needed. That cuts out an unnecessary process.

Concepts such as *Kaizen* and total quality management have migrated into other sectors, such as the health sector.

It is worth thinking about how to introduce meaningfulness into jobs. This entails enabling job-holders to see how their tasks fit into the whole purpose of the organisation; whether that be to put men on Mars or to provide dignity in later life. You may be able to help achieve meaningfulness by enabling employees to see the end product, by internal communications or by ensuring that feedback, from customers or those who use the services, is shared.

The opportunity for employees to exercise judgment and to have some control over how the job objectives are achieved are other ways of creating meaningfulness, and hence motivation, into work. Discuss this with managers when analysing or designing jobs.

'Just in time' is a related but slightly different concept. Instead of maintaining large stocks of pre-made products, each particular product is made when there is an order. The aim is to complete each stage of a production process 'just in time' to complete the order. This helps individual employees relate to the end customer of the product.

Take, for example, buying a hot drink from a coffee shop, which is likely to be made 'just in time'. You choose from a selection of options, the size of cup, sometimes the particular blend. Your drink is made 'expressly' for you there and then – 'just in time' It did not exist before you ordered it. By contrast, a filter coffee may have been made some time ago and sat on a heater awaiting an indiscriminate purchase.

So 'just in time' means designing manufacturing processes so that each product, and indeed each stage of the product, is made just in time for the order. This can produce very significant savings by reducing the amount of stock held and often the customer is offered a wider choice. It also has important implications for how jobs are designed. 'Just in time' is usually achieved by redesigning processes and often requires continuous improvement techniques to achieve that.

Many of these concepts may have been regarded as management fads, but the reality is that business processes, both in manufacturing and repetitive forms of service delivery (such as serving coffee), are now organised very differently to how they were in the twentieth century.

Customer experience is another increasingly used component in continuous improvement. There is hardly any product or service that you can buy online without being asked to provide feedback.

CASE STUDY 4.1

The story is apocryphal, but illustrates a point about producing quality at the point of manufacture, rather than through inspection. A manufacturer placed an order for 10,000 components with a Japanese manufacturer. In the contract was a clause specifying that they would be inspected on receipt of the delivery and only 2% faulty components would be acceptable. The components were duly delivered on time: 9,800 perfect components and 200 faulty components provided in separate packaging. The supplier used no inspection process – the faulty parts were made to order!

Investigate how quality is managed in your organisation. Does your organisation use inspection techniques? If so, are the inspectors employees of the organisation or working on behalf of external regulators? How effective are these processes, in your view? Forming a view will help you understand the processes better. You may agree with them or not, but it would be useful, also, to discuss your opinions in a 'safe' environment – perhaps with others on a CIPD or management course.

If your organisation does not use inspection techniques, how does it control the quality of the product or the service provided? Are there processes of traceability? These latter processes enable the final product to be traced back to and along the production line so as to be able to troubleshoot quality problems. Is the quality of service assessed by other criteria, such as customer feedback? Again, it would be useful to discuss this with others and to form a view – are the processes effective, for example?

4.3 ADMINISTRATIVE AND TECHNICAL WORK, AND DELIVERY OF SERVICES

This type of work necessarily requires more in terms of mental processes. In consequence, the concept of discretion in performing the job becomes more important. Many of the concepts described above, such as allowing control and use of judgement, apply equally to this group of employees.

However, the number of administrative jobs is also falling, as are many skilled trades. Much is due to technology. There is, however, still growth in employment in the care, leisure, and other service sectors.

Analysis of these jobs involves considering such concepts as the numerical and written content of the job, the need to communicate with others and the amount of technical knowledge required for the tasks in the job. It may also involve considering pressures such as the level of potential conflict with other functions, the severity of deadlines and the need for accuracy.

In situations where there is a variety of tasks, activity sampling (which we discussed earlier) can, therefore, be particularly relevant.

There are other approaches to the analysis of these types of jobs.

4.3.1 INTERVIEWING THE JOB INCUMBENT(S)

Apart from the benefit of obtaining valuable and relevant information, this approach involves individuals in the process. It is, therefore, more likely to bring about acceptance of any future outcomes, such as a job grade that determines the person's salary. Of course, this latter possibility will inevitably lead to individuals seeking to represent their role as being demanding, important and adding value, perhaps to the point of exaggeration.

Interviews therefore need to be carefully structured and conducted similarly from job to job. That said, there is also a need to establish a rapport with each person and to explore aspects that may be crucial to a particular job. Interviewing – as we will see in Chapter 5 – is an imprecise art. As well as the incumbent, the interviewer is necessarily a factor in the information gathered and in the importance that might be attached to particular aspects of the job. For example, an interviewer from an engineering background may have difficulty relating to the work of someone in a creative role.

Notes should be taken of the interview either during the interview (which can inhibit good listening) or immediately afterwards. If you share your notes with the job-holder, any misapprehensions can be corrected. These processes should be open and transparent in any event.

4.3.2 QUESTIONNAIRES

In questionnaires, the information-seeker becomes remote and is, therefore, less a factor in the outcome.

Like interviews, these should be structured so as to bring out the importance of the various potential aspects of the job – the concepts such as interpersonal skills that we listed at the beginning of this chapter. A difficulty with questionnaire design is that the person answering the question may not interpret the question in the same way as the individual who asked it. If the question is 'What is the most important activity that you undertake?', the people answering may interpret both 'important' and 'activity' in different ways. In an interview the meaning can be clarified, but a questionnaire rarely provides such an opportunity.

Furthermore, the answers themselves will be subject to interpretation when they are analysed, so the overall picture of the job could be distorted.

Bias in interpretation may be overcome to a degree by means of a multiple-choice style of questionnaire. But the questionnaire designer has to be very careful to ensure that the questions are answerable, or provide an additional box for 'other' responses. The latter means interpreting each response again. So designing a questionnaire is a very skilled task and not to be undertaken lightly.

There are a number of proprietary questionnaires available to answer these reservations, such as McCormick's Position Analysis Questionnaire and Saville and Holdsworth's Work Profiling System. The great advantage of these systems is that question design has been carefully addressed, responses may be cross-validated, the systems themselves are checked for their validity (do they measure what they claim to measure?) and their reliability (are they valid in a wide variety of different circumstances?).

4.3.3 WORK LOGS/DIARIES

Asking job-holders to record on a regular basis the tasks that they do can reveal valuable information about how they spend time. Various time-recording software programs and smartphone apps are available for this purpose. The resultant work logs are often used to improve time management and the two purposes can often be combined into one task.

Again, a structure is required so that tasks and time taken are revealed in a consistent way.

Where many jobs are to be analysed, the way in which a work log is completed may vary from individual to individual, making analysis more difficult.

4.3.4 DO THE JOB YOURSELF

This can be useful in getting some insight into the situation and perhaps building the respect of the job-holder – but it needs caution. If you are not a technician, you will probably not have the knowledge required. If you are not skilled, you may be unable to perform the job effectively.

4.4 PROFESSIONAL AND MANAGERIAL JOBS

These three distinctions – jobs with repetitive activities, administrative and technical work, and professional and managerial jobs – are to some extent artificial. Many technical and administrative jobs include professional and managerial aspects, and vice versa. Indeed, some aspects of professional and managerial jobs can also include repetitive elements, such as responding to emails or filling teeth. And we have already seen how *Kaizen* introduces a measure of managerial responsibility into otherwise repetitive jobs.

These are the jobs that are growing and which demand the greatest cognitive, literacy and numeracy skills.

Furthermore the importance of building relationships, relating to others, communicating and collaborating effectively with different people, exercising judgement, balancing conflicting interests, thinking on one's feet and a range of other job requirements becomes more important in this category.

Analysis of professional and managerial jobs lends itself to the addition of further techniques which are still, to some degree, applicable to other categories too.

4.4.1 DOCUMENTATION

Managerial jobs are often characterised by responsibilities, performance targets and objectives. Minutes of meetings may, therefore, be relevant as may also be documentation surrounding the creation of the job in the first place. Indeed, in all categories we have considered there may be existing job descriptions, operating standards, service-level agreements, training manuals, and so on.

4.4.2 CRITICAL INCIDENTS

Examining these would commonly be done during an interview. The technique is essentially a method of enquiry into particular events that have been seminal in achieving success in reaching targets or fulfilling objectives. Additionally, mistakes are also critical incidents and valuable to analyse too. Gladstone's words – 'No man ever became great or good except through many and great mistakes' – may seem a little daunting for us lesser mortals in corporate life, but they emphasise the fact that mistakes are excellent learning experiences and good for insight into job analysis. The culture of the organisation will influence how willing a job-holder might be to discuss mistakes.

In the critical incidents approach, the analysis explores what skills are needed to respond effectively to those incidents, and it helps to define the requirements of the job.

4.4.3 REPERTORY GRID

This is a specialist technique which has its origins in clinical psychology. Typically, in job analysis it consists of asking a manager to distinguish three individuals who report to them by saying how two are similar to each other but different from a third. So a manager might say that reports A and B are very focused, whereas report C 'thinks outside the box'.

By asking the manager to distinguish individuals along a variety of lines or 'constructs', it becomes clear what is important in the job. In practice, this works well if a significant number of constructs are identified and compared with success in the job. But this rapidly becomes complex, and for this reason, computer programs are generally used to manage repertory grids. Additional levels of sophistication can be added, such as statistical analysis, and a very clear picture of what is needed to be successful in the job emerges.

Jobs do not exist in isolation and so it is important to consider a job not only in terms of its own role and demands, but in the context of its inter-relationship with others in the organisation.

4.5 THE ORGANISATION CHART

This shows the formal interrelationship between the various jobs in an organisation. Typically, it shows who reports to whom and provides a reference point to discover who has responsibility for main aspects of the organisation's function. It can also help show where the power lies within an organisation – who has a seat on the board, for example.

As we discussed in Chapter 2, there are different organisation structures and a chart is useful for giving a pictorial representation. Often the responsibility for preparing it falls to the HR department. In all but the smallest of organisations, computer software is valuable in making the task manageable.

4.5.1 THE INFORMAL ORGANISATION

Not charted is the informal organisation, which can be as important. Who actually has access to whom, individual personalities, past history and personal relationships are all part of the informal organisation. Recent research in neuroscience is re-emphasising human beings as social animals. Meeting social needs at work interacts both with team and peer relationships and with the concept of the informal organisation. Understanding the importance of this in managerial and professional jobs (particularly) is a requirement in analysing these jobs. Common social interests outside work can often forge links across internal boundaries; a good HR professional will recognise this.

Returning to the formal structures, you may think that the aims of the organisation are determined first, and then the main functions follow from these. Within each function the tasks are split up into departments and departments into jobs. Thus each job has a relationship to the main aim of the organisation and is somehow a subdivision of that main aim.

This would be very hierarchical – described by Rosabeth Moss Kanter of Harvard as an 'elevator structure' or, more recently, as the 'silo structure'. Thus to get a decision, the question for resolution has to go up in an elevator (or up the silo) to the top floor (where the senior management resides) and then the decision goes down in another elevator (or silo) to the relevant department for action. But even within a hierarchical organisation it does not usually work quite that way.

The various functions need to interact with each other. For example, a sales department needs to work with a production department without every decision being referred to the managing director. The processes by which the various departments and functions interact, how they make decisions together, and the business process itself are important factors in the competitiveness of that organisation.

So the inter-relationship between jobs is a significant factor in job design. A typical graduate training scheme and good induction processes for managers place heavy emphasis on the needs of these people to form relationships with key people in other departments and functions. This is why graduate training schemes place graduates in a variety of departments over, say, a year. There has therefore always been recognition of informal structures.

? REFLECTIVE ACTIVITY 4.2

Examine the informal structures that exist in your organisation. Look for people who have relationships that somehow do not fit with the formal structure. Who talks to or socialises with whom? Does anyone wield power or authority that appears out of line with their apparent position? Why is this?

4.6 CHANGE AND JOB DESIGN

Although job analysis is an important part of job design, it is not the only factor. For example, in 2003 PricewaterhouseCoopers performed job analysis on schoolteacher workloads and identified 25 administrative tasks (such as photocopying) which they said should be performed by support staff rather than by teachers. Opinions vary as to how effectively that job analysis has been transformed into the job design of a schoolteacher. In particular, the main aim of the study was to reduce teacher workloads by removing these tasks from the teaching job. Today, most would argue that this has not been achieved. Many factors – such as local politics, industrial relations, insecurity, management training and the availability of resources – have impacted on the practical reality of implementation.

Job analysis is valuable, and it does impact on an organisation. But there are many factors in the reality of designing a job, and job analysis is only one – even if arguably the most important one.

A job that is designed using these techniques should be documented. This may be in the form of an operating procedure, a job description or simply a set of agreed performance objectives. A person specification, defining the qualities, experience and qualifications sought in the job-holder (as discussed in Chapter 5), is also a valuable document.

Job descriptions typically define the person to whom the job-holder is accountable, the duties (the tasks the job-holder will probably carry out himself or herself), the responsibilities (the tasks delegated to others but for which the job-holder is accountable) and potentially the job-holder's level of authority and sometimes performance criteria.

But in a rapidly changing world job descriptions should never be 'set in stone'. In other chapters we look at the impact of change and how it might be managed. Job descriptions (and person specifications) need to allow for continual change arising from L&D, performance review and organisational change. Job descriptions that are too rigid and specific can be an obstacle to change.

We haven't yet discussed managers as leaders and the distinction between the two roles. Very broadly, leaders set direction (which means change) and managers execute the direction set. But it will be a poor leader who doesn't listen to her managers and a poor manager who doesn't listen to their employees. So the distinction is blurred. Leadership is a separate topic in itself. As an HR practitioner, as opposed to a manager or director, you are unlikely to be involved in job analysis at the most senior levels. What it is worth keeping in mind though, is that managerial, professional and (to the extent in which you might be involved) senior posts need to allow for leadership and thus require flexibility in how they are defined.

The more senior the position, the more any job description will focus on performance and objectives and the less it will detail tasks and processes.

CASE STUDY 4.2

Some years ago a board of trustees appointed two employees – one titled 'manager' and the other 'supervisor' – to run a small residential home on behalf of a charity. Although the manager was nominally the more senior, both employees reported to the board. Personal circumstances led to the manager working fewer hours and eventually being granted extended leave, although he ensured continuity of his essential responsibilities remotely from his home.

During his period of leave, serious problems arose with the management of

staff. Three left, two went on sick leave citing anxiety-related conditions, and another staff member raised a complaint under the home's bullying and harassment policy. Agency staff were being employed to run a home that had previously been run by employees alone, and costs were mounting. Whose responsibility was this?

By examining the job descriptions of each, the board was able to answer the question. The manager's responsibility was to manage the home and make sure that supplies were ordered, accounts were kept, and the overall care standards were met. All staff matters were with the supervisor, including the relevant part of care standards. The words 'day-to-day management of staff' were written in her job description. The responsibility for problems that were arising from human relationships (not resources) was hers, and the board of trustees was able to investigate and make decisions accordingly.

While job descriptions may be helpful in determining responsibility, it is important also always to look at the reality of the situation. Indeed, if job descriptions do not reflect reality, their value in this type of situation would be undermined. Therefore job descriptions should be reviewed regularly and updated to ensure they reflect current reality as much as possible. We discussed, above, the impact of continual change.

These details together with other details arising from the job analysis are frequently used to determine a salary, and often via a process of job evaluation – to which we now turn.

4.7 JOB EVALUATION

Job evaluation has the advantage of providing an objective platform on which to determine the earnings of an individual job. The emphasis is on the job. However, the job content, role and authority of the job is sometimes determined more by the person who holds the job than by the paper description – so job evaluation is an inexact science.

It also rests heavily on job descriptions, which are themselves inexact – as we hope you will realise if you carry out Reflective Activity 4.3. One factor that you may uncover in your discussion during this activity is that some managers and job-holders are more articulate than others in describing their duties and responsibilities. Furthermore, if managers or job-holders have prior knowledge of what will advantage them in terms of job points (and hence salary), they may be tempted to slant their job description accordingly.

? REFLECTIVE ACTIVITY 4.3

Who should write the job descriptions? There are several options. The job-holders themselves can do so – after all, no one should know the job better than they do. But then, their manager knows far better what it is that needs to be done, doesn't he or she? Yet if we allow either of these parties to write the description, there will be no consistency with job descriptions written across the organisation – and that would pose serious questions for job evaluation. So a job analyst or HR practitioner may be best, perhaps. But then the analyst or practitioner will need to rely on the techniques we outline in this chapter.

Discuss with a learning source the feasibility and merits of these three different approaches in the context of your organisation.

There are a number of proprietary job evaluation systems; some consultants specialise in using such systems, and many organisations develop their own systems to meet their particular needs. Some of the proprietary systems have the added advantage that they link into regional and national pay surveys, enabling easy comparison of jobs with the external market.

There are also a number of approaches to the process, of which we will discuss three:

- ranking
- paired comparisons
- points profiling.

4.7.1 RANKING

This is the simplest and essentially consists of putting jobs in rank order of their importance to the organisation and additionally assigning a rank to each different level within each function. Whether completed formally or informally, the ranking method is very common in smaller organisations. There the task of ranking is manageable. But ranking is also frequently used in those larger organisations where there is no formal job evaluation. Ranking can be related to different salary grades, as discussed in Chapter 5. There is no real examination of the demands of the job, the skills needed or necessarily the qualifications required. The ranking can be subjective, and there is little basis for resisting an average performer who feels strongly that he or she deserves a higher ranking. Then there are cross-department comparisons. Should an HR practitioner be ranked higher or lower than a qualified technician in the research department? There is little basis for deciding.

4.7.2 PAIRED COMPARISONS

As an approach this is designed to deliver acceptance by involving a broad range of evaluators and working on their perceived valuations of a job. A computer program presents pairs of jobs to those participating. They then have to say which of the two jobs is more valuable in their opinion, and select it, and then the program presents another pair.

The individual's own job is not included, but a wide selection is provided on a broad basis. Because many participants are involved, the program developers claim high levels of acceptance. While the authors find this an interesting approach, neither has used it in earnest.

4.7.3 POINTS PROFILING

This well-proven approach to job evaluation is more thorough, complex and expensive than most. Our outline here is just that, an outline. Proprietary and other schemes may be constructed slightly differently.

The first task is to develop a points scheme that is appropriate to the organisation, that mirrors what the organisation regards as important, and that is equal-pay-proof.

Consultants and other sources can provide a typical scheme that an organisation adapts.

Points are ordinarily awarded for factors such as the discretion allowed to the job-holder, the level of knowledge or experience, the qualifications required, accountability for the work of others, pressures of the job such as regular deadlines or critical decision-making, accountability to others outside the organisation (such as HMRC), and so on. Care has to be taken that none of the factors chosen is discriminatory in any unlawful sense and, especially for equal pay considerations, discriminatory against women.

Sometimes there are two points systems. For example, a system for salaried staff and one for hourly paid may be appropriate. Using two or more points systems is problematic and can be difficult to defend in equal pay claims. This would be particularly so if one system applies mainly to jobs occupied by women and one to jobs mainly held by men.

Given that the points profiling system is a popular method, we shall look at the actual job evaluation process based on this system.

The evaluation process

The points profiling system in private sector organisations is sometimes kept confidential so that employees cannot write job descriptions designed to maximise their own points. In practice, this does not necessarily work, because such information has a habit of leaking out. Sometimes it is disclosed to an independent party to demonstrate its fairness. It may have to be disclosed if there is an equal pay claim made to a tribunal. In the public sector, job evaluation schemes (many of which are points-based) are usually open and transparent, and often designed and agreed in partnership with trade union representatives so that all affected are clear how decisions will be reached and what factors go to make up the particular job evaluation system.

Points can be allocated for various job characteristics and responsibilities. Many of these characteristics will have a rating scale. For example, points added would be different if a particular qualification was required and may also be different according to the level of the qualification. So the need for a professional qualification such as a certified and chartered accountant (ACCA) would carry more points than the need for an associate of accounting technicians (AAT) qualification. Experience might be allocated points according to years of experience in a particular field, and so on.

These are some examples of characteristics/responsibilities:

- qualifications
- experience
- a need to be proactive
- interpersonal skills
- responsibility for decision-making
- responsibility for problem-solving
- responsibility for managing people/money/other resources.

Then a number of benchmark jobs must be selected across the organisation. These should cover the range of functions and the various levels of jobs performed in the organisation.

The number of benchmark jobs must be sufficient to give a representative cross-section of the organisation.

A panel of people within the organisation is selected and trained to evaluate the jobs. The panel would include some senior people – ones with wide experience and minimal bias (HR, for example) and, where recognised, usually trade union representatives. Indeed, in the public sector there is often a requirement for job evaluation to be conducted in partnership with a trade union.

Then each of the benchmark jobs is evaluated against the points system by the panel. Ideally they will make decisions by consensus. This can be a daunting task. These benchmark jobs are then assigned to appropriate salary (or wage) levels to reflect the points that they have been allocated in each case. As a general principle, the aim is that the average salaries as determined by the evaluation system will match the current average salaries paid. Inevitably, that means that some jobs' salaries should go up and some down.

Then the remaining jobs are slotted into the structure that has been provided by the benchmarked jobs, and thus to appropriate salaries.

Some drawbacks

A problematic aspect of job evaluation in general, and the points system in particular, is that of market demand and supply (see the CIPD factsheet, 'Market pricing and job evaluation' listed under 'References and Further Reading' at the end of this chapter). There are always some skills shortages. An organisation which needs scarce specialist computer skills (or any other scarce specialist skill) cannot ignore the need to pay higher salaries to attract and retain such staff. But market forces fluctuate, and it may be unwise to include them in a points system.

One of the reasons that job evaluation is so expensive is that those who are already being paid more than the salary determined by the job evaluation scheme will have their earnings 'red-ringed' or protected. That is, each time there is a general salary rise, their own salaries will remain the same. However, the underlying salary rate for their job will gradually increase. Eventually there will be a point where the underlying rate matches the rate individuals are actually earning. Only at that point will a 'red-ringed' job be eligible for the annual rise. Whereas those who are earning less than the job evaluation determines will receive an increase, usually immediately. For the organisation, there is therefore invariably a net increase in salary cost.

Most schemes allow employees to appeal against their job evaluation rating. Market forces are a common reason for employees to appeal a job-evaluated salary grade. Employees have little to lose, especially if they have been red-ringed, so appeals are frequent. They have to be heard by another small panel. Indeed, sometimes appeal panels are not small. This can be time-consuming and adds to the cost.

In a world of rapid change, a typical job evaluation scheme has a life of only a couple of years simply because tasks and technology change and the relative importance of skills and knowledge fluctuates over time. This can create drift in evaluated levels, and eventually, inequalities. Then the process will have to commence all over again.

There are those who believe it is simply not worth it, and prefer subjectivity, negotiating and bargaining with individuals. Although this may work in a small to medium-sized private company, the larger and more complex an organisation is, or becomes, generally, the more likely it is to have job analysis, job design and job evaluation.

4.8 THE ROLE OF THE HR PRACTITIONER

The role expected of the HR practitioner will vary considerably from one organisation to another. It is very likely that the drawing up of job descriptions, person specifications, and job evaluation will involve the HR practitioner to a greater or lesser degree. Work measurement, method study, productivity improvement and job analysis may well be part of a specialist function and, in any event, be aligned more closely with the operational functions than with HR. But there are no set rules. Should it be your role, you may be challenging line managers as much as serving them. The status of one's job and that of one's subordinates is very close to one's personal image, so having it examined, or analysed, is a very sensitive matter. Managers will usually seek to use what political power they have to create the best outcome for themselves. This can hinder the objectivity of the processes: be alert!

4.8.1 AN ANALYTICAL ROLE

If analysis is expected of you, you will need to become familiar with appropriate techniques that have been outlined in this chapter. You may be able to take advantage of one or more of the proprietary systems on the market, which provide both training and support.

4.8.2 AN EVALUATIVE ROLE

As an 'honest broker' you may be called on to evaluate jobs. You are unlikely to be doing it on your own. Evaluation is usually carried out by a small, confidential group with a cross-section of experience related to the jobs to be evaluated. If you get the opportunity, it is an interesting role which will give you insight into the wider organisation.

4.8.3 DOCUMENTING JOB AND PERSON SPECIFICATIONS

Elsewhere, we have asked you to consider who should prepare job descriptions where no specific job analysis is being undertaken. In our view you should be very wary of taking on too much responsibility for determining job descriptions. A more appropriate role for HR is to take responsibility for ensuring consistency between descriptions that may have been prepared by different managers. In relation to person specifications, you may be able to make a valuable contribution with respect to the qualifications and attributes required, taking particular care that no unlawful discrimination is enshrined in the specification (or indeed in the job description).

4.8.4 FACILITATING CHANGE

Change management is an area of expertise in its own right, and the ability to drive change is an invaluable skill. On the whole, HR practitioners are less likely to be drivers of change and more likely to facilitate change initiated at senior levels of the organisation. Indeed, without support at the most senior level in an organisation, any change programme is liable to flounder. We look at change management in Chapter 11.

So if job analysis and design produce the need for serious change, you may be involved in retraining activities, redundancies, industrial relations issues and even some serious internal politics. Many of these matters will be the province of experienced practitioners, but that may depend on the resources of the organisation. Many of our colleagues have been through a 'baptism of fire' at some point in their HR careers.

4.8.5 AN ADMINISTRATIVE ROLE

Apart from job descriptions there is often a significant administrative role in simply keeping the whole process fully documented, arranging meetings, recording outcomes and ensuring the steady progress of a complex project. Because these can be sensitive areas, these tasks may well fall to the HR department and invariably require some involvement on your part.

? REFLECTIVE ACTIVITY 4.4

Square pegs – should the round hole be redesigned?

There is an assumption in this chapter – and, indeed, in this book – that jobs are designed and people fit them, or are recruited and selected to fit them. This is not always the case.

Often, particularly at more senior levels, jobs are restructured to fit the particular qualities brought by a promising candidate. Discuss this with a learning source. Is this a sensible approach and, if it is, in what circumstances?

What implications does it have for job analysis?

Does it have implications for equal opportunities?

If you want to consider the implications of this activity in more detail, google the term 'job-sculpting', read up on it and revisit the activity.

4.9 SUMMARY

In this chapter we have examined the value of job analysis by looking at the main areas where it can have an impact on HR activities, such as recruitment, performance appraisal and redundancy pool selection. It has both a wide and deep application in HR and in the operation of the business generally.

We've seen how jobs may be categorised as repetitive, technical and administrative (including service delivery), and managerial and professional. There is a broad range of analytical tools that can be used across these categories, although some are more applicable to one category than another. This should give you a reasonable number of techniques to use in any analysis, although some would require specific training.

You've been alerted to some established approaches to job design that are based on continuous improvement.

Fitting jobs into the organisation is important and you will now have some awareness of the issues created by how this is done.

Finally, job evaluation has been described in some detail, providing you with three approaches, and looking at one of these – points profiling – to understand the process and also to consider some of the potential drawbacks.

It's a fascinating area and addresses the question that many who are first leaving full-time education ask: 'The company employs one thousand people. *What do they all do?*'

EXPLORE FURTHER

References and further reading

BERGGREN, C. (1992) *Alternatives to Lean Production: Work Organisation in the Swedish Auto Industry*. Ithaca, NY: ILR Press/London: Macmillan.

CRESSEY, P. and TAYLOR, S. (2011) *Contemporary Issues in Human Resource Management*. London: CIPD.

LIEBERMAN, M.D. (2013) *Social: Why Our Brains Are Wired to Connect*. New York: Crown Publishers.

TAYLOR, S. (2008) *People Resourcing*. London: CIPD.

See also Factsheets on the CIPD website, available at www.cipd.co.uk/hr-resources/factsheets:

- Job Design (July 2015)
- Leadership (June 2015)
- Market Pricing and Job Evaluation (March 2015)
- Workforce Planning (October 2015)

Websites

Business process management: en.wikipedia.org/wiki/Business_Process_Management

Time tracking software: www.officetime.net

Repertory grid software: edutechwiki.unige.ch/en/Repertory_grid_technique#List_of_Software

www.job-analysis.net

Reflective Activity 4.2

Power and authority can be founded on a number of different bases. The ability to reward or carry out sanctions against another gives power. Denying access is an example of a sanction, whereas promotion would be a reward if it is a promotion that the individual would want.

Knowledge, personal confidence (or, conversely, insecurity), personal relationships, stereotyping and prejudices all have an impact on who can influence whom and hence on the informal structure.

Reflective Activity 4.4

A candidate may bring opportunities for business development, processes or organisation that have not been considered by the job designer, perhaps because the candidate has brought special experience that would be valuable. A candidate who has a disability may be able to carry out the central part of the job to an excellent level, but not be able to perform other parts. It may well be justified to redesign the job around him or her.

Job analysis would still contribute because it allows redesign of the jobs on a structured basis – not losing sight of critical aspects of the job that may need to be reassigned.

An *ad hoc* approach to designing the job around the person does have implications for equal opportunities. It will become harder to meet a challenge from an unsuccessful candidate who might have been a better match for the original job description. So care must be taken to be able to justify objectively amending the job to the candidate, because changes 'on a whim' could lead to accusations of discrimination and these could be difficult to defend. You can, though, make reasonable adjustments for a candidate with a disability without facing a legitimate claim from a person without a disability.

Recruitment and Selection

5.1 INTRODUCTION

Many HR practitioners spend a great deal of their time engaged in activities associated with the recruitment and selection of staff – often also called 'resourcing talent'. This can range from one-off recruitment episodes to major recruitment campaigns carried out to recruit and select replacement staff, staff with specialist skills, trainees, graduates, etc. HR practitioners often thus gain a great deal of experience in the range of administrative, interviewing and other selection activities associated with staffing the organisation. In larger organisations specialist recruitment officers may be appointed within the HR team or recruitment services may be delivered from a recruitment service centre, whose primary role is to ensure that (to borrow a time-honoured expression) 'the right people with the right skills are employed at the right time and in the right place' by the organisation. Other HR practitioners have little involvement in recruitment and selection because these activities have been devolved to line managers or outsourced to specialist agencies. The in-house practitioners may only get involved in limited activities or in overseeing the process.

Although recruitment and selection are core activities for many HR practitioners, they are activities that are affected by the organisation's policy and the external environment – such things as business expansion or contraction, developments in employment legislation, the general economic climate and skills shortages. Whatever the economic climate, the workforce planning process is by no means simple. Organisations need to predict their workforce requirements (numbers, skills and competencies, etc.) in accordance with future corporate objectives. In times of business contraction, even if it is obvious that fewer staff members will be required in the future than currently, it is highly unlikely that a recruitment freeze would deliver the changes in workforce make-up where they are required. Freezes can normally only be effective for a limited period of time if the organisation is to remain viable.

There are many factors to be taken into consideration in meeting the people needs of the organisation (for instance, existing skills, training and development provision, retention, career progression and workforce turnover), and it would be a rare – and fortunate – employer that did not need to look to the external labour market to 'buy in' new skills and abilities for key posts.

The employment situation over the years shifts from a seller's to a buyer's market and back again and the approach of HR practitioners and the amount of time spent on recruitment and selection activities must reflect and anticipate this. However, this effect is not always evenly balanced across different employment sectors. At any one time, some sectors may be downsizing operations or removing hierarchical tiers and this leads to losses of jobs through redundancy exercises. In others, relocation of manufacturing and/or service facilities to areas, often outside the UK, where labour costs are cheaper (and employment legislation may be less restrictive) leads to more radical approaches to recruitment and selection. Meanwhile, in certain sectors, growth and the development of new business, new technology or changing markets can mean real skills shortages in the face of which recruitment and selection become of prime importance. The general economic climate also has an impact here. During 'austerity', Government plans to reduce the deficit may lead to a contraction in the size of the public sector with consequent job losses, and an expectation (and hope) that the private sector will expand and recruit new workers to fill the gaps created.

In this section, we will consider the context within which recruitment happens and the factors impacting upon recruitment, the place and impact of employment legislation and the importance of equality and diversity in recruitment and selection practice. Broadly speaking, 'diversity' means understanding that each individual is unique, and recognising and valuing those individual differences. A diverse workforce will contain a broad range of differences of all kinds. See later in this chapter for a comparison between the terms 'equal opportunities' and 'diversity'. We will also provide an overview and detailed information on the recruitment and selection processes, considering both activities and skills, and will look at the transition from successful candidate to employee.

5.2 THE CHANGING NATURE OF THE WORKFORCE

Two significant factors can be seen to be having a continuing impact on the character of the labour force in the UK, both have implications for recruitment and selection activities: the first is demographic change, and the second the use of more flexible, less traditional working patterns and practices, including the growth in part-time employment, especially zero-hours contracts, self-employment, internships and outsourcing. A third factor is the changing nature of work itself, which threatens to have an impact on low skilled workers.

5.2.1 DEMOGRAPHICS

Over the coming years the workforce is set to become more diverse in terms of gender, age and ethnic balance, building on changes that have already happened:

- In relation to gender, there is a continuing trend for more women to enter the workforce. In 1952 females made up 30% of the UK workforce, but in 2012 it was 46%. This means you will need an ongoing focus on issues such as equal pay, flexibility and the provision of childcare/eldercare.
- In relation to age, falling birth rates in the 1990s and greater longevity mean that, by 2030, 46% of the UK population will be over 50, compared with 33% in 2002. Pension changes, health improvements and the removal of the default retirement age is already having an effect, leading to many people working for longer.

- In relation to ethnicity, government predictions indicate that by 2020 net migration will account for more than 40% of the growth in the working-age population. Migration also has an impact on birth rates making assessments of future birth rates more difficult.

All of these matters are important and complex and you will need to keep them in mind during recruitment as well as during other employment activities. You will need to give consideration to attracting and retaining a more diverse workforce. It is worth looking at age in more detail.

In order to maximise the participation of different age groups within an organisation's workforce and encourage age/generational diversity, the particular needs and expectations of each age group will have to be taken into account in designing jobs, in recruitment activities and in induction into the workplace.

Although not homogenous in their expectations, there are some common themes that are apparent in the different generations at work.

Generation Y

The younger age group (born 1978–1997), often referred to as Generation Y, have been the subject of much recent research because they are perceived by many to be very different from previous generations in their approach to work.

Research has shown that although Generation Y people's expectations of work are not homogenous, there is some common ground. The dominant expectation of this group about work is for fulfilling roles and career development. Other things found to be of importance are work–life balance, opportunities for longer periods of time off, the working environment and organisational values, a need for challenge, stretch and change, the organisation's approach to social responsibility, having motivating and inspiring managers, and having opportunities to work from home. Pay and location of work, although important, were not high on the list. Research has also shown that boundaries (of place and time) between work and life outside work for many in this generation are breaking down. Also, many expect to use technology at work, particularly social media (social networking, forums, blogs, webcasting, etc.). For this generation, being able to be yourself, feeling highly valued and being in a supportive and inspiring workplace drive satisfaction and happiness at work. They are excited by career development, particularly the opportunity to gain transferable skills and knowledge through professional and academic qualifications.

However, many younger people have been struggling to enter the labour market; with youth unemployment rates at a high level in the UK, there are 'greater proportions of young people from Generation Y entering the labour market in less skilled and less stable employment than previous generations' (Joseph Rowntree Foundation 2015).

Generation X

Workers within the middle age group (born 1958–1977) are the most likely to have the dual responsibilities of dependent children and dependent parents. Characteristics of this group include not wanting to work long hours, being keen to learn new skills and stay employable, a lack of trust in institutions, feeling increasingly uncomfortable in corporate or large organisation life, a desire to see fairness in approaches to promotion based on performance not tenure, and a preference for an entrepreneurial or independent style of working, as is also seen in older generations.

As a generation, they are strongly sought after by employers, possibly for their experience and qualifications, and represent the least disadvantaged group in the labour market.

Employees in this group (particularly women) can suffer poor career progression. Typically this is due to part-time hours, the challenge of balancing childcare responsibilities, and limited access to training. Full-time employees often benefit from more training opportunities.

Baby boomers and war babies

This older generation (1940–1958) has approached retirement much more flexibly than previous generations. The younger end of this group may have the dual pressures of ageing parents and supporting children through early adulthood. However, at the older end, there are increasing numbers of baby boomers working beyond the previous retirement ages of 60 (women) and 65 (men).

> Remaining in employment in later life can be greatly influenced by job quality and content. [These] employees are more likely to leave jobs with low levels of autonomy and those that are felt to be unsatisfying.
>
> Joseph Rowntree Foundation

The Joseph Rowntree Foundation also reports that the presence of older workers in the labour market is concentrated among those with higher levels of qualifications being retained longer by long-term employers, rather than recruitment of older workers.

However, we do see other older people take on so-called 'retirement jobs'. The reasons for this can include financial need and/or security, enjoying work, an ongoing need for the friendship and companionship found at work and a fear of full retirement as a new experience. Those with qualifications are often better placed to take advantage of such opportunities, although we see increasing numbers in low-skilled occupations that might otherwise be taken by school leavers and Generation Y.

? REFLECTIVE ACTIVITY 5.1

Consider the age/generational diversity in your own team/department/organisation. Do the issues outlined above seem familiar to you? Have you interviewed people of different ages recently? Did any of these differences come across during the recruitment process? Talk to some people of different ages. What things are most important to them in relation to their job and work situation? What things are most important to you?

5.2.2 FLEXIBILITY

The trend away from a reliance on permanent, full-time contracts of employment to the increasing use of more flexible and atypical working arrangements (for example, homeworking, compressed-hours working, term-time contracts, zero-hours and part-time arrangements, as well as outsourced services and contracts for services) is continuing. The reasons for this include:

- legislation – for example, minimum (and living) wages, holiday pay and other worker rights
- the economic climate and companies needing to be more innovative in their use of their people resource
- employee expectations about work–life balance
- changes in career paths as knowledge workers move to self-employment
- organisations utilising a range of options to resource their non-core functions
- organisations requiring increased flexibility in terms of hours of work, location, skills development and the duration of the employment relationship in order to respond quickly to market demands
- organisations taking a greener approach to work and their impact on the environment– for example, through employee travel

- government policy on outsourcing and efficiency in the public sector
- business gurus – notably Tom Peters – encouraging companies to concentrate on what they are good at and to outsource the remainder.

We have thus seen many organisations move towards greater flexibility in their relationships with employees and how work gets done and delivered. Employers often retain a core group of primary workers who are likely to be permanent employees (including part-time and other flexible working posts, as well as full-time posts). Numerical and functional flexibility is then provided by employing a range of temporary, zero-hours, casual, fixed-term and agency workers as well as outsourcing activities to other companies and self-employed individuals.

However not all employers, maybe in the smaller employer sector particularly, welcome flexible working.

The risk in resisting flexible working is that of losing valuable employees through them prioritising care responsibilities or simply through those employees seeking a better work–life balance.

Those who seek flexible working are often less well regarded by employers, perhaps in part because it is more challenging to integrate part-time or homeworkers into a team. Other challenges include the need for continuity in providing a service, arranging complex rotas to ensure coverage of (say) nursing care, or matching a continuous a production line to variable availability of workers. How much you can embrace flexible working will depend on the nature of the work, and your ability and others in your organisation's ability, to meet the challenges presented.

Please note that whatever the make-up of your workforce, the same level of care and attention has to be paid to the recruitment and selection process (of employees and other workers) in order to ensure that the organisation's workforce requirements are satisfied in as cost-effective a manner as possible. See Case Study 5.1 for further verification of this point.

CASE STUDY 5.1

A company director in a FTSE-100 company learned his lesson the hard way about the dangers of compromising good practice with regard to recruitment and selection. After the resignation of his PA/secretary, he used a secretary supplied by a local recruitment agency as a temporary measure while seeking to recruit a permanent replacement. It was an especially busy time of year and the temp coped well in the circumstances. She put in a lot of effort and worked long hours because she was keen to impress. As the weeks passed, the director decided not to bother with a proper recruitment and selection process, but to offer the permanent position to the temp. She gratefully accepted – and that was when the situation took a turn for the worse. As the workload of the department settled back to normal, it became apparent to the director that the secretary did not possess the full range of skills that were expected of a PA. A capability procedure was adopted as a late measure, but the situation was irredeemable. Eventually, they reached a mutual decision to part company – but in the meantime, there had been months of disruption and soured relationships. The secretary felt that she had been misled, badly treated and was conscious that this experience would be viewed as a black mark on her previously good employment record.

As can be seen from the sections above, it is important for organisations to know what type of posts they need in their business and to know something about the labour market they are operating in. We shall now look at workforce planning as a means of obtaining this knowledge.

5.2.3 THE CHANGING NATURE OF WORK

In the year 2000, knowledge working accounted for 37% of all occupations; by 2020 it is predicted to be 46%. By comparison, the percentage of jobs for administrators, skilled tradespeople, production workers and the unskilled has fallen from 47% in 2000 to a prediction of 36% by 2020.

So the growth in jobs in the future is in management jobs, professional occupations, and higher skilled jobs.

Against this background, over 70% of the 2020 workforce will have already completed compulsory education by at least ten years (Leitch Report). So the changing nature of work and the availability of a workforce capable of meeting these needs is going to be a challenge not just for you as a recruiter but also for assessing learning and development needs.

5.3 WORKFORCE PLANNING

There are many components to the process of workforce planning (for example, succession planning, flexible working, talent management, outsourcing, etc.) and a need for such planning to sit as part of wider business planning processes, integrated with the rest of the enterprise. For the purposes of this chapter, we will focus on two aspects of workforce planning: analysing and managing the demand for staff; and anticipating and managing the supply. An effective plan keeps the two in balance.

5.3.1 DEMAND

One source of demand arises from the organisation's activities requiring more resources. As a general rule, managers like to increase their staff numbers. The fact of having more subordinates signifies an increase in power and influence, boosts self-esteem and, quite possibly, leads to a higher salary level or increased prospects. 'Empire-building' is a mark of success in both public and private sectors, although a reputation for the activity can be damaging. However, an increase in employment costs invariably leads to an increase in overhead costs. There is a downward effect on overhead costs from shareholders and business-owners (who expect the organisation to make a profit) in the private sector, and from the Treasury, and ultimately the electors, in the public sector. From time to time, there can be pressure to reduce overheads, and this is particularly likely to arise if there is a reduction in demand for the organisation's products or services, such as during recession. When it comes to cutting overhead costs, the number of options can be limited and a reduction in staff (usually the greater part of these costs) is the inevitable outcome.

Another source of demand arises from the organisation's strategy. If it is expanding – opening more branches or services, opening new hospitals, serving new markets, for example – then it will require more people to staff those activities. There is, of course, a converse to this – namely, downsizing, where it may be closing branches or services, or relinquishing markets. The longer the timescale on which these actions are planned, the better placed the HR practitioner will be to respond effectively. This applies just as much whether it is a recruitment drive or a redundancy programme. The key for HR professionals is gaining the confidence of the decision-makers so that the HR function can be involved at an early stage in the decision-making. Often it is necessary to prove your mettle in other areas of HR activity before you can gain the trust of the strategists.

An easier source of demand to manage is that resulting from the routine turnover of employees (the attrition rate). If this is steady, it provides a guide as to how much recruiting is likely to be required in a year. You need to keep an eye on changes in the rate that might be anticipated, such as the activities of competitors in your labour markets (see the discussion on supply at 5.3.2 below).

The labour turnover rate is a useful figure to calculate for this purpose. This is calculated thus:

$$\text{Labour turnover} = \frac{\text{Number of employees leaving in a year}}{\text{Average number of employees in a year}} \times 100$$

Labour turnover rates are also a good measure of the 'health' of an organisation. The best way to make a judgement is by benchmarking organisations in the same sector, industry, and locality. You may be able to find the information you require from networking, on the Internet or from industry sources.

Very low turnover rates (especially if they reflect the recruitment rate) may be a cause for concern. It is important for organisations to bring in 'new blood' from time to time as part of a process of keeping up to date with skills and experience available in the labour marketplace.

High turnover rates are invariably bad news. Recruitment costs vary but are, typically, 10–20% of the first year's salary for each person recruited. On top of this, the leaver may have left a position vacant while the new employee is hired. The new employee is likely to need training and time to establish relationships. He or she will not be performing at maximum capacity during this period.

If your organisation is experiencing high turnover rates, it is important to establish whether this arises from new recruits leaving the organisation in the first few weeks of employment (the induction crisis) or whether employees with longer service are leaving. The most valuable statistic in deciding this will be the labour stability rate:

$$\text{Labour stability} = \frac{\text{Number of those employees still in employment today}}{\text{Number of employees in employment a year ago}} \times 100$$

A high labour stability rate (combined with a high turnover rate) means that most employees stay for many years, yet despite this in some job roles or functions there must be a high turnover rate. This may suggest an induction crisis, and attention should, therefore, be paid to recruitment and induction. (See later in this chapter for further information on both of these subjects.) Another possible explanation is that in some job roles or functions employees simply do not stay because of poor management practices. If the turnover is several times a year, the effect will not show up fully in the stability rate. Apparent inconsistencies are always worth investigating.

However, the figures must be viewed in the context of the industry. In the hotel and catering industry, high turnover and low stability rates are not unusual. In a specialist research unit, on the other hand, it could mean that valuable skills and knowledge – the lifeblood of the organisation – are draining away.

Unless the organisation has well-developed HR IT systems and sound workforce data and analytics, both these figures can be difficult to calculate. This is because finding and interpreting the raw data on which they are compiled requires persistence, judgement, and significant resources on the part of the HR department. Consequently, they are often not calculated. But the critical point is that they enable the HR practitioner to assign costs to particular organisational shortcomings. By doing this, the practitioner can raise the perceived value of an effective HR function.

5.3.2 SUPPLY

Although the level of control over demand may be problematic at times, it is harder to exert much control over the provision of employees. The external environment has a major influence here, and anticipating changes can be valuable.

What practitioners can do is to increase their knowledge and understanding of their labour markets. Most organisations operate in a variety of labour markets and you should identify and research the ones that are relevant to you – these may be geographical or skills-based, for example. Increasingly, particularly in larger companies, labour markets are global and HR practitioners will need to develop expertise and strategies to deal with this. These labour markets can be defined using the following factors, which must be considered in conjunction with each other.

Skills shortages – short-term

Short-term skills shortages arise because the demand for particular skills exceeds the numbers of people trained in those skills. Periodically, national shortages are reported in the press and this raises the profile politically. Consequently, the Government has sought to address these problems over the years through a variety of initiatives. Current at the time of writing this chapter are the Government's Work Programme (which provides tailored support for people in receipt of unemployment benefit who need help to undertake effective job-seeking), and the UK Commission for Employment and Skills. An HR practitioner can make a significant contribution by keeping in touch with such initiatives.

In particular sectors, at particular times, skills shortages do arise. Training existing staff can do much to avert skills shortages, but it takes time. For example, it takes years to train an engineering apprentice and unexpected shortages will not therefore be rectified quickly. So HR planning needs, in part, to consider, and where possible to address, shortages that can be anticipated arising from retirement, changes in technology or from the social perception of certain types of work, for example.

Be aware, though, that some shortages can be very specific and relatively transient. Searching for skills shortages on the Internet can produce current information about skills and occupational types in which there may be shortages; see References and Further Reading at the end of this chapter for an example of what is available online.

Skills shortages – overall

Overall, there is a national issue with skills as the nature of work changes, as we highlighted above. A relatively large proportion of our population has low cognitive skills. We lag behind other countries in the Organisation for Economic Co-operation and Development for literacy levels and numeracy skills. Generation Y is also well below average on problem-solving. We will return to these matters in Chapter 9.

Geography

Here you need to clarify where your employees travel from in order to work for you. Manual workers and junior staff may be very locally based, and this is where you would seek them. Some of the skills you seek may also be local, and this can be an issue if your organisation is considering relocating its activities. Managers and directors may travel from much further, especially if you are in a metropolitan area. In addition, when you come to seek senior or specialist/expert staff, the market can be national or international. Your strategy for finding employees will depend in part on where you believe they are living now.

Economic situations

You should keep in touch with the unemployment rate within the markets in which you are interested. This is particularly necessary if you envisage a recruitment drive in which you are seeking a significant number of employees.

Occupational types

The UK labour market is very diverse when it comes to occupational types. By thinking widely, you may be able to identify sources of employees that others miss. When solving supply problems remember to include possibilities such as part-timers, job-shares, shift-workers, students, new graduates, the over 60s, outsourcing, homeworkers, teleworkers, self-employed workers, agency workers, recent (legal) immigrants and workers from abroad. As mentioned above, an Internet search can provide information on occupational types and their current availability.

Online comfort

Use of, and familiarity with social media and online job search generally varies, at least in part, with the different generations (as described above). How you decide to search for new employees will influence which groups you reach. Getting to know employees who come from your target market(s) will help you to learn which approaches they use. In turn, that will assist you in reaching others.

Competitive positions of organisations

You compete with other organisations not just for sales, but also for employees. Some employers take this so seriously as to create employer brands, just as there are product brands. Your organisation may have a monopoly in its product marketplace or its labour market. Its goods and services may be in newer growing markets, in well-established markets or in a declining sector. These factors all influence your ability to find and attract employees and emphasise the importance of understanding your organisation in relation to its potential or actual labour markets. If you don't stay up to date, you could find your employees leaving very rapidly. Valuable information on labour market competitors can come from local sources, such as Chambers of Commerce, HR discussion groups and networking. Desk research from sources such as the Internet and Incomes Data Services can also be very helpful for the wider market. More detailed information and guidance on the broader workforce planning process can be found in the CIPD factsheet 'Workforce Planning'.

Having considered workforce planning, we shall now explain why the interlinked activities of recruitment and selection are so important, before outlining the relevant legislation and the practical issues involved in the recruitment and selection of staff. (See also job analysis in Chapter 4 as a necessary precursor to recruitment.) We shall be covering the key recruitment stages of advertising, selection (candidate data collection, interviewing and other selection methods), assessment and comparison. Finally, the induction and evaluation processes and the various roles played by HR practitioners will be considered.

5.4 WHY ARE RECRUITMENT AND SELECTION IMPORTANT?

As we saw above, it is crucial that selection choices result from a thorough and systematic process. As HR practitioners, you will need to be knowledgeable about the wider issues involving recruitment and selection decisions, such as legislation and good practice, and the range of recruitment sources and selection methods, as well as being skilled in interviewing and assessing potential employees.

Some examples of good practice in recruitment and selection decisions are listed below:

- When a job becomes vacant, you need to question whether it ought to be redesigned by making changes to, say, the level of responsibility, remuneration package, hours of work, working methods or reporting lines. Indeed, also question whether it should be filled at all (could the work be absorbed by existing members of staff or technological solutions found?). If you recruit when there are better alternatives to recruiting then not only will this have cost implications but down the line you may be called on to make those very people redundant. Jobs need to be designed to suit current needs; do not ignore the possibility of potential savings.

- Take care with advertising copy. It needs to give a good impression of the organisation, provide accurate information for potential applicants and encourage the right candidates to apply (see the discussion of AIDA in 5.8.3). Keep in mind, though, that online advertisements can be amended 'live' so you can change your copy if you wish, in the light of the applicants coming forward.

- Research your choice of advertising media so you get the right level of applicant and avoid needing to re-advertise and waste time.

- Remember that interviewers project a public relations image of your organisation to prospective employees. So ensure your interviewers are trained, at the very least so they avoid inadvisable lines of questioning (such as family circumstances) which may lead to claims of discrimination.

- If you are using an assessment centre (see below), you need to have trained, and, at least, some, experienced observers. Assess a manageable number of candidates against a limited number of criteria so as to avoid information overload and poor assessments. Equally, the group exercises should be short enough for assessors to remember the key points that they observe.

- If candidates fall short of the requirements defined as essential for performing the job satisfactorily then resist the temptation to appoint one regardless. Essential criteria (see 'Person specification' in 5.8.1) considered away from the pressure of the selection process are likely to be sound. Hastily revamped essentials may result in selecting a candidate who then leaves or is dismissed in the short term. That can be painful.

Adopt good practices and you will save your organisation your own salary many times over. Cut corners and you may have to repeat the whole scenario sooner than you think. There are other risks too such as unsuitable employees who remain with the organisation indefinitely or even mistakes that could incur the cost of an employment tribunal case.

5.5 THE LEGISLATION

Before considering the important issue of good practice, we need to outline the relevant legislation. The legislation is referred to and commented on throughout this chapter as well as being specifically referred to in Chapter 3. You should be aware of the impact of the following main pieces of legislation:

- Equality Act 2010
- Agency Workers Regulations 2010
- Part-time Workers (Prevention of Less Favourable Treatment) Regulations 2000
- Data Protection Act 1998
- Freedom of Information Act 2000.

You may also need to be aware of the Disclosure and Barring Service for employment positions that involve working with vulnerable people (see 5.11.1 'Employment checks').

Employing immigrants is a complex area for which there has been much legislation in recent years. If this latter area is relevant for you, then it is important to take specialist advice or, at least, consult the most recent information available on the CIPD, GOV.UK or Acas websites.

Other relevant legislation concerns amendments to the above legislation, fixed-term contract workers and flexible working arrangements. There are also specific public-sector equality duties, outlined in the 2011 public-sector equality duty. In simple terms, the equality legislation makes it unlawful for organisations to take into account a person's sex, marriage or civil partnership, race, age, disability, sexual orientation, religion or belief, pregnancy or maternity, or gender reassignment in making employment decisions. Here we are specifically concerned with decisions at the point of access to the organisation. Thus, you should ensure that you take account of equality and diversity at all stages of the recruitment and selection process, from job analysis and advertising, the choice of selection methods and the making of selection decisions through to induction into the organisation. You should note that this protection from discrimination applies before, during and after employment, so training, promotion and termination decisions (even references) are also covered.

The advisory and enforcement agency associated with the advancement of equality and diversity in the workplace is the Equality and Human Rights Commission (EHRC). The role of the EHRC is to promote equality and human rights, which it does by providing advice and guidance, working to implement an effective legislative framework and raising awareness of rights and responsibilities. Codes of practice giving guidance to employers on how to comply with the legislation are available from the EHRC. For instance, it is recommended that employers have written equality and diversity policies, procedures for making complaints and monitoring arrangements, and that they take positive action to redress any imbalances in the make-up (for example, sex or race profile) of their employees by, for example, wider advertising, flexible working hours arrangements and help with childcare.

The immigration, asylum and nationality legislation creates a legal requirement for employers to check the entitlement to work in the UK of all prospective employees in advance of their start date. Failure to do so is a criminal offence. You need to check, copy and retain certain documents. These are listed on the GOV.UK website (see 'References and Further Reading' at the end of this chapter).

Finally, in Chapter 3 we covered the Rehabilitation of Offenders Act 1974, which provides protection from discrimination for ex-offenders with spent convictions. However, certain sectors where employees work with children and vulnerable adults are exempt, notably the health and care sectors and education, where there are stringent requirements for pre-employment checks. The Disclosure and Barring Service (DBS; formerly the Criminal Records Bureau (CRB)) helps employers to obtain information on job applicants in order to screen out unsuitable candidates. For details of the full requirements and information on vetting and barring, see the Protection of Freedoms Act 2012. See the website references at the end of the chapter for details.

And for more information on both freedom of information and data protection, see Chapter 10.

? REFLECTIVE ACTIVITY 5.2

Have a look at your organisation's equality and diversity policy. Is it readily available? What impact does it have on recruitment and selection activities in your organisation? How are new employees made aware of it and their responsibilities under it? How are the responsibilities contained in the policy monitored in relation to recruitment activity?

5.6 EQUALITY VERSUS DIVERSITY

So far we have considered in any detail only those groups of employees who are covered by legislative provisions. Many leading organisations in the equal opportunities field have policies that include reference to groups not specifically protected by legislation. Recruitment and selection decisions are thus based on objective criteria only. For instance, factors such as background, appearance, social class and regional accents are not taken into consideration unless they impact on ability to do the job. Here we are moving towards a distinction between an 'equal opportunities' employer and an organisation which embraces diversity.

You are strongly advised to read the CIPD factsheets listed in the References and Further Reading section at the end of this chapter for more guidance on best practice in the fields of recruitment and selection, equal opportunities and managing diversity.

We will now take a few minutes to examine a case study relating to this subject and provide an associated activity.

CASE STUDY 5.2

An organisation in the environmental field publicises itself as an equal opportunities employer on all of its job vacancy notices. Last year the equal opportunities policy was replaced with a diversity statement, which reads as follows:

'To fulfil our vision of a better environment for present and future generations, we will develop an organisation where all employees are actively supported in giving their best contribution to corporate aims and objectives. This means attracting people from all parts of the community, valuing the differing skills and abilities of all our employees and responding flexibly to the needs of individuals in achieving organisational goals.'

The organisation recently lost an employment tribunal claim in which the claimant alleged race discrimination. The employment judge commented that there was little evidence that the organisation was an equal opportunities employer or embraced diversity in its workforce.

? REFLECTIVE ACTIVITY 5.3

What are the differences between equal opportunities and managing diversity? If you are not sure, discuss this question with one of your learning sources or look it up on the CIPD website.

List at least four things the employment judge would have looked at in considering whether the organisation employed true equal opportunities or diversity management practices.

Compare your responses with the feedback provided at the end of this chapter.

5.7 RECRUITMENT AND SELECTION – AN OVERVIEW

Continuing on the theme of good practice, we are now at the stage of considering the practical issues relevant to recruitment and selection. We shall, for simplicity's sake, be reviewing these processes separately – the recruitment process, selection, making the appointment, and induction – but it is obvious they are closely interlinked, as demonstrated by the simple flowchart in Figure 5.1.

5.8 THE RECRUITMENT PROCESS

The key activities here are job analysis and attracting applicants. We have already looked at the importance of genuine need, the complexity of the process and the need for careful attention in the section above on why good recruitment and selection is so crucial. As seen in Chapter 4, prior to any attempt to attract applicants it is important to have undertaken a thorough job analysis. It may be preferable that line managers retain responsibility and ownership for this activity for their own staff and do not view this purely as an HR function. Nonetheless, HR may wish to be involved in an advisory capacity. Since their experience will extend beyond that of an individual line manager, they will usually have a contribution to make. Regarding advertising, the task of designing and placing advertisements is often handled centrally – by HR practitioners – to maximise control (to ensure consistency and management of organisation image) and minimise costs.

Job analysis is looked at in detail in Chapter 4. In this chapter, we provide just an overview/reminder of job analysis and look at attracting applicants in detail.

Figure 5.1 Recruitment and selection flowchart

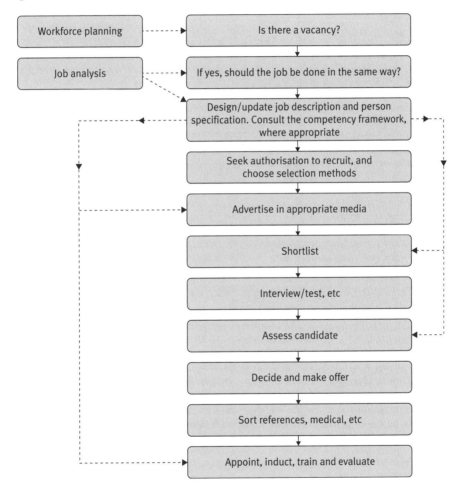

The solid arrows indicate the sequence of events, and the dashed arrows indicate where information from one stage is fed into another. For instance, the scrutinising of the job application for shortlisting purposes should not be carried out as a separate event but should be based on the information provided by the person specification on the characteristics and qualities that are being sought. In fact, application forms, if well designed, can help you make a judgement as to whether applicants possess the characteristics or qualities that are deemed to be essential.

Note: It is important to examine at each stage areas where discrimination could occur, and take preventative action.

5.8.1 JOB ANALYSIS

We will be concentrating here on the role of job analysis in recruitment and selection, but – as seen in Chapter 4 – it is also relevant to work design, organisation structures, job evaluation, the identification of training needs and performance management issues, especially the setting of objectives.

There are three elements in job analysis that are important in the recruitment process:

- research
- job descriptions
- person specifications.

We shall take each in turn.

Research

The first stage is to determine whether there is a genuine vacancy – because a new post has been created or an existing post-holder is leaving/has left. You need to define accurately and clearly the nature and purpose of the job and whether you need to fill it. Thinking about the need for an appointment and asking yourself some questions will allow you to weigh up the alternatives such as:

- treating the position as redundant (not filling the vacancy)
- redesigning the job
- distributing the work among other positions
- subcontracting or outsourcing the work
- whether the process can be changed to remove the need for the position
- whether the work can be done using computer software.

The importance of this stage is that it allows you to challenge some of the assumptions you may have about the job – for example, about the way it should be done, the time or place it should be done or even the kind of person who should do it.

This task may take you into the political arena. Some line managers can be inclined to seek to 'build empires'. A counter-pressure, to reduce the employee headcount, can exist where the organisation has shares that are traded or where a business owner runs a 'tight ship' – meaning it demonstrates acute cost-awareness. So far as you reasonably can, it is best to deal with facts and seek to resist what may be emotional reactions.

Let us assume you have decided that there is a genuine job to be filled. In order to acquire information about the job and the skills and qualities required of a person suited to that job, you need first to carry out a thorough analysis of the job and its organisational environment. There are various techniques for so doing and these include:

- observation
- interviews
- group discussions
- reviewing critical incidents (where interviewees are asked to focus on aspects of their behaviour which make the difference between success and failure)
- questionnaires
- work diaries.

Each has its own advantages and disadvantages, as demonstrated in Table 5.1.

Table 5.1 Job analysis techniques

Technique	Main advantages	Main disadvantages
Observation	Comprehensive information can be gathered about observable activities.	Very time-consuming. Those observed may act differently from the norm.
Interview	Skilled interviewers can probe areas that require clarification.	Interviewees may seek to impress the interviewer by 'talking up' the job.
Group discussion	Provides more balanced information than an individual interview because exaggeration by job-holders will be discouraged.	Time-consuming and logistically complicated to arrange.
Critical incidents	Forces an interviewee to focus on specific occurrences rather than to generalise. Helps to identify the types of behaviour that lead to success.	A complex and time-consuming process.
Questionnaire	Objective, efficient and straightforward way to gather a wealth of information. Less opportunity for interviewer bias.	If questions are not carefully designed, the information gathered may be difficult to analyse.
Work diary	A systematic way of gathering comprehensive information. Most suitable for higher-level jobs.	Very time-consuming for the individual, and if not structured, may be difficult to analyse.

Note that although the techniques listed above can be used on their own, the outcome of the job analysis will be more reliable if a combination of techniques is used.

The aim of job analysis is to answer the following questions:

- What is the job-holder expected to do?
- How is the job performed?
- What skills are required, and what is the level of those skills?
- Should the job be reorganised, for example by changing hours or level of responsibility, or incorporating duties into other posts?

The research stage should provide information that can then be formulated into a user-friendly job description and person specification.

Job description

In simple terms, this describes the job. Organisations usually have their own standardised formats for job descriptions and although they vary enormously (or may not exist at all in some organisations), they generally include the following sections:

- identification data: job title, department, pay grade, main location
- organisational data: stating to whom the job-holder is responsible and other working relationships (this could be visually presented as an extract from the organisation chart)
- job summary: a brief statement of why the job exists
- job duties and responsibilities: duties describe tasks that the job-holder does themselves, whereas responsibilities indicate those tasks they may delegate but for which they remain responsible
- performance criteria: while targets are not usually in the job description there is an opportunity to indicate those matters on which the job holder may be judged such as cash-flow or volume of sales

- miscellaneous: unusual arrangements such as shift-working, a need to be mobile, casual car-user allowance plus a reference to any other documents (collective agreements, etc.) which provide further details.

Recent years have seen a move away from this traditional approach to job descriptions in some organisations. Some have questioned whether they are necessary at all in that increased flexibility, empowerment, and the sheer pace of change mean it is hard to summarise many jobs. Further, some organisations now use generic job descriptions for job groupings rather than drafting job descriptions for each job type. There is, however, a strong argument that detailed job descriptions are still necessary for effective recruitment, job evaluation, training and performance management purposes (to name but a few). It is essential that the unique features of the job – particularly shift patterns and the need for mobility – are spelt out to job-holders and potential recruits in some way, even if not in a job description.

We also see the use of terms such as 'key accountabilities' and 'role profiles' in place of job descriptions. Both documents cover the information listed above, but the former also emphasises performance measures (indeed, performance standards have been included by some organisations for their more senior posts for many years). Role profiles tend to combine the information required for job descriptions and person specifications, and often make use of competencies (see below).

Person specification

Another commonly used term is the 'job specification', which describes the ideal person for the job. We would recommend, however, that you use the term 'person specification' because it is the potential job-holder, rather than the job, which is being specified.

Once again, person specifications vary in content and format depending on the company's house style. We see, in examples of person specifications, the terms 'skills', 'experience', 'qualifications', 'knowledge', 'personal qualities' and, increasingly, 'competencies' used, but their purpose is essentially the same: to set down the minimum requirements that an applicant must possess before being considered for a vacancy.

Further, most person specifications go beyond stating the minimum (essential) requirements and also state other (desirable) requirements, as demonstrated in Table 5.2. (In this example, you will see that the methods of assessment are also suggested. Please note that these are not the only choices, and – as a note of caution – the application form would have to be very well designed to ensure that sufficient information was available for assessment against all these criteria. References too have their limitations.)

Table 5.2 Example person specification form

Job title	Care assistant		
Category	Essential	Desirable	Method of assessment
Qualifications		• Diploma in Health and Social Care (or equivalent, such as NVQ2)	• Application form / CV and certificate check
Experience		• Worked in an environment with high standards of care provision and / or • Worked in a professional environment meeting	• Application form / CV and reference check

Job title	Care assistant		
		needs of customers, clients or service users	
Knowledge and skills (can usually be developed through training)		• Familiar with regulations and legislation within the care sector • Familiar with safeguarding principles	• CV and checks at interview
Personal qualities	• Understands instructions • Compassionate, patient and empathetic • Stays calm in emergencies and when under pressure • Attentive to detail	• Communicates well both linguistically and in manner	• English test if not first language • Competency interviewing • Situational tests • Practical tests • Questionnaires
Motivation and expectations	• Positive attitude • Team player	• Self-motivated • Able to use initiative • Committed to professional and personal development	• Competency interviewing • Situational tests • Evidence of CPD

Thus, a successful candidate will be expected already to possess all the essential requirements and to be capable of, or have the potential to be trained to, an acceptable standard in the desirable ones. You should take note that all the requirements must be realistic, justifiable and non-discriminatory. For example, if you are going to demand fluency in English you need to be sure that you have a valid reason for doing so. If you were recruiting an editor, then fluency would be essential. But if you were recruiting a manual labourer then it would not – although you might be justified in requiring the person to be able to understand safety instructions given in English.

In any event, care must be taken to ensure that person specification requirements do not discriminate either directly or indirectly in relation to the protected characteristics and other points outlined in 5.5 'The Legislation'.

?   REFLECTIVE ACTIVITY 5.4

Taking into account best practice, study your own job description and person specification. If there isn't one, then prepare one. In any event, carry out a systematic analysis then draft out accurate, up-to-date and comprehensive versions of the documents. Discuss their contents with one or more of your learning sources. You may be surprised at how much you do!

We shall now consider the role of competencies in this area.

5.8.2 COMPETENCIES

Competencies are used in many organisations and provide an outline of the skills and abilities an employee must have (or acquire) to do a job and achieve the required standard of performance. They provide an individual with an indication of the skills and abilities that are expected and that will be valued and recognised within an organisation. Competencies are often expressed in competency frameworks, which may contain both the behavioural and technical competencies required. Such frameworks are common in large organisations but less so in small private sector organisations. Competency frameworks provide a common set of criteria (which must be measurable) across a range of activities.

They can assist managers in:

- recruitment and selection decisions
- performance appraisal discussions
- career development planning
- the distribution of rewards.

Person specifications, such as the example provided in Table 5.2, have some limitations. These have resulted in a growth in the number of organisations using competency frameworks for recruitment and selection (including job analysis) purposes. So what are the limitations of traditional person specifications? They tend to use expressions such as 'communicates well' and 'team player' and expect everyone to know exactly what is meant. This is not necessarily the case, and these terms can be more precisely defined so that interviewers and assessors, in particular, have a common understanding and will be able to assess candidates accordingly.

Thus, competencies are used to describe the typical behaviours that we would expect to see when we observe a good performer (for example, a good communicator or team player). This area is a complicated one and you will find some excellent reading in Whiddett and Hollyforde (2003). They provide the example of a competency framework, showing the various levels of competency applicable to different jobs (see Table 5.3).

Table 5.3 Typical content of a competency framework

Competency cluster: SHOWS THE WAY
COMPETENCIES with levels
DIRECTION
Level 1: develops strategies that account for the short-, medium- and long-term needs of the business
Level 2: keeps others informed of business goals and inspires buy-in to them
Level 3: supports business goals by addressing issues likely to affect achieving them.
LEADERSHIP
Level 1: is consistent with expectations of others and provides clear leadership
Level 2: operates openly, is accessible and approachable to others.
PLANNING
Level 1: ensures that business plans are achievable and integrated with business goals
Level 2: ensures that plans meet local needs and that they account for the needs of other teams
Level 3: uses appropriate planning to succeed in their own role.
BEHAVIOURAL INDICATORS (for Direction)

Level 1: Develops strategies that account for the short-, medium- and long-term needs of the business	Level 2: Keeps others informed of business goals and inspires buy-in to them	Level 3: Supports business goals by addressing issues likely to affect achieving them
• Produces and regularly communicates three- to five-year plans to ensure that strategies remain relevant • Balances long-term goals with short-term deliverables to achieve business goals • Ensures that business goals are communicated and understood across the business	• Develops local goals to support wider business goals • Inspires buy-in to business goals by showing how individual efforts contribute to them • Provides timely and appropriate information to support achievement of business goals.	• Focuses and encourages others to concentrate on delivering the business goals • Regularly reviews and communicates progress on business goals • Uses the business goals to prioritise work

Source: Whiddett and Hollyforde (2003) *A Practical Guide to Competencies*. London: CIPD. Reproduced by permission.

In summary, assuming that we have decided there is a vacancy to be filled and we have permission to do so, we must ensure that:

• we carry out a thorough job analysis and design working documents (job descriptions and person specifications)
• we consult the competency framework, where this is available, to determine exactly what sort of behaviour signifies good performance in the job.

Armed with this information, we must choose appropriate methods to attract candidates before we are ready to advertise the vacancy.

5.8.3 ATTRACTING APPLICANTS

Attracting applicants can be a very expensive activity – especially if we get it wrong. It can be tempting to sit back and congratulate ourselves on a thorough job analysis that has resulted in workable and user-friendly job descriptions and person specifications. We need, however, to be just as systematic and methodical in our approach to attracting applicants to the vacancy and in managing their contact with the organisation for the duration of the process. The key is to promote the job in a way that attracts a small number of suitable candidates rather than a large number of less suitable ones. That can be a challenge if recruiting from a labour market where unemployment levels are high. But, conversely, it can be a challenge to attract any at all if there are skills shortages or if your labour market is very competitive.

The prime method of attracting applicants is often through advertising. Increasingly, advertising is done via online job boards. A quick search on Google (try 'job sites uk') will reveal the most popular job boards and some specialised ones.

These sites offer a variety of services to both companies and candidates/job-seekers – job search (by sector, job type, location for instance), CV uploading and job-matching – and usually have a presence via social media such as Twitter, Facebook and YouTube. We have found them useful because they provide easy tools to decline applicants, place applicants on hold, shortlist applicants and other, perhaps obvious, benefits such as being able to alter your job advertisement during the process in response to the applicants coming forward.

You can also post to social media sites yourself. Social media management systems (SMMS) enable you to post jobs to a number of sites at designated times as well as providing other facilities for managing a social media presence.

Each of the social networking sites needs to be used slightly differently to gain the most from it and, of course, this is an area that is constantly evolving. Exploring the tools available on a routine basis may yield new ways of maximising your recruitment efforts. Here we will look briefly at three main sites.

Twitter

Success with Twitter can depend on your followers. Building up a network of followers for your company depends on whether or not your tweets are interesting to those in jobs and sectors from which you want to seek talent. Frequent tweets and chatting on Twitter will take time and, of course, you may want to hit different sections of the job market on different occasions. Engaging with and getting known in relevant job markets might be effective only if you generally recruit in very specific areas. Twitter is very transient so posting at particular times, such as at lunchtime, as people arrive home from work, or after children have gone to bed, can pay off. Programs such as Hootsuite can assist in taking advantage of this.

Facebook

Perhaps needs little comment. If your company does not already have a company Facebook page, you can build one at www.facebook.com/business. Once you build up followers (perhaps by inviting employees or suppliers), job vacancies can be posted in the 'Share' section of your page.

As with Twitter, keeping your Facebook page current, engaging and informative will build up your company profile and reach out to more potential employees.

LinkedIn

This is the most professional social network as it focuses on business and career people. Its nature may make it the most suitable network for professional and senior vacancies. Again, building up a network of suitable connections is invaluable.

?   REFLECTIVE ACTIVITY 5.5

Discuss in a group of HR practitioners or HR students how they use social media to recruit. If they don't recruit, then have they used social media for job searching themselves? How did they use it?

Make a list of what you have learnt to help you recruit employees now or in the future.

In addition to job boards, organisations themselves are increasingly making use of their own websites or linked job websites; for example, NHS Jobs.

Although online advertising is increasingly popular and cost-effective, companies do still use other methods. Other sources of possible recruits include:

- existing employees (internal recruitment)
- existing employees' contacts (word of mouth)
- universal job match (www.gov.uk/jobsearch)
- employment agencies or recruitment consultants

- advertising
  - in the workplace
  - local and national newspapers
  - professional, specialist or technical journals
  - local radio/TV
- graduate careers fairs
- outplacement agencies
- armed forces (and police/fire service) resettlement programmes
- traditional social networking – CIPD, Chambers of Commerce, Soroptimists
- word of mouth (personal recommendations from other contacts)
- headhunters
- waiting lists or speculative applications
- liaison with schools and colleges.

Different sources are appropriate depending on the group of potential applicants that you wish to target. For instance, you may decide to use the free facilities of the jobcentre for semi-skilled positions, especially when you expect to find a wealth of unemployed talent in the immediate locality. Social media (using SMMS) can be very effective. However, if you wish to attract managerial, specialist or technical personnel, you will probably need to spread the net further. You should make use of job boards and consider national newspapers and appropriate journals. This will obviously be more expensive, but there is also a cost attached to not filling a key post (in overtime/cover payments and missed opportunities).

You should note that, in order to comply with equal opportunities legislation, vacancies should be advertised. Relying entirely on internal recruitment, on-file applications or personal recommendations may leave the organisation open to criticism, and is highly unlikely to redress sex, race or other imbalances in its workforce profile. Adverts themselves should not contain any discriminatory language or requirements. It should also be noted that where imbalances exist in the current labour force, there are a number of positive action steps that can be taken – see 'References and Further Reading'.

Although job boards offer a far more flexible and less time-sensitive approach to recruitment, the timing of advertisements is of crucial importance when advertising in newspapers and journals. You must ensure that:

- for the press, you need to choose the day on which job-seekers know that jobs will appear
- you avoid advertising just before a holiday or shutdown period because you may miss potential applicants who are on holiday, or you may disillusion others who cannot contact the organisation for further information
- you check the dates for final copy and meet them in order to avoid unnecessary delays in recruitment (this can be protracted if using a monthly publication).

CASE STUDY 5.3

An organisation within the NHS was experiencing difficulties attracting candidates for housekeeping assistant vacancies. It had tried advertising the vacant posts in a variety of ways and was spending increasing amounts of money on adverts in the local paper without any success.

An HR adviser decided to try a slightly different approach. All adverts placed by the hospital in the local paper (including the housekeeping assistant vacancies) went into the 'display' section of the jobs pages. Here adverts are larger, include artwork, contain organisation logos, etc. The HR adviser noticed that many smaller organisations advertising for similar posts put very small adverts in the 'lineage' section of the jobs pages – no artwork/logos, just a couple of sentences

> about the job. The hospital decided to give this a try with their housekeeping vacancies.
>
> When the adverts appeared in the lineage section of the jobs pages, the hospital received a 20% increase in applicants to these posts and managed to fill nearly all the vacancies.

Now we shall concentrate on the design and content of the advertisements themselves. One of the most popular mnemonics used by HR practitioners is AIDA. This provides a guide to successful advertising by highlighting the four steps:

- **Attention**
- **Interest**
- **Desire**
- **Action.**

In order for it to work, an advertisement must catch the attention of the target audience and spark the reader's interest by establishing the relevance of the job to the individual so that the whole advert is read. Further, it should arouse a desire to pursue the opportunity offered and should stimulate action in the form of applications from the target audience.

This may be easier said than done, but studying examples of advertisements online and in newspapers and journals is very useful for highlighting good and bad practices. So what should we do to avoid making mistakes in advertising? There are no golden rules, but generally an advertisement, drawing on and summarising the job description and the person specification, should be composed as follows:

- job title/location/salary (these are of key interest to job-seekers)
- make sure the job title reflects how outsiders would recognise the job
- if using online advertising, your choice of keywords will be crucial to success
- a brief description of the job
- a short description of the nature of the organisation (unless very well-known)
- a brief description of the ideal candidate (highlighting, as a minimum, the essential requirements)
- organisational benefits and facilities (if attractive)
- unique features (such as hours of work, need for mobility, accommodation provision)
- application procedure and the closing date
- reference number (if used)
- equal opportunities statement
- reference to the organisation's web pages.

In addition to an advertisement, you could have a dedicated web page providing valuable vacancy information relating to the job and generic information about the company.

In essence, you must give enough information about the job (to target the right people) and the person required (to attract only suitable candidates). The image portrayed should be inviting but also reflective of the style and culture of the organisation. For instance, an eye-catching headline seeking an 'Action Man or Wonder Woman' would probably not be appropriate for a filing clerk's post in a local authority, but has been successfully used for a security officer's role in a large toy store. Creativity can pay off.

It is important to consider the factors outlined above about advertising wherever your organisation opts to advertise vacancies, and it is likely that an approach to advertising that appropriately uses different routes and various media will bring best results. Although online advertising is increasingly popular, there are both advantages and disadvantages to using this approach. It can look very attractive because of the relatively low cost, but the

Internet is an increasingly crowded place and the ease of applying can bring many unwanted applicants.

We will be concentrating on the use of the Internet rather than company websites in the activity that follows.

?   REFLECTIVE ACTIVITY 5.6

What factors would you take into account when deciding whether to advertise a technical post:

(a)   in a specialist journal?
(b)   via an established online recruitment website such as www.jobsite.co.uk or www.monster.co. uk?

Compare your responses with the feedback provided at the end of this chapter.

Assuming that your advertisement has attracted a manageable number of suitably qualified and experienced candidates, we shall now move on to a crucial stage; that is selecting the right candidate. Please note that as we indicated earlier, the processes of recruitment and selection are not entirely separate activities, so you should by now have made the decision on which selection methods you wish to use (see Figure 5.1).

5.9 THE SELECTION PROCESS

At this stage, before looking at selection methods and processes used by appointing managers, it is worth mentioning the range of initial selection processes that may be carried out before the candidate ever gets to meet anyone from the company. Some companies, such as Tesco, have online applications that include a requirement for candidates to respond to different customer service scenarios, the responses then being used to support shortlisting. Online job sites, employment/recruitment agencies and headhunters also use a range of techniques to assess candidates before submitting a list of matched candidates to the organisation looking to recruit.

Once you have your range of applicants, either by direct response to your company or via a job site/recruitment agency, you should make your decision on the successful candidate as a result of:

- candidate data collection
- candidate assessment
- comparison.

You should always avoid making a simple comparison of candidates with each other because this is likely to be highly subjective and will lead to an offer of the position to the candidate who was deemed to be 'the best on the day'. Instead, you should use the person specification and, at each stage, compare the candidates with the essential and desirable requirements listed. Bad selection decisions can be very costly, and it is always better to make no appointment than the wrong appointment.

5.9.1 CANDIDATE DATA COLLECTION

Information can be gathered about candidates through:

- application forms
- CVs
- interview performances

- tests (ranging from physical, intelligence and aptitude tests through to personality profiles)
- appraisals (for internal candidates)
- references
- online questionnaires
- assessment centre performances.

In order for this process to be directed at achieving your aim –to recruit the person who most closely fits your person specification profile – you should ensure that you collect only relevant information about the candidates. For example, an applicant's bizarre taste in music or socks is unlikely to be relevant and can lead, like discussions of which football team he or she supports, to unfounded prejudices.

Shortlisting (or deciding whom to invite for interview/further assessment) is the first stage of the selection process and generally takes place using information provided on the application form or CV. Assessment of the information provided by candidates in this way should be done in line with the requirements of the post as outlined in the job description and person specification, and should be as objective and consistent as possible. Shortlisting should take place as soon as possible after the closing date, many larger organisations specifying that at least two people should be involved in the shortlisting process. Some organisations use a two-stage shortlisting process, particularly where large numbers of applicants are involved or the post is a very senior one. These two stages are often referred to as longlisting and shortlisting. The first stage is where a larger number of applicants are invited to take part in an initial selection process (for example, a telephone interview or an online assessment). Longlisting is often a tool used to 'screen out' or disqualify applicants from involvement in later stages of selection. Many organisations find it helpful to aim for between four and six candidates on the final shortlist. Shortlisting also gives the first real indication of the success (or not) of the recruitment and advertising stages of the process.

Later stages of the selection process involve gathering data about candidates using some of the other methods outlined above.

We are now going to consider three of the above methods in more detail. We will start with interviews and then move on to provide summaries of the latest thinking about tests and assessment centres. These latter two methods have increased in popularity and are designed to deliver more information about the candidate than can be obtained by exclusive use of the much maligned interview. Tests and assessment centres have also usually been validated to see whether the tests and exercises used adequately measure relevant characteristics and abilities in order to predict job success. There is a wealth of reading and commentary on this area for your further enlightenment. Articles in the CIPD's *People Management* magazine would be a useful starting place; see also the CIPD publications listed under References and Further Reading at the end of this chapter.

The interview – main principles

Unlike tests and assessment centres, the interview has been much criticised as a selection tool for its lack of validity. (The results of unstructured interviewing have been found to be only slightly higher than random selection at predicting future success in the job!) Nevertheless, any coverage of recruitment and selection would be incomplete without reference to 'the interview'. Although we can see the pitfalls of its use, few appointments are made without the interview playing some role. You should note that the effectiveness of interviews can be improved by thorough preparation and by ensuring that all the questions asked are relevant (and seen to be relevant) to the job. The majority of employing organisations still use interviews as a crucial stage in deciding on new appointments because they see that interviews can be useful for:

- verifying information
- exploring omissions
- checking assumptions
- providing the candidate with information.

In fact, candidates themselves seem equally loath to dispense entirely with interviews. Many feel that the interview provides the only opportunity for them to reveal their personalities and to 'sell' themselves to the employer.

So how do we get the best out of an interview? The structure of the interview should, in simple terms, follow the mnemonic WASP:

- **W**elcome
- **A**cquire – What information do you have?
  - What else do you need?
  - What should you check?
- **S**upply – What information should you impart?
  - What will happen next?
- **P**art.

Thus, you should bear WASP in mind when drawing up your list of questions for interviewees. If you are involved in a panel interview, each member of the panel can lead a different section of issues while still maintaining a logical structure overall. A checklist for successful interviewing practice and an examination of the types of questions to be used and avoided are reproduced below. Note, however, that the interviewing checklist is likely, with some adaptation, to be applicable to a large number of interviewing situations, not just those designed for staff selection purposes.

Interviewing checklist

BEFORE

- Familiarise yourself with the job description and person specification.
- Read the application form and/or CV.
- Meet the rest of the interview panel to agree the division of question areas and roles to be played – for example, chair, scribe, timekeeper.
- Arrange the interview at an appropriate time and place.
- Book the venue.
- Inform the applicant well in advance, providing details of location, time, expected duration, any need for preparation, travel expense provisions, the number of stages in the selection process, etc.
- Ask if particular arrangements need to be made – for instance, a personal loop system for a candidate who is hard of hearing.
- Confirm the arrangements with the panel members.
- Notify security and reception of the arrangements.
- Ensure that the venue is private and that interruptions will not occur.
- Allow enough time between interviews for breaks, discussions, and completion of assessment forms and, at the end of all the interviews, for a full review.

DURING

- Start on time.
- Begin with a welcome.
- Seek to establish rapport.
- Explain the purpose of the interview, the stage in the selection process and that notes will be taken to provide a record of the interview.

- Ask relevant questions (see the box 'Types of interview questions' below).
- Allow the applicant to do the majority of the talking. Aim for an 80:20 ratio.
- Listen actively.
- Do not seek to fill silences (or you may discourage the candidate from providing more information).
- Observe non-verbal behaviour (and check anomalies between this and the verbal messages).
- Check gaps, omissions or contradictions.
- Check claims made about their level and type of experience.
- Use a logical sequence of questions and provide links between sections.
- Provide brief information about the job and organisation.
- Allow sufficient time for the applicant's questions.
- Ensure that the candidate's responses are noted by relevant panel members.
- Keep control of the content and timing.
- Summarise.
- Close on a positive note – thank the candidate and reiterate the next stage of the process.

AFTERWARDS

- Compare the information gained about the applicant with the person specification requirements.
- Complete the assessment form after reaching an agreement with the panel members.
- Follow up the interview with the appropriate documentation – for example, an invitation to the next stage, or a rejection letter.

Types of interview questions

Generally questions should be:

open to encourage full responses

eg 'Tell me about. . .'

probing to check information provided in the application or interview

eg What?, Why?, How?, Explain. . .

Probing questions include situational or behaviour-based questions to elicit practical experience or judgement; and 'contrary evidence' questions to check an assumption made about the candidate by seeking evidence to the contrary.

Closed questions – ie those demanding a yes or no response – should be used only for clarification or control – eg bringing a line of questioning to its conclusion.

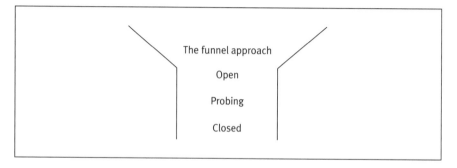

We recommend a *funnelling* approach, as indicated above. You should start with an open question – eg 'Tell me about your current responsibilities' – followed by progressively narrower probing questions – eg 'What experience have you had of formal negotiating situations?' At the end of this section of questioning you should use a closed question such as 'So would it be accurate to say that you have had limited experience in formal negotiating situations, and if you are successful in being offered this vacancy, you would welcome specialist training in this area?' The candidate is very likely to say yes, effectively bringing about a 'full-stop' to this section. You should then provide a link to the next section of questioning – eg 'Thank you for your responses to those questions; we will now move on to discuss. . .'

The following types of questions should generally be avoided:

leading   eg 'You are fully trained in the use of an XYZ HR Information System, aren't you?'

(The candidate knows exactly what answer you are looking for here!)

multiple   eg 'Tell us about your educational background, your career history to date, and your strengths and development needs.'

(By the time the candidate has finished telling you about his or her educational qualifications, you will probably both have forgotten what else you asked. Further, a clever candidate will undoubtedly tell you about his or her strengths but ignore the issue of development needs!)

If you do fall into either of the above traps, it is relatively easy to rectify your mistake by asking additional probing questions. Keeping brief notes, both of the candidate's responses and the further questions that you feel it necessary to ask, will help you here.

The above guidelines apply to a range of approaches to interviews – eg behaviour-based, situational and telephone interviews.

Competence or behaviour-based interviewing

Competence or behaviour-based interviewing has developed in line with the use of competency frameworks (see Table 5.3 for an example). It is grounded on the premise that the best way to predict future job performance is to understand a candidate's past performance and behaviour in job-related situations. It allows candidates with limited job experience to compete on equal terms with more experienced candidates (See References and Further Reading at the end of the chapter for more information on this subject.)

Let us take the example of a vacancy for a bar attendant in a hotel. There are three steps to follow:

- developing a competency profile based on the behaviour necessary to be a successful bar attendant – adherence to health and safety, hygiene and quality standards, customer service, knowledge of the hotel's products and services, selling ability and cash-handling
- developing appropriate benchmark-behaviour-based interview questions against which the interviewers measure each candidate's response to a specific situation: these are open-ended questions which focus on the candidates' describing critical incidents in their current and previous jobs as well as in their life experiences
- scoring the responses – this means measuring each candidate's answer against each of the respective profile statements.

Advocates of this approach say that their organisations have achieved financial benefits due to reductions in recruitment and training costs, improvements in productivity of newly appointed workers and reductions in staff turnover.

Draft competency/behaviour-based questions which seek to determine whether a candidate possesses the following competencies:

- effective leadership skills
- the ability to handle conflict
- problem-solving ability
- project management skills.

Compare your responses with the feedback provided at the end of this chapter.

Situational interviewing

Situational interviewing is similar to behaviour-based interviewing in that it centres on critical incidents, but instead of focusing on past behaviour, it is future-oriented. Thus, questions tend to be hypothetical and are related to dilemmas that job-holders might encounter. It is based on the assumption that intentions predict behaviour. Candidates are presented with 'What if. . .?' job-related scenarios and asked 'What would you do in this situation?' The responses are then assessed against a pre-prepared scoring guide covering the possible range of responses, indicative of poor, average or good performance.

Proponents of this approach point to its high predictive validity, reliability and freedom from bias, and there is research evidence that backs up this contention. There are, however, many dissenters who have concerns that candidates may not actually behave in the real world in the same way that they say they will in the interview. We would conclude that this approach can be useful, especially when applicants do not have experience in your industry or sector, but would suggest that it is used alongside a variety of other questioning approaches, some of which look at past performance and behaviour, as indicated above.

Telephone interviewing

Telephone interviews are often used by recruiting organisations for two main reasons:

- as an initial short-listing device, it is more cost-effective than a face-to-face interview, especially if candidates live outside the locality
- many employees now spend a significant proportion of their time communicating with customers by telephone (for instance, call centre staff) and the telephone interview provides an opportunity to start to assess skill and approach in this area.

There are drawbacks to telephone interviews, especially when candidates have not been notified that they may receive a call and that it is a crucial part of the selection process. It is possible, however, to capitalise on their use by following the rules of thumb below:

- thoroughly prepare your questions beforehand and have at hand an easy-to-complete interview assessment form
- telephone the candidate at the agreed time and explain the nature, purpose and structure of the phone interview
- first ask screening questions that candidates must answer satisfactorily before progressing on to the remainder of the interview
- next ask a range of probing questions, such as behavioural or hypothetical questions, so that you are able to assess as many skills or competencies as possible
- 'sell' the job opportunity and provide information on the company, as required
- check the candidate's understanding and continuing interest in the post

- provide details of the next steps in the selection process and tell the candidate when he or she will be notified about progression (or not) to the next stage
- make a preliminary decision on the candidate's suitability and complete the paperwork while the interview is fresh in your mind.

Those in favour of this approach point to the advantages to both parties in that neither has to travel. More importantly, they say that people are less inhibited than in face-to-face interviews and so the quality of information provided can be higher.

Online or webcam interviews

This is increasingly an option and much the same principles apply as to do telephone interviewing. There are some practical considerations:

- not all job applicants will have easy access to a webcam or be confident in using one
- tungsten filament lighting (gradually being phased out) may show you candidate in a poor light (literally)
- on a positive note, you might gain otherwise inaccessible information about their home environment (relevant if they might be working from home) or about how seriously they view the interview by how they present, prevent interruptions, etc.

We now move on to consider the use of tests in selection decisions.

Tests

The use of aptitude and psychometric tests is certainly on the increase, although they tend to be used more extensively by larger organisations with established HR departments. The main applications of such tests in the recruitment and selection field are that they can be used to measure individual differences in personality and ability, and make predictions about future behaviour.

The CIPD broadly supports the concept of testing, but recognises the many concerns about their use. It answers these by setting out six key criteria for their use:

1 Everyone responsible for the application of tests including administration, evaluation, interpretation and feedback should be trained to at least the level of competence recommended by the British Psychological Society.

2 Potential test users should satisfy themselves that it is appropriate to use tests at all before incorporating them into their decision-making processes.

3 Users should satisfy themselves that any tests they decide to use actually measure factors that are directly relevant to the employment situation.

4 Users must satisfy themselves that all tests they use have been rigorously developed and that claims about their reliability, validity and effectiveness are supported by statistical evidence. (The Data Protection Act 1998 is relevant here. If candidates are selected by an automated process, they have the right to know the logic used in the selection decision.)

5 Care must be taken to ensure equality of opportunity among all those individuals required to take tests.

6 The results of single tests should not be used as the sole basis for decision-making; this is particularly relevant with regard to personality tests.

Assessment centres

Nowadays assessment centres (ACs) are used not only for large-scale recruitment, graduates and senior positions, but across a large number of appointments to specialist, technical, customer service and other positions within organisations. The use of ACs – and development centres – is undoubtedly on the increase.

What are ACs? There is no typical AC, but a good one should include the following:

- a variety of selection methods or assessment techniques – that is, a combination of any of the following: interviews; psychometric tests; in-tray exercises; job sampling or simulations; questionnaires; team-building activities; structured discussions; presentations; report-writing; and role-playing exercises
- assessment of several candidates together
- evaluation by several trained and experienced assessors/observers
- assessments against a number of clearly defined job-relevant competencies.

ACs thus answer some of the criticisms of the use of sole techniques such as interviews and tests. This is because they enable assessors to observe and assess candidates' behaviour in a number of different situations that provide a more comprehensive and rounded picture of the individuals concerned, as demonstrated by the example AC matrix in Table 5.4.

Table 5.4 Example assessment centre matrix – project manager

Competency	Selection technique				
	Interview	Group exercises	In-tray exercise	Presentation	Written report
Leadership	×	×			
Problem-solving	×	×			×
Verbal communication	×			×	
Written communication			×		×
Time management			×	×	×
Decision-making		×	×		×
Negotiating and influencing skills	×	×		×	
Analytical ability		×	×		×

We have seen that we need to gather a range of data about our candidates using various methods such as the application form, the interview and the use of tests and assessment centres. We now consider the second key stage of the selection process: candidate assessment.

5.9.2 CANDIDATE ASSESSMENT

In assessing our candidates, we need to evaluate each one against the job-relevant criteria detailed in the person specification and reach a considered and objective judgement in every case. Here your skills in defining those criteria in very precise and measurable terms should stand you in good stead. Referring to the example person specification form shown in Table 5.2, as we have already stated, the requirements should ideally be defined further. But in the absence of a competency framework, it is necessary to define what you mean by terms such as 'good verbal communicator'. For instance, should our successful candidate be an experienced and polished presenter that could represent you at a conference, or simply have a reasonably outgoing nature?

At the shortlisting stage, you are likely to have only the information contained on the application form. If this has been well designed, it should be relatively easy to filter out those candidates who do not meet the minimum (essential) requirements. CVs are often used at this initial shortlisting stage, but because they are not standardised and often contain incomplete information, they may be much less useful here. You can help this process by giving clear instructions to candidates regarding the type of information that you want them to provide on their application forms and CVs. It may also be instructive to see whether they take any notice of such guidance.

If you still have a large number of potentially suitable candidates after considering the essential requirements, you may shortlist further by producing a list of candidates who appear to possess a number of the desirable requirements also. Interviews, tests, and exercises can then be used to gain more information on your shortlisted candidates. Depending on the number of suitable applicants and the seniority of the post, the selection process may consist of one, two or even three stages (with a different combination of selection methods and HR involvement at each stage).

5.9.3 COMPARISON

Here you are comparing the candidate assessment with the person specification and looking for the closest 'fit'. The candidate who most closely matches the 'ideal person' described in your person specification should be offered the vacancy. You should not necessarily select the individual who performs best overall; this could result in the recruitment of an overqualified person, which might present problems after appointment. Nor should you select an underqualified person (that is, if all the candidates fell short of your requirements and you take the 'best on the day'). If you are confident that you have carried out a systematic job analysis, you should recognise that those candidates who appear to be overqualified for your needs may be equally as unsuitable as those who clearly fall short of your requirements. Thus, you are aiming to achieve:

- the right person for the job

  and

- the right job for the person.

? REFLECTIVE ACTIVITY 5.8

Look back at a recent vacancy within your organisation and analyse the process of recruiting and selecting the successful candidate by answering the following questions:

- Was an appropriate choice of advertising media made?
- Was suitable documentation (job description, person specification) available?
- Was an appropriate choice of selection methods made?
- What lessons have been learned, and what suggestions do you have for improvements in the event of similar vacancies arising in the future?

Discuss your recommendations with an appropriate learning source.

5.10 MAKING THE APPOINTMENT

Once you have decided on your preferred candidate, you are in a position to make an appointment. In many organisations this involves two stages: undertaking any necessary employment checks; and making a job offer.

5.10.1 EMPLOYMENT CHECKS

Although some pre-employment checks may be made at earlier stages of the recruitment and selection process, it is likely that most will be done as the process nears its conclusion – either for all shortlisted candidates or just for the chosen candidate. There is a range of different checks that may be undertaken. These may include references, qualifications and professional registration. You will also need to confirm identity and the right to work in the UK. In some cases, you will need to check criminal records. In larger organisations, there may well be established procedures for undertaking such checks; in any event, these and the associated tasks often sit with the HR department. It is likely that you will want to take up references from previous employers to confirm a candidate's employment history. Where particular qualifications (for example, GCSEs or an HGV licence) or professional registration (for example, as a teacher or nurse) are required, the organisation would be wise to check, and in some cases will need to check, that the candidate possesses these by inspecting certificates or contacting the relevant registration body.

There is a legal requirement for employers to verify an individual's right to work in the UK. Many overseas nationals have the right to work in the UK (for example, EU nationals and some Commonwealth nationals). Others require full employment-based permission to work in the UK. It is advisable to check the up-to-date requirements for those who require permission and the circumstances in which such permission will be granted as the rules are subject to regular change and updating. A starting point would be on the GOV. UK website – see 'References and Further Reading' at the end of this chapter.

Criminal record checks are currently undertaken by the Disclosure and Barring Service (DBS) and apply to posts that are exempt from the Rehabilitation of Offenders Act 1974. Many such posts are found in the health, care or education sectors, although not exclusively. Further details can be found on the DBS website, the address of which is in the References and Further Reading list at the end of this chapter.

Under the Equality Act 2010, it is unlawful, except in certain circumstances, for employers to ask candidates questions about their health. Such questions are only allowed if it is necessary to determine whether the candidate can carry out a function that is a core and intrinsic part of the job; for example, heavy lifting for a warehouse operative. Job offers can still be made conditional on satisfactory health checks, but to withdraw a job offer made to a person with a disability would be risky. You would need to show that the health issue means that, even after reasonable adjustments, the job would be beyond the candidate's reasonable capability.

5.10.2 JOB OFFERS

It is likely that you will initially make a verbal offer if you are authorised to do so, but you must be careful to emphasise any 'subject to' conditions. Conditional offers most commonly refer to some of the checks outlined above.

A probationary period may also be stipulated.

All these areas are fraught with difficulties and it is not our intention to cover them all here, but you should note the following:

- It is advisable to make job offers conditional on receipt of references which are 'satisfactory to the company'. If the references you subsequently obtain are weak, the offer of employment can then be withdrawn without the employer being in breach of contract.

- As already indicated, evidence of health problems should not be used for withdrawing an offer unless it can be justified on material and substantial grounds. For example, a food factory may be justified in not employing someone with a serious nut allergy if they could not make reasonable adjustments for the applicant to avoid contact with nuts. Medical information can help the employer to ensure compliance with the Equality Act 2010 (see Chapter 3 for more information).
- Despite requests by line managers to bring new recruits on board as soon as possible, you would be wise to await references and medical information before confirming start dates (see Case Study 5.4).

CASE STUDY 5.4

You have probably read over the years a number of stories in the press about employees – particularly in the medical, educational and caring professions – who have lied about their backgrounds and qualifications in order to obtain work. Some of these stories have had alarming outcomes; hence the press coverage. It would appear that due to the competitive nature of today's job market, there is more temptation for some applicants to embellish the contents of their CVs.

One medium-sized organisation found itself in difficulties when it appointed a finance director. His CV indicated that he had an impressive array of qualifications and was experienced in the industry sector in question. It quickly became apparent, however, that he was not up to the job. The HR manager was notified and was concerned to learn, four weeks after he commenced employment, that a reference request to his former employer had been returned as 'not known at this address'. Further investigations showed that the finance director did not have the qualifications that he claimed, and that he had been dismissed by one of his previous employers for alleged fraud, although he had not been prosecuted. The finance director remained unaware of the HR manager's investigation until it had been completed and the decision was taken to dismiss him. This 'damage limitation' strategy was successful in that the company was not financially exposed, but the experience did cost the company time and money, and they then had to start the recruitment and selection process all over again.

The simple expedient of seeing original qualification certificates (and copying them for the record) could have saved the cost (and embarrassment) of this situation.

Turning back momentarily to employment contracts – fuller detail of which is provided in Chapter 3 – do contracts have to be written to be enforceable? In essence, a contract comes into being once a verbal offer has been made and accepted. It is important, therefore, that you do not give an indication of an offer until you are ready to make an explicit one. Good practice suggests that you should also ensure that the following occurs:

- Once a successful candidate has been chosen, make a verbal offer promptly, if your company policy allows this *and state any conditions.*
- You follow this up with a written conditional offer accompanied by written particulars or, as a minimum, the main terms and conditions of employment –salary, hours, location, benefits, etc.
- You keep in touch with the chosen candidate during the time he or she takes to make the decision, providing additional information as necessary.
- If he or she does accept, you continue to keep in touch with the successful candidate, notifying him or her when the conditions of the offer have been satisfied, when they

can start their new job with you, and the arrangements for induction and any necessary job training.

- Unsuccessful candidates are treated with respect and notified promptly of your decision.
- If not sent with the offer, a written statement of particulars is provided for the selected candidate as early as possible in the process (but no later than two months after the commencement of employment).

We now move on to consider the induction and evaluation processes for our new employee before summing up the role of the HR practitioner.

5.11 INDUCTION

Successful organisations will ensure that this process is treated as a significant activity and has sufficient resources devoted to it. The main reason is that new employees who have undergone an effective induction programme are likely to be competent performers at their jobs more quickly than those whose induction was minimal or non-existent. Also, the former group are less likely to leave the organisation at an early stage. There is a phenomenon which is commonly known as the 'induction crisis' and it signifies a dissatisfaction with the job or the organisation or both. In consequence, the number of people leaving an organisation in the first few months of their employment is often disproportionately high.

Different employees have different requirements, but they are all likely to need:

- to learn new tasks and procedures
- initial direction
- to make contacts and begin to develop relationships
- to understand the organisational culture
- to feel accepted.

There are, however, certain groups of employees who may need particular consideration, such as:

- school- and college-leavers
- people returning to work after a break in employment
- employees with disabilities
- management/professional trainees
- people from minority groups
- recent immigrants, especially if from a very different culture
- employees who have undergone internal transfer or promotion.

The Acas advisory booklet 'Recruitment and Induction' provides guidance on these needs and how they can be accommodated.

The commencement of the induction process is hard to pinpoint because, for employees new to the organisation, the imparting of information begins with the job advertisement. We could, therefore, argue that the process starts at this early stage and plan accordingly. Usually, however, when designing an induction programme, we begin with the first day of employment and then timetable activities to be included in the first few weeks and months.

Induction programmes vary between two extremes – from the simple 'tick box' approach (covering the essential organisational information that an employee must be told) to comprehensive induction packages (which include, for example, video messages from the chief executive, guest speakers, 'getting to know you' exercises, and group activities). Some induction processes, particularly in larger organisations, may combine the two approaches with a simple induction carried out in the relevant department and a more comprehensive induction done on an organisation-wide basis.

The former approach is likely to be brief, take place at the workstation, and involve the new employee and his or her line manager only. The latter, more sophisticated (and initially more costly) approach is likely to take place away from the workplace and involve more people at a senior level in the organisation. Also, in accordance with economies of scale, organisations are inclined to provide this programme only periodically (usually monthly or quarterly) – that is, when there are sufficient numbers of new employees who can attend.

Neither of these approaches is preferable to the other: their worth is gauged by how successful they are in helping the new employee to settle down quickly and become effective in the job. Often employers combine these approaches with other methods of delivery in providing a comprehensive induction programme for new appointees. See Table 5.5.

Table 5.5 Example methods of delivery and their key applications in the induction process

Method	Key applications
Welcome pack containing information on the organisation, main terms and conditions, joining instructions, etc.	Generally provided pre-employment to aid the gathering of essential employment information and promote good first impressions of the organisation
Face-to-face meetings between the new appointee and people who are key to the role in question, both from within and external to the organisation	Usually arranged in the first few days of employment to facilitate good working relationships and impart formal information about the job and informal information on the organisational culture
Formal sessions aimed at groups of new appointees	Held periodically, as a cost-effective means of instilling organisational values, providing consistent core information and allowing for networking opportunities across functions
Information provided on the organisation's intranet or YouTube	A useful backup to the information provided elsewhere. Should be an up-to-date and detailed source of reference
Interactive e-learning activities	Enable individuals to learn at their own pace, place and time, and provide an evaluation mechanism to ensure that the learning cycle has been completed

Finally, let's consider the information that should be supplied. As a minimum, employees should be informed about:

- the organisation's background and structure
- the organisation's products, services, markets, and values
- the terms and conditions of employment (stated in the written particulars of their employment – see Chapter 3).
- the organisation's rules and procedures; for example, how to report in sick and disciplinary protocol
- the physical layout of the organisation
- health and safety issues (note: it is crucial that these are covered in the very early stages of employment)
- first aid arrangements
- data protection policies and practices
- equal opportunities policies and practices

- employee involvement and communication arrangements
- trade union and/or employee representative arrangements
- welfare and employee benefits and facilities
- access to the organisation's computer facilities and its security processes
- access to assistance with the English language where appropriate.

There could be a lot for your new appointee to take in on the first day. You may be able to make them feel more at home if you find some tasks that they can do that will form part of their job; this enables them to go home feeling they have accomplished something.

Note that we have concentrated on general induction above (that is, core induction programmes applicable to all new recruits). We must not forget that this should be combined with induction that meets the individual's needs as well. During the recruitment and selection process, you will have gathered a lot of information about the candidate's skills, abilities and development needs. Instead of filing this information, use it to agree on a personal development plan with the individual, which will involve planning on-the-job and specialist skills training as well as other development activities.

The use of a buddy – the pairing of the new appointee with someone else who was appointed a little while ago – might also be considered. In some circumstances, care may need to be taken to be sure that the buddy is one who will pass on good habits!

Relationships can be crucial, so introduce the appointee to those with whom they will be working. If this is a wider circle of colleagues, then it may need to be planned.

Finally, other activities aimed at integrating the new appointee into the team should also not be forgotten.

?   REFLECTIVE ACTIVITY 5.9

Look back at a recent appointment made within your organisation and analyse the induction programme carried out when the selected candidate took up his or her post. (This exercise can still be applicable if the successful candidate was an internal one.) What suggestions do you have for improvements in the induction process for the future? Discuss your recommendations with an appropriate learning source.

5.12 EVALUATION

As with the majority of activities that HR practitioners become involved with, there is a strong argument for evaluating the success of your recruitment and selection procedures. This is, however, not just a simple matter of concluding that, for instance, an advertisement for a clerical officer's post was successful because 250 applications were received. In fact, it is likely that the reverse is true because sifting through 250 application forms will have been a time-consuming and costly exercise. Every stage of the recruitment and selection process should be reviewed to see whether mistakes were made, whether a repetition of them can be avoided in the future, and what can be learned.

It would be good practice to consider the following questions – but note that some may be more appropriately addressed or re-addressed in three, six or 12 months' time:

- Did you get the job analysis stage right? That is:
  - Did you carry out a thorough field study?
  - Is the job description an accurate reflection of the range and type of activities and the level of responsibility involved?

- Are the person specification requirements defined in specific and measurable terms?
- Are there any significant omissions or unnecessary inclusions in the person specification?
- Was a new recruit justified or should the work have been organised differently?
- Are the selection criteria too restrictive or potentially discriminatory – for example, are age limits implied or is an unnecessarily high level of qualifications called for?
- Have you considered flexible working arrangements to encourage applications from people who are unable to work conventional office hours?
- Is the total employment package sufficiently competitive?
- Did you get the recruitment stage right? That is:
  - Is recruitment being targeted too narrowly – eg have you concentrated only on those sources that you have used in the past?
  - Did the advert give sufficient information about the job and the person required to encourage suitable applicants only?
  - Was the advert eye-catching?
  - Did you choose the most appropriate media?
  - Did you get the timing right?
  - Have you carried out an analysis to see which media produced the most cost-effective results?
- Did you get the selection stage right? That is:
  - Did you choose the most appropriate methods for selection?
  - Did you ensure that the information generated by each method was cross-checked for validity?
  - Did you ensure that only relevant information was considered in decision-making?
  - Have you carried out an analysis to see which of the methods used were the most fruitful and cost-effective?
- Did you get the induction stage right? That is:
  - Did the induction programme run smoothly?
  - Was the employee properly assisted to settle in and quickly learn the job?
  - How much did the induction process cost?
- Did you select the right person? That is:
  - Did the employee become effective as quickly as expected?
  - Did the employee require more assistance, training or support than expected?
  - Is the employee still in the post and performing at a satisfactory level?
  - Has the employee made satisfactory progress regarding salary reviews or career progression?
- Did you ensure compliance at all stages with equal opportunities legislation?
- What would you do differently next time?

?   REFLECTIVE ACTIVITY 5.10

After studying the section above on evaluation, consider which methods your organisation uses to evaluate the success or otherwise of the recruitment and selection process. Suggest two or three major improvements. Put these down in the form of an action plan with, if possible, timescales and the names of persons responsible. Discuss your recommendations with one of your learning sources.

Having considered this important but often forgotten issue of evaluation, we now summarise the many roles played by HR practitioners in carrying out the activities associated with the recruitment and selection of staff.

5.13 THE ROLE OF HR PRACTITIONERS

In considering the activities above, we have touched on a number of the roles performed by HR practitioners at various stages of the recruitment and selection process.

5.13.1 AN ADVISORY ROLE TO LINE MANAGERS

It is rare – and, indeed, would be inappropriate – for all of the above activities to be performed solely by HR practitioners. In any event, it is generally wise for line managers to lead the job analysis stage because of their specialist knowledge, and be very involved at the selection stage so that they play an integral part in selecting their own member of staff and are therefore more likely to be committed to the new employee's success. Following on from this, it is worth noting that interview panels commonly consist of the line manager and an HR practitioner. This may involve you in an influencing role when, say, the line manager is tempted to offer the post to a candidate for subjective reasons (for example, the manager and the candidate attended the same school) rather than objective reasons (ones linked to the person specification).

5.13.2 AN ADMINISTRATIVE ROLE

This is to ensure that information is sought, chased and checked; that appropriate records are kept; and that all interested parties remain in touch with the timetable of events. It would be sensible to be assisted in this role by using appropriate software either online or on the organisation's computers.

5.13.3 A TRAINING ROLE

This may cover the design, organisation and delivery of skills training for interviewers/ assessors or coaching for inexperienced managers during the recruitment and selection process. There will also be an educational or possibly a compliance role to ensure that equal opportunities principles and policies are adhered to at all stages of the process.

5.13.4 A PUBLIC RELATIONS ROLE

This arises owing to the need to attract suitable candidates, and involves conveying information about the job, the person required and the organisation itself. Also, the way in which candidates are dealt with in making enquiries, pursuing applications and attending interviews may confirm or contradict their first impressions of the organisation. Attention to these matters assists in creating a positive employer brand, encouraging promising candidates to apply in the future.

5.13.5 AN ASSESSMENT ROLE

HR practitioners play a role in assessing candidates by interviewing, observing, testing and evaluating them using a range of selection methods.

5.13.6 AN EVALUATION ROLE

Finally, HR practitioners are likely to be responsible for ensuring that the process of recruitment and selection is periodically evaluated against its objectives – that is, did you employ the 'right people in the right jobs at the right time'?

5.14 SUMMARY

- You should by now be familiar with the key issues involved in the recruitment and selection of staff. We have looked at why recruitment and selection are important (regardless of the economic climate), the relevant legislation, the various stages involved and the importance of a thorough job analysis. We pointed out the importance of a robust and systematic process for all appointments and not just those concerning your core group of employees. We also considered the keys to effective induction and evaluation processes and the various roles played by HR practitioners.

- You should note that even if your experience of recruitment and selection is limited, it is likely that you will have applied for at least one position for which you were granted an interview or were invited to attend an AC. Thus, if you are unfamiliar with the whole process from the viewpoint of the interviewer or assessor, you will be familiar with it from the candidate's perspective. Nothing can replace the experience of actually conducting your first interview, administering a test or being involved in running an AC. In the latter case, you are likely to have an opinion on the good and bad practices that you observed. Reflect on such experiences to ensure that you do not make the same mistakes that others may have made. Continue this learning process by – if you have not already done so – attempting some of the Reflective Activities above before moving on to Chapter 6.

EXPLORE FURTHER

References and further reading

ACAS (2015) 'Recruiting staff': www.acas.org.uk/media/pdf/q/e/Recruiting-staff.pdf

CMI (2008) *Generation Y: Unlocking the talent of young managers*. London: Chartered Management Institute.

GEORGE, A., METCALF, H., TUFEKCI, L. and WILKINSON, D. (2015) *Understanding age and the labour market*. York: Joseph Rowntree Foundation.

ROBERTS, G. (2005) *Recruitment and Selection*. 2nd edition. London: CIPD.

TAYLOR, I. (2008) *The Assessment and Selection Handbook: Tools, Techniques and Exercises for Effective Recruitment and Development*. London: Kogan Page.

TAYLOR, S. (2008) People Resourcing. London: CIPD.

WHIDDETT, S. and HOLLYFORDE, S. (2003) *A Practical Guide to Competencies*. London: CIPD.

YEUNG, R. (2010) *Successful Interviewing and Recruitment*. 2nd edition. London: Kogan Page.

Websites

Acas: www.acas.org.uk

CIPD: www.cipd.co.uk

Disclosure and Barring Service (DBS): www.homeoffice.gov.uk/dbs

Equality and Human Rights Commission: www.equalityhumanrights.com

Immigration: www.gov.uk/government/collections/immigration-rules-statement-of-changes

Eligibility to work in the UK: www.gov.uk/legal-right-work-uk

Generations and the ageing workforce factsheets: www.talentsmoothie.com/insights

Leitch report: www.gov.uk/government/publications/prosperity-for-all-in-the-global-economy-world-class-skills-executive-summary-and-foreword

Legislation: www.legislation.hmso.gov.uk

Positive action: www.equalityhumanrights.com/your-rights/employment/applying-job/positive-action-and-recruitment

Skills at Work in Britain survey (2012): www.cardiff.ac.uk/__data/assets/pdf_file/0009/118683/1.-Skills-at-Work-in-Britain-mini-report.pdf

See also factsheets on the CIPD website at www.cipd.co.uk/hr-resources:

- Competence and Competency Frameworks (August 2015)
- Diversity in the workplace: an overview (October 2015)
- Equality Act 2010 (April 2014)
- Induction (October 2015)
- Pre-employment Checks (May 2015)
- Recruitment: an overview (November 2015)
- Selection Methods (November 2015)
- Understanding the economy and labour market (August 2015)
- Workforce planning (October 2015)

REFLECTIVE ACTIVITIES FEEDBACK

Reflective Activity 5.3

The differences between equal opportunities and managing diversity are summed up in Table 5.6.

Table 5.6 Equal opportunities versus managing diversity

Equal opportunities	Managing diversity
• entails removing discrimination against specific groups • is primarily an issue for HR specialists • relies on positive action • has a moral/legislative focus • is driven by domestic and EU discrimination legislation • can be adapted to the existing organisation	• entails maximising employee potential through an appreciation and utilisation of people's differences • involves all managers • is unlikely to rely on positive action because this will not be inclusive • has a business focus • has a global application in that it supports a variety of cultures • challenges the nature, values and structure of the existing organisation

An employment judge would have looked at areas such as:

- the demographic make-up of the workforce in terms of gender, race, disability, age, etc., across the various functions and levels, and whether this reflected the outside population
- signs of support from top management – for example, diversity champions, value statements which incorporate diversity principles, publicity for policies and practices
- attitudes within the workplace as evidenced by witnesses' responses to questions at the tribunal hearing

- recruitment sources, to see whether positive steps were taken to encourage applications from under-represented groups – for instance, advertising in ethnic minority publications
- selection methods, to ensure that they were not tainted by discrimination and that selection decisions were based on fair and objective criteria
- working arrangements – are part-time, term-time, homeworking and other flexible working arrangements available?
- training provision – have managers received appropriate skills training and has awareness training been provided for all employees?
- the handling of complaints about discriminatory matters – are grievances dealt with appropriately, and are offenders disciplined?
- the provision of equal access to training and promotion opportunities for all employees – for example, are adjustments made to the timing of training events in order to include part-timers?
- an integration of relevant policies with each other, backed up by company practices – for example, employee involvement in establishing a dress code that respects differing cultures and needs; a policy on religious observance that is actively promoted rather than tolerated by line managers.

Reflective Activity 5.6

In Table 5.7, there are a number of factors listed, and a tick indicates, in general terms, where one avenue has the advantage over the other.

Table 5.7 Factors to take into account when advertising a technical post

Factors	a)	b)
Speed in placing an advertisement		✓
Speed in receiving and processing applications		✓
Size of target population		✓
Access to international labour market		✓
Ease of access to additional company information		✓
Security of information, eg CVs	✓	
Less likely to attract poor-quality applicants/time-wasters	✓	
Ability to correct and update information in the advert		✓
Less costly		✓
Facility to use an online selection questionnaire		✓
Established source for this type of vacancy	✓	
Increasing trend to use this medium		✓

Reflective Activity 5.7

Your questions should be on similar lines to those listed below. Supplementary questions can then be asked, depending on the responses received.

Table 5.8 Behaviour-based questions

Competencies	Questions
Effective leadership skills	Give me an example of a situation in which you were responsible for helping others to complete a task or project. What steps did you take to motivate the team members?
The ability to handle conflict	Describe a situation where you were faced with views that differed from your own. How did you deal with this conflict?

Competencies	Questions
Problem-solving ability	Give me an example of a problem you had to solve recently. What was the outcome, and what steps did you take in solving the problem?
Customer focus	Tell me about a difficult situation which involved you in dealing with an internal or external customer. How did you ensure that you understood the customer's needs and that they were met?

CHAPTER 6

Performance Management

After reading this chapter you will:

- understand the importance of effective performance management in delivering successful business outcomes
- understand that performance management is a broader concept than performance appraisal and involves a number of people management activities
- appreciate the wide variety of performance appraisal schemes within organisations and be able to take steps to ensure that your own scheme is working effectively
- be able to identify the activities and skills involved in conducting appraisals and the links with motivation
- recognise the legal complexities surrounding performance appraisal.

6.1 INTRODUCTION

The latest available CIPD survey of performance management shows that many organisations claim to operate a formal performance management process, although the mix of activities involved varies greatly from one organisation to the next. Further, there was little agreement on what successful performance management looks like. Thus the impact of performance management on the achievement of organisational goals is debatable: some organisations fail to evaluate it in either quantitative or qualitative terms. It is also possible to see differences in how employees view their organisation's performance management processes: the CIPD's Employee Outlook (Spring 2014) found 39% of employees thought that their organisation's process was fair whilst 30% thought it was unfair. Similarly, over half of employees (56%) believed communication with their managers regarding objectives and expectations was effective to some degree, whilst 20% felt that it was ineffective. As with most HR and development activities, experiences vary greatly and in addition to success stories there are also accounts of poorly designed and implemented performance management systems. In the next section we consider what performance management is, why performance management is important for HR practitioners, line managers and the organisations they work for, and note the reasons for some of the difficulties that arise, before looking at the differences between performance appraisal and performance management. We then go on to look at performance appraisal in more detail: its purposes; trends; the move towards competence-based performance review; the various components of schemes, including the issue of objective-setting; good practice considerations; and some of the skills involved in undertaking performance appraisals. We thereafter provide sections on good practice in giving and receiving feedback, motivation, dealing with problem performance and the legal considerations.

Finally, we examine the differing roles played by the HR practitioner and the skills necessary for effective appraisal interviewing.

Before doing this, we draw your attention to the distinction between the terms 'performance management' and 'managing performance'. The first term tends to be used in reference to activities designed to motivate and encourage employees to work towards objectives that are in line with organisational goals. The second term includes managing good and poor performance, and therefore encompasses activities such as disciplinary procedures and absence control. In this chapter we provide an overview of dealing with poor performance while concentrating on performance management, and refer you to Chapter 8 for guidance on managing poor performers via disciplinary or capability routes. (Chapter 8 also provides guidance on absence management tools.)

Note that the processes of disciplinary or capability procedures and performance appraisal should complement each other in these circumstances. (See 6.8 'Legal Considerations'.)

6.2 WHAT IS PERFORMANCE MANAGEMENT?

In broad terms, at its best, performance management is an integrated and all-encompassing process comprising many elements of what makes up good practice in managing people. It operates as a continuous cycle rather than a one-off annual event. Effective performance management:

- is strategic with a focus on long-term issues
- is future-focused
- aligns the effort of individuals and teams with the goals the organisation is trying to achieve
- ensures individuals and teams know what is expected of them
- ensures feedback on achievement is provided
- ensures a developmental approach is taken to individuals' skills and capabilities.

This reflects the findings of the CIPD Employee Outlook Survey 2015, which found that employees want an approach to performance management that is individually based, future-focused and looks at *how* people undertake their roles as well as *what* they achieve. Because it can cover so many aspects of people management practice, it is useful – indeed, some may say vital – to have a structure and framework in place to support the process. However, any such structure and framework must be flexible to allow for individual and managerial freedom and discretion, and to avoid performance management being seen as just a bureaucratic form-filling exercise.

As a critical part of an integrated approach to managing people, performance management is a key role and activity for line managers and one in which they frequently look to HR departments for support and help. An effective performance management process enables line managers to undertake their people management responsibilities well and get the best from the people they manage.

Features of a performance management process may include:

- appraisal/performance review
- assessment of competence
- clarifying roles and expectations
- objective-setting and review
- learning and development activities
- performance-related pay
- coaching and mentoring
- succession and talent planning
- personal development planning.

6.3 WHY IS PERFORMANCE MANAGEMENT IMPORTANT?

Performance management is important for a number of reasons, both for the individual and the organisation. In relation to the organisation, suffice it to say here that without performance management, individual and team work may not be organised to achieve the optimum results for successful organisation performance. Some of examples of this are:

- Sales people may be achieving their sales targets, but the discounts and special incentives that they offer customers in order to do so have a detrimental effect on the profit margins – profit being the driving force of the company they are working for.
- A university lecturer whose brief is to recruit a certain number of students to a full-time course of study may find a smaller pool of potential candidates with the requisite qualifications than in previous years. The college tutor decides that rather than failing to reach the target, he or she will lower the entry requirements to the course. This will satisfy the immediate intake requirement, but is likely to lead to problems later on (the output), because a larger percentage of students may fail to attain the qualification. The university's finances (and business goals) will be dependent on the overall intake and output targets being reached – both of which have long-term implications.
- Computer helpline staff may point to the numbers of users they have helped over a period of time as an indication of their hard work and efficiency. However, this figure does not take account of those users who failed to get through to the busy switchboard system and had to seek assistance elsewhere. If the main aims of the computer company are to increase market share and maintain customer loyalty, this aspect of after-sales service has to be re-evaluated. The dissatisfied group of customers will be less inclined to buy from the same supplier again and will also not recommend friends and colleagues to do so.

Thus we can see that the employees concerned were all seeking to do what they had been told to do – that is, they were probably being efficient – but were they being effective?

Efficient: doing things right.
Effective: doing the right things.

The answer is no – in each case, insufficient thought had been given to ensuring that employees' individual targets and objectives were geared towards the overall business goals. The key is to ensure that there is a clear link between the tasks and activities that employees are involved in and the achievement of organisational goals. It is also crucial that evaluation methods are set up to assess whether this happens. We shall return to this question in a later section.

In relation to individual employees, performance management is a key aspect of being managed well. For employees, among other things, effective performance management leads to clarity about their role and the expectations the organisation has of them and where that role fits and contributes to the organisation. Performance management helps employees build a positive relationship with their manager, ensures they get feedback on how they are performing, and highlights learning and development needs. All of this contributes to an employee who is more likely to be motivated, engaged, productive and committed to the organisation. (For more on employee engagement, see Chapter 8. Those interested in the link between performance management and employee engagement might like to follow up the 2011 report by Farndale et al (see References and Further Reading at the end of this chapter.)

It is a fact, however, that many organisations do not adopt performance management processes, and even where they do, the process may come in for criticism or be counterproductive. Next, therefore, we examine why this might be the case.

6.4 WHY IS PERFORMANCE MANAGEMENT NOT ALWAYS SUCCESSFUL?

There are many reasons; for instance:

- Employees recognise that there is a lack of management commitment to the process and become cynical about its intentions.
- Managers lack the commitment and/or skills necessary to carry out effective appraisal interviews.
- The organisation doesn't have a culture of giving/receiving feedback and so employees are unaware of how their work and performance is viewed.
- Individual objectives are not reviewed often enough. For example, a six-month objective to recruit a specific number of people can quickly become inappropriate if there is a downturn in the organisation's market. Performance management favours what can be measured, and there is always the danger of leaning towards efficiency rather than effectiveness, as in the examples above.
- Even within those performance indicators that can be measured, individual performance in a large organisation is often outside the control of individuals. For instance, if the main employer in a small town makes its workforce redundant, the effect on retail sales in retail organisations in the town is outside the control of individual store managers.   Success often rests on qualitative, intangible matters such as the quality of relationships built up by an employee, an understanding of commercial realities or the ability to motivate others. Purely quantitative measures that focus on shorter-term results can compromise long-term benefits.
- When performance management is linked to reward, such as salary increases, the process can be problematic. In these circumstances individuals may tend to deny their weaknesses, may bury mistakes and may even blame others for any perceived shortfall in performance.
- Managers need training in performance management and in performance appraisal. All too often this is not provided and managers come to dread an annual appraisal round.

In taking everything into account managers can end up paying 'lip service' to the appraisal process. Sometimes this creates a negative effect, undermining the employee's confidence in both the process and the manager. Sometimes matters that should be tackled are not.

The employee may then be understandably unaware of his or her own shortcomings.

6.5 PERFORMANCE MANAGEMENT VERSUS PERFORMANCE APPRAISAL

In very simple terms, performance appraisal (or 'review', as it is sometimes called) is the 'tail that wags the dog' in its relationship with performance management. The exercise of appraising performance is necessarily retrospective because it concerns making a judgement about the past performance of employees. Appraisals can be used to improve current performance by providing feedback on strengths and weaknesses. (Note that 'weaknesses' are probably better labelled 'areas for improvement' or 'developmental needs' if we wish to emphasise the positive and constructive nature of this feedback.) Appraisals, done well, can therefore be effective in increasing employee motivation and, ultimately, organisational performance.

Performance appraisal can, and should, be linked to a performance-improvement process, and can then also be used to identify training needs and potential, agree future objectives, focus on career development and solve problems. Building on the overview and introduction to performance management given above, we can see that performance management is a vehicle for the continuous and evolutionary improvement of business performance via a co-ordinated programme of people management activities. Most commentators agree that these activities include:

- strategic planning
- the definition of organisational goals, priorities and values
- the translation of organisational goals into department, team and individual goals, targets or objectives
- the development and application of a performance assessment process based on the achievement of the above
- an appraisal process
- personal development planning
- learning and development activities
- various forms of contingent pay.

CASE STUDY 6.1

The company is an architectural lighting manufacturer that designs and manufactures LED lighting products that have been used in some high-profile projects around the world – the London Olympics, the Royal Botanic Gardens at Kew, the Royal Ballet School in London, Bitexco Tower in Ho Chi Minh City, Vietnam and the Burj Khalifa in Dubai, amongst others. It is a successful and growing business employing 125 staff across five different locations. As well as staff in head office functions – sales, procurement, finance, HR – the company also employs mechanical engineers, product designers, production operatives, stores and dispatch personnel.

As a company they had a good reputation, a strong brand and product range and were creative and innovative, but felt they weren't quite realising their full potential. They didn't have a clear business strategy or objectives, had inconsistent business information, inaccurate and unspecific key performance indicators (KPIs), a lack of cohesion in their company processes and some problems with communication. They also needed to ensure they had the right workforce for the future in terms of roles, skills and capability. In relation to their staff, the company didn't always deal with conduct and capability matters well, or appoint the right people with the right skills, and didn't always develop people.

Following some key appointments to the leadership team, including an HR and people development manager, a project was launched to address these issues. They took a coordinated approach with work across a number of activities: defining company vision and values; setting company strategy and business objectives; clarifying roles and responsibilities; introducing a new performance review process; introducing regular structured one-to-ones for all staff; developing and sharing new KPI measures and information; improved communication processes; and planned programmes of training and development activity – a holistic and co-ordinated approach to performance management across the whole company.

The new performance review process was a key part of the project. The old system was described by the HR manager as very mechanistic and seen by most as a tick-box exercise in form-filling – a common view of performance review or appraisal processes. The company wanted to link company objectives and performance with departmental and individual objectives and performance. They also wanted to encourage honest dialogue between managers and staff about how the member of staff feels the year has gone and how the manager feels it has gone. The new performance review process includes objectives – but no more than five each year for staff in head office functions and no more than three for staff in the production facility. Importantly the process also has a significant focus on what support and development people need in order to help them deliver their objectives and realise their potential as individuals. Crucially for the company, they wanted to encourage ownership of the new process amongst employees and so made them the owners of the forms that supported the process, trained everyone and ensured managers were clear about their responsibility to encourage employees to complete the process comprehensively. In a complete change to the previous approach, the company also included company values as part of the review and asked staff to review not just *what* they had achieved, but also *how* they had achieved it and whether their approach was in line with the company's values. As part of the whole process staff are asked to be open and honest in their evaluation of their own performance and approach and managers are asked to support this with open and honest feedback. All staff now have clear objectives that have a clear link to departmental and company objectives, know what is expected of them and what deadlines they are working to, have regular one-to-ones and an annual review and an individual training plan linked to their identified development needs.

The company made a decision to not link the performance review process with pay in order to encourage greater openness and honesty in both the individual staff member's assessment of their own performance and the manager's feedback.

In terms of impact on overall company performance, the company has seen greater role clarity for individuals and function clarity for departments, a more effective senior management team, an improved company structure and design, improved communications and reporting, a more focused approach to training and development, a greater focus on company culture, a lower level of customer complaints, more innovation across the company and an approach they call 'focus to fix', where everyone has a role in and is empowered to think about process and product improvements. On the more quantifiable aspects of workforce measurement, sickness absence has reduced, staff turnover has gone down and engagement has increased.

In the words of one of their employees, he now understands 'why I've been given this objective, how that supports my manager's objectives and how that supports the company to achieve its goals'.

As we have already stated, there is no universally accepted definition of 'performance management, but we can safely say that it is a much broader concept than that of performance appraisal. To demonstrate some of these points, consider the example of the LED lighting company in Case Study 6.1.

One of the main lessons that the company learned in Case Study 6.1 was that there should be clear and co-ordinated two-way links in all the stages between the company's strategic plan and individual objectives (see Figure 6.1).

This model does not mean that individuals cannot seek to satisfy their own personal objectives, but it does help to focus them on their own roles and contribution to the overall business performance. The result will hopefully be a motivational one because their efforts are directed at those activities which best serve organisational goals. (Further consideration of this motivational aspect is provided below.)

The issues are the same regardless of the size of organisation; the key is to ensure that there are feedback mechanisms in place, as demonstrated in Figure 6.1. To return to Case Study 6.1, the company was able to ensure the new and revamped approach to performance management was fully co-ordinated and geared towards the achievement of business objectives.

Figure 6.1 The two-way links model

There are a number of learning points we can draw from this case study:

- the company took a holistic approach
- its scheme included a manageable number of objectives for individual staff
- there was a clear 'line of sight' between the company objectives and individual objectives
- employees were fully involved in the process and given ownership of the new process
- the process is built on regular dialogue and feedback
- the process considers what people do and how they do it.

6.6 PERFORMANCE APPRAISAL

Performance appraisal is one tool for managing individual performance and is more appropriately used by line managers than HR professionals. It can help in reinforcing the values of the organisation and in maintaining employee loyalty and commitment. The appraisal process is about providing an opportunity for a manager and member of staff to get together and have a conversation about the member of staff's performance, development and the sort of support they need from their manager. Done well, it should be a constructive and positive two-way process.

6.6.1 PURPOSES

Performance appraisal often serves three different purposes (and most schemes incorporate at least two of these):

Performance reviews – managers discuss with employees their progress in their current posts, their strengths, and the areas requiring further development in order to improve current performance. This purpose focuses on past performance.

Potential reviews – managers discuss with employees opportunities for progression, the type of work they may be interested in and capable of in the future, and how this can be achieved, by identifying their developmental needs and career aspirations. This purpose is future-focused. This can be an important part of a talent management programme.

Reward reviews – these are usually separate from the appraisal system but the decisions on rewards such as pay, benefits, promotion and self-fulfilment are fed by the information provided by performance appraisal. This purpose will only apply where reward in the organisation has a performance contingent element. (Further information on reward, including performance-related reward, can be found in Chapter 7.)

Well-conducted performance appraisal interviews therefore usually involve a manager and an employee in a constructive discussion concerning the employee's recent performance (say, over the previous 12 months), plans for improved performance – which will probably involve agreeing future objectives or targets (see below) – and plans for meeting the developmental needs of the employee. At a later stage, a reward review interview may be arranged if appropriate so that the manager and employee can openly discuss, for instance, the level of performance-related pay (PRP) that has been awarded. However, conducting performance appraisal is often ranked by managers as the most disliked managerial activity and is often viewed by employees (and some organisations) as the least effective HR policy – often due to the way it is carried out by managers. This indicates the need to pay attention to appraisal and strive for the most effective approach for the organisation's culture.

As HR practitioners, you are likely to know already that appraisals do not always go according to plan. For instance:

- Work pressures or a lack of skills or training may result in managers' seeking to avoid the regular performance appraisal interview, thereby leaving interviews to the last minute when they are poorly prepared, and they then rush the process.
- Not all managers are good at people management activities and as a result may be inconsistent or subjective in their approach and base the appraisal on their relationship with the individual employee rather than on performance.
- Not all employees are good performers and managers may not be as clear or constructive as they should be in their delivery of feedback.
- In an organisation in which there are few promotion opportunities, employees (and their managers) may view learning and development activities as somewhat pointless.
- If a high-performing individual's expectation of PRP is not realised (often through factors outside his or her own control), he or she may decide not to try so hard to achieve targets or objectives in the future.
- The organisational context and climate may not suit traditional annual cycles – in many businesses the goal posts move rapidly, objectives change, many employees work across projects and departments and in a variety of different teams and appraisal just cannot keep up.

The motivational effect of performance appraisal is thus often debatable. In order to have some positive effect on motivation, performance appraisal needs to be done well, with a fair process and outcome. Table 6.1 shows how appraisal, done well, can increase levels of individual motivation at work.

Table 6.1 Performance appraisal and employee motivation

Aspects of motivation	Role and impact of performance appraisal
Need to know how you're doing	Provides opportunity for formal feedback on performance
Need for recognition of the contribution you make	Formalises and provides structure and time for your manager to discuss your efforts and achievements
Need to know you are valued	Demonstrates an investment of time and effort in you from your manager
Need for growth and development	Facilitates the setting of stretching and challenging goals and provides a focus on your future role, career and development

We shall discuss the skills of performance appraisal interviewing, applicable in both good and poor performer situations, and provide more detail about motivation in a later section.

6.6.2 TRENDS IN PERFORMANCE APPRAISAL

Developments in performance appraisal see a much greater focus now on how individuals contribute to organisational performance and success through the behaviours and capabilities they deploy. For organisations there is a significant interest in how performance appraisal can contribute to employee engagement, to increasing motivation and to increasing involvement, ownership and responsibility. This changing focus creates interest in alternatives to the traditional (often annual) conversation (and form-filling) between a manager and an employee about the employee's achievements. Some of these alternatives are set out below.

Ongoing feedback, coaching and development

A 2014 report from Deloitte University Press found that a number of organisations are now using ongoing feedback and coaching as part of a process of continuous development for employees in preference to an annual evaluation or appraisal cycle. This is often seen hand in hand with a move away from annual ranking approaches in appraisal where every employee is given a grade or score, and in some cases limits are placed on how many employees can be in each rank or grade regardless of how well or badly they have performed. A process of continuous feedback, coaching and development clearly requires something different along with a new approach from managers. This development very clearly presents some difficulties for organisations that link pay and reward with appraisal and again new approaches will be needed.

360-degree appraisal

In some organisations appraisals have moved on from a fairly simple manager–subordinate (or top-down) relationship (possibly including self-appraisal) to 360-degree appraisals, involving stakeholders who provide feedback on an individual's performance. However, this is still not a widespread practice – the CIPD Employee Outlook Survey 2015 reports that only 19% of employees report getting feedback from people other than their manager.

Figure 6.2 Stakeholders in 360-degree appraisal

Figure 6.2 shows an example of the stakeholders that might be involved in an individual's appraisal. There is great variety in the way in which 360-degree appraisal is implemented in organisations. On the one hand, the appraisal interview may include all the stakeholders giving face-to-face feedback to the appraisee (who may well feel that the term 'victim' is more appropriate here!). On the other hand, some organisations operate systems whereby the collection of feedback from the chosen stakeholders is done via formally constructed questionnaires. This information is then collated and fed back to the individual by a neutral third party (possibly an HR practitioner). Larger organisations have even invested in computer packages to cut down on the administrative burden attached to collecting and collating this information on a large scale. To appreciate the potential benefits of 360-degree appraisal, see Case Study 6.2.

CASE STUDY 6.2

An HR director in a large public sector organisation was concerned about the level of staff turnover in his own department. He was satisfied that the department was appropriately resourced, had clear objectives, and was, on the whole, well regarded by others in the organisation. He had a very effective deputy who managed the HR team on a day-to-day basis. As part of a wider development programme, he participated in a 360-degree appraisal process, using a number of staff in his department as stakeholders. The results were collated and fed back to him by an independent third party. The feedback he received through this process indicated that his team members had a fairly negative view of their relationship with him. He was seen as distant, very externally focused, not accessible and uninterested in the day-to-day activities of his department and team.

As a result team members felt their contributions weren't valued by the senior managers in the organisation, and this was a major factor in decisions to leave. The 360-degree appraisal gave the director a perspective and some feedback he had not received through any other source, and enabled him to start building stronger, more personal relationships with members of his team.

Review of competencies and behaviours

We have seen a move from just concentrating on *what* a job-holder achieves to also assessing *how* the job is carried out. Thus many organisations now review the achievement of objectives and targets and also the behaviour exhibited by the job-holder.

Not only does this take a wider view of the role the individual employee is undertaking, but it also considers the impact of behaviour on colleagues and customers. The importance of behaviours can be seen just within the HR profession through the CIPD Profession Map (see Chapter 12), a large component of which identifies the behaviours needed for HR professionals to carry out their activities successfully. The authors are aware of more than one organisation which has started to use these behaviours as a formal part of considering effective performance in their HR professionals.

6.6.3 THE PERFORMANCE REVIEW CYCLE

As a result of the above trends, most performance appraisal schemes nowadays follow the stages of the performance review cycle, as set out in Figure 6.3.

According to Whiddett and Hollyforde (2003, p 75), competencies can make significant contributions to all stages of the performance review process – that is, by:

- identifying factors relevant to performance in the job
- collecting information on performance

- organising the information
- discussing or reviewing the information (for example for solo reviews)
- agreeing outcomes.

We shall discuss the much-debated issue of objective-setting shortly, but first let's look at the various components of performance appraisal schemes.

Figure 6.3 The performance review cycle

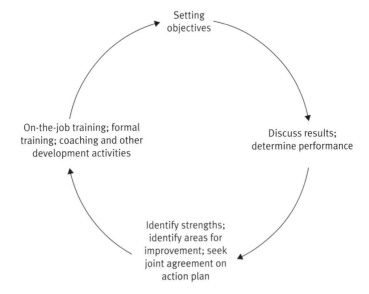

6.6.4 THE COMPONENTS OF PERFORMANCE APPRAISAL SCHEMES

If you are designing a performance appraisal scheme, you need first to determine its purpose (or purposes) and seek to integrate the new scheme into your performance management process, if one exists. Against this backdrop you must then make the following decisions, depending on the organisational circumstances:

1 Who is to be appraised? That is, you must decide what levels or functions of employees are to be involved.

2 Who appraises? This could be the employee, the manager only, the manager and subordinates, or other stakeholders (see the previous section regarding 360-degree appraisal).

3 What is to be appraised, and what criteria will be used? The options include results versus competency-based versus behaviour-based assessment, and achievement of objectives.

4 What assessment methods will you employ? You could opt for a descriptive or narrative report, a checklist, ratings or gradings, comparison with objectives, comparison with others (ranking individuals in order of performance), critical incidents (recorded incidents of positive and negative behaviours), or competence-based assessment (assessment against the achievement of set standards). An example of this last method is provided in Table 6.2. (Please note that you may need to define different levels or standards for each competency, according to the level and responsibilities of the job under consideration.)

5 Will you incorporate assessment of promotion potential? A link to reward or a salary review? A means of appeal against a (perceived) unfair assessment?

6 How often is a formal appraisal interview to be carried out – for example, once every three, six or 12 months? Will you include interim reviews to accommodate the pace of change? Will you introduce ongoing review and feedback rather than scheduled formal sessions?

7 How will you ensure that the action points are implemented (for example, the meeting of development needs)?

8 How will you evaluate success (that is, the achievement of the purpose(s) of the scheme)?

Table 6.2 Competence-based assessment

Competency: Meeting customer needs	
Anticipates, responds to and seeks to exceed the expectations of existing and potential customers	
Competent	**Needs developing**
Strives to provide the best customer service	Unhelpful to customers, not taking time to understand what they need, and then jumping in with any solution
Adopts a positive and professional approach to meet the needs of customers	
Provides advice that is beneficial to both customers and the company	Sees customers as 'not part of my job' – focuses instead on internal or administrative requirements
Always ready to help by anticipating and responding to customers' needs in the most appropriate way	Does not ensure products meet customer needs
	Is target-driven, ignoring customers' real needs
Competency: Self-control	
Performs effectively by keeping emotions under control, particularly in stressful and difficult situations	
Is patient and even-tempered	Is easily flustered – runs around panicking
Remains calm; does not appear to become irritable or anxious	Takes the reactions of other people very personally
Does not panic under pressure	Appears childish, petulant
Does not react to provocation – maintains poise and professionalism when challenged	Loses cool; becomes aggressive or defensive
Accepts refusals and rebuffs; does not take things personally	Bottles up stress and then explodes – takes out frustrations on others

? REFLECTIVE ACTIVITY 6.1

Find out as much as you can about the appraisal scheme(s) used by your organisation (or another organisation with which you are familiar) and how it is viewed by managers and employees. Investigate any paperwork, talk to your manager and other line managers, talk to other employees, and use other learning sources to compare your practices with those of outside organisations. Then answer the eight questions above.

Acas have suggested the following key points for successful appraisal schemes:

- Make sure that senior managers are fully committed to the idea of appraisals.
- Consult with managers, employees and trade union representatives about the design and implementation of appraisals before they are introduced.
- Monitor schemes regularly.
- Give appraisers adequate training to enable them to make fair and objective assessments and to carry out effective appraisal interviews.
- Keep the scheme as simple and straightforward as possible – don't let the paperwork take over.

We add the following suggestions:

- Before implementing the scheme across the whole organisation, carry out a pilot run (for example, in one department) in order to gain invaluable feedback on possible teething problems that can then be solved before the main launch. Start with the most senior people in your pilot area, so that you gain their commitment, and encourage them to lead by example and to cascade their learning downwards.
- Ensure that appraisers and appraisees jointly identify strengths and areas for improvement, and that appraisers provide constructive feedback on performance and support the appraisee in meeting his or her development needs in line with business goals.
- Provide familiarisation training for appraisees so that they understand the purpose of the scheme and are able to gain the maximum advantage from their participation.

> **? REFLECTIVE ACTIVITY 6.2**
>
> Following on from Reflective Activity 6.1, think about how managers and employees viewed your appraisal scheme and how useful (or not!) they find it. Suggest some improvements that could be made to the scheme(s) you have chosen for your analysis. Present them in the form of a written report to senior management, making sure that you justify your proposals.

We have mentioned the place of objective-setting several times within the context of performance appraisal and performance management. We now seek to examine this concept further.

6.6.5 OBJECTIVE-SETTING

Objective-setting is one way in which current expectations of employees can be made clear and allows the focus of an individual's work to be integrated and aligned with the overarching goals of the organisation. Objectives are about improvement, and there are a number of levels:

- business objectives
- team/division/departmental objectives linking with the above
- individual objectives linking with all of the above as well as
- individual objectives resulting from developmental needs
- project objectives
- training and development objectives.

However, rather than trying to set objectives, managers would be better advised to seek to agree objectives with their staff. The CIPD Employee Outlook Survey 2015 indicates that only 56% of employees have formal objectives and only 45% of these employees mutually agree *all* their objectives. It is our view that during the course of the appraisal process the manager and employee should jointly agree objectives for the forthcoming period which comply with the mnemonic SMARTS:

Specific
Measurable
Agreed
Realistic
Time-bound
Stretching.

Which of the following two objectives complies with SMARTS?

- To improve supervisory skills by taking responsibility for the training and development of a new apprentice over the coming year.
- To research, design and implement a new sickness absence monitoring system that differentiates between certified and uncertified absences and that records frequency, duration and reasons for absence. (This new system would be linked into a company-wide initiative to reduce costs by appropriate absence management techniques.) The budget for this exercise is x, the ongoing maintenance costs should be limited to two clerical labour hours a month, and the timescale for implementation is y months.

The first example is not SMARTS because it is not specific and its outcomes would be difficult to measure. However, the second example provides a specific task with several measurable outcomes for the evaluation of success. The objective is presumably (barring disasters) realistic for the employee working with available resources, and is clearly time-bound.

It would also be stretching if it involved the employee in areas of work that he or she would not normally encounter in day-to-day activities. Thus he or she would be able to build on new experiences and develop new skills and would be more likely to agree to it. This individual objective is also clearly linked to an organisational goal: cutting costs.

Obviously, not all objectives can be defined in this way because many lean more to qualitative rather than quantitative measurement, which is necessarily more subjective. Nevertheless, the mnemonic SMARTS provides an ideal to which you should aspire as far as possible.

?   REFLECTIVE ACTIVITY 6.3

Think about your own job role and what you would like to achieve over the next 12 months. Write down three to six key objectives for this period. Make sure that the majority of them tie in with the business goals of your organisation and that they all comply with the SMARTS guidelines. Discuss them with one of your learning sources.

We shall now return to considering performance appraisal in general terms by looking at the benefits of a well-designed and implemented scheme before we summarise good-practice issues.

6.6.6 THE BENEFITS OF PERFORMANCE APPRAISAL

Employees are often suspicious of new or revised appraisal schemes, particularly during times of rapid change or rationalisation. If you are faced with the task of introducing a new or updated scheme, you should pick your timing carefully, because many employees (sometimes rightly) view such innovations as a cynical way of selecting candidates for redundancy.

In any event, if the design incorporates the list of key points provided in 6.6.4 on the components of performance appraisal schemes, the benefits for both the organisation and the individual should include the items listed in Table 6.3.

Table 6.3 The benefits of performance appraisal

For the organisation	For the individual
• Improved communication of business goals • Improvements in work performance and therefore overall business performance via, for example, increased productivity or customer service • Identification of potential to aid succession and talent planning • Training provision or development activities targeted at identified needs rather than provided on an *ad hoc* or 'first come, first served' basis • Evaluation of effectiveness of selection criteria for new or newly promoted employees • More objective distribution of rewards • Improved retention of employees	• Increased understanding of strategic aims and own role in organisational success • Increased motivation • Increased job satisfaction • Development of potential • Better-informed career planning • Increased ability to meet own individual objectives as well as wider department or business objectives • Opportunity to publicise ambition • Better understanding of the link between effort, performance and reward

The benefits listed in Table 6.3 demonstrate why organisations should seriously consider the value of introducing performance appraisal – but they should also bear in mind the many potential pitfalls. A half-hearted attempt to introduce formal performance appraisal may be more damaging in the long run than no attempt at all.

In order to help you to avoid the pitfalls suffered by some performance appraisal schemes, we have summarised a list of good-practice features.

6.6.7 GOOD PRACTICE IN PERFORMANCE APPRAISAL

There is no right or wrong in relation to appraisal and how it is established or conducted, but effective schemes and approaches will generally incorporate the following:

- support from top management
- systems that are open and participative
- agreement at all levels about the purpose(s) of the scheme
- separation of reward reviews from the appraisal interviews
- clear, specific and well-communicated (SMARTS) objectives that are jointly agreed
- line managers' recognition of their critical role in this process – that is, it is not seen as an HR function
- clear links to the disciplinary and/or capability procedure when handling conduct or poor performance issues so that the messages to the employee are the same
- training for appraisers and appraisees, including giving and receiving feedback
- a 'maintenance' programme to ensure that follow-up action is taken – for example, training or development programmes are arranged as agreed
- a flexible approach to cater for individual and organisational needs
- simple administrative procedures with minimal paperwork

- ongoing open dialogue between managers and employees regarding performance and progress.

Finally, you should ensure that there is vertical and horizontal integration of the performance appraisal scheme within the business. Vertical integration means that there must be a link between the purposes of performance appraisal and the business strategy.

Horizontal integration means there has to be a fit between performance appraisal and other HR and development activities.

In relation to conducting a performance appraisal meeting, good practice would indicate that the person being appraised should do most of the talking, with the appraiser being an active listener – this will be a good starting point for a system to be participative.

There should be opportunities for reflection, clarification and summarising to ensure shared understanding. The whole period under review should be covered, not just recent or 'big' events, with a focus on performance in the job rather than on the personality of the appraisee. Feedback should be both positive and constructive, with achievement being recognised as well as agreement on areas for further development. Agreement should be sought at the end of the meeting about next steps and actions needed. Additionally, all the logistical matters relating to any type of interview – quiet location, no interruptions, good preparation, and so on – should be fulfilled.

In the list above we pointed out that appraisal training should include development in giving and receiving feedback. We now consider this important issue.

6.6.8 GIVING AND RECEIVING FEEDBACK

Here we are referring not only to the giving and receiving of feedback in formal performance reviews, but also to the regular and informal feedback that employees should be able to expect throughout the year. Feedback is a critical part of knowing how you're doing at work; however, the CIPD Employee Outlook Survey 2015 shows that 18% of employees never get any feedback. Obviously, not all feedback will be positive, although anecdotal evidence suggests that managers are reluctant to give negative feedback and employees are poor at receiving it. Poorly handled feedback can have a detrimental effect on future performance and working relationships, so we must work hard to try to get it right.

In Table 6.4 we seek to identify how feedback, whether negative or positive, can be given in a constructive way.

Table 6.4 The dos and don'ts of giving constructive feedback

Do:	Don't:
<ul><li>Be specific, precise and objective – describe what you see</li><li>Give examples where you can</li><li>Focus on behaviour (that can be changed), not personality</li><li>Give feedback in a timely fashion, as soon after the event as possible</li><li>Agree what needs to be done/changed</li><li>Be supportive but challenging</li><li>Be self-aware about the impact you are having</li><li>Encourage reflection</li><li>Make it part of an ongoing dialogue</li></ul>	<ul><li>Be apologetic</li><li>Ignore a situation when feedback is needed</li><li>Dilute the message to feel more comfortable</li><li>Assume you know best</li><li>Deliver feedback when you are feeling angry, stressed, etc.</li><li>Bring up old concerns and mistakes unless it's to highlight a pattern of behaviour</li></ul>

Following the advice in Table 6.4 can be very powerful in terms of getting your message across in the right way and in helping the recipient to understand and accept what you are saying. This is demonstrated in Case Study 6.3.

CASE STUDY 6.3

The owner of a number of children's nurseries had some concerns about the manager she had employed to run one of the nurseries on a day-to-day basis. The manager had been in post for approximately 18 months but had never had a performance appraisal or review. The owner of the nursery had never had a one-to-one sit down with the manager to discuss how she was performing in her role or to clarify the owner's expectations. The owner dropped into the nursery on a weekly basis, but only discussed general issues concerning the day-to-day running of the nursery and issues concerning the children and their parents.

Following an Ofsted inspection visit, the owner was notified that there were a number of concerns regarding the management of staff at the nursery including staff frequently using their mobile phones whilst on duty, staff taking excessive numbers of smoking breaks during the working day and the daily record-keeping of the children's activities (which was shared with parents) not being comprehensive or up to date.

The owner approached an external HR advisor for advice and support; she indicated that she wanted to take disciplinary action against the manager on the basis of poor performance and the critical Ofsted report. On questioning from the HR adviser, the owner indicated that she had been aware of the smoking and mobile phone issues but had not raised this with the manager. She had told the manager that the standard of paperwork wasn't good enough and that she was lazy and disorganised on one occasion 12 months ago, but this had turned into an argument and the owner had not subsequently followed up on this.

? REFLECTIVE ACTIVITY 6.4

In Case Study 6.3:

- What feedback 'sins' did the owner commit?
- How might she have tackled this situation differently?
- Compare your responses with the feedback provided at the end of this chapter.

In Case Study 6.3 we saw how counterproductive poor feedback can be, and how, in such a situation, it would be difficult for the recipient to react in a constructive way and bring about the required improvements. In any event, even where feedback is given well, employees often lack the skills to receive feedback effectively, even positive feedback. For instance, when someone unexpectedly praises or thanks you, you may be inclined to reply with such statements as 'It was nothing,' or 'It's just part of my job.' What's the result?

That person may be less inclined to praise or thank you next time!

So how *should* we receive feedback?

TIPS FOR RECEIVING FEEDBACK

- Listen carefully to the message – seek to understand what's being said.
- Don't become emotional, defensive or argumentative (take a deep breath!).
- Ask questions to clarify anything you are unsure of.
- Give the person a chance to speak.
- Accept the feedback.
- Pause and think before responding.
- Be open to suggestions for improvement.
- Learn from it.
- Respect and thank the giver – he or she has just taken a risk for you.

6.6.9 DEALING WITH POOR PERFORMANCE

As noted throughout this chapter, performance management is a positive process aimed at improving individual and thereby organisational performance. However, in all organisations there will be instances of poor performance. This can result from a whole range of factors – for example, lack of skill or knowledge, problems with attitude and behaviour, poor management, lack of resources, poor systems or processes of work or external factors. As is evident, not all of these relate to or are within the control or influence of the individual employee, and it is very important to be clear why the poor performance is occurring. An effective performance management system can help to identify the causes of poor performance and ensure that an appropriately broad view is taken of how performance might be improved. This might range from interventions in learning and development to changing systems of work, ongoing discussion and supervision with managers, and so on. Where the reason for the poor performance does lie with the employee – perhaps related to conduct, performance or health – then, in most organisations, there are separate procedures for dealing with it. Further information on this is contained in Chapter 8.

6.7 MOTIVATION

We saw in Table 6.1 some of the links that can be made between performance appraisal and motivation. Individual performance depends on a number of factors – skill, knowledge, competence, aptitude, attitude and behaviour, among others. Underpinning the application of these factors by an individual employee in the workplace is the level of motivation, which itself is affected by a range of variables. Motivation is a very complex and individual issue – what motivates one person won't necessarily motivate another, and for each individual, motivating factors fluctuate in their importance according to the changing circumstances of his or her life. Motivation is important because it directs, energises and sustains behaviour in the workplace driving individual performance and ultimately impacting on productivity and organisation success. Many studies have been carried out into motivation and many theories have been developed as a result. There is a variety of ways to classify these theories, but here we shall look at just three broad categories: reinforcement theories; needs theories; and cognitive theories.

6.7.1 REINFORCEMENT THEORIES

These theories propose that behaviour is shaped by its consequences – that positive reinforcement (for example, praise, approval, promotion or bonuses) increases the likelihood of that behaviour being repeated, whereas negative reinforcement (for example, punishment or reprimand) motivates behaviour by leading to the avoidance of the undesired behaviour. The proponents of these theories believe that positive reinforcement is a more effective motivator than negative reinforcement. In principle, this theory is fairly simple, but in the real world it doesn't usually operate so smoothly because reinforcement at work (for example, praise for a job done well) is often inconsistently applied or not forthcoming at all. There is also the question of which reinforcements are appropriate for which workers. One example of a reinforcement theory is Herzberg's motivation-hygiene theory, which looked at a range of factors and concluded that satisfaction and dissatisfaction arise from different factors – motivators (for example, achievement and the work itself) providing positive reinforcement, and 'hygiene' factors (for example, pay and work conditions), if not handled well, having a negative effect.

6.7.2 NEEDS THEORIES

A number of theories of motivation suggest that people have needs that are satisfied (or not) by working. These needs might be tangible, such as the need for food and housing, or less tangible, such as the need for respect from others. Some approaches suggest that individuals usually have a preference or bias towards particular needs, the motivational impact varying for each individual, while others have suggested that needs occur at different levels and individuals move through these levels as lower-order needs are satisfied. One example of a needs-based theory is Maslow's hierarchy of needs, in which he identified five levels of need, from physiological needs (for example, hunger, thirst) at the bottom to the need for self-actualisation (for example, realising your potential) at the top. As needs at the bottom are satisfied, they cease being primary motivators and an individual becomes motivated to satisfy higher-level needs. The different levels and associated needs can be seen in Table 6.5.

Table 6.5 Maslow's hierarchy of needs

Self-fulfilment:	realising potential, creativity and self-development
Ego needs:	autonomy, esteem, self-respect, confidence, sense of achievement, recognition/status, appreciation
Social needs:	sense of belonging, association, being accepted, giving and receiving, love and affection
Safety needs:	protection from danger and deprivation, physical and psychological security
Physical needs:	food, drink, shelter, rest

The theory acknowledges that people don't necessarily move in a continuous direction through the different levels of need, and also may be at a different place in different aspects of their lives at work and outside work. As with everything, there may also be exceptions to this theory and some people may be happy to remain at a level below the top.

6.7.3 COGNITIVE THEORIES

These theories recognise individuals as rational thinking beings with differing views about reward, which therefore puts motivation on a much more individual basis. Such theories suggest that workers bring inputs to a job – for example, experience, qualifications, energy and effort – and expect to receive outcomes in return – for example, pay, recognition, benefits and interesting work. The inputs and outcomes are weighed up and perceived as either fair or unfair by the individual both at his or her own level and in comparison with others. One example of a cognitive theory is Adams' equity theory, which states that workers are motivated by a desire to be treated equitably or fairly. If workers perceive that they are being treated fairly, the motivation to work will be sustained and effective performance can be expected.

Now consider Reflective Activity 6.5.

REFLECTIVE ACTIVITY 6.5

Think about what affects your motivation at work. Try to write down a number of different factors and their impact on you – do they motivate you or demotivate you? Try to arrange these factors in order of how important you think they are in motivating you.

Now talk to a couple of colleagues – see what motivates them and what priority order they come up with. How does that compare with yours?

Now think about the factors that you and your colleagues have come up with. How good is your organisation at addressing these factors?

6.8 LEGAL CONSIDERATIONS

The two main pieces of legislation relevant to the area of employee reward (where performance-related pay is used) are the Equality Act 2010 (which covers, amongst other things, equal pay) and the National Minimum Wage Act 1998. Both are summarised in Chapter 3.

With regard to performance appraisal, it would appear at first sight that there is no specific legislation. Yet Acas advice on employee appraisal, summarised (and updated) below, leaves little room for doubt concerning the relevance of certain legal considerations.

APPRAISAL – THE LEGAL CONSIDERATIONS

Trade unions

Employers who recognise one or more trade unions are required (if requested by a union) to disclose information for the purposes of collective bargaining. In these circumstances, particularly where merit pay schemes are in operation, they may be requested to explain how appraisal systems operate and to describe the criteria against which employees are rated.

Further, under the Employment Relations Act 1999, recognised trade unions have a statutory right to be informed and consulted on training policies and plans.

Data protection

The Data Protection Act 1998 (supplemented in the public sector by the Freedom of Information Act 2000) gives individual employees a legal right of access to personal data (such as appraisal details). 'Personal data' includes not just factual information but also opinions expressed about employees. Employees could therefore have access to opinions recorded about their performance or attitude at an appraisal. See Chapter 10 for further details on data protection.

Equal opportunities

Under the Equality Act 2010, employees who feel that they have been refused promotion or access to training on grounds such as their race, age, sexual orientation, disability status or sex, etc., have the right to make a complaint to an employment tribunal.

In discrimination cases, appraisal forms and procedures may be used by employees to support their complaints. It is important for employers regularly to monitor their appraisal systems and promotion policies to ensure that criteria used to assess performance are non-discriminatory in terms of age, disability, gender reassignment, marriage and civil partnership, pregnancy and maternity, race, religion and belief, sex and sexual orientation.

Poor performance

Employees dismissed on the grounds of inadequate performance and who subsequently complain of unfair dismissal sometimes indicate in their applications that they have received little or no indication of alleged poor performance while in employment. Appraisal schemes should not be used as a disciplinary mechanism to deal with poor performers, but it is important to establish a procedure for informing employees in writing of unsatisfactory ratings. The consequences of failure to meet the required standards should be explained to the employee and confirmed in writing. The appraisal form is not, however, the place to record details of a verbal or written disciplinary procedure. There should be space on the appraisal form to record unsatisfactory performance together with the notes of action to be taken, both by the individual and by management, to remedy these deficiencies. See Case Study 6.4. (Many organisations now choose to have separate capability procedures to cover this eventuality – see Chapter 8 for more guidance on this.)

Equal pay

Men and women are entitled to equal treatment in respect of pay and conditions of employment. A person who wishes to bring a claim that they are not being paid equally must show that, on the face of it, they are being paid less than a person of the opposite gender doing the same work. The employer is then required to give a non-discriminatory reason for the difference in pay. Proactive employers are wise to consider carrying out equal pay audits which examine all aspects of their reward policies and practices with a view to eradicating bias. For instance, the basis upon which managers have reached decisions on the awarding of contingent pay to their teams would be closely scrutinised. (See Case Study 6.4.)

CASE STUDY 6.4

This is exactly what happened in one City-based securities organisation. The manager was then surprised to receive a grievance claim and equal pay questionnaire (subsequently abolished in April 2014) from his female member of staff. She had taken exception to the fact that her annual bonus, supposedly based on individual performance measures, was considerably lower than that received by her male colleagues.

Although there were grounds for arguing that her performance was inferior in terms of outcomes, the legal advice was that this was not a claim that could be defended because of:

- the complete lack of objectivity in awarding bonuses throughout the organisation

- the fact that no action, formal or informal, had been taken to notify the employee that her performance was unacceptable and plan a course of corrective action
- the disparity between her performance appraisal rating and the level of bonus paid.

The manager learned his lesson the hard way as protracted negotiations then took place, and a settlement agreement (a legal agreement that can be entered into when a member of staff leaves employment in certain circumstances) was the eventual outcome. The organisation also realised that a more open and transparent approach to rewarding staff was required in the future. They decided to carry out an equal pay audit.

In our experience, managers are often loath to tackle poor performance. They turn a blind eye when substandard work is produced by a team member and do not communicate their discontent. Although the appraisal process should not be the starting point for tackling poor performance issues, it does provide an opportunity to discuss examples of where an individual's performance must be improved. For some managers, however, there may be a temptation to duck the issue entirely and, for example, rate the employee concerned as 'good'.

This area is a complex one, but the Acas advisory handbook, 'Discipline and Grievances at Work' provides excellent guidance on how to handle problems concerning poor performance; it is essential reading in this area.

We next consider the role of HR practitioners in designing, administering, maintaining and evaluating performance appraisal within their organisations.

6.9 THE ROLE OF HR PRACTITIONERS

HR practitioners adopt a multifaceted role in the area of performance appraisal and within the wider remit of performance management in their organisations. Those of you in generalist roles are likely to get involved, with varying degrees of support from more senior and experienced staff or even outside consultants, in a number of the following stages:

- identifying the need for a new or revised scheme
- designing the scheme
- implementing and communicating the scheme
- designing and organising training for appraisers and appraisees
- administering the scheme
- monitoring the scheme
- maintaining the scheme (that is, is it working efficiently?)
- evaluating the scheme (that is, is it working effectively and does it meet its objectives?).

You will thus carry out all or some of the following roles (or possibly assist outside consultants in undertaking their roles).

6.9.1 A RESEARCH ROLE

This covers finding out about current thinking and good practice in performance management, the various types of scheme in other organisations, their purposes and links to the achievement of business objectives, and their effectiveness, and so on. (See 6.6.4 'The Components of Performance Appraisal Schemes'.)

6.9.2 A CREATIVE ROLE

The aim here is to design a scheme that is tailored to your organisational circumstances and culture and the needs of your employees.

6.9.3 AN INFLUENCING ROLE

The purpose of this role is to sell the benefits of the scheme to senior managers, to the line managers who will be operating it, and to each and every employee who will be appraised.

6.9.4 A TRAINING ROLE

This may cover the design, organisation and delivery of training for both appraisers and appraisees in relation to their familiarisation with the scheme and the skills of appraisal interviewing.

6.9.5 AN ADMINISTRATIVE ROLE

This involves implementing the scheme, communicating with all those affected at each stage, ensuring that all the paperwork flows through the system according to the requisite timescales and that action points are followed up.

6.9.6 AN ADVISORY ROLE

Advice has to be given to managers regarding, for example, giving feedback or developmental opportunities for their staff.

6.9.7 A MONITORING ROLE

You need to oversee consistency in applying standards, allocating rewards and ensuring that appeals are handled fairly and constructively.

6.9.8 MAINTENANCE AND EVALUATION ROLES

These ensure that the scheme continues to enjoy a high priority and that feedback on the success of the scheme (in reaching its objectives) is acted upon in amending, updating and enhancing it.

6.9.9 AN APPRAISAL ROLE

This is both as an appraiser for your own staff and as an appraisee in your own right. Further, if your organisation operates a 360-degree appraisal scheme, you may be involved as the neutral third party to provide feedback for a number of employees on the collated information provided by all the stakeholders involved in the process. (See Figure 6.2)

6.10 INTERVIEWING SKILLS

Chapter 5 provides general guidance on interviewing techniques and skills. The majority of these are also applicable in an appraisal situation, although the purposes of appraisal interviews are of course different from those of selection interviews. Here we are concentrating on the skills necessary to be an effective appraiser.

We tackle appraiser skills by referring to the 'dos and don'ts' of appraisal interviewing: see Table 6.6.

Table 6.6 Appraisal interviewing – the appraiser

	Do	**Don't**
Before	<ul><li>give the appraisee notice of the meeting and any preparation necessary</li><li>book a suitable venue (checking whether any particular arrangements need to be made for appraisees who have a disability)</li><li>allow sufficient time</li><li>read the job description</li><li>identify suitable competencies if you intend to use these as the basis for discussion, and provide the appraisee with details of the competencies</li></ul>	<ul><li>wait for the formal appraisal interview to tackle performance issues (good or bad)</li><li>be swayed by the 'halo or horns' effect (that is, when one feature exhibited by the appraisee governs your perception of his or her overall abilities. An example of the 'halo' effect would be a belief that because an employee has a business studies degree she is</li></ul>

	Do	Don't
	• review past appraisals and achievement of objectives • review performance over the whole period • check on development opportunities • collect facts and examples, perhaps using any chosen competencies as a framework • reflect on what you are trying to achieve • consider future objectives • plan the agenda	highly numerate. On the other hand, the 'horns' effect would apply when you assume that an employee who is persistently untidy lacks commitment and is unproductive. The beliefs may be correct but need to be verified by more objective methods) • be overly influenced in your assessment by recent events
During	• seek to establish rapport • state the purpose and structure of the interview • check whether the appraisee wishes to add any other relevant items to the agenda • invite the appraisee's views on his or her own performance • keep notes • praise strengths and discuss areas for improvement • listen actively and maintain eye contact • ask open and probing questions • jointly seek solutions • invite the appraisee to summarise first • agree an action plan and future objectives • end on a positive note	• be afraid to tackle difficult issues • be bullied • be afraid to use silence • concentrate on weaknesses at the expense of strengths • concentrate on personality issues at the expense of results • make assumptions – for example about ambitions • argue • give vague responses to questions • make false promises • impose future objectives
After	• complete and return paperwork and ensure that the appraisee and other authorised parties receive copies of the form • ensure follow-up to action points • carry out regular reviews • hold frequent discussions with regard to progress	• file the papers and give the matter no more thought until the next review!

? REFLECTIVE ACTIVITY 6.6

If you are inexperienced in appraisal interviewing – either as an appraiser or as an appraisee – set up a role-play with a likeminded individual so that you can both practise and receive feedback on your skills in appraisal interview situations. (See Table 6.4, the Tips for receiving feedback box, and Table 6.6 for guidance.)

6.11 SUMMARY

In order to achieve the learning objectives of this chapter we have sought to distinguish between the broad concept of performance management and the part played by performance appraisal within this framework. We have also explored the importance of the link between individual objectives and business goals, and have concluded that a lack of integration is a major stumbling block towards truly effective performance management for many organisations.

Performance appraisal has been examined in detail – its purposes, motivational effect and trends. The differing components of performance appraisal schemes have been highlighted, such as the setting of objectives, and the major benefits and good-practice issues, including those concerning feedback, have been detailed.

The legal considerations, the role of HR practitioners and the skills necessary to be an effective appraiser have been identified.

You will by now be familiar with the terms used and will be able to relate your learning to the scheme or schemes with which you are familiar. References and further reading are provided below, and you are encouraged to complete some, if not all, of the Reflective Activities in this chapter in order to reinforce and apply your learning.

EXPLORE FURTHER

References and further reading

ACAS (2014) *How to Manage Performance Booklet*. Leicester: Advisory, Conciliation and Arbitration Service.

ACAS (2015) *Discipline and Grievances at Work, The Acas Guide*. Leicester: Advisory, Conciliation and Arbitration Service.

ARMSTRONG, M. (2012) *Armstrong's Handbook of Reward Management Practice: Improving performance through reward*. 4th edition. London: Kogan Page.

ARMSTRONG, M. (2014) *Armstrong's Handbook of Performance Management: An Evidence-Based Guide to Delivering High Performance*. 5th edition. London: Kogan Page.

ARMSTRONG, M. and BARON, A. (2004) *Managing Performance: Performance management in action*. London: CIPD.

CIPD (2014) *Employee Outlook*. London: CIPD.

CIPD (2015) *Employee Outlook Survey*. London: CIPD.

CIPD (2009) *Performance Management in Action: Current trends and practice*. London: CIPD.

FARNDALE, E., HOPE HAILEY, V., KELLIHER, C. and VAN VELDHOVEN, M. (2011) *A Study of the Link Between Performance Management and Employee Engagement in Western Multinational Corporations operating across India and China*. Cass Business School, Tilburg University and Cranfield University.

HUTCHINSON, S. (2013) *Performance Management Theory and Practice*. London: CIPD.

NABAUM, A., BARRY, L., GARR, S. and LIAKOPOULOS, A. (2014) *Performance Management is Broken*. Available online at: dupress.com/articles/hc-trends-2014-performance-management

WHIDDETT, S. and HOLLYFORDE, S. (2003) *A Practical Guide to Competencies*. London: CIPD.

WRIGHT, A. (2004) *Reward Management in Context*. London: CIPD.

See also survey reports on the CIPD website: www.cipd.co.uk/hr-resources/survey-reports

See also research reports on the CIPD website: www.cipd.co.uk/hr-resources/research

See also podcasts on the CIPD website: www.cipd.co.uk/hr-resources/podcasts:

- (2012) *Implementing Effective Performance Management*. Podcast 72.

See also factsheets on the CIPD website: www.cipd.co.uk/hr-resources/factsheets:

- Competence and Competency Frameworks (2012)
- Feedback – 360-degree (2012)
- Performance Appraisal (2012)
- Performance Management: An Overview (2012)
- Performance-related Pay (2012)

REFLECTIVE ACTIVITIES FEEDBACK

Reflective Activity 6.4

What 'sins' did the manager commit?

It's difficult to find anything that this nursery owner did get right, so you will probably have highlighted the facts below:

- She didn't give regular constructive feedback to the manager.
- The owner ignored the issues about the use of mobile phones and smoking breaks.
- The feedback given about the paperwork was not precise and did not encourage discussion.
- The feedback given was not a two-way dialogue, the owner *told* the manager what she'd done wrong.
- No specific examples of the concerns were given.
- The owner focused on generalised personality traits rather than specific behaviours.
- There was no agreement about what need to be changed/improved and how.

How should she have tackled this situation?

She should have:

- held regular one-to-one discussions with the manager during which regular constructive feedback could have been discussed
- related what she observed – that is, that it appeared staff were using their mobile phones whilst on duty and taking too many smoking breaks
- been specific about what paperwork was a concern, reinforced the importance of this and sought explanation about it
- discussed with the manager what changes and improvement were necessary and set a timescale
- jointly agreed with her a plan of action
- monitored and followed up on that plan of action.

CHAPTER 7

Reward

LEARNING OUTCOMES

After reading this chapter you will:

- understand that reward is a broader concept than just pay and includes a range of both financial and non-financial features
- appreciate the differences between different pay systems and pay structures and be able to identify the pros and cons of different approaches
- be able to make clear links between reward and other aspects of managing people at work
- understand the law as it relates to reward and have a clear appreciation of equal pay
- appreciate the variety of pension schemes available and the differences between them.

7.1 INTRODUCTION

Reward is a broad concept and one in which there has been a lot of change in recent years.

Traditionally, reward is thought of as pay (including performance-related pay) and other contractual-type benefits, such as holidays, sick pay and pensions, the aim of these being to attract, motivate and retain employees. The purpose of each element of reward was thought to be clear – for example, performance-related pay (PRP) was considered to be about motivating people. More recently, these very clear distinctions about purpose – and, in fact, the definition of what elements are considered to make up reward – have changed.

For very many people reward is one of the most important aspects of working life: it is certainly one in which many HR practitioners will be involved. In this chapter we aim to provide an overview of reward, considering what is meant by the term 'reward', giving an introduction to different reward systems and structures, and looking at the links between reward, motivation, and performance management. We then look at some of the legal issues connected with reward, and consider how pay decisions are made and the different roles that HR practitioners can play in reward.

The reward system in an organisation is about rewarding people fairly and consistently for their individual contribution and value to the organisation and for their skill and performance. A good reward system will ensure that individual employees' efforts are directed to those activities that will help the organisation to achieve its goals and objectives. Reward clearly has an ethical dimension – think of the introduction of the national minimum wage and national living wage, or the question of bonuses in the banking sector and how that did or did not contribute to inappropriate risk-taking in that sector. It can be a very sensitive subject – the way in which reward is handled can have a big impact on morale, motivation and productivity.

A useful definition of reward is provided by Michael Armstrong (2002, p4):

a reward system consists of financial rewards (fixed and variable pay) and employee benefits, which together comprise total remuneration. The system also incorporates non-financial rewards (recognition, praise, achievement, responsibility and personal growth) and, in many cases, performance management processes. The combination of financial rewards, employee benefits, and non-financial compensation comprises the total reward system.

This introduces the concept of a 'total reward package', which many organisations consider when thinking about their reward policy and strategy, and shows a broader, more inclusive approach to reward than that indicated by the more traditional approach outlined above. In effect, it means the combination of financial and non-financial rewards available to employees, and covers a much wider range of issues than just pay and other contractual-type benefits such as holidays and pensions.

7.2 WHAT DO WE MEAN BY 'REWARD'?

As noted above, reward is a broad concept covering both pay and non-pay items. The increasing number of organisations taking a total reward approach reflects a growing evidence base and understanding that performance, productivity and motivation are influenced by a much wider range of factors than those addressed in the past. Looking at total reward requires consideration of such elements as basic pay, any contingent pay (that is, any element of pay based on individual or team factors such as performance, results, skill, competence, and so on), non-pay benefits and wider non-financial rewards, such as the work environment, job security, company culture, employee recognition practices, opportunities for personal development and growth, and factors intrinsic to the job. A survey of 455 employers conducted by the CIPD in 2012 showed that around one-fifth of employers had adopted such a total rewards approach, while a further 22% were planning on taking that approach. Table 7.1 features the most commonly used individual performance-related schemes and non-pay benefits in the survey.

Table 7.1 Commonly used performance-related schemes and non-pay benefits

Performance-related schemes	Non-pay benefits
• Individual bonuses • Merit pay rises • Combination • Sales commission • Individual non-monetary recognition awards • Other individual-based cash incentives	• Flexible/homeworking • Annual leave in excess of statutory minimum • Training and development • Childcare vouchers • Free tea/coffee/cold drinks • Christmas party/lunch • On-site car parking

Source: CIPD (2012) 'Reward Management', survey report

The latest Annual Reward Survey 2014–15 shows little has changed in this respect.

The place of reward in the employment relationship is too important to be left to chance. It is advisable for organisations to adopt a managed approach to reward, which, if done well, will ensure:

- that people are rewarded in line with what the organisation wants to pay for
- that rewards are linked to business objectives
- that messages about organisation culture, values and desired behaviours can be communicated, and desired outcomes rewarded

- the development of a performance culture
- that the right people with the right skills are attracted and retained
- that employees are motivated and engaged
- the development of a positive employment relationship and psychological contract (see Chapter 8).

> **?   REFLECTIVE ACTIVITY 7.1**
>
> Consider your own organisation. How is reward dealt with? Does your organisation take a total reward package view or not? Is there a reward strategy or policy? What elements currently make up the total reward package? What information is collected about how successful these elements are in attracting, retaining and motivating employees? What ethical considerations are taken into account in determining pay levels? Discuss your thoughts with one of your learning sources.

Clearly, reward is about far more than just pay. However, pay is a critical component of reward. In the next section we go on to consider the different ways in which pay is organised through a consideration of pay systems and structures.

7.3 PAY SYSTEMS AND STRUCTURES

There are many different types of pay system and structure in place in different organisations; which ones are used will depend very much on the organisational context, size, and sector. 'Pay systems' tends to refer to the way in which individual employees are rewarded for their contribution, whereas 'pay structures' refers to the way in which different levels or groupings of pay are organised linking related jobs and providing a framework for making payments.

7.3.1 PAY SYSTEMS

There are two main categories of pay system: basic rate schemes and variable or incentive schemes. The systems in use in some organisations include a combination of the two, whereas in other organisations only one of these systems is used. In basic rate schemes the pay does not vary according to achievement or performance, whereas in variable or incentive schemes, either all or part of the pay of an individual will vary depending on things such as team or individual performance, company profits, level of skill or competence. Some of the most commonly used incentive schemes are listed in Table 7.1. Within public sector organisations basic pay schemes are more common, whereas incentive schemes are found more frequently in the private sector.

Basic rate systems

Here, an employee has a fixed rate of basic pay set in reference to a particular time period – for example, per hour, per week or per year. There may be other payments in addition to basic pay, such as overtime or additional pay for working shifts or nights, for example, but the basic pay rate will not vary according to individual contribution or performance.

A basic pay system can be illustrated by looking at the example of a nurse working in the NHS. An individual nurse's job is allocated to a pay band with a number of pay points by undertaking job evaluation. Each pay band attracts a basic annual salary on an incremental scale. Individual nurses progress up the pay band and receive an incremental increase in their basic salary each year until they reach the top of their pay band. In addition, they may also receive an annual cost-of-living pay increase, negotiated nationally, to reflect increases in inflation. (Although in recent years, as part of work to reduce the national deficit, we have seen these cost-of-living payments in the public sector removed or reduced.) All nurses on the same pay band are treated in the same way and any differences in their effort or performance are not reflected in their basic pay. Although there is no performance or contingent pay, nurses can add to their basic pay in a number of ways:

- those working in the London area will receive a high-cost area supplement
- those who are on call outside their normal working hours will receive an additional percentage of their basic pay depending on the frequency of the on-call commitment
- those who work additional hours over and above full-time hours may be eligible for overtime pay
- those who work nights, weekends or on bank holidays will receive percentage enhancements to basic pay for the 'unsocial hours' element

Basic rate systems apply to many employees in the UK and are used in a significant number of different organisations. There are both pros and cons of using a basic rate system.

? REFLECTIVE ACTIVITY 7.2

Think about the pros and cons of a basic rate pay system. Make a list of what you think the pros and cons are.

Compare your response to the feedback provided at the end of this chapter.

Basic rate schemes relate to the job rather than the individual doing the job and are frequently determined using reference to the 'going rate' for that type of job in that locality, sometimes supported by job evaluation. Further information on job evaluation can be found in Chapter 4.

Variable or incentive pay systems

Here an employee's pay – or, more usually, part of their pay – will vary depending on his or her individual performance, the performance of the team they are in, or the whole company's performance. The most common types of scheme relate to individual performance and apply only to part of the employee's wage or salary. Examples of variable or incentive pay systems include sales commission, appraisal-/performance-related pay, payment by results (for instance, piecework) and skills-based pay. Again, there are both pros and cons associated with variable or incentive pay systems.

A variable-rate pay system can be illustrated by looking at the example of a financial adviser. Posts such as these may be found in either large financial institutions, such as banks, or in smaller companies dedicated to providing financial advice. The financial adviser will generally receive a basic salary, expressed as a 'per annum' figure, from the company they work for. In smaller companies, any increases in the basic salary tend to be negotiated on an individual basis, whereas in the larger companies, financial advisers may get an annual salary increase in line with the national average earnings index. In addition, financial advisers earn income for their companies by providing advice and selling financial products to customers. If an individual financial adviser achieves a predetermined level of income earned over a given time period (each month/quarter/year, for example), he or she will receive a bonus, which is usually a percentage of the amount of income earned. Thus, the more income that individuals earn for their company, the higher the level of bonus they will receive. Such bonuses may be paid to each individual on a monthly, quarterly or annual basis. In addition to the basic salary and the performance-related bonus, the financial adviser will often also receive other benefits, such as a company car or car allowance.

> **? REFLECTIVE ACTIVITY 7.3**
>
> Think about the pros and cons of a variable rate system. Make a list of what you consider the advantages and disadvantages are.
>
> Compare your response to the feedback provided at the end of this chapter.

Many organisations use a combination of both types of pay system in order to increase the degree of flexibility they have to respond to changing circumstances. In this way a lot of employees will have both a basic pay rate and some element of variable pay (such as a bonus scheme).

7.3.2 PAY STRUCTURES

Pay structures provide a framework for defining different levels of pay for jobs or groups of jobs. This is often done in relation to the external job market, the internal value placed on various types of jobs and how different jobs relate to and compare with one another. Employees and their individual competence, experience and standards of performance should fit into, and be valued by, the structure.

In smaller organisations (fewer than 200 people) formal pay structures may not exist, but they are generally found in larger organisations across all sectors. Pay structures often consist of grades or pay bands, individual jobs being allocated to a particular grade/band depending on the responsibilities of the job. The purpose of using pay structures is:

- to create a framework for pay that is transparent and easily understood
- to make sure that payment reflects what the organisation is trying to achieve
- to help ensure fairness and lawfulness – particularly in relation to equal pay.

Pay structures can be multiple, so that there are different pay structures for different categories of workers within one organisation (for example, one structure for manual workers and a different one for non-manual workers), or, increasingly, single structures where the same structure applies to all employees. Many larger organisations and public sector bodies, such as local authorities, have implemented 'single-status' schemes that are equally applicable to all employees. However, even where single status has been introduced, you will still often see separate arrangements for senior executives.

The different types of pay structures in use include:

- graded structures
- broadbanding
- spot salaries/individual pay rates
- job families
- pay spines

We shall now look at each of these in turn.

Graded structures

These structures involve a sequence of job grades in which the pay for each grade is identified and jobs of equivalent value are placed in each of these grades. Such grading structures can be narrow-graded, usually involving ten or more grades, or broad-graded, usually involving between six and nine grades. Narrow-graded structures typically have either narrow pay ranges or a single salary point, whereas broad-graded structures have a single salary point or slightly wider pay ranges – although progression through these wider pay ranges is sometimes controlled so that not everyone in the grade can reach the top of the pay range. In both graded structures, progression through the pay range is generally linked to performance, competence or length of service. With graded structures, employees can often reach the top of the pay range quite quickly, which can lead to pressure for upgrading or grade drift. The 2014–15 CIPD survey on reward showed that 32% of organisations use narrow-grading structures – a slight increase from the 29% found in the 2012 survey.

Broadbanding

This involves the use of a smaller number of pay bands or grades than in traditional graded structures – typically, four or five pay bands. Within these bands pay can be managed more flexibly: they can be more responsive to things such as changes in market rates for particular jobs. The pay range within a broad band will necessarily be quite wide and the band can sometimes incorporate a number of different grades. The effect of broadbanding is to flatten the pay and grade hierarchy. Because of the wide pay ranges associated with broad bands, some organisations have introduced 'zones' or 'bars' so that not all employees in a particular band can expect to move right through the band to the top. The 2014–15 CIPD survey on reward showed that 26% of organisations use broadbanding.

Spot salaries/individual pay rates

This involves the setting of one fixed rate of pay for one job, which allows for no progression in basic pay, although there will often be incentive payments (for example, bonuses) in addition to the spot salary basic pay rate. In practice, spot rates might be amended from time to time in line with such things as inflation or changes in the job market for a particular type of job. Spot rates are seen most often in relation to low-skill/ low-pay occupations, perhaps where the minimum wage is used as the spot rate, and at the opposite end of the job spectrum in executive pay, where the total reward package might be made up of a spot rate salary and a range of other benefits. The 2014–15 CIPD survey showed this type of structure as the most popular, with 50% of respondent organisations using spot salaries or individual rates.

Job families

In this structure, similar types of jobs (for example sales, finance, and so on) are grouped together and have a pay structure with a number of different levels (similar to a graded structure). The basic skills and knowledge required for jobs within the family are the same but there are different levels of responsibility that attach to individual jobs. Such a structure can be appropriate when there are distinct job markets for certain types of jobs (for example, IT specialists). This makes it easier for the organisation to respond to market forces in the labour market. For example, it may be necessary to pay a higher salary to attract scarce skills than might have to be paid for an equivalent level of skill in another job family. Progression within a level in a job family is often linked to contribution or competence. The 2014–15 CIPD survey showed 29% of organisations using this approach.

Pay spines

This structure exists where a pay spine with a wide range covers all jobs from the lowest to the highest paid. Different grades or pay bands are often superimposed over the pay spine, in effect meaning that no one moves from the bottom to the top of the whole spine. Progression within a pay spine is frequently linked to length of service. Pay spines allow greater certainty and control over pay than some of the other structures, and are common in the public sector. The 2014–15 CIPD survey showed 31% of organisations using this approach.

7.3.3 FLEXIBLE BENEFITS

In some organisations, regardless of the type of pay system or structure used, there is flexibility in the total reward package that an individual can receive. In flexible systems employees can exchange certain elements for others – for example, exchanging an amount of pay in return for childcare vouchers. In this way reward packages can be tailored and individualised to suit the circumstances of the employee. Common considerations for employees in opting for flexibility and exchanging benefits are personal circumstances (for example, in the case of childcare vouchers) and the tax implications (for example, in the case of company cars). This is sometimes referred to as the 'cafeteria system', by analogy, with an employee being able to choose the elements of a meal according to their own preferences. Common flexible benefits are:

- buying and selling holidays
- childcare vouchers
- advances and loans
- company cars
- mileage expenses
- company shares
- private health schemes
- medical insurance
- gym membership.

? REFLECTIVE ACTIVITY 7.4

Consider what sort of issues must be thought about when an organisation is considering introducing flexible benefits. Compare your response to the feedback given at the end of this chapter.

7.4 LINKING PAY WITH PERFORMANCE

Performance is not always linked to pay – far from it. Indeed, there is an ongoing debate about how effective pay is as a motivator of performance. The CIPD Reward Management Survey 2014–15 shows a continuing decline in the use of performance-related reward, with only 49% of organisations using it compared with 65% in 2012. However, if pay is linked with performance, then – as seen in Chapter 6 – for a performance management scheme (PMS) to be successful, each and every aspect of it must be clearly linked and work towards the overall aim of continually improving business performance. This can be achieved only through your employees, who will expect to be rewarded for their loyalty, hard work and contribution both extrinsically (factors generated by others) via promotions, salary, fringe benefits, bonuses, stock options, and so on, and intrinsically (self-generated factors) via feelings of achievement, responsibility, personal growth, competence, and so on. The satisfactory integration of reward into the PMS is undoubtedly a difficult thing to achieve – not least because the factors that motivate employees vary from individual to individual. Further, for each individual, motivating factors fluctuate in their importance according to the changing circumstances of their lives – for example, at the start of an individual's working life the level of pay might be the most important factor, whereas for someone with childcare responsibilities work–life balance might be the most important factor. There is even disagreement about whether some extrinsic rewards have any motivational impact at all, but here we shall proceed on the assumption that they do have a short-term effect in increasing effort and, therefore, productivity.

7.4.1 DEFINITIONS

While base pay most often relates to the job itself – for example, the responsibilities included in a job as determined by job evaluation – performance pay relates most frequently to factors to do with the individual: it is contingent on matters such as individual performance, skill, competence and contribution. In some instances performance pay may be based on other variable factors such as how the team or company as a whole are doing; however, it is most frequently related to the individual factors mentioned here.

7.4.2 THE LINK TO MOTIVATION

In linking pay to performance, we are concerned with the types of reward system available to organisations to encourage their employees to make worthwhile contributions towards the achievement of business goals. For reward systems to act as real incentives to employees, they must be:

- timely in relation to when the reward is paid compared with the effort/performance being rewarded
- objective and fair
- sufficiently valuable to the employees in receipt of them for the effort made
- simple, so as to be easily understood by employees, while still being seen as fair.

Thus rewards such as salaries, fixed hourly rates and profit-sharing do not satisfy all of the above requirements. However, many contingent reward schemes are designed to succeed on all four counts. For instance, merit pay schemes may provide salary or wage increases in recognition of excellent job performance during the review period, and incentive or bonus schemes may provide payments in addition to base salary or wages related to the satisfactory completion of a project or the achievement of an individual or group target.

But PRP, for example, is not without its problems, mainly because of the difficulties encountered in trying to measure individual or team performance objectively and in establishing the most appropriate pay-out levels. For instance, working hard all year to be eligible for a maximum merit award of 4% would probably be less motivating than seeking to achieve, say, three specific targets and a bonus payment of 10% to 20%. With careful thought, contingent reward can be introduced as an effective strategic tool linked to business needs, but it should not be relied upon as the sole motivator for employees.

? REFLECTIVE ACTIVITY 7.5

Think about the key components of your organisation's reward system – for example, hourly rates of pay, incremental rises, shift premiums, competence-related pay, PRP, recognition schemes.

List three financial and three non-financial rewards that you feel help to motivate individuals to improve their performance.

Compare your response to the feedback provided at the end of this chapter.

PRP schemes are not the only motivators and, as we have seen, it is debatable whether they are motivators at all in some instances. There is a broad range of other financial and non-financial rewards at the disposal of employers when they are seeking to motivate staff and, generally, a mix of both is to be recommended.

We shall now consider non-pay rewards.

7.5 NON-PAY REWARDS

We have addressed the topic of a total reward package above and have outlined a variety of pay systems and structures. To ensure a full consideration of reward requires us to look at non-pay rewards. 'Non-pay rewards' usually refers to those items that are not pay or benefits but still have a role to play in recruiting, retaining and motivating employees and generating loyalty and commitment. Such forms of reward are often intrinsic to the job itself and reward employees by giving them opportunities for growth and development and by recognising contribution. The main non-pay rewards include:

- achievement
- recognition
- responsibility/autonomy
- influence
- personal growth.

There is a significant amount of agreement that non-pay rewards are often the most important to individual employees, and this is particularly true in the public sector. An Audit Commission study of public sector workers looked at the factors influencing individuals' decisions to join, remain in or leave a public sector organisation. The five most common reasons for joining a public sector organisation were:

- making a positive difference
- working with people
- a career people had always wanted to do
- interesting work
- career progression.

Pay was not indicated as an important factor in decisions to take public sector jobs, although it was important to employees in making a decision to stay in or leave a job.

From this we can see the importance of the non-pay aspects of the reward package, and the fact that different rewards are important not only to different people but also to the same people at different points in their life/career.

What we have outlined above in relation to both pay and benefits and non-pay rewards shows just what a complex area reward is, individual choice and differing views about what is important at different life stages just adding to this complexity. Case Study 7.1 gives a picture of this in one public sector organisation.

CASE STUDY 7.1

A survey was carried out in an NHS trust looking at how important different benefits were to employees, and how satisfied employees were with these benefits. A range of 15 different benefits which existed within the trust were included in the survey. The most important benefits to employees were support from managers and open and honest communication. Opportunities for career development and for training came sixth and seventh respectively, while having a competitive salary was ranked as the ninth most important benefit, and a good pension scheme was ranked as tenth. When reporting how satisfied these employees were with these benefits, the pension scheme was ranked as the benefit employees were most satisfied with, training and career development opportunities came fourth and tenth respectively, support from managers came eighth, open and honest communication came twelfth, while salary came thirteenth.

Employees were also given the opportunity to respond to an open question about what additional benefits they would like to see introduced. The largest percentage of comments (24%) was made about pay; for example:

● Benefits and services can be nice, but proper pay and suitable working conditions are what is important.
● Increasing pay to recognise the growing problems for lower-paid staff dealing with the rising cost of living. We are losing bright young staff in whom we have invested time and money who are forced to leave to (a) work in agencies or (b) move to jobs in cheaper areas of the UK.

These comments were made despite 'having a competitive salary' being relatively far down the list of which benefits were important.

This shows the complexity, for organisations, in understanding what to include in their benefits package and also delivering on what matters to their employees.

We will now move on to consider the law as it applies to reward.

7.6 THE LEGAL ASPECTS OF PAYING EMPLOYEES

7.6.1 NATIONAL LIVING WAGE/NATIONAL MINIMUM WAGE

The national living wage (NLW) became law in April 2016. It applies to workers aged 25 and over. For staff under the age of 25 the national minimum wage (NMW) will continue to apply.

At the time of writing the NLW was still to be introduced and was before Parliament in the form of The National Minimum Wage (Amendment) Regulations 2016. Many of the arrangements in the current Minimum Wage Act, apart from the age at which the new NLW applies and the rate, will continue to apply. The National Minimum Wage Act provides a minimum wage for all workers, including employees, many apprentices, employees of subcontractors, agency staff and homeworkers.

Only a few workers are excluded, and these include those who are genuinely self-employed, certain students and trainees on particular government-funded training schemes. Because the exact categories of who is included and who is not change from time to time, it is important to check with authoritative sources such as the Department for Business, Innovation and Skills (BIS) website.

In many cases it will be simple for you to assess whether your workers are being paid the NLW/NMW, but in some instances you will need to check carefully to see that you are complying with a minimum wage. Circumstances such as piecework, commission-only payments, on-call or stand-by elements, or project work may demand careful attention because the rules and calculations of pay and hours differ depending on the type of work. HMRC make random checks from time to time and small employers, particularly, do get caught out.

Individuals also have the right to apply to a court or tribunal for non-payment of the NMW. So you must keep sufficient records to show that you are paying your workers this minimum wage for all the activities they are engaged in on your behalf. There are a number of criminal offences under the Act, including refusing to pay the NMW – so be careful!

CASE STUDY 7.2

In advance of the introduction of the NLW, a local council decided to pay the living wage to all of its employees who were earning below that level. They said they were using the rate set by the Centre for Research in Social Policy because that is set at a level considered to be the basic cost of living to provide a minimum income standard.

A local councillor was quoted as saying, 'We already paid more than the national minimum wage, but we believe it is only right that our staff, who work extremely hard to provide excellent services, receive at least a living wage.'

Use of the words 'only right' indicates that some value judgements have been used in taking this action – an ethical consideration on the part of that council.

7.6.2 MATERNITY AND PATERNITY, STATUTORY SICK AND REDUNDANCY PAY

Here, minimum rates are determined by legislation. The rates themselves are reviewed annually. Each also has qualifying conditions and periods for which payments are due. These change from time to time as new legislation is enacted. See Chapter 3 for more details.

7.6.3 A WEEK'S PAY

For the purpose of some statutory requirements, such as notice pay and redundancy pay, there are precise rules for calculating a week's pay. While broadly this is an employee's normal pay for their normal hours, without overtime, it is important to follow the rules that are current at the time. Consult the BIS website. Incidentally, for redundancy purposes there is a maximum amount, reviewed annually.

7.6.4 THE RIGHT TO BE PAID

An employee must be paid a wage per hour, a salary per annum, or some variation (per week, for example). Piecework – once common in some UK industries – must be related back to an hourly rate to demonstrate that it complies with the NLW/NMW. Although there is no longer the right to be paid in cash – as applied many years ago – the minimum payment (at least) must be in monetary value: it cannot, for example, be made up of the company's products. The right to be paid in currency is very important and is enshrined in the contract of employment.

An employee's remuneration must be stated in writing in the written particulars, as we have seen. The statement of written particulars is valuable to an employee because it prevents the employer from making unilateral changes to the amount an employee is paid.

Pay is part of the contract and it cannot be unilaterally varied. That means an employer cannot reduce an employee's pay without the employee's agreement. To do so would be a breach of the contract. It would give the employee the right to claim constructive dismissal and very likely it would be found to be unfair (but see below).

7.6.5 RIGHTS ON THE TRANSFER OF AN EMPLOYEE'S EMPLOYER

In some sectors employees transfer from employer to employer quite frequently. For example, a cleaner may work for a school on a full-time basis. The school then contracts the work to a cleaning company and the cleaner has the right to 'follow the work' and become an employee of the cleaning company. Later on, the school becomes dissatisfied with the cleaning company and so engages another. Once again the employee follows the work and becomes an employee of the new company. These are transfers under the Transfer of Undertakings (Protection of Employment) Regulations 2006 (TUPE).

The definition of a transfer of an undertaking is quite technical and the interpretation has changed from time to time under case law. The latest changes to the legislation about transfers occurred in 2014 – a useful summary of the changes is available from Acas (see References and Further Reading at the end of this chapter). There are many technical aspects concerned with transfers, such as the need for consultation. Because it is a complex area, we should let others decide whether the legislation applies in any particular case – or if you need to decide, take advice. For this reason we have not examined the concept in the legal background to HR. But when it comes to pay, there are important considerations that you must not ignore.

Employees' pay and terms and conditions are protected after a relevant transfer. They can be improved by the new employer but no aspect can be reduced – even if there is compensation provided elsewhere. Furthermore, employees lose the right to agree on any detrimental change to their pay whatsoever. This protection to terms and conditions applies to most employees indefinitely. Collective agreements, however, may be renegotiated after 12 months. Even here though, any new collective agreement must not, on balance, disadvantage the employees affected.

In the above sections we have looked at legislative protection for an employee's pay. There are other areas where an employee's pay can, nevertheless, still come under threat.

7.6.6 SHORT-TIME WORKING

Employers can put employees on 'short time' – that is, they can reduce the hours that the employees work and reduce their pay accordingly. The right to put an employee on short-time working is sometimes put into the contract of employment (and documented in the written particulars) as a right to vary hours. Without this variation, short-time working would be likely to enable the employee to claim constructive dismissal and, again, this would very likely be unfair dismissal.

However, usually overtime hours can be cut or stopped altogether without breaching the contract of employment, and this is often a first step in periods of austerity.

7.6.7 LAY-OFFS

As with short-time working, the right to lay employees off (that is, tell them to go home or stay at home) without paying them is sometimes put into the contract of employment (and documented in the written particulars). Lay-offs or short-time working cannot continue indefinitely. After a few weeks employees may be able to insist that they are made redundant (and claim redundancy pay).

7.6.8 REDUCING PAY RATES

It is not unusual for employers in hard times to ask employees to take a pay cut. The prospect of a 10% cut is more attractive than a 100% cut! Employees often agree, especially if there is a reasonable hope of saving their employment by doing so. The important word here is 'agree'. Employers should not put employees under duress to obtain such agreement. Additionally, note that employees cannot agree to be paid less than the NLW/NMW and they may not be free to agree if their employment is protected by transfer from a previous employer, as we explained above.

7.6.9 AGREEING PAY REDUCTIONS

In some industries – particularly some manufacturing industries – lay-offs, short-time working and even short-term pay cuts are part of the culture. In those circumstances the employees' 'agreement' might be implied into the contract. If there have been such events in the past, you may be able to consider them as options in the future.

Collective agreements can also provide an avenue where these determine the employees' terms and conditions of employment. An agreement with the recognised trade union may therefore provide the opportunity for pay reductions to be agreed.

As we have said, employees may agree to any of these austere measures in order to protect their employment. If an overwhelming number of employees do agree, you may be able to impose the change on the remainder. If they leave and claim constructive dismissal, it is reasonably likely that such a dismissal will be held to be fair on the grounds of sound business reasons (that is, 'some other substantial reason'). It is good to be aware of this, but unless you are very experienced, it is wise, first, to take further advice on how to handle such situations.

7.6.10 UNLAWFUL DEDUCTIONS

There are a few purposes for which you can deduct money from an employee's wage or salary without their permission – tax and National Insurance (where due) being examples. But to make a deduction for other purposes – say, to deduct parking fines – you must have the employee's explicit permission to make the deduction *before the incident occurs* – not just before the deduction. If you do not have the permission, ask the employee to write you a cheque. Advance permission for this type of deduction and others, such as union dues, can be put into the written particulars (or a separate document), but these must be signed so that there is no question over the explicitness of the permission. If you deduct an amount in contravention of the employee's rights, you will have to pay the amount back (if the employee makes application to an employment tribunal) and it will no longer be lawful to obtain it in any other way.

As you will have seen, the law relating to pay can be quite complicated and is very detailed, so we would always advise you to seek further advice where in any doubt. Getting pay wrong is a serious problem.

7.7 EQUAL PAY LEGISLATION

Employers are obliged to pay men and women equally where they are doing the same (or equivalent) work. If the rates are different, the employer has to show there is a genuine reason that is not related to their gender. On the face of it this seems very simple, but if disputes arise, it does become extremely complicated. An aggrieved woman (or, in principle, a man) has to establish a comparator – that is, someone of the opposite gender who is in the same employment as they are.

Usually this is someone working at the same establishment as they are working in, but in some circumstances a person can select someone at a different establishment. The next question to arise is whether the work is equivalent, and this would generally require determination by a job evaluation scheme. The work could be of equivalent value even if it is different work – for example, enabling a cook to compare herself with a warehouseman.

The landmark case in equal pay was *Hayward v Cammell Laird Shipbuilders*. Ms Hayward was a canteen cook and she observed that she earned less than a warehouseman. She felt what she did was of equal value to her employer and so challenged this at the Liverpool industrial tribunal (the forerunner of employment tribunals). The tribunal found that she could compare her pay with another employee who was doing a job of equal value to the employer, irrespective of whether it was the same job. At the time (the 1980s) this caused a stir – could any woman compare her job with any job? Where would this end? Cammell Laird appealed. Accepting that the work was of equal value, they appealed on the grounds that when the overall package was taken into account Ms Hayward was treated as favourably as the men. However, while this was accepted by a higher court, the House of Lords (the highest court in the UK at that time) overruled the decision. They determined that Ms Hayward was entitled to equal pay without evaluation of the total package. Equal pay claims are now considered contract clause by contract clause.

If there is no job evaluation scheme, or if there is more than one, the employee has to compare herself with another and show that the work is of equal value, in effect carrying out a job evaluation exercise on her job and that of the comparator. For this purpose the tribunal may require a report from an independent specialist. As we have already seen, pay may be made up of many different components and it is not unusual for the woman's pay package to be made up differently from that of her male comparator. The law allows the woman to compare herself on every term in the contracts of employment. It is not the package as a whole that counts.

The employer has one major line of defence and that is to show that there is a genuine material factor to explain the reason for any difference in pay. Examples might be a different level of skills, qualifications and experience of the people being compared.

This is a complex and increasingly important area. In the first three months of 2015, 17% of employment tribunal claims were for unfair dismissal, 15% were unauthorised deductions from wages claims and 21% were equal pay claims. Because these claims are expensive to defend and, as we have seen, complicated, equal pay principles cannot be ignored.

In spite of the equal pay legislation, there is still what is known as a 'gender pay gap' in existence. The Annual Survey of Hours and Earnings – 2015 Provisional Results by the Office for National Statistics shows that for full-time employees this gap is 9.4%, whilst for full-time and part-time workers combined it is 19.2%.

7.7.1 EQUAL PAY CLAIMS

There are complex reasons why pay can be unequal. Market forces and historical trends are not necessarily sound as a defence, but are often a reality. There is a tendency for part-time work to be low-paid, especially where there is no full-time comparator (which would render the difference unlawful), and to attract women with families, rather than men. Breaks to bring up a family can interrupt a career and damage salary prospects as well as leading to the need to catch up with skills and experience in a rapidly changing world. Claims relating to equal pay are generally dealt with by an employment tribunal. There is non-statutory Acas guidance for employees to follow if they are considering making a claim (see References and Further Reading at the end of this chapter). Since October 2014, employers who lose an equal pay claim can be forced to conduct an equal pay audit and publish the results.

One of the most effective ways of establishing whether your organisation is providing equal pay is to undertake an equal pay audit. The Equality and Human Rights Commission (EHRC) recommends that every organisation should conduct such an audit. The purpose of conducting an audit is to:

- compare the pay of men and women doing equal work
- identify any gender pay gaps
- eliminate any such pay gaps that are based purely on gender.

The EHRC publishes a code of practice on equal pay and suggests a policy for employers. It also provides an equal pay toolkit to assist in creating an equal pay environment. See Table 7.2.

Table 7.2 An equal pay audit: the five-step process

STEP 1 Decide the scope of the audit and identify the data required	
STEP 2 Identify where protected groups are doing equal work: like work/work rated as equivalent, equal value	Check job evaluation
STEP 3 Collect pay data to identify gaps	No equal pay gaps Go to Step 6
STEP 4 Establish the cause of pay gaps and decide whether they are free from discrimination	
Pay gaps not free from discrimination	Pay gaps free from discrimination
STEP 5 Redevelop an equal pay action plan	

Source: www.equalityhumanrights.com/private-and-public-sector-guidance/employing-people/managing-workers/equal-pay/equal-pay-audit-toolkit

(The copyright and all other intellectual property rights to 'Equal Pay Audit – 5 Step Process and Flow Chart' are owned by, or licensed to, the Commission for Equality and Human Rights, known as the Equality and Human Rights Commission ('the EHRC'))

? REFLECTIVE ACTIVITY 7.6

Should sleeping dogs be left to lie?

Discuss in a group the pros and cons of initiating an equal pay code of practice and an equal pay audit in your organisation.

Compare your response on the pros and cons with the feedback provided at the end of this chapter.

7.7.2 TRANSPARENCY IN EARNINGS

Some employers have used pay secrecy clauses that stop employees discussing their pay with their colleagues. However, the Equality Act 2010 outlawed pay secrecy and introduced a requirement which prevents employers using punitive measures to enforce pay confidentiality clauses in employment contracts. The purpose of the legislation is to encourage pay transparency. The CIPD 2014–15 Reward Management survey showed, however, that the majority of organisations (56%), while saying they are compliant with the law, nevertheless prefer to keep pay information as confidential as possible. Although there was a big difference between the private sector (which prefers confidentiality) and the public/voluntary sector (which prefers transparency).

We now go on to consider the different factors that influence decisions about pay.

7.8 MAKING PAY DECISIONS

Employees' wages and salaries are not determined in isolation. Individuals themselves make comparisons of their benefits packages with those they perceive as being their peers (inside and outside the organisation, with jobs they see advertised and with numerous other sources). In some labour markets employees will leave quite quickly if there is a better offer available nearby, whereas in other markets they may accept poor rates relative to the market because of other redeeming factors in the total reward package.

The appropriate rate is important, not just to retain employees – although that is important in itself – but to have motivated employees. Dissatisfaction arising from a feeling of being underpaid or undervalued can be a major demotivator, whether the low pay is real or perceived. It is for the latter reason that some organisations provide a total pay statement. In such a statement the organisation puts a value on each aspect of the reward package and totals it up. This helps reassure individuals who may see better salaries elsewhere. For example, the true value of a good pension scheme, usually with life assurance included, can be hard to grasp in our early twenties. But an organisation can show employees how much they would have to earn to obtain such benefits if they bought them personally. Adding such figures into a total pay statement helps employees think carefully about what may, at first sight, seem a more attractive employment proposition in another company. It also helps to curb dissatisfaction.

Many wage rates are locally determined to ensure that they are competitive in the local labour market. Others – for example, many rates in the public sector – are determined nationally to reflect the national job market and national job evaluation schemes. Pay rates for many senior jobs are more regionally, nationally or even internationally determined.

7.8.1 INFORMATION TO DETERMINE PAY DECISIONS

The labour turnover rates and the labour stability rates that we looked at in Chapter 5 are good indicators of how your pay and salary rates fare in the marketplace. Indeed, high labour stability and low turnover may indicate that you are paying too much!

In considering salary rates, the contribution that an employee is making becomes an important factor. Performance management (which we looked at in Chapter 6) and job evaluation (which we examined in Chapter 4) assist us in making relative internal comparisons. Job evaluation in particular can also help in external comparisons. There are proprietary systems, such as Hay, that have their own job evaluation system so that jobs can be related to local, regional and national rates directly. Other salary survey systems, for example payscale.com, can nevertheless give good comparisons based on the job function, the level of responsibility and location. It is best to acquire a little understanding of some basic terms such as 'median', 'upper quartile' and 'percentiles' to get the most from such data.

These sources of information are available for a fee or subscription (see Case Study 7.3). Local discussion groups are free in that they require only time. Data such as the Retail Prices Index and the Consumer Price Index is widely available. Local CIPD groups, Chambers of Commerce and newspaper articles can be valuable as well as the Internet and social media/discussion forums.

Recruitment agencies should be treated with caution, since they have a vested interest, but they do have a shrewd idea of the salary levels that are necessary to attract good candidates. Indeed, advertisements themselves can give you an idea of how much others are prepared to pay to attract your employees away!

CASE STUDY 7.3

The position of shipping manager is a complex and critical role. The term 'missing the boat' has real and serious implications for anyone in such a position. There can be great stress in making sure that everything goes together, the container arrives on time, the product fits into the container and the container arrives with all the necessary documentation completed at the port on time. If you are exporting to remote parts of the world, the next boat may be weeks or even months hence.

You can understand that anyone with that responsibility needs to feel they are getting the salary they deserve. So when one company's shipping manager felt the job evaluation was not leading to the salary he thought he deserved, he complained. The company looked carefully at their purchased salary survey data (which contained salary levels for that very position) and considered the level of the job and their location in the UK. He was comfortably above the median salary for the post. Of course he would have liked to be paid more, but the company were able to satisfy him that he was being fairly rewarded.

7.9 PENSIONS

7.9.1 THE STATE PENSION

The basic state pension changed in April 2016 and is based on an individual's National Insurance contribution record. As a result of the change there are different rules that apply to people who have made National Insurance contributions before 6 April 2016 to those that apply to people who start making contributions after 6 April 2016. More information is available on the GOV.UK website, which includes a calculator to work out what an individual employee might be eligible to receive. State benefits are paid out of current contributions; there is no pool of investments to provide this income. Thus those in employment now are paying the pensions of those who are currently drawing their pension.

Prior to April 2016, some employers offered an alternative to the state scheme called a 'contracted-out' scheme. This will no longer be the position under the new state pension scheme. As the scheme is in transition at the time of writing, you would be well advised to seek up-to-date information from a reliable source such as GOV.UK if you require further detail.

7.9.2 DEFINED BENEFIT (FINAL SALARY) SCHEMES

These are becoming much less common because most members of such schemes entered employment some years ago and the schemes are often closed to new employees. In defined benefit schemes the employees' pension is based on their salary (usually their final salary when they retire or leave the scheme) and their length of service. They may also receive a lump sum within HMRC limits and the restrictions of the scheme. In the past, inflation has eroded the benefit of a fixed pension. Thus defined benefit schemes often provide for increases either in line with inflation or according to a simple formula.

These pensions are paid out of funds accumulated from past contributions that have been invested by fund managers, and it is partly their responsibility to ensure that the return on the money invested is sufficient to meet the fund's liabilities for paying pensions. Employers have to pay in sufficient amounts to ensure that the benefits employees (members) are entitled to can be met when an employee retires. A shortfall will have to be met by the company. In a final salary scheme it is the employer who takes the risk as to whether investments rise or fall.

The value of the pension fund has to be shown on the annual report of a private company – which can affect the share price of that company. This is one reason why many employers are ceasing to offer defined benefit schemes to new employees.

7.9.3 DEFINED CONTRIBUTION (MONEY-PURCHASE) SCHEMES

In a defined contribution scheme, the employee's contributions (together with those of the employer) are invested. The pension the employee gets is based on the total payments into the pension fund, and how well these investments have done. In general, the longer the funds have been invested, the larger the pension the employee gets when he or she retires.

The difficulty here is that the performance of the fund largely determines the final pension that the employee receives at the time an employee retires.

The employee uses the money built up in a defined contribution scheme as a lump sum to buy an annuity from an insurance company – an agreement to pay him a pension for life – when he retires. The final pension can be very dependent on the financial environment over the lifetime of the contributions. Annuity rates vary based on the timing when it is bought and the health of the individual at the time of purchase. The employee can choose when (or whether or not) to buy an annuity once they take the pension.

With defined contribution schemes it is the employee, rather than the employer, who takes the risks, but who could, on the other hand, gain if there are fortunate improvements in the financial world.

7.9.4 PENSIONS AUTO-ENROLMENT

The Pensions Act 2008 will eventually require all employers to enrol employees into a pension scheme. Both employer and employee will be obliged to make contributions to a scheme. Known as 'auto-enrolment', this is being phased in and will include all employers by 2018. In many cases employers will already have a suitable pension scheme, particularly larger employers.

Other employers will either have to set up a scheme with a pensions provider or enrol employees into an independently run scheme known as the National Employment Savings Trust (NEST). Employees can opt out if they wish, but unless they do so they will be auto-enrolled into a pension scheme. They are re-auto-enrolled every three years and have to opt out each time, if they wish. The NEST scheme is a money-purchase pension scheme and it enables employees to move from one employer to another without needing to move from one pension scheme to another.

7.9.5 COMMUNICATING WITH THE EMPLOYEE

The Financial Services Act 1986 and subsequent legislation restricts those who can advise on investment matters to appropriately trained independent financial advisers. This means that as an HR practitioner you can advise employees of the options that exist, but you cannot advise them as to which option to take. You cannot advise them to take an employer's scheme, for example, although you can set out the financial benefits, how the scheme works and factual differences such as who pays the administration charges for the scheme.

When it comes to decisions such as purchasing an annuity, that is a very serious financial decision. It may affect a person, and perhaps their family, for decades to come. Many individuals have a limited understanding of such financial decisions. The temptation is to help them. You must remember that, as an HR practitioner, you must never advise them yourself. If you work in a large organisation there may be qualified, professional, advice available in the organisation. Otherwise, direct retiring employees to an independent financial adviser.

> ### ? REFLECTIVE ACTIVITY 7.7
>
> This applies if you are in a pension scheme. Look at your latest pension statement or ask your pension provider for a statement. Take time to understand every aspect of it. It is possible that there will be figures that you do not quite understand. So ask questions of your provider if you are unsure. If you are early in your career, it may not seem important now – but it is likely to be so in time. In any event, as an HR practitioner you should understand the essentials of your organisation's pension scheme.

7.10 THE ROLE OF HR PRACTITIONERS

Reward can be a complex and specialist area of HR work. Indeed, many very large organisations have individuals or whole teams of reward specialists ensuring that their reward strategy, systems and approaches are at the leading edge of reward practice. In contrast, many smaller organisations rely on general HR practitioners to provide the necessary advice about reward. In some organisations there are salary and wages departments (or, indeed, paying staff may be an outsourced function) to do the administrative work associated with paying people. The different roles HR practitioners are likely to play in reward are as follows.

7.10.1 AN ADVISORY ROLE

You may need to provide both managers and employees with advice about the reward package in your organisation – how it works, what it includes, how decisions are made, and so on. This role might be one you need to fulfil on a face-to-face basis, in meetings or by developing written materials (for example, for a staff handbook) to explain the reward system. You may also need to explain your pension scheme to employees. Take care not to stray into the realm of giving financial advice.

7.10.2 A RESEARCH ROLE

This covers finding out about pay rates and reward packages in competitor organisations and the labour market you are operating in. It may involve researching different pay systems and structures and making recommendations or decisions about which will be appropriate for your organisation.

7.10.3 AN ADMINISTRATIVE ROLE

This could mean implementing your organisation's chosen pay system, some involvement in paying wages and salaries, and administering other aspects of the total reward package, such as holidays or gym memberships.

7.10.4 A MONITORING ROLE

There will be different aspects of the reward system in your organisation that need monitoring. You may have to make sure that the way in which your pay system operates is fair and equitable, and you may have a role in monitoring how competitive your reward package is in your local labour market.

7.10.5 A TRAINING ROLE

You may be called upon from time to time to train others (HR colleagues, line managers, trade union representatives, etc) in how various aspects of the reward system work. You may also have some involvement in raising awareness about the reward package at events such as induction training programmes for new employees.

7.11 SUMMARY

In this chapter we have sought to address the objectives by outlining the key components of reward within an organisation. The various different reward systems and structures available to organisations have been outlined, and some of the pros and cons of each addressed.

We have introduced the concept of total reward, which shows that reward is about much more than just pay, and that how reward is dealt with has many links to other aspects of HR work, such as performance and motivation.

The law as it relates to pay, including equal pay legislation, has been considered along with the need for specialist advice in this area.

We have also provided an overview of one very important aspect of the reward package – that is, pensions, an area in which there has been a lot of significant change and which will continue with the changes to the state pension and the full roll-out of auto-enrolment.

You will by now be familiar with some of the terminology used in the field of reward and be able to make links with what happens in your organisation. We have suggested a number of different roles for HR practitioners, and you will be able to use this as a means of assessing the role that you play in reward in your organisation.

References and further reading are provided immediately below for your information and activities have been suggested throughout. You are encouraged to complete some, if not all, of these activities in order to reinforce and apply your learning.

EXPLORE FURTHER

References and further reading

ACAS (2006) *Pay Systems*. Advisory booklet. Leicester: Advisory, Conciliation and Arbitration Service.

ACAS (2014) *2014 Changes to TUPE*. Leicester: Advisory, Conciliation and Arbitration Service.

ACAS (2014) *Asking and responding to questions of discrimination in the workplace: Acas guidance for job applicants, employees, employers and others asking questions about discrimination related to the Equality Act 2010*. Leicester: Advisory, Conciliation and Arbitration Service.

ARMSTRONG M. (2002) *Employee Reward*. 3rd edition. London: CIPD.

ARMSTRONG, M. (2015) *Armstrong's Handbook of Reward Management Practice: Improving Performance through Reward*. 5th edition. London: Kogan Page.

AUDIT COMMISSION (2002) Recruitment and Retention: A Public Service Workforce for the Twenty-first Century. London: Audit Commission.

OFFICE FOR NATIONAL STATISTICS (2015) *Annual Survey of Hours and Earnings, 2015 Provisional Results*. Available online at: www.ons.gov.uk/releasecalendar/annualsurveyofhoursandearnings

PERKINS, S. and WHITE, G. (2011) *Employee Reward: Alternatives, consequences and contexts*. 2nd edition. London: CIPD.

ROSE, M. (2014) *Reward Management (HR Fundamentals)*. 1st edition. London: Kogan Page.

WRIGHT, A. (2004) *Reward Management in Context*. London: CIPD.

See also survey reports on the CIPD website: cipd.co.uk/hr-resources/survey-reports:

- Reward Management 2014–15
- Employee Attitudes to Pay (January 2013)
- Employee Outlook: Focus on Pensions (January 2012)
- Employee Outlook: Focus on employee attitudes to pay and pensions (February 2014)

CIPD factsheets: www.cipd.co.uk/hr-resources/factsheets:

- Bonuses and Incentives (2015)
- Employee Benefits (2015)
- Equal Pay (2015)
- Flexible and Voluntary Benefits (2015)
- Market Pricing and Job Evaluation (2015)
- Occupational Pensions: A strategic overview (2015)
- Pay Progression (2015)
- Pay Structures (2015)
- Performance-related Pay (2015)
- Reward and Pay: An Overview (2015)
- Strategic Reward and Total Reward (2015)

Websites

Acas: www.acas.org.uk

CIPD: www.cipd.co.uk

Equal pay audit toolkit: www.equalityhumanrights.com/private-and-public-sector-guidance/employing-people/managing-workers/equal-pay/equal-pay-audit-toolkit

Auto-enrolment pensions: www.thepensionsregulator.gov.uk

REFLECTIVE ACTIVITIES FEEDBACK

Reflective Activity 7.2

Table 7.3 provides some of the pros and cons of basic rate pay systems.

Table 7.3 Basic rate pay systems

Pros	Cons
<ul><li>Relatively cheap and simple to administer and operate</li><li>Certainty and stability in pay for the employee</li><li>Relative simplicity in how pay progression happens</li><li>Costs of the workforce can be more easily forecast</li><li>Potentially fewer grounds for disagreement and dispute at an individual level</li></ul>	<ul><li>No incentive for improved performance or quality</li><li>Individual employees may feel aggrieved if they perceive themselves to work harder or perform better than others</li><li>Can be rigid and hierarchical</li></ul>

Reflective Activity 7.3

Table 7.4 provides some of the pros and cons of variable rate pay systems.

Table 7.4 Variable rate pay systems

Pros	Cons
• Rewards individual contribution and performance more directly • Can be more flexible and responsive to changing business priorities • Can be self-financing and linked to productivity • Easier to control increasing pay costs by managing the variable element	• Potential subjectivity and perceived bias and unfairness • Can be damaging to long-term business success in the achievement of short-term results • Can work against effective team working

Reflective Activity 7.4

Before introducing flexible benefits, an organisation would be well advised to consider: how employees feel about the current reward package and whether they are open to change; whether the benefits under consideration will be attractive to the employees in that organisation; whether the resources are available to design, introduce and maintain a flexible benefits package; whether external expert help should be sought in designing the flexible benefits; and the level of senior management support for the concept.

Reflective Activity 7.5

You are unlikely to have listed financial rewards such as hourly rates of pay, service-related benefits, profit-sharing and other team- or company-based rewards where the links between individual effort and the reward are difficult to establish. The list below indicates some of the financial and non-financial rewards that would be more likely to have a motivational impact:

- individual PRP
- bonuses
- incentives
- commission
- accelerated service-related pay
- skill-based pay
- competence-related pay
- praise
- employee of the month title
- feedback
- prizes/awards
- training and development opportunities
- responsibility
- autonomy
- self-development.

Reflective Activity 7.6

Some pros:

- If you know what is wrong, you can address it.
- Better to be driving change than be driven by it.

- It gives a chance to negotiate proper remedies rather than being forced into them by an adversarial process.
- In the event of a claim it may help your defence if a policy is in place.
- In the event of a claim it may help your defence if you have done a review.

The following pros are put forward by the EHRC:

- complying with the law and good practice
- identifying, explaining and eliminating unjustifiable pay gaps
- having rational, fair, transparent pay arrangements
- demonstrating to employees and to potential employees a commitment to fairness and equality
- demonstrating your values to those you do business with.

You may think of more, equally valid, pros.

Some cons:

- Organisations have more important things to do – like survive.
- You immediately alert workers to the possibility that they may have a claim.
- You may be giving workers ammunition that they could use in a claim.
- Once a claim is made, you lose control.
- Claims are very expensive to defend.
- Remedies can be very expensive too – potentially six years' back pay with interest.
- A code of practice and/or a pay review that is then ignored will be used against the organisation – you could be hoisted by your own petard!
- It is important for you – if badly handled, it could be a career-breaker.
- You may think of more, equally valid, cons.

CHAPTER 8

Employee Relations

LEARNING OUTCOMES

After reading this chapter you will:

- understand the changing nature and continuing importance of employee relations
- be able to define the differences in the purposes, content and operation of disciplinary, capability and grievance procedures
- understand the good practice steps and statutory requirements that ensure the effective handling of conduct or capability cases
- be able to assess the suitability of a range of tools for managing long- and short-term absences
- appreciate the importance of responding appropriately to employee grievances concerning individual and collective matters
- understand the growing importance of and interest in employee engagement.

8.1 INTRODUCTION

In this chapter we will be considering employee relations within organisations. It is a very broad area of practice and one that people describe and define very differently. How employee relations is defined and practised will often be organisationally specific, with the context of, and culture and climate in, a particular organisation having a significant bearing on what constitutes employee relations and how it is practised. As indicated in the CIPD 'Managing Employee Relations' research report (2012), employee relations can be viewed as a series of activities either more narrowly focused on managing the employment relationship or more broadly focused on the whole area of managing and developing people.

However it is defined, it is a field of HR practice and an approach that has changed much over recent years and it is worth considering different views of what employee relations is. From commentators including the CIPD, the work of the Workplace Employment Relations Study and academic research it is clear that employee relations is still an important aspect of HR work, but without a single definition. It can be seen as a field of work that comprises:

- managing the employment relationship and contract
- ensuring compliance with employment law
- communication with employees and the employee 'voice'
- promoting employee engagement and involvement
- addressing conflict in the workplace
- collective processes of negotiation and consultation.

The 'snapshot' of employee relations taken by the CIPD in the 2012 research (after the global financial crisis) suggests that the challenges faced by HR professionals in the field of employee relations are similar to those faced five to ten years ago. The CIPD Profession Map, mentioned in earlier chapters, states that 'the professional working in this area of HR ensures that the relationship between an organisation and its staff is managed appropriately within a clear and transparent framework underpinned by organisation practices and policies and ultimately by relevant employment law'. Thus employee relations involves seeking to gain the commitment of employees to organisational goals, dealing with situations where the conduct or performance of employees does not demonstrate this commitment and managing conflict situations. These aspects will be addressed in this chapter.

Conflict, potential or actual, may be of an individual or collective nature. In this chapter our emphasis will be on individual conflict situations, because these are the ones most likely to be faced by the majority of the readers of this book. Such individual conflict is likely to be born out of differences between employers and employees on matters such as conduct, performance, absence, working relationships, individual employment rights and contractual matters and communication. Formal procedures will exist in most organisations for dealing with discipline and grievance matters that arise. Procedures may also exist, particularly in larger organisations, on issues such as capability, bullying and harassment, absence and whistleblowing. It should be noted, however, that employee relations does not just operate at a formal level, nor is it solely the preserve of the HR practitioner, indeed, much of the interaction between managers and staff can be construed as employee relations and this is an area of people management practice where line managers potentially have the greatest influence. There has also been a growth in the use of less formal and less procedural approaches to dealing with conflict – for example, workplace mediation.

Later in the chapter we will be referring to strategies aimed at averting collective conflict – that is, situations that involve groups of individuals or the whole workforce. Our contention is that collective conflict is often triggered by organisational changes such as restructuring, changes in ownership or working arrangements and relocation. Managers must take care to ensure that they comply with their legal obligations in their communications, consultations and other means of involving employees as well as adopting good practices.

In the opening sections of this chapter we set out to explain what we mean by disciplinary rules and disciplinary, capability and grievance procedures. We highlight the importance of the Acas Code of Practice 2015 and the Acas Guide. We consider good practices in disciplinary, capability and grievance-handling as well as exploring bullying and harassment, whistleblowing, mediation and a number of absence management tools.

We then move on to consider effective strategies for employee engagement and involvement, including those involving trade unions. We also briefly cover the impact of the psychological contract on the management of employee relations. All of the above is set against the backdrop of relevant legislation, much of which has been covered in Chapter 3. Finally, we look at the complex nature of the role of HR practitioners in employee relations. Suggested activities to develop your knowledge and skills in this important area can be found throughout the chapter. More information on the associated skills can be found in Chapter 12.

First, we shall consider how employee relations has been changing and why it is so important that potential individual conflicts, such as disciplinary incidents and employee grievances, and potential collective conflicts, such as plans to introduce new technology, are handled with skill and according to laid-down procedures.

8.2 THE CHANGING NATURE AND FOCUS OF EMPLOYEE RELATIONS

The term 'employee relations' gradually came to replace the term 'industrial relations' and, in doing so, reflected a change in the nature and focus of relationships in the workplace.

Recent developments see a number of organisations using the term 'employee engagement' interchangeably with employee relations, which shows the continuing changing nature of this area of work and the increasingly wide focus of what people understand by employee relations. We can also see the growth of new types of contractual relationship – use of outsourcing and agency workers and zero-hours contracts, for instance – which also influence how employee relations will be managed. As the CIPD has outlined in previous surveys, 'industrial relations' is generally used and understood to mean relationships in the workplace that are collective – that is, between the employer and groups of employees. 'Employee relations' tends to be used more in connection with matters to do with individual employment. Further development can be seen from the 2012 CIPD research report, with employee relations being increasingly seen as being about preventing and managing conflict, managing workplace relationships, and even managing and developing people in the widest sense to 'release potential and drive performance'.

The focus of attention in employee relations can also be seen to have changed and developed over time:

- from attention being devoted to the mechanism and 'machinery' of formal employee relations to a greater focus on organisational culture and the key role this has to play in employee relations and the working climate
- from negotiation playing a key part in employee relations to communication and consultation, often with individual employees, coming to the fore
- from pay, terms and conditions being the fundamental issues dealt with to a greater interest in considering motivation and performance and how to achieve flexibility to enable change in structures and working patterns
- from managing problems and conflict in the employment relationship to preventing it in the first place through initiatives such as employee engagement and the use of tools such as mediation.

In recent years there has been a decline in the number of matters dealt with on a collective basis and an increasing focus on relationships with individual employees. A number of different factors indicate this shift:

- a significant decline in trade union membership
- a significant decline in the number of employees covered by collective agreements
- a significant decline in the range of matters addressed by collective bargaining
- a shift in what union officials spend their time on – from negotiating pay and conditions to individual representation and support
- a reduction in industrial action
- the increasing importance attached to the employee 'voice' and employee involvement
- growing interest in the use of mediation to resolve disputes.

It is also possible to see a change in the nature of collective action when it is taken. There are now fewer strikes and other forms of direct industrial action, and greater use of ballots. The threat of industrial action ballots is used to prompt negotiations and there is increasing use of mass action campaigns involving marches and demonstrations. Where direct industrial action is seen it is often in the public sector or former public sector organisations, such as the unrest and action at Royal Mail, London Underground and Network Rail in 2015.

Individual employee relations activity is a key aspect of managing people in all organisations and will be something both managers and HR professionals spend a significant amount of time on. Additionally, in certain sectors and types of organisation – for example, the public sector, some larger private sector organisations and former public sector bodies – collective employee relations and trade unions still play a major role. Further information on the collective aspects of employee relations is included later in this chapter.

8.3 WHY IS IT IMPORTANT TO MANAGE EMPLOYEE RELATIONS?

It is important to have a focus on and positive approach to employee relations for a number of reasons, including creating a climate for productive relationships at work and to fulfil legal obligations. We consider here a couple of the formal mechanisms for managing employee relations.

Concentrating on discipline first, rules and procedures exist to help employees to improve their performance. They should not be regarded as just a means of punishing employees or a means by which managers can dismiss employees legally. There are several potential consequences of poor practice in addressing disciplinary matters:

- A lax approach to potential disciplinary incidents will lead to an ill-disciplined workforce who do not respect management's authority and are likely to 'play the system' to their own advantage – for example, by making their own decisions about working methods and break times. When managers do want to assert their authority by, say, enforcing break times, employees will rightly point to the fact that established custom and practice have overridden written policy and procedure.
- An overenthusiastic or inconsistent use of the disciplinary rules and procedures will lead to employee discontent and complaints of unfairness and is unlikely to be beneficial in realising employee potential and thus maximising productivity.
- Ultimately, management may be faced with a decision to dismiss an employee. If their reason is insufficient (for example, they have overreacted to the incident), or if they act unreasonably in dismissing that employee (for example, by failing to follow the procedure correctly), the chance of the employee's making a successful claim of unfair dismissal to an employment tribunal is increased. Fighting such claims will be costly and time-consuming and, regardless of the outcome, does little to enhance the reputation of the organisation in the eyes of its employees and outside parties.

Turning now to grievance-handling, procedures exist to enable employees to have a formal means of complaint about their terms and conditions, working environment and related issues. Failure to encourage use of this provision or to respond appropriately to grievances will result in:

- discontent among the workforce because they feel that management are not interested in and do not value their views. This may lead to poor motivation and low productivity
- missed opportunities to tackle problems at an early stage to ensure that they do not continue, thus creating difficulties for other employees. For example, claims of harassment, discrimination and bullying should be handled quickly and carefully and be fully investigated to avoid accusations of unreasonable delay or indecision. Failure to do this could lead to constructive dismissal claims
- the threat of industrial action when complaints about issues which affect several employees – such as health and safety matters – are perceived by the workforce to have been handled badly.

Similarly, with regard to collective conflict situations, failure actively to involve employees, listen to their requests or concerns and/or seek their buy-in to proposals can result in a range of responses from apathy and lack of commitment to employment tribunal claims, strikes and other forms of industrial action.

We will now look at these matters in more detail.

8.4 DISCIPLINE

The legislation relevant to the handling of disciplinary matters (and grievances) is referred to and commented on throughout this chapter. The major pieces of relevant legislation are the Trade Union and Labour Relations (Consolidation) Act 1992, the Employment Rights Act 1996 (ERA) and the Employment Act 2008. These Acts contain most of the legislation applicable to the individual rights of employees, including the right not to be unfairly dismissed and the legislation about procedures.

Obviously, not every disciplinary situation will result in a dismissal, fair or unfair, but HR practitioners and line managers would be well advised to bear in mind the provisions of ERA and the guidelines provided by Acas (see below). This is because the manner in which previous disciplinary situations have been handled will be taken into account by employment tribunals when considering unfair dismissal applications.

Let's consider two examples of this:

- A manager who claims that a dismissed employee was previously warned about the consequences of continued poor timekeeping will have to be able to produce the requisite records, the notes of disciplinary interviews and letters of confirmation to the employee concerned.
- In a case of poor performance, the manager will need to produce evidence that he or she reviewed the situation with the employee at regular intervals, communicated the standards of performance required, set realistic targets for improvement, provided the necessary support mechanisms to help the individual to improve, monitored the situation and kept records of subsequent performance before any decision to dismiss. Further, the manager will have to show that the messages given out to the employee at formal appraisal interviews did not contradict those issued in the disciplinary context.

All organisations, large or small, should have in place written disciplinary and grievance procedures and, we would recommend, a separate capability procedure to deal with poor performance and ill-health cases. In unionised environments, these documents must be agreed with the trade union(s). The Acas Code of Practice 1: Disciplinary and Grievance Procedures gives guidance to employers on the content and operation of disciplinary rules and procedures, and the Acas Guide – Discipline and Grievances at Work – provides good practice advice for dealing with discipline and grievances in the workplace.

8.4.1 DISCIPLINARY RULES

We shall deal first with disciplinary rules. These set the standards of behaviour and conduct expected in the workplace. The contents of the rules vary greatly depending on the size of the organisation, the industry, management style, the history of employee relations, and so on. It is likely, however, that they will refer to the following:

- general conduct
- health and safety
- security
- time-keeping and attendance.

Examples of disciplinary rules under each of the above might include:

- 'Disorderly conduct, threatening behaviour, insubordination or playing practical jokes is strictly forbidden in any part of the company.'
- 'Any defects in personal protective equipment must be reported immediately by the employee to his or her supervisor.'
- 'Employees are strictly forbidden to take from the workplace any materials, tools, equipment, or other company property unless written permission is first obtained from their departmental manager.'
- 'Employees must follow the company's sickness reporting procedures on each occasion of sickness absence.'

Disciplinary rules help to ensure a consistent and fair approach to the treatment of employees. Managers obviously wish to have a disciplined workforce, but the majority of employees are likely to be just as keen to have a set of rules in operation so that they are clear about the behavioural standards expected of them.

Breaches of disciplinary rules vary in their seriousness. It is always a good idea to consider whether an informal discussion is appropriate to resolve the issue before moving into the use of formal procedures. However, once a decision has been made to deal with an issue formally, the types of action you should consider are:

- Minor infringements – for example, an occasional late arrival at work – might merit a verbal warning.
- More serious infringements – for example, failure to complete quality checks properly – might result in a written warning.
- Gross misconduct – for example, theft, fighting, negligence or fraud – will probably result in summary dismissal (dismissal without notice or pay in lieu of notice).

You should always point out to an employee that failure to heed warnings by engaging in repeated breaches of the rules – for example, continued poor attendance – may ultimately result in dismissal.

Whilst management must seek to be fair and consistent in applying the disciplinary rules, no two disciplinary incidents are ever identical. Thus managers must always ensure that they take into account the circumstances of the case before them. For instance, they are likely to deal less severely with a previously satisfactory employee whose poor attendance is due to temporary domestic commitments than with a newer employee who has already had some attendance problems. Depending on the circumstances of an employee's case, the manager may decide that disciplinary action is inappropriate and that an informal approach is more appropriate. This might include the manager arranging for counselling to take place (see Figure 8.1). Some may see this as a soft option (putting off the inevitable), but this approach is entirely consistent with the aim of disciplinary rules and procedures – that is, assisting employees to improve their performance rather than providing the means for managers to punish employees or dismiss employees legally.

? REFLECTIVE ACTIVITY 8.1

Talk to a manager or HR practitioner in your company who has been involved in a number of disciplinary processes; find out which of the disciplinary rules in your company is broken most often. Discuss why this might be the case. Is there something that could be improved – for example, company policies or communication with employees – that could help change this situation?

We shall now consider disciplinary procedures.

8.4.2 DISCIPLINARY PROCEDURES

We have seen that where standards of conduct are not met, management may decide to take some form of disciplinary action against the employee(s) concerned. Disciplinary procedures provide guidelines for adherence to the rules and a fair method of dealing with infringements.

The Acas Guide 2015 lists the following essential features of disciplinary procedures. Good disciplinary procedures should:

- be put in writing
- be non-discriminatory

- provide for matters to be dealt with speedily
- allow for information to be kept confidential
- tell employees what disciplinary action might be taken
- say what levels of management have the authority to take the various forms of disciplinary action
- require employees to be informed of the complaints against them and supporting evidence, before any meeting
- give employees a chance to have their say before management reaches a decision
- provide employees with the right to be accompanied
- provide that no employee is dismissed for a first breach of discipline, except in cases of gross misconduct
- require management to investigate fully before any disciplinary action is taken
- ensure that employees are given an explanation for any sanction, and allow for appeal
- apply to all employees.

The procedures should also:

- ensure that any investigatory period of suspension is with pay, and specify how pay is to be calculated during such period. If, exceptionally, suspension is to be without pay, this must be provided for in the contract of employment
- ensure that any suspension is brief, and is never used as a sanction against the employee prior to a disciplinary meeting and decision
- ensure that the employee will be heard in good faith and that there is no pre-judgement of the issue
- ensure that where the facts are in dispute, no disciplinary penalty is imposed until the case has been carefully investigated, and there is a reasonably held belief that the employee committed the act in question.

The Guide also advises that all formal disciplinary actions should be confirmed in writing to the employee concerned. Further, when deciding on the level of disciplinary action (if any), managers should take account of the employee's record and any other relevant factors (often referred to as extenuating circumstances or mitigating factors).

Acas is empowered by the Secretary of State for Business, Innovation and Skills to issue codes of practice such as the one referred to above. Failure to observe the provisions of a code of practice will not of itself render a person liable to any proceedings. However, a code of practice is admissible in evidence in any tribunal proceedings, and if any provision is relevant to any questions arising in the proceedings, it will be taken into account in determining that question. Furthermore, a failure to follow the Acas Guide can lead to an award for unfair dismissal being increased.

The message here is very clear: regardless of the size of your organisation, you should ensure that you incorporate the 'essential features' listed above in your disciplinary procedure. Further, once disciplinary rules and procedures have been formulated in conjunction with interested parties, managers must ensure that the written procedure matches up with the actual practice within the organisation (or employees will have a head start in pursuing their claims at an employment tribunal).

Failure to follow the correct procedure is one of the most common arguments put forward (often successfully) by representatives of unfair dismissal applicants. Examples of such failures include:

- not distinguishing between misconduct and poor performance – for example, a failure to achieve performance targets may be the result of inadequate training or poor supervision, rendering a disciplinary sanction inappropriate. Alternatively, the shortfall in performance may be due to a medical problem, in which case a capability procedure should be followed (see 8.5.1 'Capability Procedures' below)

- an incomplete or prejudiced investigation – for example, managers ignoring the evidence of a key witness or failing to keep an open mind about the possible outcome of the investigation
- the improper constitution of a disciplinary hearing – for example, a supervisor on night-shift making a decision to issue a final written warning when he or she is not authorised to do so
- the absence of a person suitably independent to hear an appeal against a disciplinary decision – for example, because the manager who should hear the appeal has been involved in either the investigations or the discussions leading up to the disciplinary decision
- an employee not being accompanied – for example, because the manager assumed that the employee was familiar with this right and would make his or her own arrangements
- an employee not being reminded of the right to appeal and the procedure for so doing (this is an illustration of the importance of keeping accurate notes of all disciplinary hearings so that the validity of such an allegation can be checked).

The ERA also states that employers must give new employees written particulars of employment within two months of their starting date, including dismissal and disciplinary procedures. The written particulars must specify the disciplinary rules.

(Note that the term 'dismissal procedures' also applies to non-disciplinary terminations such as with capability cases or fixed-term contracts.)

Managers should not, however, assume that 'offending' employees are fully conversant with the contents and operation of the organisation's employment policies. It is often the case that our working lives are so busy that we are forced to adopt a 'need-to-know' approach regarding the information that we take in. Thus previously exemplary employees would have had no need to know intimately the workings of the disciplinary procedure.

So what can the employer do to bring the disciplinary rules and procedures to the attention of the workforce? There are several options: incorporate this subject into the induction programme; make copies readily available to all employees (using appropriate means, including the company intranet); or provide training for newly appointed line managers and refresher training for existing ones (organisations often wait for disasters to occur before doing this; for example, a finding of unfair dismissal at a tribunal hearing).

Further, if management decide to clamp down on certain activities – for example, careless time-keeping, 'casual' sickness absence or private work during company time – they should publicise this by, say, including it on the agenda of team meetings, issuing emails and compiling reports highlighting statistical trends.

?   REFLECTIVE ACTIVITY 8.2

Have a look at your organisation's disciplinary policy and rules. Are they clear and easy to follow? How are they brought to the attention of new and existing employees? How far do they contain the essential features identified by Acas? See if you can identify any changes needed and discuss these with one of your learning sources.

We will now summarise the key elements in implementing disciplinary procedures.

Good practice in implementing a disciplinary procedure

It is advisable for disciplinary procedures to reflect the principles of the Acas Code of Practice and Guide and to ensure that the following guidance is adhered to:

- Disciplinary processes should be carried out promptly and consistently.
- All necessary investigation should be carried out to establish the facts.
- The employee should be informed of the basis of the problem and be given an opportunity to put his or her side of the story.
- The employee should be informed of the right to be accompanied by a work colleague or by a certified trade union representative or employed trade union official, and allowed to be so accompanied.
- The employee should be allowed to appeal.

It is important to note that, wherever possible, the different elements of investigation, putting the case to the employee and hearing their side of the story, and the appeal should be handled by different people. This avoids the possible criticism that a manager has prejudged the situation and is not, therefore, of an independent mind.

It is worth pointing out that in disciplinary situations, including dismissal, managers are not expected to prove that an employee is guilty of an offence (as in a court of law) but to establish, after a full investigation, a 'reasonable belief' that the employee committed the offence.

With regard to the first stage – that of investigation – you will need to collect evidence of the relevant acts, omissions or conduct under consideration and accompanying documentation. As well as the disciplinary procedure itself, you will need copies of relevant rules and company policies – for example, health and safety, equality and diversity – and the employee's written particulars and employment records on, say, attendance, training, appraisal and previous disciplinary incidents. Factual data such as customer complaints, production figures and cost or quality information may also be needed, along with physical evidence such as copies of emails, 'stolen property' and video recordings.

If you need to interview the employee during this stage, ensure that he or she is aware that it is an investigatory meeting and not a disciplinary hearing. Further, make sure that in practice this distinction is a clear one. Often an investigatory meeting will be referred to as a 'fact-finding' meeting to make this distinction clear.

Next, if on the face of it disciplinary action seems to be warranted, you should write to the employee outlining the allegations made and inviting him or her to a disciplinary meeting to discuss the matter. You must then hold a meeting, for which detailed guidelines are provided in Table 8.3.

With regard to the equally important stage of conducting the disciplinary appeal, the Acas Guide, Discipline and Grievances at Work (2015) recommends that an internal appeals procedure should:

- specify a time limit within which the appeal should be lodged
- provide for appeals to be dealt with speedily, particularly those involving suspension or dismissal
- wherever possible, provide for the appeal to be heard by someone senior in authority to the person who took the disciplinary decision and, if possible, who was not involved in the original meeting or decision
- spell out what action may be taken by those hearing the appeal
- set out the right to be accompanied at any appeal meeting
- provide for the employee, or a companion if the employee so wishes, to have the opportunity to comment on any new evidence arising during the appeal before any decision is taken.

CASE STUDY 8.1

Is it possible to get it right? One organisation – a charity – did. The organisation found that pornographic images were stored on the computer of a member of the IT team and there was evidence to suggest that such material had been passed between the members of the department. There was a concern among the managers that if they were not seen to take decisive action, they might be viewed as condoning similar behaviour in the future as well as running the risk of receiving harassment claims and, possibly, a criminal conviction. After an investigation, the IT manager was unable to identify the guilty party or parties, and so reluctantly decided to dismiss all four employees in the department. One employee appealed, but the appeal was turned down and subsequently the same employee submitted an unfair dismissal claim.

In summarising the reasons for the finding of fair dismissal, the tribunal chair pointed out that:

- the organisation did have an established Internet and email policy that clearly specified what was 'acceptable use' and which actions were prohibited
- infringement of this policy was listed as an example of gross misconduct in the organisation's disciplinary procedure
- a thorough investigation had taken place, but the employer had not been able to discover which employee(s) were to blame, and so had dismissed all four employees on the grounds of a reasonable suspicion
- it was noted that the employees had been unhelpful during the investigations and there were no mitigating factors to be taken account of.

? REFLECTIVE ACTIVITY 8.3

If you are inexperienced in handling disciplinary situations, ask if you could sit in on a disciplinary interview as an observer only. Try to identify good and bad practices (diplomatically, of course). Did you agree with the decision reached? If not, seek to discuss the reasons for the decision with the manager concerned.

We have now looked at the content and operation of disciplinary rules and procedures as well as the effect of relevant employment legislation. Before moving on to the issue of capability procedures, we must consider when disciplinary action is necessary. The flowchart in Figure 8.1 should help.

In Figure 8.1 we can see that although conduct is unsatisfactory in some manner, there may be extenuating circumstances that merit consideration and render disciplinary action unwise or unjustifiable. The manager may decide that counselling is a more appropriate option and either personally undertake this role or arrange for a 'specialist' to do so (see Chapter 12 for more information on counselling). In this process the manager is likely to have asked whether the unsatisfactory conduct is within the control of the employee or not. If not, then disciplinary action is rarely appropriate because there is an underlying assumption that the employee has the ability to change and the use of a capability procedure is generally more advisable. (See the CIPD 'Policies and Procedures for People Managers' manual listed in 'References and Further Reading' below for in-depth advice on discipline and capability-handling.)

Figure 8.1 Disciplinary action checklist

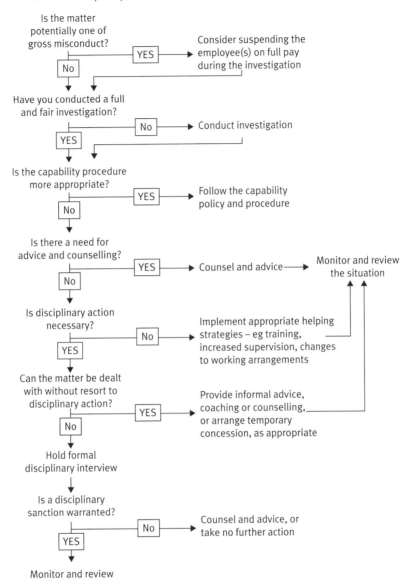

A breach of disciplinary rules has occurred – is disciplinary action necessary?

Is the matter potentially one of gross misconduct?
YES → Consider suspending the employee(s) on full pay during the investigation
No ↓

Have you conducted a full and fair investigation?
No → Conduct investigation
YES ↓

Is the capability procedure more appropriate?
YES → Follow the capability policy and procedure
No ↓

Is there a need for advice and counselling?
YES → Counsel and advice → Monitor and review the situation
No ↓

Is disciplinary action necessary?
No → Implement appropriate helping strategies – eg training, increased supervision, changes to working arrangements
YES ↓

Can the matter be dealt with without resort to disciplinary action?
YES → Provide informal advice, coaching or counselling, or arrange temporary concession, as appropriate
No ↓

Hold formal disciplinary interview
↓

Is a disciplinary sanction warranted?
No → Counsel and advice, or take no further action
YES ↓

Monitor and review

8.5 CAPABILITY

8.5.1 CAPABILITY PROCEDURES

These may be designed to cover poor performance and ill-health. We will deal first with poor performance cases.

Poor performance

Employers are entitled to expect their employees to produce work of good quality and in accordance with sensible deadlines. Where an employee fails to meet the required standards, the manager concerned may decide to invoke disciplinary action. This would be appropriate if the employee is simply not trying and has the ability to change his or her behaviour. Our suggestion, however, is that poor performance is generally not a conduct issue, and a separate capability procedure would therefore be more appropriate. An investigation or review should be carried out to determine the causes of underperformance.

The Acas Guide, 'How to Manage Performance' (2014) stresses the importance of using alternative strategies where poor performance is concerned – ensuring effective feedback (see Chapter 6), support and coaching and having difficult conversations with employees where necessary (see Chapter 12).

Where poor performance is identified, then it is vital to be absolutely clear in discussions with the employee exactly what the problem is, what improvements are required and the timescales for achieving this improvement. This will often be formally recorded in a performance improvement plan (PIP).

An employee should not normally be dismissed because of unsatisfactory performance unless warnings and a chance to improve have been given, with additional training if necessary.

If the main cause of the unsatisfactory performance is the changing nature of the job, employers should consider whether the situation may properly be treated as redundancy rather than as a capability issue.

Further, where poor performance may arise from a disability, consideration must be given to any reasonable adjustment that could enable the employee to reach a reasonable standard of performance. In a manufacturing assembly environment, for example, a reasonable adjustment could mean providing special seating for an employee with back problems. It is essential that the performance is monitored at all stages and that full records, including notes of meetings, are kept.

This is particularly important if you need to tackle underperformance in older employees. Consistency in the way in which you tackle this is crucial. The procedures should be essentially the same for a 20-year-old, a 40-year-old or a 70-year-old, and you may need to demonstrate that if challenged. The Acas good practice steps are demonstrated in Case Study 8.2.

CASE STUDY 8.2

A company selling electrical goods had employed one sales executive for three years. He reported to one of four regional sales managers (RSMs) who, in turn, reported to the sales director. In the last six months, the RSM had issued the sales executive with two written warnings for minor incidents.

One concerned the late submission of a report and statistics, and the other his failure to follow the notification of sickness absence procedure. More recently she issued him with a final written warning (FWW) because she couldn't contact him during working hours. The sales executive felt that he had been badly treated and lodged an appeal.

At the appeals hearing, which was conducted by the sales director, the sales executive said that his problems with his job had several causes. He hadn't told the RSM anything about them because he didn't get on with her and felt that she would be unsympathetic. The causes were:

- He had a number of personal problems, not least trying to gain access to see his children since his marriage break-up.
- There had been a change in the computer package used for his work

and he was really struggling to adapt to it.

- He was feeling very stressed and insecure, and at the suggestion of his GP had been visiting a counsellor when the RSM had tried to contact him. He had a letter confirming his state of health from his GP, and pointed out that he had made up the time the following day.

The sales director concluded that this case had been inappropriately dealt with under the disciplinary procedure to date, although there were understandable reasons for this. She upheld the appeal and withdrew the FWW. Nevertheless, she informed the sales executive that his performance still needed to improve. In future, this would be handled in accordance with the company's capability procedure and the company would do its best to help him with regard to IT training and his personal and health problems.

Ill-health (long-term and short-term)

Case law suggests that disciplinary procedures are inappropriate in most circumstances relating to sickness absence, whether it is long-term or short-term. Ill-health capability procedures follow a rather different route from disciplinary procedures (although both may have the same conclusion – that is, dismissal of the employee). The key elements of an ill-health capability procedure are:

- consultation with the employee – that is, maintaining regular contact throughout the period of absence and fully involving the employee in the decision-making process. Remember that for meetings which may result in actions such as warnings, demotion or dismissal, the employee has a statutory right to be accompanied. This right does not apply to informal or investigatory meetings or counselling sessions
- a medical investigation – that is, gathering medical evidence on the likelihood of an early return to work and the suitability of the current position
- consideration, where appropriate, of alternative employment (and/or reasonable adjustments in the case of employees who have a disability) before any decision to dismiss the employee.

In tribunal proceedings, the panel, in reaching their decision on whether a dismissal was fair or unfair, will consider whether these elements were provided by employers. Unfortunately, there are other pitfalls in store for you in ill-health dismissals. You may have followed the above good practice guidelines, but what if the dismissal occurred during the employee's contractual entitlement to sick pay? In such a case, the employee may have a claim for breach of contract if there is no express term to permit this. You should note the following approach to dismissing an employee on the grounds of sickness:

1 Check the written particulars for relevant clauses and seek legal advice if there are ambiguities.

2 Ensure that you follow a correct procedure (see the key elements listed above).

3 Ensure that the provisions of the Equality Act 2010 are taken into account before making your final decision.

We have mainly concentrated above on long-term sickness absences. What about short-term absences?

Sometimes we tend to forget that employees may genuinely be sick and, if these are infrequent occurrences where proper notification and certification procedures have been followed, no further action is likely to be necessary. If the absences are genuine but frequent, you should follow the capability procedure as set out above.

On the other hand, if investigations show that absences are not genuine (for instance, an employee returning from a period of absence with a deep suntan might lead you to investigate more fully), you should follow the normal disciplinary procedure because this is a conduct issue. However, it is often the case that suspected 'casual' absences cannot be proven, so you should be wary of treating absences as misconduct. Do not despair, though, for unacceptable levels of attendance can be dealt with by ensuring a fair review of the attendance record, allowing the employee to make representations, gathering medical evidence (which could reveal genuine underlying causes), seeking to help the employee to improve his or her attendance record and warning him or her of the consequences should that improvement not occur. If there is no adequate improvement, dismissal should be a justifiable option.

8.5.2 SICKNESS ABSENCE MANAGEMENT TOOLS

Whatever the cause, duration or validity of sickness absences, it is undisputed that the cost to industry is very high. A survey of 518 UK organisations conducted by the CIPD in 2014 revealed that UK employees take an average of 6.6 sick days off every year, at an average cost of £609 per employee per year.

According to the survey, more than half of employers have an employee well-being strategy in place, in which the most common benefits are:

- access to counselling services
- employee assistance programmes.

So what can you do to reduce sickness absence? You would be advised to adopt the good practice steps outlined above alongside a combination of absence management tools. You may wish to make your choice based on the conclusions of the CIPD survey, which looked at a range of absence management tools and drew conclusions on their effectiveness, as shown in Tables 8.1 and 8.2.

Table 8.1 The most effective tools for managing short-term absence

Most effective part of short-term absence management approach	Percentage of organisations specifying this as one of the most effective tools
Return-to-work interviews for all absences	62
Use of trigger mechanism to review attendance	57
Disciplinary procedures for unacceptable absence	26
Sickness absence information given to line managers	21

Source: CIPD (2014) 'Absence Management', annual survey report

Table 8.2 The most effective tools for managing long-term absence

Most effective part of long-term absence management approach	Percentage of organisations specifying this as one of the most effective tools
Occupational health involvement	46
Trigger mechanisms to review attendance	28
Return-to-work interviews	26
Restricting sick pay	17
Rehabilitation programmes	15

Source: CIPD (2014) 'Absence Management', annual survey report

Consider your own organisation. Which absence management tools are currently used? How successful do you think they are? If you were to adopt a different approach, which tools would you recommend, and why? Discuss your thoughts with one of your learning sources.

8.6 HANDLING GRIEVANCES

Case law dictates that employees must be provided with a means by which they can officially raise complaints and seek redress. As with disciplinary procedures, the ERA declares that details of the grievance procedure must be contained in the written particulars of employment. It is good practice to have a written grievance procedure.

Employers should encourage employees to raise concerns so that problems can be dealt with at an early stage before they become intractable or start to affect other employees. In theory, then, managers should welcome grievances, but the experience of many employees is that management view those who raise them as nuisances or troublemakers.

What is your view?

You should ensure that employees are aware of the existence of the grievance procedure by publicising it through the induction programme for new employees, making copies readily available to all employees, making known the results of successfully resolved grievances where appropriate and providing specialist training for all levels of management likely to be involved in handling grievances.

It cannot be stressed enough how important it is for grievances to be dealt with in an appropriate and timely manner. If an employee has decided to make a complaint formal, it usually means that he or she feels strongly about the issue and will not, therefore, appreciate a manager attempting to trivialise the complaint. Further, if employees perceive that managers never seem to respond to formal complaints, the incidence of grievances may fall. This does not then mean that there are no problems, but that employees are too demotivated to raise them. It is unlikely to result in an energised and productive working situation.

Examples of issues likely to be raised under grievance procedures include:

- working conditions/patterns – for example, rotas, lighting, heating
- use of equipment – for example, poorly maintained tools
- personality clashes
- refused requests – for example, timing of annual leave, shift changes
- shortfalls in pay – for example, late bonus payments, adjustments to overtime pay
- allocation of 'perks' – for example, Sunday overtime working
- the imposition of company policies or practices
- terms and conditions.

More serious matters would include:

- complaints about deductions from pay
- allegations of bullying or harassment
- allegations of sex or race discrimination.

The types of issue included within the scope of grievance procedures vary from one workplace to the next. We shall now look more specifically at the content of grievance procedures.

8.6.1 GRIEVANCE PROCEDURES

Grievance procedures are the means by which employees can formally raise complaints with management. The aim is to resolve these issues as near as possible to the location of the original complaint. Grievance procedures should be:

- equitable in the way in which employees are treated
- simple to understand
- rapid in their application.

Further, in the interests of natural justice, the investigation of a grievance should be conducted by an unbiased individual.

The outcome of a successfully handled grievance would be a solution that satisfies all the parties. For example, an employee with a justifiable complaint about the unequal distribution of overtime would probably be satisfied if a new written procedure was drawn up to avoid this in the future. Management are also likely to be happy, because this should minimise the likelihood of similar complaints in the future. Sometimes, though, there is no satisfactory solution available, so management's job becomes one not of problem-solving but of explanation and persuasion. Employees will often initially view the effect of a decision as unfair but will be more likely to accept it if they know why it was made. (See Chapter 12 for more information on the important skills of negotiating, persuading and influencing.)

As for the content of grievance procedures, the procedures often follow the stages set out below:

Informal stage – The employee should first raise the matter with his or her immediate manager, or a manager from another department if that is more appropriate.

Stage 1 – If the matter remains unresolved, the employee can raise the matter formally in writing with the relevant manager. A meeting will be arranged with the employee, the companion (if applicable) and the relevant manager. The decision will be confirmed in writing.

Stage 2 – If the employee wishes to appeal against the decision, a meeting will be arranged with the employee, the companion (if applicable) and the relevant senior manager. The subsequent decision will be confirmed in writing.

Stage 3 – If the employee wishes to appeal against *that* decision, a meeting will be arranged to include the functional director and the companion/union regional officer (if applicable). The subsequent decision will be confirmed in writing.

Note that:

- Each stage will be time-bound so that a speedy resolution can be sought.
- In a smaller organisation, the grievance procedure may contain only two formal stages.
- In non-unionised organisations, it is likely that the decision given by the authorised officer at the final stage is a binding one – that is, there is no further internal right of appeal.

In unionised organisations, if there is a failure to agree at Stage 3, the arrangements outlined in the organisation's disputes procedure may come into play – for example, independent conciliation or arbitration or, possibly, a ballot for industrial action. Thus the grievance procedure and the disputes procedure dovetail at the final stage. Any form of industrial action is precluded until all the stages have been completed and a failure to agree recorded – that is, the procedure has been exhausted.

CASE STUDY 8.3

A company was faced with a grievance submitted by a female employee who had been nominated to attend a weekend training event. The employee did not want to go and approached her immediate manager to complain that she was only given two weeks' notice and would find it difficult to arrange for childcare. The line manager followed the procedure, met with the employee to clarify the problem and sought expert advice on a range of possible options. He realised that the training was necessary and would be expensive to cancel. He found it difficult to reach a decision that was satisfactory to all parties. In this instance, the employee was not satisfied by the response she received at this informal stage, but did agree to the compromise solution proposed at the formal Stage 1 meeting.

? REFLECTIVE ACTIVITY 8.5

Consider Case Study 8.3.

In carrying out his investigations, what questions did the supervisor need to find the answers to before reaching a decision? Compare your response with the feedback given at the end of this chapter.

HR practitioners often feel that they are in a difficult position in handling grievances. Often, their only formalised role is to take receipt of grievances at Stage 1 and onwards. A good record-keeping system should assist them in determining whether any previous decisions have established precedents for handling similar grievances. Some HR practitioners will, however, initiate the investigations and discussions necessary in order to address grievances and may also attend grievance hearings. These actions will help them to keep a tight rein on such matters so that line managers do not seek resolutions to grievances without thinking through the consequences for the rest of the organisation. For instance, in our previous example regarding the unequal distribution of overtime, it is unlikely that changes to overtime allocation arrangements within one department could be taken in isolation of all other departments. Dependent on the organisational position of the HR department (and personal standing of its members), HR practitioners will have varying degrees of success in seeking to influence such decisions.

8.6.2 WHISTLEBLOWING

'Whistleblowing' is the term used to describe a situation in which an employee perceives a wrongdoing at work and reports it to an outsider. The Public Interest Disclosure Act 1998 contains employment guarantees for employees who have made a protected disclosure so that they may not be dismissed or suffer detriment for so doing. The types of disclosure covered by the Act concern criminal offences, failure to comply with legal obligations, miscarriages of justice, health and safety risks, and environmental damage. If an employee feels safe and confident to raise the matters of concern with his or her employer, this is invariably to the employer's advantage. It may be that there has been a misunderstanding.

But more importantly, it enables the employer to deal with the matter before other agencies become involved. Employers must, of course, comply with the terms of the Act but could be more proactive by reviewing the arrangements that would be necessary to allow employees to raise these types of concern. It may be that the existing grievance procedure can simply be revised or that a separate policy and procedure should be implemented to reflect the greater sensitivity and seriousness attached to such matters. This can be particularly valuable in the care sector where a 'whistleblowers policy' can protect employees who report those colleagues who are abusing vulnerable people. However, abuse of the policy itself (by malicious reporting) would result in disciplinary action.

8.6.3 BULLYING AND HARASSMENT

An employee relations issue that has been growing in importance and has had more attention given to it by employers over recent years is bullying and harassment. Both bullying and harassment can be very damaging in the workplace and can lead to a negative impact on individual health, levels of motivation and morale, the employee relations climate at work and individual relationships. It is an issue that must be taken seriously and be seen to be taken seriously by employers – it should not be tolerated in the workplace. In the Acas guide for managers and employers on bullying and harassment it is stated that those making a complaint often define bullying and harassment as something that has happened that is unwanted, unwelcome and has a negative impact on them. They advise that any such complaints should be treated as a grievance which must be dealt with. The normal grievance procedures should be used for this, although in many larger organisations there will be specific procedures for dealing with bullying and harassment. The legislation on discrimination (covered elsewhere in this book) also provides protection from harassment on the grounds of age, sex, race, disability, sexual orientation, gender reassignment, religion or belief, marriage and civil partnership, and pregnancy and maternity.

?   REFLECTIVE ACTIVITY 8.6

What sort of behaviours would you consider to be bullying and harassment? Do some further reading and research to see what behaviours are generally held to be bullying and harassment. How does your list compare?

8.6.4 MEDIATION

Conflict between individuals at work, which may result in the use of formal procedures, such as grievances or claims of bullying and harassment, can in many circumstances be addressed through mediation. Mediation is aimed at helping the parties in conflict to reach their own resolution (thereby generating greater ownership and buy-in to the solution and way forward) by exploring the matters over which they are in conflict with the help of an independent person through a voluntary and confidential discussion process. A key part of mediation, and often a significant difference between mediation and other more formal processes, is that mediation is future-focused with the aim of helping the parties to work together more constructively in the future. It can be particularly effective in addressing absence where such absence relates to conflict at work and where there are issues of management style that have caused conflict. It is often most appropriate where individual relationships and behaviour towards others are at the heart of the conflict.

For more information on grievances in the workplace, see the CIPD 'Policies and Procedures for People Managers' manual listed in 'References and Further Reading' at the end of this chapter.

8.7 THE RIGHT TO BE ACCOMPANIED AT HEARINGS

As we have already stated, the Acas Code of Practice on disciplinary and grievance procedures provides guidance on the statutory right for workers when they face certain disciplinary or grievance hearings to be accompanied by either a fellow worker or a trade union official.

This right applies to any disciplinary hearing at which action may be contemplated against an employee. Thus it may be that it would not apply to an investigation, especially if that is solely concerned with obtaining facts. It would apply to a consultation on ill-health absence, if continuation of employment could be an issue – even though this is not a disciplinary matter.

With regard to grievance hearings, the right applies to meetings at which employers deal with complaints about duties owed by them to workers, whether the duty arises from statute or common law.

Your disciplinary and grievance procedures and practices should reflect these rights. Perhaps you should check to ensure that this is the case. Before moving on to consider the case for employee involvement, we will deal with the skills necessary for successful disciplinary, capability and grievance hearings.

8.8 INTERVIEWING SKILLS

We have seen that HR practitioners and line managers need to acquire a great deal of knowledge in order to be competent in handling disciplinary, capability and grievance situations. They also need certain skills – written and oral communications, investigatory skills, persuasion, judgement, taking responsibility, decision-making and analytical reasoning, to name but a few. At no time is the need for this knowledge and these skills more evident than when carrying out the disciplinary, capability or grievance interview, and we shall now examine accepted good practice.

Thorough preparation will help to ensure that interviewers are as professional as possible, regardless of their level of experience. It can safely be said that few managers actually relish the idea of conducting a disciplinary or capability interview: most, as has already been suggested, are more likely to view grievance-handling as an unpleasant chore than as a rewarding experience (a visit to the dentist might engender only slightly less enthusiasm).

Many of the skills required to carry out satisfactory selection interviews (see Chapter 5) are equally applicable to disciplinary and grievance interviewing – for example:

- preparing for the interview
- preparing the environment
- using open and probing questions
- active listening
- maintaining good eye contact
- using appropriate body language
- using silence
- keeping control of the subject matter and timing
- taking notes
- remaining unemotional
- providing clarification
- summarising.

There are obviously differences in the purposes of these types of interviews. It is good practice, in selection interviews, for instance, to establish a rapport with the interviewee. This generally involves a warm welcome and friendly exchange in an attempt to relax the interviewee so that he or she can perform at his or her optimum during the interview.

Such behaviour is obviously not entirely appropriate in a disciplinary or capability interview, and also, to some extent, a grievance interview, although it is advisable to establish the appropriate degree of rapport to ensure trust and confidence as far as possible. If you are too familiar or too personal, there is a danger of not being taken seriously, or of possibly being drawn into arguments and straying into personality issues.

A lack of perceived seriousness could:

- invalidate a disciplinary warning
- give sick employees the impression that their employment is not at risk if their absence continues
- lead employees with a grievance to the conclusion that their views are unimportant.

Conversely, an overly formal and impersonal style may seem to compromise reasonableness. Implementation of procedures in ways that are devoid of humanity is likely to lead to dissatisfaction and, in the case of dismissals, successful employment tribunal claims. You need to strike a balance between the two approaches.

In summary, the key points applicable to disciplinary, capability and grievance interviews are to:

- stay calm and in control
- be reasonable and objective
- be factual and unemotional.

There is no one correct and precise way to conduct a disciplinary or grievance hearing, but you should find that Tables 8.3 and 8.4 provide useful step-by-step approaches.

Table 8.3 The disciplinary interview

Before	During	After
• Ensure that you are familiar with the disciplinary procedure; for example, the disciplinary penalties, the limit of your authority, the employee's rights to accompaniment and to appeal. • Suspend the employee on full pay if this is a case of suspected gross misconduct. • Carry out a thorough investigation and gather facts. Record all the information you acquire in accordance with the requirements of the Data Protection Act 1998. • Consider any relevant precedents, and the employee's disciplinary record. • Inform the employee in writing of the time, date, location and type of hearing, the nature of the	• Convene the disciplinary hearing and make the necessary introductions. • Explain the purpose of the hearing, present the allegations and the evidence. • Request that supporting witnesses give their statements and are prepared to answer questions from both parties, if appropriate. • Listen to the employee and/or the employee's companion as they give their side of the story, and allow them to call supporting witnesses. • Ask questions of the employee and the employee's witnesses (and allow your management colleagues to do the same). • Take comprehensive notes (or arrange for someone else to).	• Confirm the decision to the employee in writing, and write up the notes of the interview. Provide the employee with a copy, and place copies of all the relevant documents on the personal file. Complete the disciplinary record. • Monitor and review.

Before	During	After
allegations and the right to be accompanied. Provide copies of evidence, such as witness statements, preferably prior to the meeting. • If the employee has a disability or English is not his or her first language, check whether any particular arrangements will be needed at any time during the procedure; for example, access to facilities, a reader or interpreter. • Decide on the sequence or structure of the interview. Invite all the relevant parties – that is, companions and witnesses – and arrange for their release from duties. Be prepared to agree a postponement to the hearing should individuals be unavailable. • Arrange a suitable venue for the hearing – that is, a quiet place free from interruptions – and allow sufficient time in your diary. • Ensure that the hearing will be properly constituted according to the procedure; for example, in a potential dismissal case, a senior manager must take the decision. It is always preferable that different managers conduct the investigation and hear the case.	• Seek clarification of the key issues. • Give the employee and/or the employee's companion the opportunity to reiterate any aspects that they wish to emphasise. • Adjourn the hearing to allow consideration of the points raised and any mitigating circumstances (or to allow further investigation). Agree an extension to the schedule for the hearing if necessary. • Consider the appropriate action to be taken. • Reconvene, and inform the employee of your decision and the reasons for it. Highlight the change in behaviour needed, if appropriate, and the consequences of a failure to improve in the future. • Specify a review date, if there is to be one. • Inform the employee of the appeals procedure.	

Note: halt the proceedings at any point where it is apparent that:

• the use of the disciplinary procedure is inappropriate and, say, counselling or the capability procedure should be used
• there is no case to be answered by the employee.

Table 8.4 The grievance interview

Before	During	After
• Ensure that you are familiar with the grievance procedure, any required timescales and with what happens if you fail to resolve the grievance at this stage. • Request that the employee (or companion, if applicable) provide full details of the grievance in writing. • Carry out a full investigation. Seek to establish the facts; for example, dates, times, places, witnesses. • Request details of the nature of any prior discussions from appropriate managers. • Question other parties relevant to the grievance. • Consider any information pertinent to the issue raised; for example, policies and procedures, statistical information, custom and practice, notes of interviews, written particulars, personal records, employment legislation, codes of practice. • Record all the information you have acquired, ensuring compliance with the Data Protection Act 1998. • Inform the employee, in writing, of the subject matter, time, date, location and nature of the interview, and of the right to be accompanied. • If the employee has a disability or English is not his or her first language, check whether any particular arrangements will be needed at any time during the procedure; for	• Convene the grievance interview. • Listen objectively to the employee's complaint. • Regardless of the eventual outcome of the grievance, thank the employee for bringing the matter to your attention. • Hear witness evidence and allow for examination and cross-examination, as appropriate, by both sides. • Consider any documentation provided by the employee. • Be prepared to answer questions/explain current practices, and so on. • Seek clarification of the key issues, including any solutions sought. • Summarise your understanding throughout the interview. • Arrange for comprehensive notes to be taken. • Allow time for the employee to confer in private with his or her companion at any point in the proceedings. • Adjourn the interview to allow consideration of the points raised, and the circumstances. If the case is particularly complex, or if further investigations are necessary, request and agree an extension to the time allowed before a response is expected. • Consider the appropriate action to be taken, if any, bearing in mind any relevant procedures and possible repercussions. • Reconvene, and inform the employee of your decision, giving your reasons and seeking agreement, if possible. If an immediate	• Record the results and write up the notes of the interview. Arrange for confirmation of the decision to be sent to the employee and his or her companion. Depending on the nature of the grievance, in the interests of good employee relations, and bearing in mind data protection provisions, you may wish to publicise any resultant changes to all workers. • Monitor the situation by, for example, maintaining informal contact with the employee or arranging a formal review meeting (whichever is more appropriate). • Evaluate the success or otherwise of any actions that have been taken as a result of the grievance being raised.

Before	During	After
example, access to facilities, a reader or interpreter. • Decide on the sequence or structure of the interview. Invite all the relevant parties – that is, companions and witnesses – and arrange for their release from duties. Be prepared to agree a postponement to the hearing should individuals be unavailable. • Arrange a suitable venue for the interview – that is, a quiet place free from interruptions – and allow sufficient time in your diary. • Ensure that the meeting will be properly constituted, according to the procedure.	recommendation cannot be given, ensure that it is communicated to both parties within the appropriate timescale, and confirmed in writing. • If a mutually acceptable agreement has not been/is not likely to be reached, inform the employee of his or her right to appeal at the next stage, and of the procedure for so doing, if the procedure has not been exhausted.	

8.9 EMPLOYEE VOICE AND EMPLOYEE ENGAGEMENT

We consider the two linked concepts of employee voice and employee engagement here because they have been and continue to be an area of growing interest and activity for HR practitioners and managers alike. Both issues (but particularly employee engagement) are increasingly receiving attention in organisations and have been a vehicle for HR to engage in debate with employees, managers and senior leaders in their organisations about good people management practice. In some instances we have seen the phrase 'employee engagement' used interchangeably with 'employee relations' as if one is a development of the other. A lot of the available debate and research about employee engagement understandably looks at what can broadly be described as aspects of the employment relationship, hence the link to employee relations. Similarly, many of the aspects of people management practice that need to have attention paid to them to promote and sustain engagement are the very ones looked at elsewhere in this chapter, such as effective communication, having fair and just management processes, dealing well with conflict, and having managers who can effectively manage the relationship with employees.

As the CIPD's 'Employee Engagement' factsheet (2014) asserts, employee engagement is increasingly mainstreamed – in both the work of HR practitioners and in organisational activity.

8.9.1 EMPLOYEE VOICE

The concept of employee voice – where employees actively share their views and opinions and are really listened to and have influence – is part of any effective two-way communication process within an organisation. It is about how employees get heard and have a say in their employment relationship with their employer. That voice may be heard in the:

• decision-making processes

- formulation of company strategy and direction
- the contribution of ideas and opinions about company plans.

It may be individual voices that are heard, recognising the unique position employees have, often at the front line of an organisation, in really understanding how the organisation works on a day-to-day basis. Or, the collective voice may be heard through representative participation and mechanisms such as:

- formal partnership agreements (common in the public sector)
- European Works Councils
- joint consultation arrangements
- employee forums.

Increasingly, there is a role for social media in employee voice, with organisations looking for new ways to encourage employee input and employees using different platforms to share views and make input. See Chapter 10 for further information on the use of social media in the workplace.

Purcell (2014) suggests that it is not about *ad hoc* or one-off communication activities: real voice is about a 'culture of participation'. He also suggests that employee voice is a forerunner of employee engagement and something that should return to mainstream focus after falling somewhat out of favour.

8.9.2 EMPLOYEE ENGAGEMENT

Employee engagement is a broad concept and area of practice – indeed, we are now seeing jobs for employee engagement specialists being advertised alongside the more well-established roles of HR business partners, learning and development and reward specialists. As with employee relations, there are many different definitions of employee engagement, but some common features indicate it is a field of practice concerned with:

- levels of organisational commitment from employees
- the extent to which employees are willing to 'go the extra mile' (discretionary effort)
- levels of pride, enthusiasm and motivation (see Chapter 6 for more on motivation)
- job satisfaction.

One definition provided by the Kingston Employee Engagement Consortium in its CIPD-published research report, 'Creating an Engaged Workforce' suggests that employee engagement is 'being positively present during the performance of work by willingly contributing intellectual effort, experiencing positive emotions and meaningful connections to others'.

This is surely the holy grail of HR?

As with employee relations, the role of line managers in employee engagement is key. Many organisations now measure employee engagement and the things that are measured – how happy/satisfied employees are; how effective communication is; how employees view managers and leaders; and so on – are things that managers have a huge impact on and are often driven by the state of the relationship between managers and their staff. It is possible to see how the manner in which managers deal with disciplinary and grievance matters, for instance, will have an impact on how employees feel about the managers and leaders in their organisation.

In building and sustaining employee engagement the CIPD in its 'Employee Engagement' factsheet suggest organisations should pay attention to:

- communication processes, ensuring they are effective and keep employees informed about company performance, purpose and vision
- ensuring employees have an effective 'voice'
- role-modelling by managers and leaders
- fair processes and procedures.

Some people have, however, suggested that employee engagement is merely a repackaging of old concepts, albeit one that has brought issues such as job satisfaction and motivation back into the spotlight. It is clear that employee engagement has done a lot to highlight and drive good people-management practice in many organisations, with many now investing heavily in assessing what engagement means for them, what drives engagement and how it can be measured effectively. At the same time, many of the leading thinkers and researchers on employee engagement are beginning to question how sustainable engagement is. Emphasising the need for engagement to go hand in hand with work on employee well-being, they point to the risk of employee burnout and question what it is the employee is engaged with – their job, their manager or their organisation? Without knowing the answer to this, it is difficult for organisations to assess the effectiveness of their policy or approach.

? REFLECTIVE ACTIVITY 8.7

Find out if employee engagement is an issue that gets any attention in your organisation. What do people understand by employee engagement? Is it measured and, if so, how? What impact has paying attention to employee engagement had? If it is not an issue that gets any attention in your organisation, think about how you might get the conversation started: what aspects of communication, motivation and job satisfaction do you think need attention in your organisation?

Employee engagement is an evolving area of practice and readers would be well advised to keep up to date with developments in this field.

8.9.3 TRADE UNION INVOLVEMENT

Throughout this chapter we have mentioned the role that may be played by trade unions in employee relations – particularly in terms of representing employees. Here we will be concentrating on the specific roles played by trade unions in the context of employee involvement in the workplace. Trade unions share in the decision-making within unionised organisations in five main ways:

1   Collective bargaining – this constitutes negotiations between employers (or employers' organisations) and trade unions. Traditionally, collective bargaining in the UK has centred on substantive terms and conditions of employment – for example, pay, hours and holidays. In many cases there has also been bargaining over the allocation of work and job duties and the physical working environment. From time to time there may be negotiation over procedural matters, such as the criteria to be used for redundancy selection.

2   Statutory consultation – this covers areas where employers are obliged to consult with a trade union, where they are recognised (see Chapter 3). In addition, recognised unions can require the appointment of a safety representative or representatives who have wide powers to access the workplace and to table questions to which management has to respond.

3   Joint consultation – this complements the collective bargaining arrangements in unionised environments and involves managers and trade union/employee representatives meeting regularly to discuss items of mutual concern, such as health and safety, welfare, training, efficiency and quality.

4   Dispute resolution – as we have discussed, trade union representatives frequently accompany employees at disciplinary and grievance hearings and may also raise collective grievances.

5   Partnership arrangements – these are based on agreements between management and trade unions and are symbolic of a desire to move away from the old adversarial approach to employee relations (or industrial relations). Gennard and Judge (2005, pp 278–279) summarise six key principles on which partnership arrangements are based.

These are paraphrased below:

● Both management and trade union are committed to the success of the enterprise and have a shared understanding of its goals.
● Each side has legitimate and separate interests.
● There is a joint responsibility to maximise employment security and improve the employability of employees via training and development.
● The quality of working life will be improved by creating opportunities for personal growth.
● There needs to be a real sharing of 'hard' information.
● Tapping into new sources of motivation, commitment and resources will 'add value' to the business.

8.10 THE PSYCHOLOGICAL CONTRACT

In Chapter 3 we covered the legislation governing the contract of employment. It was pointed out that the contract terms may be explicit – that is, written down and/or agreed between the parties – or implicit – that is, implied by statute, custom and practice, and so on. An even more subtle feature of the employment relationship relates to the unwritten expectations that employers and employees have of each other. This is referred to as the 'psychological contract'.

What do we mean by this term? In the past, employers expected loyalty and obedience in exchange for providing employees with job security and regular pay increases. As 'jobs for life' (and inflation-linked pay increases) have become increasingly rare, the exchange of expectations nowadays tends to centre on factors such as those in Table 8.5.

Table 8.5 The psychological contract

Employers expect:	Employees expect:
● commitment to goals and values ● hard work and flexibility ● creativity and innovation ● team-playing capability	● skill development to aid employability ● fair and respectful treatment ● involvement in decision-making ● good working relationships

It is an inevitable fact that changes – minor and major – in the work situation will be necessary. Such changes frequently have an impact on the 'health' of the psychological contract. All of the expectations listed in Table 8.5 are relevant to the management of change within organisations. Also, many conflicts within the workplace are related to the way in which change is managed. Forcing changes on individuals is not only bad practice but is likely to have detrimental consequences. Neglecting the psychological contract will inevitably impact on the state of employee relations within the organisation.

If you want to contribute towards an improved psychological contract in your organisation, you might like to give attention to the following:

- the expectations that are created at the recruitment stage; for example, in advertisements
- the expectations that are created on appointment, including the terminology used (some of these are created by the legal contract itself)
- the expectations created at the induction stage, and the extent to which there is fulfilment of some of the earlier expectations
- the extent to which all these expectations are realised as the job and employment unfolds
- the amount of trust shown in employees
- the extent to which openness and honesty is encouraged
- the attitude to mistakes – are they an opportunity for learning or an opportunity to blame?
- other related cultural factors (see Chapter 2).

8.11 THE ROLE OF HR PRACTITIONERS

Whilst we have tended to concentrate on the role of line managers in implementing the rules and procedures applicable to discipline, capability and grievance handling and in managing employee relations, as an HR practitioner you will obviously adopt the same role when dealing with your own staff and are also likely to carry out the following roles, depending on your organisation.

8.11.1 AN ADVISORY AND SUPPORTIVE ROLE TO LINE MANAGERS

In this capacity your advice is sought when employee relations incidents occur or before disciplinary action is taken or grievances are addressed. This will help to ensure a consistency of approach across the organisation as, in this role, you need to be familiar with relevant employment legislation, case law and accepted good practice. You should also have an appreciation of how such situations have been dealt with in the past and the likely repercussions of decisions taken for the future, as well as being the 'authority' regarding the operation and interpretation of your own rules and procedures. (It has already been stressed that industrial action could result from poorly managed disciplinary and grievance situations – most managers would agree that troubleshooting is generally preferable to firefighting!)

8.11.2 AN OVERSEEING AND CO-ORDINATING ROLE

In this you bring possible disciplinary infringements and performance problems to the attention of line managers for their action; for example, following a periodic check on attendance records and/or sickness notification and certification records. This again serves to ensure a standardised approach to organisation-wide problems, but difficulties may arise when line managers use this as an opportunity to abdicate responsibility back to the HR department.

8.11.3 A SECRETARIAL ROLE

You often carry out this role in communication and consultation meetings as well as disciplinary, capability and grievance hearings to ensure that detailed and accurate records are kept. This is especially necessary in the event of appeals against disciplinary action or unresolved grievances that are progressing to the next stage and (every HR practitioner's nightmare) employment tribunal hearings. See the Appendix to this chapter for a checklist on taking notes of disciplinary interviews. (This checklist could also, with some slight adaptation, be used for capability and grievance interviews.)

8.11.4 A DECISION-MAKING ROLE

This concerns the action that should be taken in addressing an employee relations issue or a disciplinary situation, or in concluding a grievance application (hopefully) satisfactorily. The authority for this role must be stated in the appropriate procedures (except where, as an HR practitioner, you are acting as the line manager for your own staff). This role is more likely to be adopted in a smaller organisation where, for instance, the HR manager has the authority to dismiss, and the managing director reserves the independence of a third party of higher status in order to be able to hear any appeals.

8.11.5 A TRAINING/EDUCATIONAL OR COACHING ROLE

This is to ensure that managers follow the procedures correctly and are trained to carry out interviews and to obtain other requisite skills such as counselling and negotiating. Training may be formal or informal, as appropriate. Most managers, unlike HR practitioners, do not have a wide experience of handling conflict situations; they may have undergone formal training some time previously, but need some coaching to give them the confidence to lead an interview or meeting.

8.11.6 A PERSUADING, INFLUENCING OR NEGOTIATING ROLE

Depending on the job role, you may find that you need to:

- persuade managers that they must pay heed to your advice on employee relations incidents
- 'sell' the benefits of organisational changes or the results of disciplinary or grievance proceedings to appropriate personnel
- consult or negotiate directly either with individual employees or union/employee representatives over a range of issues affecting the employment relationship
- 'set the tone' by the way you phrase correspondence, policies and other communications with employees
- manage expectations by influencing what is put in job advertisements or appointment letters, said at interview or outlined at induction.

See Chapter 12 for more information on the requisite skills. It is essential that the HR practitioner identifies which 'hat' (or 'hats') he or she is wearing in disciplinary and capability matters and grievance-handling. Employment tribunal cases regarding unfair dismissal claims have been lost by employers when it became apparent that the decision to dismiss was taken by someone other than the person named in the procedure as having sufficient authority.

8.12 SUMMARY

You should now be familiar with the theory and practice of handling conduct, performance and grievance issues. We have looked at the content and operation of disciplinary rules and disciplinary, capability and grievance procedures, as well as their importance, relevant legislation and accepted good practice.

We have also highlighted a range of absence management tools that organisations have found to be effective in reducing absenteeism and its associated costs.

We have considered the nature of the employee voice and employee engagement and the impact they can have on the relationship employees have with their manager and the organisation

We have considered the role that trade unions play in employee relations in the workplace.

We then highlighted the need to take account of the psychological contract in seeking to manage employee relations.

The knowledge and skills necessary for dealing with employee relations issues have also been examined, specifically with regard to the role(s) played by HR practitioners.

Finally, note that a list of legislative Acts is included within the References and Further Reading at the end of this chapter, Reflective Activities have been suggested throughout the chapter, and you are encouraged to complete some, if not all, of these activities in order to reinforce and apply your learning. The Appendix checklist follows the activities feedback at the very end of the chapter.

EXPLORE FURTHER

References and further reading

ACAS (2009) *Bullying and Harassment at Work: A guide for managers and employers*. Advisory Booklet. Leicester: Acas.

ACAS (2009) *Employee Communications and Consultation*. Advisory booklet. Leicester: Acas.

ACAS (2009) *Managing Attendance and Employee Turnover*. Advisory booklet. Leicester: Acas.

ACAS (2015) *Code of Practice 1: Disciplinary and Grievance Procedures*. Leicester: Acas.

ACAS (2015) *Discipline and Grievances at Work. The Acas Guide*. Leicester: Acas.

All of the above are available from: ACAS Publications, PO Box 235, Hayes, Middlesex, UB3 1HF; tel: 08702 429090. They can also be downloaded at www.acas. org.uk

ALFES, K., TRUSS, C., SOANE, E., REES, C. and GATENBY, M. (2010) *Creating an Engaged Workforce. Findings from the Kingston Employee Engagement Consortium Project*. Research report. London: CIPD.

BRINER, R. (2014) *What is Employee Engagement and Does it Matter? An Evidence-Based Approach*. Bath: University of Bath, School of Management.

DUNDON, T. and ROLLINSON, D. (2011) *Understanding Employment Relations*. 2nd edition. London: McGraw-Hill Higher Education.

EINARSON, S. (ed) (2010) *Bullying and Harassment in the Workplace: Developments in Theory, Research and Practice*. 2nd edition. London: CRC Press.

GENNARD, J. and JUDGE, G. (2010) *Managing Employment Relations*. London: CIPD.

GENNARD, J. and JUDGE, G. (2005) *Employee Relations*. 4th edition. London: CIPD.

LEWIS, C. (2009) *The Definitive Guide to Workplace Mediation and Managing Conflict at Work*. Weybridge: Roper Penberthy Publishing.

PURCELL, J. (2012) *The Limits and Possibilities of Employee Engagement*. Warwick: Industrial Relations Unit, University of Warwick.

PURCELL, J. (2014) *The Future of Engagement: Thought Piece Collection – Time to Focus on Employee Voice as a Prime Antecedent of Engagement: Rediscovering the Black Box*. Institute of Employment Studies and CIPD.

SPURGEON, P., MAZELAN, P., BARWELL, F. and FLANAGAN, H. (2007) *New Directions in Managing Employee Absence: An Evidence-Based Approach*. London: CIPD.

The CIPD publications listed below are available from: 151 The Broadway, London SW19 1JQ; tel: 020 8612 6201:

- CIPD *Policies and Procedures for People Managers* manual.
- CIPD (2005) *What is Employee Relations?* Change agenda. London: CIPD.
- CIPD (2011) *Conflict Management*. Survey report. London: CIPD.
- CIPD (2012) *Managing Employee Relations in Difficult Times*. Research report. London: CIPD.
- CIPD (2014) *Absence Management*. Survey report. London: CIPD.

Acts of parliament and codes of practice

Equality Act 2010

Employment Rights Act 1996

Public Interest Disclosure Act 1998

Acas (revised 2009) *Code of Practice 1: Disciplinary and Grievance Procedures*. Leicester: ACAS (reproduced in full in the Acas publication *Discipline and Grievances at Work* above).

Websites

Acas (Code of Practice): www.acas.org.uk/media/pdf/l/c/Acas-Code-of-Practice-1-on-disciplinary-and-grievance-procedures.pdf

Department for Business, Innovation & Skills (Employment Relations): www.gov.uk/government/organisations/department-for-business-innovation-skills

Legislation: www.legislation.hmso.gov.uk

See also the following CIPD factsheets, available at cipd.co.uk/hr-resources/factsheets:

- Discipline and Grievances at Work (2012)
- Dismissal (2012)
- Employee Engagement (2014)
- Employee Relations: An Overview (2012)
- Employee Voice (2012)
- The Psychological Contract (2012)

REFLECTIVE ACTIVITIES FEEDBACK

Reflective Activity 8.5

Before reaching a decision, the supervisor needed to answer the following questions:

- Do the written particulars contain a clause referring to out-of-hours training?
- Which legislative Acts are relevant – for example, the Equality Act 2010 (regarding indirect sex discrimination)?
- What has happened in the past in similar circumstances (that is, custom and practice)?
- Has the employee been willing to attend previous training events?
- What is known about the employee's domestic circumstances (taking into account the employee's right to privacy)?
- Can the company provide any help and assistance regarding childcare?
- Can alternative arrangements be made to accommodate this training; for example, rescheduling the event to weekdays, changing the attendance requirements?
- What are the likely repercussions of all the possible solutions?

APPENDIX TO CHAPTER 8

CHECKLIST FOR TAKING NOTES OF DISCIPLINARY INTERVIEWS

The following checklist should assist you in ensuring that your written notes fully meet the need to:

- provide sufficient information for whoever is responsible for issuing the confirmation letter to the employee (if this is necessary)
- provide a useful justification and record of the action taken at this stage should the situation deteriorate further (possibly resulting in an unfair dismissal claim being heard at an employment tribunal).

Do the notes include: **YES/NO**

1 the date, venue, and start time of the interview?

2 an account of those attending the interview and their roles?

3 details of the allegations stated to the employee and of the supporting evidence; for example, witness statements?

4 details of the employee's response and of the supporting evidence?

5 a record of any adjournments and approximate timings?

6 consideration of the employee's previous record?

7 the decision on whether disciplinary action was appropriate or not and the type of action taken with the appropriate timescale?

8 the review date and a clear statement of intent if improvement does not occur?

9 reference to the right to appeal and the finish time of the interview?

10 reference to the note-taker's name plus a date and signature?

Learning and Development

9.1 INTRODUCTION

In recent years there has been an increasing tendency to talk about learning, rather than training. It emphasises a subtle but important difference in approach. Training is a process through which individuals are helped to learn a skill or technique. The emphasis is very much on the responsibility of the trainer or the employer to assist the employee. It implies that the process is effective (sometimes it is not) and that the employee can be a passive recipient in the process. The latter explains why training does not always succeed in its objectives. But when computer-based training (CBT) was developing, it became apparent that the user had to take responsibility for learning, not the computer for training. So using the term 'learning' switches responsibility and carries the further implication that the employee himself or herself can initiate the learning whether or not the organisation provides any specific assistance. Learning is very broad-based, encompassing minor and major pieces of information, skills, judgement and personal growth.

The opportunities for learner-driven, rather than trainer-driven, learning are increasing. Software can be learned through online tutorials (through the Help key or via Google) whereas conferences, YouTube, forums and other forms of social networking are allowing us to learn (cautiously, it should be said) from the practical experience of others whom we have never met and whom we probably never will meet.

Training tends to focus on skills or techniques. These are areas where one person (the trainer) can more easily guide another (the learner) than ones where the learner might guide himself or herself. A skill may be primarily manual, as in using a keyboard, or essentially intellectual, such as negotiating a house sale. The latter is often referred to as a 'soft skill' since no 'hard' equipment is involved. Instruction is a very typical form of training, but there are many others. There is often an end point – perhaps the achievement of a specific data-entry speed.

Development places emphasis on the growth of the individual. It relates to acquiring a very broad range of soft skills through planned activities and experience. Management of people, handling work relationships and leadership are typical of broad ranges of skills that are developed. Success in all these areas requires maturity of judgement. There is no fixed end point to development, because individuals can continually improve, for example, their leadership skills.

This chapter is included because training, learning or human resource development typically sits within the HR department. In small organisations it may be the direct responsibility of the HR manager or officer. However, these responsibilities are often treated as a major function in themselves. So this chapter focuses on matters of interest to the HR practitioner rather than on the broader needs of a dedicated learning and development practitioner. For these needs, please see the companion publication, *Learning and Development Practice*.

The structure of this chapter follows the steps in the *learning cycle*, which we shall look at in a moment. First, though, we consider the importance of learning and development activities.

9.2 WHY ARE LEARNING AND DEVELOPMENT IMPORTANT?

We shall be looking at the unrelenting pace of change in the world and at its implications for learning needs. If our organisations respond to change early, they will prosper and gain rewards in terms of security, profit or attainment of their goals. Today, commercial products and services can be imitated – some almost immediately. So technological advantage may give one producer an edge over others, but these other producers can catch up quickly. In a free-market economy all organisations have similar access to capital, to customers and to employees. It is their effectiveness in operating, as organisations of people, that primarily distinguishes one from another. Key factors in operating effectively are the knowledge and skills of people.

In the commercial world, then, if we train our people and continually ensure that they have up-to-date knowledge and up-to-date skills, it follows that we shall be able to compete effectively, and reasonably expect to prosper. Few, if any, jobs today are protected from commercial realities. Even those not originally viewed as commercial organisations – for example, charities – now place considerable importance on obtaining well-trained professional people to run their operations.

As an HR practitioner you have an important role to play. You should be able to relate to commercial needs and your corporate mission, using them to help identify suitable learning. Like every other operation, learning and development has to be managed. HR practitioners need to acquire advanced skills and knowledge if they are to manage it effectively.

We shall commence with a look at the learning cycle, which helps identify the main principles involved in managing learning and development activities.

9.3 THE LEARNING CYCLE

Figure 9.1 demonstrates how learning is managed. It is a continuous cycle. We shall look first at how learning needs are identified, usually referred to as 'learning needs analysis'. Then we shall look at how to plan a learning programme, highlighting the ingredients available to satisfy those needs that have been identified. Last, and not least, we shall look at how the effectiveness of learning can be evaluated.

Consider how this might work in practice.

At an annual appraisal you decide that an improved knowledge of employment law would add to your effectiveness. You will want to assess what level of knowledge you need and the areas of knowledge that are important to your particular role, whether recruitment and selection, policies and procedures or employee termination matters. You should compare what you know already with what you need to know. This would identify the learning needed. You should set some objectives for the outcome of the learning.

Figure 9.1 The learning cycle

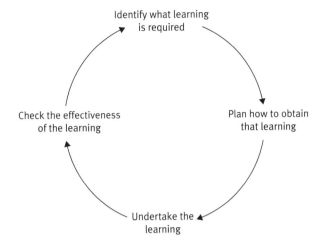

Planning could involve discussions with colleagues, investigating short courses in employment law, private study or even considering the CIPD Awards in Employment Law. You will need to assess the appropriateness of the options, how much time would be involved, when you will be able to go, and what the cost will be.

You implement the learning by going on the course(s), doing the reading, completing any coursework.

Checking the effectiveness of the learning is often the most difficult. How effective has your learning been? Are you confident of actions that you might have previously referred to others? How does it match up to the original outcomes? Is this saving your organisation time, cost, disputes and grievances, exposure to tribunal claims, and so on? It doesn't stop there, because as you review the learning you will probably uncover other learning needs – and the cycle continues.

?   REFLECTIVE ACTIVITY 9.1

Work through the learning cycle by using your own example, as below.

Realistically identify some skill need(s) of your own; for example, improving your typing speed (there are many online tests; just google 'typing test'). Set some objectives and write them down.

Plan how to satisfy that need, examining a range of options for achieving your objectives and selecting one or more possibilities.

Undertake the learning and/or development that you have planned.

When you have completed the learning and/or development, assess its effectiveness against your original objectives.

1   Have you achieved your objectives?

2   Did you learn as fast as you expected?

3   Were the options you chose the best?

4   Have you discovered additional skill needs?

Although learning is a continuous cycle, we shall look first at how learning needs arise.

9.4 LEARNING NEEDS ARISE BECAUSE THE WORLD CHANGES

Change is continuous; it affects the environment in which organisations operate and it exists within organisations themselves. Employees are affected by change and they must adapt, learn new skills, cope with different pressures, acquire new knowledge and forge new relationships. Learning brings additional resources to individuals to enable them to change and develop. When we looked at the organisational context (Chapter 2), we briefly identified some of the types of changes that affect the corporate environment.

In recent years *political change* has brought about the need for new management skills in many different industries. The Government increasingly manages sectors of both the public and the otherwise private economy through regulations, inspections and standards. The extended government involvement in the banks and the standards to be met by care homes are particular examples where managers and employees have to learn how to respond to changes brought about by political philosophies. Politicians also seek to influence the participation of organisations and individuals in learning. This has led to initiatives such as National Vocational Qualifications (NVQs).

The *economic conditions* of the early twenty-first century favoured the creation of many small businesses encouraged by tax advantages, new technologies and a healthy economy generally. This created the need for wider business skills on the part of many people who had previously worked only as part of a larger enterprise. The subsequent recession placed further demands on those same people.

Social change creates learning needs. For example, information is becoming available to all as never before. Among many other effects it changes the way people buy, what they buy, or how they complain. Second, as a society we now acknowledge women's right to occupy jobs at the highest levels in companies and institutions. Both these examples indicate the need for learning: the first example, in terms of customer care and skills in information access, and in the second, management skills for women (to help redress the imbalance at senior levels).

Technological change is relentless. The learning needs it creates in computer skills, in advanced technical skills and in entirely new ways of doing things are widespread and substantial. The ability to develop and exploit opportunities provided by cloud technologies is critical for business and such new technology will mean the need for learning. Social networking (see Chapter 10) has far-reaching implications for the availability of information, for education, for retail trade and for many more activities.

It is already changing the way we work and creating many new businesses around technology. The development of social networking is continuing and will result in changes that are still difficult to predict. At the same time, all this technology also provides new techniques for trainers and learners to use in the process of learning itself; for example, virtual learning environments (see References and Further Reading at the end of this chapter).

The law changes continually as well, and HR practitioners are only too aware of the learning needs it creates for them. Keep in mind that employment is only one area affected by the law. Product liability, labelling of consumer goods and the regulation of financial services are just a few examples where the law creates learning needs for employers.

Environmental issues are increasingly to the fore. Fair trade, organic foods and green products are responses to consumer demand. The need for re-use, recycling and reduced landfill is creating new industries. These changes create threats for some companies and opportunities for others. In many industries, environmental pollution can be reduced by the better training of operatives.

Globalisation is a factor for many businesses both in trading and in outsourcing goods and services. It also creates competition and the UK lags seriously behind other developed countries in its levels of productivity. As we outlined in Chapter 5 jobs growth is in management jobs, professional occupations and higher skilled jobs where cognitive skills are paramount. Unfortunately, a relatively large proportion of UK workers have low cognitive skills (OECD; see 'References and Further Reading at the end of this chapter') and it is especially so among 16–24 year olds. It is going to fall to employers and to government initiatives to address the challenges this situation creates.

These changes lead to new products, services and standards of expected performance that, in turn, demand new skills and abilities. Organisations that can respond to these changes quickly by training their employees appropriately steal an advantage over their competitors.

Listening to and reading suitable media material and cautious social networking will raise your awareness of the corporate environment. We recommend:

- *People Management*
- other specialist training or learning publications
- quality daily or Sunday newspapers
- quality magazines covering business or current affairs
- BBC Radio 4
- the CIPD website
- a wide range of other websites on the Internet
- LinkedIn
- Twitter – where you can follow an incredible range of valuable sources, including all of the above.

Note: In a changing world the best social networking sites will also change, as some grow, others contract, and new ones with new ideas come on stream.

Individual learning needs also arise internally, directly or indirectly, as a result of external changes. Even without those external changes, learning needs will arise for employees who are new to the organisation, gain promotion, relocate, are redeployed or choose to retire. So when looking at learning needs, we have to consider not only changes in the environment but also changes for individuals.

9.5 LEARNING NEEDS ARISE BECAUSE PEOPLE'S JOBS AND CAREERS CHANGE

Induction training addresses the needs of new starters and similar training is needed for all employees who transfer or are promoted within the organisation. We choose the term 'training' because the responsibility to initiate the learning here rests primarily with the organisation. Some special cases are considered below:

School-leavers have much to learn about the world of work. They need to understand the level of commitment required and to be able to assess others' expectations of them. Working with adults will be a novel experience and new attitudes must be formed. All this is quite separate from the actual mechanics of doing the job. Comparatively simple everyday tasks, such as answering the telephone, can be a major source of anxiety to those who have never been in employment before. (Perhaps you can remember your first day at work!)

Increasingly we need to be aware that some 16–24 year olds may be low in literacy, numeracy or problem-solving skills.

Young graduates, especially those who have not been in employment before, need a similar induction process to that for school-leavers, although they can be expected to learn faster. Many employers give special consideration to graduates, recognising that they may eventually become senior managers in the organisation. Building relationships with people in different departments of the organisation and having a broad understanding of what each function does is critical for those who seek a progressive career. Graduate learning schemes invariably recognise this and graduates often spend time in different functions before settling into their chosen career path.

New employees who already have experience elsewhere need to learn about the culture of your organisation – that is, 'how things are done' (see Chapter 2). They need to meet, and begin to build relationships with, those with whom they will be in regular contact.

Systems and routines will be different from those of their previous employer. At the same time, new employees usually bring alternative approaches that can benefit their new employer.

Returners from maternity leave, a career break or a period of unemployment may need time and help to build up their confidence. For example, business processes change as technology provides new systems for accomplishing routine tasks. Given support to adapt and learning in new skills, returners usually regain their confidence rapidly.

Employees who have moved from other departments, functions and sites also need time to acclimatise to their new situations. The building of new relationships and finding the right contacts can be encouraged by team-building events and by deliberate inclusion in social activities.

With the possible exception of those from other departments, all these groups are likely to need to learn to use the corporate computer facilities.

Providing mentors and associates to aid all these transitions is a popular way to assist employees. Mentors, usually more senior than the employee, can provide encouragement and support and pass on their own skills and experience as well as lead by example.

Associates may be peers of the employee, such as a graduate who joined with the last intake and who can relate easily to a new graduate entrant.

Retirement calls for a new set of life skills, and responsible employers recognise the need for learning for this. They provide preparatory courses covering subjects such as health and financial planning, as well as introducing employees to pensioners' groups.

Current employees who are not performing at the right level require specific diagnosis. The problem may lie in a lack of technical skills or in attitude, but very often other factors not directly related to learning needs may be diagnosed.

Promotion creates learning needs. Surprisingly, this is often not recognised. It does not follow that the best operative is automatically an effective supervisor, that the best salesman is a natural manager, or that an experienced schoolteacher knows how to be a headteacher. The Peter Principle, which suggests that everyone is promoted to their level of incompetence, possibly reflects the lack of learning that most employees receive on promotion.

Future potential is another reason for training and developing individuals. It particularly relates to those who are progressing to managerial or professional careers, where the responsibility for development of skills rests more heavily with the individual.

'Fast-tracking' is the term used when individuals are identified as having significant future potential. Such individuals are singled out for special development. Activities may include studying for professional qualifications, secondments to other sites, departments or companies, special project responsibilities, and mentoring from one or more senior managers.

Organisations have to try to identify the capabilities that they will need in the future. This gives them the option of developing the talents required from within the organisation – talent management. Indeed, as we have seen elsewhere in this book, the demand for well-qualified managerial and technical people is likely to exceed the supply, and so internal development may be the key to success in the future. The activities described above are equally appropriate to talent development, but the emphasis is on the needs of the organisation rather than just developing the potential of individuals (where the talents developed might not be those eventually required).

Older workers need to be considered carefully. You might be reluctant to offer training to older workers because you fear that the older worker is less able to respond or that the time for return on the investment will be shorter. There is little, if any evidence, that older people are slower learners. However, they may often need to actually unlearn techniques and skills that have served them well in the past. Recognising this need to unlearn is important for them so they can be open to learning new skills. Remember too that it is not unusual for blue-chip companies to invest substantially in new graduates, knowing many will leave after two years. The 60-year-old, however, might still be with you at 70.

Great care is needed with assumptions!

9.6 LEVELS OF LEARNING NEEDS ANALYSIS

When we look at analysing learning needs we shall see that learning is needed at three levels. These are the organisation, the job or occupation, and the individual employee.

9.6.1 THE ORGANISATION

Customer care is typical of a learning need that originates at the level of the organisation and is experienced by most, if not all, employees. It could arise from a board-level decision to change the organisation's image in this one regard.

9.6.2 JOB OR OCCUPATION

Learning in electronic 'point of sale' equipment (for example, the scanners familiar at supermarket checkouts) is an example of learning that applies to everyone in a specific job; in this case, checkout operators.

9.6.3 INDIVIDUAL EMPLOYEE

Here there may be an opportunity for learning where an individual has a particular need or the organisation requires an individual to be trained in a specific area. For the HR officer, an employment law course or secondment to another organisation might be examples.

9.7 MAKING LEARNING NEEDS ANALYSIS COMPREHENSIVE

Jill Fairbairns has provided a model that emphasises three matters that must be addressed in making decisions about appropriate training and hence learning. We shall use this model to describe our approach to identifying where training should be concentrated. In part, it links the three levels above, but it can also be applied to evaluating the suitability of learning solutions at each level. Because of its early development it refers to training rather than learning, but the principles are still highly relevant today.

Throughout our working lives we increase our levels of knowledge and skills in order to perform work activities well. The acquisition of relevant knowledge and skills opens up opportunities to individuals for increased job performance, career development and personal development. Organisations continually seek the best return on their limited funds, so it is necessary to be selective and to identify those areas that will be important in the particular job in question ('Important in my job' – see Figure 9.2).

Most jobs today need a wide range of skills and knowledge: some are critical and others desirable for top performance. Job-holders usually possess the majority of those skills and knowledge already, but for the reasons outlined above there will always be areas that can benefit from additional training ('In need of training' in Figure 9.2). So at this point we would be looking for the overlap between importance in the job and need of training.

The third factor involves the culture of the organisation. We looked at culture in Chapter 2 and observed that businesses are characterised by different attitudes and priorities – that is, the corporate culture. Learning knowledge and skills that do not fit comfortably with the corporate culture will either put the trained person at odds with that culture or, more probably, lead to the learning being rejected on the basis that 'it does not work here'. For example, learning in customer care may be misplaced if it is immediate additional sales (rather than repeat business) on which success is judged. Another example of a cultural factor is the attitude to NVQs or Scottish Vocational Qualifications (SVQs); some organisations are more enthusiastic about these than others. In an enthusiastic organisation an NVQ initiative will receive a better reception and more support from senior managers. Identifying the cultural direction in which your organisation is going will help identify the most relevant training ('Likely to be encouraged and rewarded' in Figure 9.2).

Figure 9.2 Factors in the selection of training (Fairbairns' model)

HR practitioners will benefit from taking these three factors into account in selecting suitable learning activities. It is where such activities address the overlap between all three factors that the most benefits are likely to be realised (again, see Figure 9.2).

The person being trained is a further factor to be considered. Offering training can imply weakness or that an individual has a problem with some aspect of his or her performance. Unless individuals see training as a valuable learning opportunity or believe it is important in their jobs and relevant to their organisation, they are likely to reject it. So individuals should be involved in the plans for their learning to encourage their commitment to it.

9.8 GATHERING THE INFORMATION

To carry out a learning needs analysis for your organisation you will need information that can be evaluated against the factors mentioned above. The information must relate to the level at which you are doing your analysis: organisation, occupation or employee.

Suitable source material for the analysis is likely to include some of the following:

- mission and values (formal culture)
- business plans
- succession plans
- competency framework (for example, NVQs)
- views and observations about 'how we do things around here' (this is the informal culture, not necessarily the same as the formal culture)
- appraisal records
- evidence of competence for individuals (for example, portfolios)
- opportunities for improvement (for example, development opportunities)
- minutes of meetings (for example, action points that highlight needs)
- questionnaires
- job descriptions
- performance targets
- observation of employees at work

- recorded conversations, such as on a customer care line
- other relevant NVQs or SVQs
- interviews with:
  - managers
  - staff
  - subordinates
  - internal customers
  - external customers.

Using sources such as these is important because you start with the needs that relate to the business. Once you know what is needed, you can start to consider the best way to meet those needs.

When you have gathered the source material and feel well informed, it is time to carry out your analysis. This could be at the level of the organisation, job or individual. To illustrate the process we shall consider examples at the job level.

You have to ask what job performance is needed in the particular situation. The answer should be in the form of a level of performance. This could be quantitative (for example, the number of calls handled per hour) or it may be qualitative (for example, all telephone calls are to be answered politely, competently and effectively).

Another way of defining the required performance may be to use an NVQ/SVQ standard or other competency framework that directly defines the competence – for example, to select candidates for jobs within agreed timescales and budgets.

Competencies can be invaluable in helping you decide on desired levels of performance. An accepted framework will provide a sound basis on which line managers and trainers can discuss what is needed.

We shall assume that in these examples learning is a suitable remedy. That may not be the case in all circumstances – for example, if operations are under-resourced, learning is an inappropriate solution.

Next you need to ascertain what performance or competence is being achieved at present. Perhaps applicants responding to a recruitment advertisement are kept waiting for a reply with no apology offered when the call is answered. Maybe the person answering does not understand how to handle some of the enquiries, or incomplete messages are taken. In the second example, selection of candidates may regularly overrun both timescales and budgets. More critically, you may lose a good candidate. The difference between this and the level of performance needed is known as the 'learning gap'.

You may have to try to estimate what that gap is costing the organisation, or the gain and benefits of closing that gap. We may be able to get information about sales lost owing to poor telephone technique, or estimate the costs of taking an extra day to fill a vacancy.

This is important because these costs will provide the justification for the learning costs or, perhaps, lead to the conclusion that training is not justified in a particular instance.

CASE STUDY 9.1

A manufacturer of plastic pipes found that a market opportunity existed for providing not only pipes but also a variety of equipment associated with customers' use of them. The sale of a 'package of pipe and equipment' enabled higher margins since pipes had often been sold to an intermediary who then put its own package, and margin, together for industrial customers.

This diversification of its operations was a significant change for the manufacturer.

As a buyer of raw polymers the manufacturer was a major customer of the polymer supplier. Consequently, negotiations were carried out at a very senior level and favourable terms were the norm.

The change in product range meant that as well as processes the manufacturer was also carrying out assembly work. This created a learning need that was recognised. However, components had to be purchased from a variety of sources and by junior purchasing staff. Furthermore, the pipe manufacturer was not a significant customer so far as the individual component manufacturers were concerned. Delays began to occur.

Deliveries for large orders of pipe were being held up because the equipment to be shipped with them was not ready.

The equipment, in turn, was being held up because minor components had not arrived from local suppliers in good time.

Fortunately, the company recognised the problem as one of negotiation. It was not sufficient to get the best price for components – reliable delivery had to be part of the deal. Purchasing staff that had been treated well by large polymer manufacturers now had to learn to deal with owners of small engineering works. The process of learning how to work in these circumstances had to be accelerated and a training programme in negotiation skills was initiated.

9.9 LEARNING AND DEVELOPMENT PLANS

Here, a balancing act is required between available resources, which may be influenced by the benefits that have been estimated, and the identified needs. Achieving such a balance is a matter of skill. As we saw in the Fairbairns model (Figure 9.2), you will have to weigh up needs in the context of the political considerations, style and culture of the organisation.

Let's look at some of the factors that will have to be considered.

9.9.1 GOVERNMENT INITIATIVES

Successive British governments have recognised the need for training if Britain is to compete internationally. They have developed and supported initiatives to encourage employers and employees to take responsibility for training and learning. Investors in People (IiP) provides a detailed approach to training and to its integration within the organisation, thereby assisting thinking on policies, procedures and action.

IiP status requires an organisation to meet specific standards, demonstrate that it is doing so and submit to an inspection process. Vocational qualifications (NVQs/SVQs) are another example of an initiative designed to encourage learning. The UK Government is keen to encourage these achievements, and there are invariably financial incentives such as grants and subsidies provided for organisations and individuals, particularly where growing a business is concerned.

In addition, there are government schemes on offer to encourage employment of particular groups, such as school-leavers (that is, apprenticeships), and to help fund employee training for organisations.

There is a huge variety of funding to assist training in specific industries, such as rural, maritime or sport. Then there is funding to support training for specific purposes, such as innovation or carbon reduction.

It is therefore wise to investigate the current availability of grants and subsidies for learning. You can search the Internet (some references are given at the end of this chapter), or approach universities, colleges or local authorities. In many cases funds for learning can come, via these bodies, from European sources such as the European Social Fund. Networking with your learning sources can also reveal useful opportunities. At the same time you should assess the requirements placed on your organisation by such bodies as a condition of providing grants or subsidies. For example, you might be expected to train your HR administrator to an NVQ/SVQ standard and to train your HR officer as an assessor. While it may be worthwhile to do such training, it might be time-consuming.

Even if no special conditions apply, it is still important to assess the amount of time you may need to spend on administration and documentation. Wise use of the funds has to be demonstrated to those who provide them, and this often means significant documentation.

9.9.2 THE INTERNAL LEARNING AND DEVELOPMENT RESOURCES AVAILABLE

You must understand the size of the budget and how it is structured. Structure can be important. For example, some budgets may apply only to amounts invoiced – thus the use of a supervisor to train call-centre operators may well not be counted against such budgets. This does not mean that using the supervisor would be without cost, but it may save some of the budget for use elsewhere.

You may have some facilities available internally, such as a learning centre well-equipped for craft learning, management learning, computer learning, or for all of these.

On the other hand, there may be very limited facilities. Nonetheless, in most cases there will be equipment available that could be used for learning. Production departments, for example, may have idle production lines that could be used for learning purposes. Setting up a work station for call-centre learning or an additional computer on the corporate system may be straightforward.

Consider the availability and capability of specialists and trainers within the company. These may be increased by training supervisors in the techniques of instruction, for example. In addition, experienced employees may be available for training-based activities. At more senior levels, experienced managers may be willing to coach or mentor more junior managers or staff. This can be a valuable development activity for both the senior and the junior.

Another valuable development activity is secondment to another section, site or associated company. Equally, these locations and jobs themselves may provide project opportunities. A local non-competitor may have a good call-centre operation and be willing to share expertise. Some organisations are very innovative and engage in formal partnership arrangements, sometimes including a training provider, to share employee development opportunities.

9.9.3 THE EXTERNAL LEARNING AND DEVELOPMENT RESOURCES AVAILABLE

Using external resources invariably has an opportunity cost. There will be absence from the workplace and, in consequence, temporary loss of production, sales, service or contribution to the business. Often these costs are hidden in that they do not appear in any financial calculations, but they are there nonetheless. In addition, there will be the cost of course fees, travel and accommodation. These latter costs are rarely hidden and are likely to need justification. If there are grants or subsidies available, these may help. As we discussed above, you have to know the conditions laid down by the bodies providing them. Expect questions as to whether the external resources are in fact available internally or could be more economically provided internally. Investigate, also, the availability of grants and subsidies for external training from the bodies we mentioned above.

Finally, you need to evaluate the quality of such training, its relevance and its relationship to the culture of the organisation and to the quality standards demanded in the workplace. For example, a local telephone techniques course might not be sufficient to meet your expectations if you work in an international marketplace. Specified competencies can help you and any external provider identify appropriate learning objectives. A discussion that centres on these can help you and your training provider decide if they can, in fact, meet your expectations. You should also consider the relevance of learning to an individual's career. Qualifications, in particular, can be relevant to the needs of both the organisation and the individual – we look at these next.

9.9.4 QUALIFICATIONS

In many organisations it is important to have qualified people; in some cases, third parties may impose such requirements. Hospitals are obvious examples, where qualifications are necessary for doctors and nursing staff. In industry, accountants and engineers are examples of professional people who are frequently required to be suitably qualified. Even when not a statutory requirement, qualifications help to show that responsibilities are taken seriously. Health and safety qualifications, for example, indicate a responsible approach to an important issue – one for which a company may be held liable for injuries and occupational ill-health.

Indeed, as we highlighted earlier, the number of jobs in occupations needing higher level qualifications is the greatest employment growth area.

Qualifications provide external verification of skills, competence or knowledge. This can be helpful, for example, where pay is related to level of qualification.

Examination-based qualifications provide evidence of knowledge and ability to examine issues and solve problems. High performance in examinations may also imply judgement. However, such a guide is not always reliable, and furthermore, examinations rarely assess practical skills.

Competence-based qualifications depend on providing evidence of ability to carry out specific tasks to the standard expected in the workplace. Evidence is assessed by a qualified assessor who judges whether it provides sufficient evidence of competence. Typical evidence might include documents prepared by the 'candidate', reports, copies of correspondence and witness testimony about carrying out activities to a specified standard. Competence can also be assessed by observation.

NVQs and SVQs are nationally recognised competence qualifications. They provide detailed descriptions (standards) of vocational competencies, breaking them down into units of competence, then into elements of competence. Units of competence can be accredited individually, accumulating into a qualification. Elements of competence describe activities (such as leading a meeting) and have performance criteria against which competence in the activity can be judged (for example, handling conflict). The detailed descriptions can be invaluable in preparing learning activities for specific skills and for checking achievement. Colleges and other local and national government bodies can help employers identify relevant NVQs/SVQs for their employees.

The use of competence-based workplace learning can involve the use of internal advisers and assessors. While these would naturally be supervisors and experienced employees, the cost of training advisers and assessors, of administering the system and of providing the learning may be substantial. One point of caution on competence-based learning and NVQs/SVQs: take care not to allow the collection of evidence to develop into a paperchase, because this may obscure the need to develop skills and impart relevant knowledge.

Qualifications in the UK have eight levels and the differing forms of qualification can be related to these levels. See 'Qualification levels' in 'References and Further Reading at the end of this chapter'.

One benefit of qualifications is that they provide individuals with the incentive to learn – a point we take up now.

9.9.5 CHOOSING APPROPRIATE LEARNING EXPERIENCES

This choice should take into consideration the range of techniques available.

9.9.6 LEARNING AND DEVELOPMENT TECHNIQUES

There is a temptation to associate learning with the provision of 'training courses'. In practice, the majority of learning takes place outside such courses, is often 'on the job' and is frequently left to chance. Learning opportunities abound and the learning specialist should seek to manage these as effectively as possible. So 'learning and development techniques' include using naturally occurring or deliberately created learning opportunities. The examples of techniques and opportunities that we list here can also help you to address your own learning and development needs.

On the job

- job instruction
- coaching and mentoring
- work diaries and log books
- records of continuing professional development
- rotating a person's job with someone else at a similar skill level
- enlarging the job by providing more tasks or responsibilities at the same level
- enriching the job by adding tasks at higher level of responsibility
- group meetings
- projects and assignments
- NVQ/SVQ programmes

Off the job

- seminars and workshops
- attending talks and presentations
- guided reading
- local discussion groups
- local meetings of professional bodies, such as the CIPD or Institute of Administrative Management (IAM)
- visits to other organisations
- business games
- delivering talks and presentations
- programmed learning in books, computers, interactive videos or DVDs
- computer simulation
- assignments prepared for a course
- action learning
- outdoor development.

Online

- YouTube
- webinars and podcasts
- web meetings
- computer help facilities, online and offline
- Internet information resources such as Wikipedia
- networking forums such as those provided by the CIPD and others
- social networking
- virtual learning environments
- online training programmes.

The intention here is simply to highlight some of the various training techniques available. For more detail of these techniques, see 'References and Further Reading at the end of this chapter'.

? REFLECTIVE ACTIVITY 9.2

? REFLECTIVE ACTIVITY 9.2

Look at the lists of on-the-job and off-the-job learning techniques above. Are any of those listed new or unfamiliar to you? Discuss any that you are unclear about with a learning source and undertake further reading, as appropriate.

CASE STUDY 9.2

An assembly factory found itself continually running into problems meeting its delivery targets. It had a full manufacturing requirements planning system in place, reliable suppliers and excellent industrial relations. On the face of it the planning system should have enabled the targets to be met comfortably, but it was not happening. The training officer became involved and he went to talk to the supplier of the planning system.

There was, it seemed, a familiar problem. The system worked, but senior people circumvented it. If a customer asked for a special delivery, an improvement on an existing delivery date or a change to the order, it would be granted – even if it meant tweaking the system. Any attempt to resist on the part of the planning staff would be referred to the managing director, who invariably supported the sales staff.

Indeed, he tended to bypass the system himself. If the system were overridden for special circumstances, it clearly could not be blamed if delivery dates went awry.

To deal with this problem the computer supplier developed a computer simulation program. Rather like a flight simulator this provided the opportunity to experiment with the system and experience the effects of different options. The appropriate senior managers were persuaded to take part in a simulated exercise. Because it wasn't the real factory (any more than a flight simulator is a real plane) they could 'crash' the system again and again until they learned that if they followed the rules of the system, the planning worked. The process took several days, but it convinced the managers that if the system was followed, and everything was put through the system, the delivery targets would be met.

9.10 IMPLEMENTING LEARNING AND DEVELOPMENT ACTIVITIES

The key to successful learning activities is planning and preparation. In planning, it is helpful if you can regard people at events as participants in a learning process. Use of terms such as 'attenders', 'trainees' or even 'students' implies they are passive rather than actively involved in a learning process for which they have responsibility. One could, perhaps, refer to them as 'learners', at the risk of sounding patronising.

Carefully consider each of the following:

- the learning objectives of the event (these can be broad or very specific, but the accuracy with which they have been determined will be a major factor in the success of the event)
- how many will be trained at any one time
- the length of your learning sessions and how much will be learned at each session
- how much time is available and how you will divide it up
- the range of learning techniques available and their suitability
- how to involve participants in the learning process

- the pace of learning.

If you plan to run a workshop, seminar or training course, you will also have to consider:

- the practical arrangements – room, layout, and so on
- the use of support material – handouts, videos, PowerPoint slides, other visual aids
- the learning resources – flipchart, laptop, DVDs, data projection equipment, etc.

Make sure you know how to use any technology!

? REFLECTIVE ACTIVITY 9.3

Take learning or development needs at your place of work. Write some learning objectives for addressing a specific need. These may include behavioural objectives – for example: 'to be confident about "having a word" with a subordinate'. Decide the activities that might be available as options for the learning or development, and select suitable ones. Write out a plan that addresses the issues discussed in this section. Then discuss your plan with a learning source.

When we have implemented our training, there is one more task. It is not really the last task, because it is only one step in the learning cycle. It is appropriate for it to lead to the identification of further needs.

9.11 WHY SHOULD WE EVALUATE OUR LEARNING AND DEVELOPMENT?

It is important to remember that learning and development activities are not ends in themselves. The nineteenth-century biologist T.H. Huxley said: 'The great end in life is not knowledge, but action.' Our activities must result in some positive changes in the performance of our organisation; they need to be economically valuable or at least assist the organisation in achieving its objectives. We should therefore evaluate the action that results from our learning if we are to know whether it was worthwhile.

It is good practice to evaluate any business investment to learn lessons for the future.

When we look at learning, some particular reasons to consider are:

- justifying the expense
- providing the trainer with feedback
- providing feedback on techniques
- establishing whether the needs and objectives of the learning have been met
- improving future programmes
- identifying further needs
- providing data for justifying further expenditure
- helping top management understand the broad costs and benefits of developing people.

We might be prompted to ask the question 'Why is learning and development so frequently not evaluated?'

9.12 WHY IS LEARNING AND DEVELOPMENT SO FREQUENTLY NOT EVALUATED?

Looking at the answers to this question helps to identify the practical problems.

The benefits of learning and development are often intangible: effectiveness may improve, but in ways that are not immediately obvious. Development activities help people to grow, to improve their judgement and to increase their value to an employer.

Such skill develops gradually and may not become suddenly apparent on completion of the activities.

Sometimes the objectives of the learning and development have not been defined, or when they have, it may be difficult to measure whether they have been achieved.

Even where measurable change exists, it is not always easy to establish a direct link between the learning or development and the results, because there are many other factors that may impinge on the same changes.

It costs time and money to evaluate learning and development thoroughly, and that has to be weighed against what is learned from the process of evaluation. For instance, an in-depth evaluation of a management development programme that will be implemented across many parts of a large organisation is likely to be worthwhile (and essential in terms of justifying the expenditure). For a one-off training course for one particular person, a thorough evaluation is likely to be disproportionate.

The result is that evaluation is often confined to questionnaires completed by trainees at the end of a training course.

What we find particularly helpful in evaluating the effectiveness of training, and hence learning, is a model proposed by Hamblin – see Table 9.1 – in which there are examples of measures for assessing the true value of training at each of five levels.

Table 9.1 Hamblin's levels of evaluation

The levels		Methods of evaluation	
Level 1	Reactions of the trainees – to the content and methods of training, to the trainer, and to any other factors perceived as relevant. What the trainee thought about the learning exercise	• Discussion • Interviews • Questionnaires • Recommendations of trainees • Desire for further learning	
Level 2	Learning attained during the training period Did the trainees learn what was intended?	*Behaviour:*	Objectives obtained
		Knowledge and understanding:	Examinations and other tests
		Skills:	• Analysis by observation of demonstrated skill • Evidence of skills applied • Projects or assignments
		Attitude:	Questionnaires
Level 3	Job behaviour in the work environment at the end of the learning period Did the learning get transferred to the job?	• Production rate • Customer complaints • Discuss with manager/subordinate/peers • Activity sampling • Self-recording of specific incidents • Evidence of competence • Appraisal	
Level 4	Effect on the department Has the learning helped the department's performance?	• Minutes of meetings • Deadlines met • Stress indicators	

The levels		Methods of evaluation
		• Quality indicators • Interview other managers and superiors
Level 5	The 'ultimate' level. Has the learning affected the ultimate well-being of the organisation in terms of business objectives?	• Standing of the training officer • Growth • Quality indicators • Stress indicators • Achievement of business goals and targets

? REFLECTIVE ACTIVITY 9.4

Evaluation of a training programme, course or exercise should be measured against its objectives. The result of the evaluation may legitimately lead to improved objectives, but the training event itself should be reviewed against the original learning objectives.

Take a learning activity in which you have been involved recently – perhaps a group exercise on a Certificate in HR Practice (CHRP) programme if you are currently a participant. Investigate the objectives of the activity. Then discuss with others who have followed a similar activity the effectiveness of that activity.

Try to decide how that effectiveness might be measured at your place of work. Concentrate on Level 3 of Hamblin's model (see Table 9.1) and, if you feel it appropriate, Level 4 or even 5. Look for some tangible measures, remembering that it is actions that really count in the workplace. Relate these back to the objectives in order to make your decision.

9.13 THE ROLE OF HR PRACTITIONERS

Your role in learning and development activities will be largely determined by the structure and culture of your organisation. As previously discussed, an HR practitioner may be expected to take responsibility for learning and development activities. If so, then the content of this chapter will be especially relevant as will the companion publication, *Learning and Development Practice*.

9.13.1 AN INFLUENCING ROLE

If you want to influence line managers towards better training decisions, you will benefit by learning to understand their needs. That means talking to them about what they are trying to achieve. You will then be in a position to make positive and helpful suggestions. By becoming familiar with government initiatives and sources of grant support you will increase your own value and credibility and, hence, your ability to influence.

You may also want to take on board the skills shortages, at managerial and professional levels, threatened by the changing nature of work in order to make the case for more internal development.

Many organisations in the UK still give learning and development low priority. The CIPD 2015 Learning and Talent Development survey suggested a median budget spend per employee of just £201–£250 per year. Your most valuable contribution could be to research the true value of learning and development for your employer and make clear cost-justified cases for improvement. Remember that learning and development activities need to produce a return in a similar way to any other investment.

9.13.2 AN ADMINISTRATIVE ROLE

You take this on when you concentrate on making the arrangements for learning and for keeping the records. Significant costs from the budget can be saved by effective arrangements and diligent negotiation. Well-organised records on objectives and outcomes can provide valuable information for evaluating the true benefits of learning activities. In specific sectors – for example, health – records of certain training are needed for quality and safety inspection purposes. However, if you want to break out of the administrative mould, you should use your learning in this chapter and your unique access to learning records to move towards an influencing role.

9.13.3 A TRAINING ROLE

This comes into play when you are appointed an HR and learning practitioner. If you are so appointed, you will have clear training responsibilities. If this also involves delivering training on a regular basis, you may consider trying to specialise in either training or HR rather than spreading your skills and responsibilities too thinly.

Delivery of training and hence learning requires planning and thorough preparation. HR responsibilities often require you to respond to demands that arise suddenly and unexpectedly. The two responsibilities therefore do not always sit very comfortably alongside each other.

9.13.4 A DECISION-MAKING ROLE

Here you have the opportunity to make decisions about learning needs, about the response to those needs and about the effectiveness of the response. This chapter should have given you the basic understanding you require to start making decisions. If you are new to the task, commence slowly and build up your experience as you go round your own learning cycle.

9.13.5 AN OVERSEEING ROLE

This role requires you to keep in touch with all the learning activities in your sphere of responsibility, which will help you to influence others, as we discussed above. You may be able to pick out many ways of improving the relevance and effectiveness of learning.

9.14 SUMMARY

We have looked at the steps of the learning cycle and used them to examine the management of learning and development. It is the changes in the environment in which a business operates, and people's job and career changes, that create the need for learning.

Learning needs can be identified at the level of the organisation, job or occupation, and at the individual employee level. We have to consider not just what may require training, but whether that is both important in the job and likely to be recognised or rewarded within the culture of the organisation.

Learning needs are established by examining the gap between the performance that is sought and the performance currently being achieved. A wide variety of sources is available to help determine both the desired performance and current performance.

Competency frameworks can be particularly useful.

In formulating plans for learning and development it is important to examine the internal resources available, the external resources and the relevance of qualifications. We can select from a wide variety of techniques and opportunities, and should never restrict our concept of learning and development to training courses alone.

To complete the learning cycle, we emphasised the value of evaluating training and learning, considered some of the practical obstacles, and identified a model that can help structure our evaluation.

If you have the opportunity to be involved in learning and development activities, we suggest you involve yourself with enthusiasm. There is much to be gained.

EXPLORE FURTHER

References and further reading

FAIRBAIRNS, J. (1991) Plugging the gap in training needs analysis. *Personnel Management*. February. pp 43–45.

See also the CIPD's online bookshop for books and training materials. In particular, the following books contain material relevant to this chapter:

BEE, R. and BEE, F. (2003) *Learning Needs Analysis and Evaluation*. London: CIPD.

BEEVERS, K. and REA, A. (2016) *Learning and Development Practice in the Workplace*. London: CIPD.

HACKETT, P. (2003) *Training Practice*. London: CIPD.

HARRISON, R. (2009) *Learning and Development*. London: CIPD.

REID, M.A., BARRINGTON, H.A. and BROWN, M. (2004) *Human Resource Development: Beyond training interventions*. 7th edition. London: CIPD.

REYNOLDS, J. (2004) *Helping People Learn*. London: CIPD.

WHIDDETT, S. and HOLLYFORDE, S. (2003) *A Practical Guide to Competencies*. 2nd edition. London: CIPD.

Web references

Virtual learning environments: en.wikipedia.org/wiki/Virtual_learning_environment

OECD Employment Outlook 2015: www.oecd.org/unitedkingdom/Employment-Outlook-UnitedKingdom-EN.pdf

Apprenticeships: www.thetechpartnership.com

Business grants: www.ukbusinessgrants.org

Skills funding: www.gov.uk/government/organisations/skills-funding-agency

Government funding: www.governmentfunding.org.uk/

Qualification levels: www.gov.uk/what-different-qualification-levels-mean/compare-different-qualification-levels

CIPD Learning and Development survey: www.cipd.co.uk/hr-resources/survey-reports/learning-development-2015.aspx

See also Survey Reports on the CIPD website: cipd.co.uk/hr-resources/survey-reports:

- Focus on E-learning (June 2011)
- Learning and Development (May 2015)
- Learning to Work (March 2015)
- The Coaching Climate (September 2011)

See also Factsheets on the CIPD website: cipd.co.uk/hr-resources/factsheets:

- Coaching and Mentoring (December 2015)
- Costing and Benchmarking Learning and Development (April 2015)
- E-learning (September 2014)
- Identifying Learning and Development Needs (February 2015)
- Learning and Development Strategy (February 2015)
- Learning Methods (August 2014)

Websites

BBC Education: www.bbc.co.uk/learning/adults

Chartered Institute of Personnel and Development: www.cipd.co.uk

Employer Solutions Ltd: www.employersolutions.co.uk

Investors in People: www.investorsinpeople.com

Qualifications and Curriculum Authority: www.qca.org.uk

People Management: www.peoplemanagement.co.uk

CHAPTER 10

Information and Communication Technology in HR

LEARNING OUTCOMES

After reading this chapter you will:

- have an understanding of the important contribution that accurate data (stored manually or electronically) can make to the HR function
- be able to record data and information
- have given thought to how to interpret, analyse and present information clearly and accurately
- be aware of appropriate formats to support decision-making for the organisation and for HR solutions
- be able to find some suitable computer applications or apps for use in the HR function, including the role of databases and e-learning
- be able to understand and respond to the main legal requirements for confidentiality, data protection and security of data
- be able to help realise some of the opportunities provided by the social media revolution.

10.1 INTRODUCTION

No other area of HR practice is changing faster than the use of technology in accessing information and in facilitating new methods of communication. In social media attention has moved from preventing abuse to realising the benefits, especially in recruitment. Today almost all employees have a smartphone and many will be accessing their work emails via them and even using tablets to work on their employers' servers.

In commerce, small organisations or generalist HR, individuals' experience of social networking may be more personally based but the use of technology by employees, Cloud technology, for example, is driving its use by employers. In many cases, employers are working to catch up. In writing this chapter, we are addressing a diverse audience, but our intention is to focus on the relevance of information and communication technology to HR. Occasionally, we refer to basic concepts for the benefit of those who may be unfamiliar with them. In this chapter we will:

- examine some of the information of which HR is the nominal guardian
- highlight some of the technology that assists that task
- consider the legal position in relation to data protection and freedom of information
- highlight the opportunities provided to HR by social networking
- review the importance of 'big data' and its likely implications for the practitioner.

In the first place, a typical HR department is responsible for a substantial amount of information about the people employed in the organisation, as well as applicants, past employees, and workers. It needs to maintain accurate and largely up-to-date records. So let's start by examining why that should be so.

10.2 WHY RECORDS ARE IMPORTANT IN HR

We see seven main reasons why records are important:

- to satisfy legal requirements
- to provide the organisation with information to make decisions
- to record contractual arrangements and agreements
- to keep contact details of employees
- to provide documentation in the event of a claim against the organisation
- to provide information for consultation requirements
- for due diligence in the case of a business transfer.

There is an extensive body of legislation that regulates and controls the management of personal data and information. HR records have to satisfy a number of legal principles.

We look first at the importance of records in more detail.

10.2.1 TO SATISFY LEGAL REQUIREMENTS

Government departments, including HMRC, can demand information on how many people you employ, what they are paid, what they have been paid over a number of years, and how many hours they have worked.

The Working Time Regulations and the National Minimum Wage Act each require certain specific records relating to hours of work and, in the latter case, pay.

10.2.2 TO PROVIDE THE ORGANISATION WITH INFORMATION TO MAKE DECISIONS

Knowledge and information are the lifeblood of good decision-making for organisations. For individuals, access to accurate, factual and dependable information that can be used for arguments and influence is a vital factor in their ability to achieve. In the past, financial information has been highly regarded and available to considerable levels of sophistication. HR information has been harder to obtain, but because computer software is now highly developed in this area, such information is much more readily available.

It is important to record HR data clearly and accurately. Interpreting, analysing and presenting information requires critical thinking and often a broader understanding of management accounting or statistical concepts. Presenting information in an appropriate format to support decision-making is invaluable. We recommend that you familiarise yourself with bar charts, pie charts and statistical terms such as 'probability' and 'significance'.

It is also significant that in an era of advanced technology, products of all kinds are quickly and easily imitated. Consequently, products are becoming increasingly similar and therefore business is beginning seriously to value service. It is frequently service that differentiates one supplier from another. This has led business-decision-makers to appreciate the value of their employees more, because of the need for them to give good service to customers. In a healthy organisation, or in shared services, 'good service' includes internal customers (that is, fellow employees and managers). In turn, this places more emphasis on good HR information. For example, if you want to know the level of staff turnover in different departments, a good computer system will allow you to access it relatively easily. Having such information may aid in the identification of problems.

'Big data' is now providing further opportunities both in recruitment, performance and decision-making generally. We will look at the implications for HR later in this chapter.

10.2.3 TO RECORD CONTRACTUAL ARRANGEMENTS AND AGREEMENTS

Agreements that are recorded are clearer and also easier to insist upon. It is not only legal requirement to provide written particulars of employment, but it is also simply good practice to provide them. Employment problems are less likely to arise when all parties are clear about what has been agreed. Records are needed for reference purposes in the case of disputes and, as we emphasise below, for defence if, for example, claims are made to an employment tribunal.

10.2.4 TO KEEP CONTACT DETAILS OF EMPLOYEES

The simplest and most obvious reason for this is so that employees can be paid. It is not difficult to see other reasons, such as the need to call someone in at short notice to provide relief cover.

10.2.5 TO PROVIDE DOCUMENTATION IN THE EVENT OF A CLAIM

Employment protection rights demand that we keep records to protect ourselves, as employers, from claims that we have discriminated against or unfairly dismissed employees. Health and safety legislation demands that records are kept of accidents, exposure to hazardous substances, what training has been provided, and much more.

Employers must be able to demonstrate responsible management of health and safety issues. When employees feel their rights have been infringed, they may make claims to employment tribunals. Expectations of employers are increasing continually. Tribunal cases at which the employer is cross examined by an advocate, rather than it being left simply to a claimant, are increasingly common. If your employer needs to defend such a case in a tribunal, it will place heavy demands on the accuracy and comprehensiveness of HR records.

10.2.6 TO PROVIDE INFORMATION FOR CONSULTATION REQUIREMENTS

In Chapter 3 we outlined the requirements that can be put on larger organisations by the Information and Consultation Regulations, which include information on developments relating to employment within the organisation. Even if your organisation is not within the scope of these Regulations, there will still be many other areas where information for consultation is required. For example, if employees might be made redundant there is a need to consult – and if they are to be transferred to another organisation (under an outsourcing arrangement, perhaps), there are similar requirements to consult. Information on alternative jobs, pay rates and skills needs, as well as records of the consultations themselves, will be important.

10.2.7 FOR DUE DILIGENCE IN THE EVENT OF A BUSINESS TRANSFER

In the event that an organisation or the activities of part of an organisation are transferred to another organisation (the transfer of an undertaking), the employees in that organisation, or part of it, normally have their employment transferred to the new organisation. On transfer, they are entitled to precisely the same terms and conditions (as a minimum) as they enjoyed with the previous organisation. This is a complex area of legislation not least because it creates complications for the transferee (the organisation that receives the employees) as they may have other employees on different, perhaps poorer, terms and conditions. The legislation is known as 'TUPE' – often pronounced 'chew-pea' or 'two-pea', depending on regional accents. Whether or not TUPE applies in any particular case has been the subject of much case law over many years. As a general rule, employees follow their jobs.

The reason for explaining this here is that the transferor (the organisation losing the employees) is required to provide the transferee (the organisation gaining the employees) with detailed information about the terms and conditions under which those employees were employed – for obvious reasons. The detail is known as 'employee liability information' and the requirements are laid out in the Transfer of Undertakings (Protection of Employment) Regulations 2006, from which the acronym TUPE is derived.

Finally, it is worth emphasising that good organisation of records is the key to efficiency and effectiveness, and to the credibility of the HR department.

? REFLECTIVE ACTIVITY 10.1

Have a close look at the records in your department.

1   Identify what is recorded, what duplications occur, what information is routinely sought, what information is aggregated.

2   Is data recorded that is never used?

3   How much time does it take to record the data?

4   How easy is it to obtain information when it is needed?

5   What routines exist to ensure that data is kept up to date? Do they work?

6   Are your systems in 'real time'?

7   If not, how do systems cope with current information required (such as the number of people employed) before current data has been recorded (such as adding new appointees)?

8   How quickly could you access a record that an employee had attended an induction?

10.3 MANUAL AND COMPUTERISED RECORDS

You can see from the above that many records are kept and that some of these may be manual records – that is, written or printed on sheets of paper – such as application forms, copies of qualification certificates and some everyday correspondence received about an employee.

Typically, these items will be in an individual employee wallet or envelope and kept secure from threats such as fire or theft. Thought needs to be given to the filing processes.

Not only should records be easy to find when needed, but also different records should be destroyed after different periods of time. Unsuccessful application forms may be destroyed after a few months, whereas pension-related documents should be kept for 60 years or more. Guidance about the length of time records need to be retained can be found on the CIPD website.

Good document discipline is needed in HR departments – paper should not be left lying around for prying eyes and a 'clean desk at night' policy should be mandatory. In an HR department, the only flat surfaces on which papers can be placed should be personal desks.

Documents can be scanned into computers and their image stored as a computer file. The advantage of having scanned documents on a computer is that they can then be accessed by means of a computer screen rather than by going to a filing cabinet, and can be forwarded easily to others who may need the information. If placed on a central server they can be found by search processes. They can also be assigned an expiry date so they are not kept longer than necessary. Optical character recognition (OCR) software can convert text within images into electronic text for indexing or word-processing. One tip here: if you are scanning a double-sided document, make sure you scan both sides if you intend to destroy the document!

10.3.1 DATABASES

Once a database has been set up for employees, you should be able to find who is due for a long-service award, whose probationary period ends next week, whose salary exceeds £30,000, etc – all just with a few clicks of a mouse. Proprietary computer systems use databases in such fast and subtle ways that you are unlikely to be aware of the search processes or the structure of the database. (See 'Using databases for primary employee records' below.)

10.3.2 BIG DATA

As the ability to store incredible amounts of data in accessible form increases, so the possibility of identifying trends, patterns and associations becomes a reality. Online retailers, such as Amazon, are using big data already. Buy a few books on Amazon and you will soon find other books in which you might be interested being suggested to you. Walk into a supermarket with a smartphone and the chances are the retailer will be tracking which aisles interest you, that is where you pause to look. It is rumoured that the police now use big data to predict where the next crime will happen! HR cannot ignore this trend.

To understand how big data might work in HR, suppose your HR policies and procedures were digitised and held on a computer server. If you then monitored viewings of those policies and procedures, you would know which ones interested employees. That in turn could tell you whether a new policy had come to your employees' attention. This is a relatively simplistic example.

But taken further, by monitoring employees' computer activities it is possible to establish which activities are of value to an organisation and which are not. Google, as an employer, uses complex algorithms and statistical analysis to assess recruitment, their employees' performance and much more.

It is, of course, important to let employees know if you are monitoring their activities in a way in which they might be identified personally.

You can read more about big data in the EMC Education Services (2015) book under 'References and Further Reading' at the end of this chapter.

10.3.3 APPLICATIONS SOFTWARE ON COMPUTERS AND THE INTERNET (APPS)

You will have noticed that we have referred to the task which a computer is performing as an 'application'. The smartphone has subsumed the term into an abbreviation – the 'app'. There is an inestimable number of apps available on smartphones and tablets, often accompanied by what is still known as 'applications software' on laptops and standalones.

In the case of apps you use the application but don't own the software. There are also remote facilities in which your applications (software or apps) are held on a 'cloud' and accessed over the Internet. In some cases you also own the software; in others you have only the right to use it. Different facilities are being developed all the time and you will need a basic understanding of how your HR record system and facilities work because you may be responsible (and will almost certainly have to react) if it fails. Many organisations are, understandably, nervous about key data (including HR data) being held on clouds. Do you know where your data is held? What happens, for example, if a foreign power denies access (or demands its own access) to data held on its territory?

A few years ago, a large national baker maintained its policies and procedures in the company head office HR department. These were kept on paper and had been prepared in a variety of formats and by different people at different times. Some were part of negotiated agreements, others enhancements to statutory entitlements such as maternity leave.

Now all these policies and procedures are gathered in one place on the Internet. They can be accessed by all the 5,000 employees and their managers. The presentation reflects the status of the company, is consistent, and allows navigation from one webpage to another. Employees and managers can search for keywords in the documents, print out relevant policies and link directly to government websites. The whole suite is kept continually up to date; there is no haphazard search for the latest copy or being unsure of its status when found. Routine forms, such as holiday requests, can be printed out directly by employees only when needed, and in time these will no doubt be completed online too.

There is always a trade-off between the benefits available from a particular piece of software and the investment in time required to learn all the possibilities it provides or to input all the data it needs. Some priority-setting is likely to be necessary. First, let's have a look at just a few of the applications that you might use.

Word-processing

So commonplace now is word-processing that you probably take it for granted. But there is an enormous range of facilities in any typical word-processor. If you have particular needs, such as cross-referencing, or have more than one person needing to work on a document, then always investigate to see if there are facilities that would assist the task. Most of us use only a small fraction of the facilities available – even authors!

Using databases for primary employee records

The data here would typically be personal details such as name, address, date employment commenced, date of birth, National Insurance number, payroll number and salary. It could be used in its raw, unprocessed form to send out a letter, for example. In addition, it could be processed to identify who is due to retire or to calculate salary costs for a department. Aggregating data for reports to managers is a valuable computer task. As with word-processing, there are so many facilities in a typical database that you will be unlikely to use them all – but investigating them often pays off.

Absence recording and analysis

This is a popular application. Because tangible financial savings can be identified from reductions in absence level, it is easy to make a cost case for this application. Only actions taken by managers and supervisors can bring the absence level down, but good records can help them to do that job. The HR department can also monitor the situation to see that the job is being done.

Administration

HR departments need to seek to reduce administrative burdens. Computers can help with many aspects of administration, of which recruitment administration is a particularly good example. The use of online forms, intranets and self-service access to employment details can further reduce the administrative burden by allowing employees to do much of it themselves. Because of the ease with which computers can communicate, this is an application that is easily outsourced to a shared service provider (see Chapter 2).

Diaries, organisers, and workflow

Organisers can bring together the diaries of different managers, making it much easier to identify dates and venues. This can be invaluable for discovering when, for example, all members of a recruitment panel might be available.

HR personal assistants (PAs) in the past lived by their diaries. Typical tasks could be to confirm salary, send out an offer, check acceptance of a contract, confirm acceptance to the manager, notify payroll, notify security, prepare a salary card, etc. Probationary reviews, stages in the pay review process and long-service awards due are all examples of the information that would be entered. Great diligence was required to ensure that all activities were entered, all procedures followed and everything ticked off correctly when it was done.

Today's PA can rely on, for example, Microsoft Outlook as an organiser, often in conjunction with smartphones. Task lists are less necessary because Outlook provides prompts, enables flagging of priorities, etc. Tasks that require manual action can be set up individually and repetitive activities can be set up with prompts/alerts that are synchronised across different computer platforms. New information will still need to be entered, but actions can be brought to the PA's attention in advance. Tasks with relevant telephone numbers and addresses can all be programmed to appear on the screen or the phone's display at the appropriate time.

Actions not completed can be deferred to a later date. Memos, letters and emails can be written directly from the database and a record kept on the employee's file, cross-referenced to the memo, letter or email itself. Even telephone calls can be made directly from some databases. These actions can each initiate history records which, with added notes, can easily be kept for future reference. A history tagged to an employee's record can be invaluable if your organisation has to defend an employment tribunal claim.

Reference information that many employees may want to access can be placed on an intranet or the Internet.

Collaboration tools can display ongoing projects on virtual noticeboards. They keep team members 'in the loop' so team members can see what's being worked on, who's working on what, and where something is in a process.

Such applications improve workflow around the organisation, ensuring that tasks are passed smoothly from one individual to another and keeping all people in the system informed of the progress of items, subject to any access restrictions.

? REFLECTIVE ACTIVITY 10.2

In many organisations, email inboxes are becoming overwhelmed and it can be difficult to keep track of information. It is possible that the use of email may decline and other approaches take its place. Investigate some other approaches such as Trello (which you can trial within your own workgroup) or Yammer.

Payroll

This contains much of the information held in primary records and, for this reason, there is a great temptation to amalgamate the two. Unfortunately, payrolls are designed for weekly (or monthly) calculations and for 'pay history' purposes. They do not often lend themselves well to the task of providing or analysing other HR information. It is nevertheless feasible to link payroll and HR systems.

Time and attendance

Systems such as these help manage flexitime and, when linked to payroll, pay. Clocking systems are linked to a central computer and can make considerable administrative savings. Care is needed over who controls the system to ensure that there is no abuse.

Organisation charts

Drawing organisation charts by hand is a long and tedious task and one that soon needs repeating if they are to be kept up to date. People outside the HR function often ask why HR practitioners never seem to be able to cope with what they see as an easy task. Fortunately, a variety of software now exists and the task is far more manageable.

Candidate selection systems

These are a very different form of application, but there is an increasingly wide variety available. A number of purveyors of psychometric testing provide their own software; others sell selection systems to help identify suitable candidates from among your own employees. These tend to be more relevant to larger organisations. See 10.4 'The Data Protection Act' below for some cautionary notes on the logic in automatic systems. The Internet is also being used for candidate selection. There is a wide variety of systems, some of which give the applicant immediate feedback on whether he or she really is a suitable candidate. For example, GCHQ launched a code-breaking campaign to attract cyber security specialists. If they cracked the code, they could apply for the job.

Specialised processing applications

Placing primary employee records onto a computer database provides in itself no more than a computerised reference system, valuable though that might be. Specific applications offer benefits by facilitating routine calculations. Complex calculations such as those for redundancy pay, pensions, labour turnover, salary trends and time to fill vacancies are usually included in proprietary packages. Furthermore, 'what-if' calculations can be invaluable in assisting decision-making.

Other records systems

Many, many other records lend themselves to computerisation. Company vehicle records, Control of Substances Hazardous to Health records, risk assessments, and equal opportunities monitoring are just a few such. Modern databases can cross-reference these to the primary employee records and to each other. Indeed, they may be on the same database.

Expert systems

As specialised versions of reference information, expert systems can guide inexperienced individuals (by means of question-and-answer sessions) through otherwise complex decisions. One area in which they are used is in the process of medical diagnosis. In HR, such systems can be used to guide managers as they carry out disciplinary action and seek to meet legal requirements, for example.

Interactive learning

Similar in principle to expert systems, these often use the Internet and DVD to enable learning. Typically, users choose answers to questions posed and the system takes the user through learning points appropriate to the responses they give. Systems use text and a variety of illustrations and often incorporate substantial amounts of video illustration.

Podcasts, webinars, streamed and downloaded training

Podcasts are downloaded to MP3 players, computers or smartphones. There is a wealth of podcast material available for keeping pace with current affairs, being up to date on technical subjects and for use in training.

Streamed facilities – of which BBC iPlayer and YouTube are examples – provide training, allowing you to view presentations from leading experts and to access video demonstrations over the Internet, ranging from baking a cake to assembling a jet engine (well, almost). Webinars provide access to easy at-the-desk training.

Self-service

Many large organisations are beginning to allow staff to access the information held in their HR records from their own workstation and to update their own personal details, such as a change of address. Clearly, this frees the HR staff from a good deal of work of a minor nature and helps to meet many aspects of subject access as required under the Data Protection Act.

Other applications

Our list is far from exhaustive: there is an enormous range of applications and apps that can help you and your department perform well. Here are a few:

- voice recording (care!)
- employment law alerts
- time and expense recorders
- travel planning, rail timetables, TripAdvisor, taxi fare calculators.

But for HR practitioners these are the means to an end. It is important not to lose sight of the end itself!

10.3.4 COMPUTERISING HR

Few small businesses start with a computerised HR system, but as the company grows it makes practical sense to introduce one. There are many proprietary systems on the market and most will provide the facilities that we have outlined above. It is not within the scope of this book to examine the options available. However, we can indicate some of the questions you should ask if you are involved in implementing a system or in choosing a new one.

You may like to consider first which facilities are the most important to you or, if you are seeking new ones, which offer real advantage and which might be simply 'nice to have'. The latter are fine if they don't add cost or preclude more appropriate choices of computer system. Don't lose sight of the end you had in mind!

There are also technical issues such as how well any system might integrate with other applications you already have, such as Microsoft Office, or major business processes, such as resource requirements planning systems. In the latter case, it is likely that the implementation will be led by those responsible for the main business system.

10.3.5 WHERE TO START

The starting point should be your ability to meet your organisation's needs. For what information are you continually asked? To what discussions and decisions does your department contribute regularly? What would you like to influence?

Establishing your needs is a crucial first step. The better you can establish these, the less likely you are to be disappointed subsequently. Talk to others in discussion groups or on your course and find out what they do. Perhaps they will let you visit them, talk you through the system they have and explain how it meets their needs.

People Management and other HR publications generally have many advertisements for HR systems. Bear in mind that some specialise in very large systems and others in smaller applications. Cautious contacts with these organisations will help you begin to appreciate what is available. If asked, most suppliers will visit you and give an on-site demonstration. However, if they do this without much commitment on your part, they may be operating on quite high margins – that is, the system could be expensive. Looking at literature or visiting exhibitions, such as the CIPD HR Software Show, could be a better first step.

10.3.6 OBSERVING DEMONSTRATIONS

Whether at an exhibition or on your premises, you should know what to look for in any demonstration. You would be wise to be cautious. The following list is not exhaustive, but it contains some key points you may wish to bear in mind:

- Ease of use is an important area in looking at a system.
- Make sure you understand what is happening at the demonstration.
- Check how many records the demonstration is using – is it comparable with the number of records you will need?
- Ask how to do some simple tasks that you might want to do yourself (for example, a list of salaries in the accounts department).
- Ask how easy it is to tailor selections, reports and routine activities to your own needs (for example, how would it be if you wished to exclude the finance director's salary from the above list?)
- Ask how the application might link up with existing software such as word-processing or that in the accounts department or in payroll.
- Make sure you know the configuration of the hardware on which the demonstration is running. Run on different equipment it may well be slower.
- Do not reach too far. In looking at systems, it is all too easy to achieve 'conceptual overload'. Rather than try to understand very unfamiliar concepts, there is a huge temptation to take the demonstrator's word for it. Make sure you understand what you want and understand how the system will meet those needs. Take time.
- Ask how it will integrate with current business systems, Microsoft Office, the Internet and with social networking. Establish how access might be controlled to avoid abuse.
- Establish the technical support available. At the time of writing some technical support is woefully inadequate. Hours spent on technical support lines (often just waiting for a reply) will not increase your productivity.
- Where will your data be physically located? Increasingly, data is stored on 'clouds'. There are pros and cons to this as we indicated earlier in this chapter. It is important to understand that using clouds is increasingly common and you might not even realise it is happening! Ask the question!

10.3.7 THE NEXT STEPS

Once you have some feel for systems, it would be wise to stop and give further careful thought as to what you would want a system to do for your department or organisation. Have a look back through the benefits and applications above and relate them directly to the needs you identified earlier. Choose that application or those applications that are likely to realise most benefits. Read through suitable literature on computer systems generally, especially HR systems. A short section in a book, such as this one, can only give you pointers. Think through the politics of purchasing computer systems in your organisation. Do you have an IT department? Who will be able to make the decision? Who will need to be convinced? Now you know something about the subject you will want to talk to appropriate people in your organisation. We assume you will have influence in any decision, but that the responsibility to purchase will be taken by a more senior person. Your influence will be greatest if you are quite clear about the benefits, the costs and the type of system needed. Do recognise the importance of ease of use, especially if you are the person who will be using it!

?   REFLECTIVE ACTIVITY 10.3

Seek out some new software or apps that would be useful in your HR department and investigate them. You should find many possibilities in HR magazines, in an app store on the Internet or by networking with colleagues on a college course.

Prepare the outline of a case for implementing one of your discoveries into your HR function. For example, a document management system may have the potential of revolutionising the archiving of your HR records.

10.4 THE DATA PROTECTION ACT

The Data Protection Act applies to personal data that is held in a 'relevant filing system'. This means that it applies to personal data held in manual filing systems as well as email, taped telephone conversations or social networking sites and blogs. You must have legitimate grounds for processing such information. The Act places restrictions on the processing of personal data. Personal data is information that relates to an identifiable living person. It does not need to be confidential or private to be deemed personal data. An email describing an incident involving a named individual is 'personal data'. The same applies to information on successful and unsuccessful job applicants, agency and contract workers, individual customers (rather than businesses) or, for example, residents in a care home. Obtaining, recording or simply holding data is equivalent to processing it. Depending on the purpose for which personal data is held, your organisation may need to register with the Information Commissioner. There is a ready check process for this on the Commissioner's website.

Certain data is defined as sensitive information. This includes anything that relates to a person's racial or ethnic origin, political opinions, religious beliefs, trade union membership, physical or mental health or sexual life. Processing of such data requires the explicit consent of the individual (which usually means a signature freely given), unless the individual has himself or herself made it public. There are, however, some exceptions to this explicit permission where the data is to be used for health and safety purposes, for monitoring of non-discrimination in the workplace or for the protection of customers' property or funds, and for certain legal purposes.

It is also important to realise that data gathered for one purpose cannot be used for another. So, for example, if you gather information about union membership to deduct union dues (which, as sensitive data, requires explicit permission), you cannot then use it in negotiations unless, again, you have explicit permission to do so. Workers (and others on which you might hold data) are entitled to know the purpose for which data on them is held.

10.4.1 STAFF HANDBOOKS

Employers are responsible for ensuring that they and their staff comply with the data protection principles. It would, therefore, be a good idea if the staff handbook and policy provided guidance so that staff know how to comply with the data protection principles. Staff and managers can only lawfully have access to personal data where there is a legitimate need.

Disciplinary rules must indicate examples of misconduct and gross misconduct in relation to data protection. For example, you would be wise to make it a disciplinary rule that references must be given only by HR staff at a specified level. Your handbook could be a useful place to indicate what information is held on individuals, how it is obtained, how it is processed and to what purposes it is put. This would help to prevent staff requesting this information individually and creating a serious administrative burden. If your handbook is on an intranet, it will be easier to keep up to date. If you allow employees to access their own records, it will enable them to check the information held on them.

10.4.2 THE EMPLOYMENT PRACTICES DATA PROTECTION CODE

The Information Commissioner has produced a code of practice covering: recruitment and selection; employment records; monitoring at work; and information about workers' health.

The scope of this code and its various parts is wide. It often gives very specific information about how the matters in each area of employment should be handled. Its purpose is to act as a source of recommendations on how the legal requirements of the Data Protection Act can be met and good practice achieved. There is a quick guide available for small businesses – see 'References and Further Reading' at the end of this chapter.

10.4.3 DATA PROTECTION PRINCIPLES

As a data-user, you have to comply with a set of principles that are designed to protect individuals from the misuse of data. These are examined, in summary, below. The purpose of this examination is to give general guidance about the principles. You should refer to the detail in the code, or even the Act, before implementing actions.

The basic requirement of the Act is that the processing of both automated and manual data must comply with certain data protection principles.

1 *Data must be processed fairly and lawfully.*
   Examples of fairness could be advising applicants that their records are being kept on file; making available the logic of any automatic selection processes; or giving candidates the opportunity to defend themselves against adverse information obtained from third parties. There are legal restrictions on the processing of sensitive data, as we have already seen, and unjustified disclosure of private information is likely to contravene the Human Rights Act.

2 *Personal data can be obtained only for specified and lawful purposes and not processed in any incompatible manner.*
   You must have a legitimate need for obtaining information. This may mean assessing the pros and cons of what information you gather. For example, you may be justified in recording telephone conversations in order to be able to hear what happened in the event that a customer subsequently complains about a worker. However, if you use the same recordings as examples for training purposes in open class, that use might be incompatible. An unlawful purpose would be to require disclosure of spent criminal convictions (other than where provided for by law).

3 *The data must be adequate, relevant and not excessive.*
   In application forms, for example, you should seek only information that is relevant to the job in question. Records that you retain should be based on a business need.

4   *Data must be accurate and, where necessary, kept up to date.*
     In employment, one way to achieve this is to allow employees to check, and even
     update, their own records.

5   *Data should not be kept longer than necessary.*
     When it comes to employment records, there should be a clear and foreseeable need
     for retaining information. The need diminishes as time passes, so some data may be
     best destroyed after a few months (unsuccessful application forms, for example),
     whereas other data should be retained for many decades. You can avoid keeping data
     longer than necessary if you keep such data on a computer because it can then be
     cross-referenced by date. However, old manual records can pose a problem. An
     example of this is leavers' files. These may be filed more conveniently in alphabetical
     order than in the order of leaving. That is fine until you want to remove the oldest
     files. Indexing manual files to a computer system could provide an interim solution.
     Phasing manual files out altogether may provide the long-term answer.

6   *Data 'shall be processed in accordance with the rights of data subjects'.*
     Employees have a right to privacy, particularly in respect of their personal life. If you
     record private telephone calls that an employee makes, then this will breach their rights
     (unless they clearly knew such calls would be recorded). Similar rules apply to private
     emails. Facebook creates a problematic area. An employee may want a matter to be
     kept private, but what if one of their friends shares it and it is then seen by their
     employer?

7   *Data must be protected by appropriate security measures.*
     There is quite a lot here for the HR practitioner to think about. How is data stored? Is
     it protected from computer failure, fire, intrusion and unauthorised access? What
     happens when employees take information out of the organisation on laptops, on
     memory sticks or it is sent to them via a smartphone synchronisation? Are
     communications systems – such as email or remote access – secure?
     It is of particular importance that appropriate technical and organisational measures be
     taken against unauthorised or unlawful processing of personal data and against
     accidental loss or destruction of, or damage to, personal data. Data can be destroyed
     accidentally (we look at the need to take security measures to protect computer data
     below). Other forms of data recording are not so easily duplicated, so there is a need to
     consider appropriate protection where manual data is held. So, for example, fireproof
     safes may be appropriate. HR departments must be particularly careful about
     disclosure, especially when it may be unlawful. HR computer screens should not be
     visible to visitors to the department. Laptops, tablets, and smartphones should be kept
     secure. Bear in mind that telephone calls from people purporting to be building
     societies, future employers or other plausible bodies may, in fact, be from private
     investigators. Also see the section on security, below.

8   *Personal data must not be transferred to countries that do not provide an adequate level
     of data protection.*
     If you are a small company, you may need specific advice on this. Larger organisations
     are likely to have clear policies wherever this may apply.

10.4.4 REFERENCES

You will want to know whether the person asking for the reference is legitimate. Requests
on letter-headed paper, from verifiable email addresses or from people whom you know
personally, are safest.

In giving a reference in confidence, an employee (or ex-employee) is not entitled to
request it from you. However, once the reference is in the hands of the recipient, then
they may make a subject access request to see it. The question of what may, or may not,

be revealed by the recipient requires careful consideration. There is guidance on the Information Commissioner's website; see References and Further Reading at the end of this chapter.

It is important when giving references that they are factual, fair and accurate. Fair, of course, implies an obligation to the future employer as well as towards your employee or ex-employee. It is generally unwise to go into large amounts of detail or to express opinions. In most employment sectors (you may need to check whether yours is an exception), there is no obligation to provide a reference. Indeed, they are usually regarded as a final check on the authenticity of a potential employee rather than as a selection tool.

Beware that any reference given on your organisation's headed paper or from its email address will be treated as emanating from your organisation. Many data protection policies restrict the giving of references, on behalf of the organisation, to a senior level. They may make it a disciplinary offence to breach that aspect of the policy.

10.4.5 SECURITY

This covers not just password protection but also the long-term protection of data. The major threats are computer failure, viruses, fire and even sabotage. The main protection against all these is a regular programme of back-ups, and anti-virus software and sound firewalls in place. Your supplier or IT department should ensure that these are run automatically on your system. It is important that security routines are implemented where necessary. Back-up data should also be stored off-site. If large amounts of data need to be kept, then restoring over the Internet, from a remote location, might take a lot of time. Also keep the following in mind:

- Back-ups must be capable of being restored to a different machine to cover machine failures.
- Viruses usually come from software that originates from an uncertain source, such as pirated software or software downloaded from the Internet.
- Fire and sabotage can be mitigated against by using a fireproof safe for back-ups or by an off-site back-up (password-protected) at another location. If you are a 'belt and braces' person, you will do both!
- In most cases, your IT department or supplier will also have access to your system and may take responsibility for passwords and access permissions to various parts of your system. It is important to understand what is happening and who has access to what. If the supplier is external, your contract should specify how your data is still protected from unauthorised access.

> **?   REFLECTIVE ACTIVITY 10.4**
>
> Imagine that there was a serious fire at your place of work. Your office, archives and computer system were completely destroyed. What would happen? Are critical pieces of data protected? If no data is protected, then what should be? Even if back-ups were secure in a fireproof safe, would you be able to get access to key information (such as contact details) if access to the site was denied? Put forward recommendations to rectify any shortfalls.

10.4.6 WHAT ARE THE OTHER LEGAL IMPLICATIONS?

It is a criminal offence to hold personal data for certain purposes (educational records, for example) without registering with the Information Commissioner, and your employer could be prosecuted. The same applies if the data is obtained unlawfully or sold unlawfully. Individuals have rights under the Data Protection Act. They include the right to have access ('subject access') to the information you hold on them (although not to any intentions, such as promotion, that you may have). This access includes access to details of the data being processed, to a description of the data being processed, to the purposes for which it is being processed, to the names or titles of any potential recipients of this data, and to information on the source of the data.

Case law suggests that the data thus protected has to be biographical to a significant extent and have the 'data subject' as its focus. It must also be in a 'relevant filing system'. The email we mentioned earlier (about an incident where an individual is named) would be in a relevant filing system if attached to the employee's record in a computer database, and in such a case it is possible that the email will be about the individual in some biographical way. But if there is merely mention of an employee in the minutes of a meeting, the employee is unlikely to have the right of access to it, either because the data will not be in a relevant filing system, because it will not have the data subject as its focus, or because it does not say much about them.

Where the data is processed automatically and is likely to form the sole basis for any decision significantly affecting the data subject (such as a psychometric test used for shortlisting purposes), the individual is also entitled to know the logic involved in the decision-making.

It is your responsibility to supply the logic to any enquirer, so you will need to be careful to obtain it from test suppliers. You would also be wise to check that the logic is valid. Checking the validity of a test, even relying on data from the supplier, requires some understanding of statistics. If you don't understand terms such as normative data, it would be wise to get further advice.

Failure to comply means that the individual can complain to the Commissioner, who has a range of powers. Individuals can also request information to be corrected or deleted, and they can also sue for damages if they suffer financial loss (or physical injury) as the result of incorrect data.

The Data Protection Act is very important. As we warned in Chapter 3, employment law is not an area in which issues are necessarily clear-cut. Quite frequently, the precise way in which the law is interpreted changes. So although we have explained key principles, you are likely to need further advice from more senior colleagues, Acas or legal specialists.

? REFLECTIVE ACTIVITY 10.5

Data may be stored on clouds, sometimes without the individual realising it. 'Everything everywhere' programs do this automatically; indeed, so do smartphones. Should HR departments be comfortable with this? Discuss this in your group.

10.5 OTHER LEGISLATION RELATING TO INFORMATION

10.5.1 THE FREEDOM OF INFORMATION ACT

The Freedom of Information Act covers information in the public sector, but also applies to the private sector where an organisation holds data on behalf of a public organisation. The Act came into force in 2005, but it does not confer additional rights on employees, or others, for them to have access to employee records, although there may be exceptions. As an example, in 2009 a disaffected soldier used the Act to obtain information on MPs' expenses and the information was subsequently published in the *Daily Telegraph*. Because the MPs held a public office, individuals' expenses were disclosed and an enormous public outcry resulted that led to ministerial resignations.

If you are likely to need to respond to access requests under the Freedom of Information Act, you should be well-briefed by your legal department. Where you are not – in a small private company holding public sector information, for example – you must take further advice. There is no dispensation for being inadequately prepared.

10.5.2 THE HUMAN RIGHTS ACT

The Act confers the right on individuals to have their privacy respected and provides for employees in the public sector to take legal action against their employer if they consider that their rights have been infringed. Under Article 8 of the Act: 'Everyone has the right to respect for his private and family life, his home, and his correspondence.'

Some interference in human rights is permitted to prevent crime and for national security. Where monitoring occurs (of emails, for example), employees should be informed in advance that the use of the facility is not private. Across-the-board monitoring by employers is regarded as intrusive and is not likely to be justifiable.

Circumstances where monitoring may be permissible include those shown below under the Regulation of Investigatory Powers Act. Employees in the private sector might claim constructive dismissal if they consider the intrusion into their privacy breaches trust and confidence (in their employer).

The Human Rights Act also protects individuals from you disclosing private information that you may hold as a result of employing them. Disclosure without consent could lead to a grievance and a claim of constructive dismissal.

10.5.3 THE REGULATION OF INVESTIGATORY POWERS ACT

This provides for the Telecommunications (Lawful Business Practice) (Interception of Communications) Regulations 2000. There is no absolute right to privacy (some intrusion may be justified so long as it is proportionate to the circumstances), but care may be required when investigating disciplinary matters that intrude on privacy. You may be called on to show that you have a 'legitimate' and 'defined' purpose for such investigation. Other aspects of this legislation are beyond the scope of this book.

10.5.4 THE CRIMINAL JUSTICE AND IMMIGRATION ACT

This Act makes it an offence for a person to have an indecent photograph or pseudo-photograph of a child in their possession. This is a serious criminal matter beyond the scope of this book.

10.6 INFORMATION AND CONSULTATION

Employees, whether trade union members or not, have the right to be informed and consulted about issues that affect their employment. The right applies to employees in organisations of 50 or more employees. Where employers do not provide for this right, employees have the right to request it.

There will be different arrangements for this process in different organisations but there has to be an agreed method of informing and consulting employees. That method must include all employees and have been formally approved by the employees. Particular issues have to be included in the information and consultation, such as the development of the organisation, of employment within the organisation and any matter that is likely to result in substantial change. More detail is provided in the CIPD publication listed in 'References and Further Reading' at the end of this chapter.

In summary, the issues relating to information legislation are complex and the various Acts interact to a significant extent. The important points for you as an HR practitioner are to be very careful about what personal information you obtain, how you obtain it, what you do with it, how you protect and manage it, and to whom you disclose it. The Employment Practices Data Protection Code provides a helpful guide (and can also help you to defend your actions). In all areas of doubt, seek advice. The relevant legislation discussed in this chapter is:

- Data Protection Act 1998
- Human Rights Act 1998
- Regulation of Investigatory Powers Act 2000
- Freedom of Information Act 2000
- Information and Consultation of Employees Regulations 2004.

10.7 SOCIAL MEDIA

Social media sites allow users to publish material on the Internet. The most familiar sites are Facebook, Twitter, LinkedIn, Google+, Yammer, YouTube, Wikipedia and Wordpress, but there are hundreds of social media sites globally, most with many million users – Facebook alone has well over one billion users.

This creates a number of questions for the HR practitioner: if I am not already doing so, which sites should I be using both personally and/or as an employee? How can this new resource benefit the practice of HR? What are the implications of social media for the organisation for which I am working?

Here we will look at the value of this resource to HR and its impact on the organisation. In this context the terms 'enterprise social media' or 'business social media' may be gaining some ground and are, perhaps, more appropriate. However, at the time of writing, 'social media' and 'social networking' seem to do service to our subject and these are the terms we will use here.

In 2016, it is hard to predict the future role of social networking, but it is safe to say that it is only going to grow in relevance for HR practitioners. Ignore it at your peril! But first some warnings.

Many corporate organisations are still struggling to understand social networking and some are very cautious. The latter applies especially in the mid-range of company size. Unproductive social networking is estimated to cost the economy billions in lost working time and a significant proportion of organisations have dismissed employees for Internet misuse. So, before you rush off to set up a company Twitter account or Facebook page, check the prevailing culture in your employing organisation first. The view of the chief executive or the managing director is the most critical. If you spend large amounts of time on social networking at work, make sure that you can justify it.

Material placed on social networking sites is there *permanently*. What may seem fun after a few beers may not look so cool when you apply for promotion. As an individual, you may want to try to maintain separate identities for your social life and professional life, although this is not always easy to do.

10.7.1 ABUSE

Much is written about the HR problems associated with social media. These include issues with the type of material circulated, harassment of others, questions of what is to be regarded as private, breaches of confidentiality and damage to the organisation's reputation. This list is far from exhaustive; social media is increasingly a part of human life and new problems will arise over time, so it pays to be always updating your understanding of this issue.

10.7.2 INAPPROPRIATE MATERIAL

It is well understood that child pornography is a serious criminal offence. However, outside this defined area, obscenity is subjective and there have been relatively few cases of successful prosecutions for obscene publication on social networking. Accessing, or providing, adult sites is not in itself a criminal offence.

It is for your organisation, perhaps with your advice, to set acceptable standards of behaviour in a social media policy and perhaps in disciplinary rules. You might want to say that if it is not acceptable to post an image on an office wall, it should not be acceptable to circulate that image electronically (or view it where others can also see it).

Where such material offends other employees, action can be taken as it would in any similar situation where employees are offended by the action of another. There have been dismissals for employees accessing pornography at their workstation. Such dismissals are often accepted by those who are dismissed: if they were to complain to an employment tribunal, the behaviour of which they are accused would become public. However, improved filtering is reducing access to adult sites, protecting employers and tempted employees alike.

Sensitivity is required in determining what might be considered inappropriate. For example, a care worker might take pictures of residents on an organised day out. Older people do not always look as well as they would wish and so posting their photographs on Facebook, however well intentioned, breaches their rights.

10.7.3 CYBER-BULLYING OR HARASSMENT

This can be treated in the same way as any other form of bullying. Indeed, as social media and other online activity leaves a trace (which IT professionals can follow), evidence is easier to find and less dependent on cautious witnesses. Again, coverage in a social media policy or anti-harassment policy is valuable.

10.7.4 BREACHES OF CONFIDENTIALITY

Where employees have access to confidential company information, they should be subject to confidentiality covenants in which they make a solemn promise not to divulge confidential information. This may be accompanied by restraint of trade clauses in which they also make similar promises not to compete, poach employees or take clients if they should leave the company. In theory, legal injunctions can be brought to stop employees defaulting on their covenants. In practice, this cannot always be achieved.

But many employees have access to small amounts of valuable information which, spread on social networking sites, could be valuable to a competitor, compromise data protection or damage the organisation in a variety of ways, not to mention its reputation (covered below).

If these are risks for your organisation, employees need to be made aware of the risks, their responsibilities and any sanction that might be taken if there is a breach. This is another item to add to your social media policy!

10.7.5 DAMAGE TO REPUTATION

It is relatively easy for activities on social media to be considered damaging to the employer's reputation. However, it can be difficult to establish the seriousness of the damage and whether a particular action justifies dismissal. A dramatic example of this was a team leader who posted on Facebook the comment that working with others at her employer's client was like, 'working in a nursery,' and she, 'didn't mean plants'. Even her employer's managers were divided over how damaging this was to the company. She was dismissed and subsequently found to have been unfairly so (see *Whitham* v *Club 24*

Limited T/A Ventura). Where dismissal cases have held up well in court – as in *Crisp* v *Apple Retail UK Limited* – the main reason has been a robust social media policy.

10.7.6 PRIVACY

In some cases, the employee who is discovered to have posted inappropriate material or damaged a reputation claims the material was private and not circulated beyond their friends. Of course, friends can fall out. Policies need to point out that privacy is not always assured, otherwise the right to privacy might be used as a defence. In the case of *Preece* v *JD Wetherspoons plc*, Miss Preece thought her privacy settings protected her when she made repugnant comments about Wetherspoons customers. Not so, as the daughter of one of the customers saw the comments. Wetherspoons' robust social media policy was an important factor in effecting a fair dismissal.

10.7.7 SOCIAL MEDIA POLICIES

There is still suspicion about social media – hence our earlier warning – but few seminars for HR practitioners now focus on the belief that such activities can be controlled. Indeed, there will be serious limits as to how much control can be exercised. But misconduct online, just as any other inappropriate behaviour in the workplace, can be subject to disciplinary procedures. Most of the unfair dismissal cases reaching the courts stand or fall on the existence of a social networking policy and sometimes on its comprehensiveness. Acas (see 'References and Further Reading' at the end of this chapter) produces invaluable guidance on social networking polices (see Reflective Activity 10.6 for a link to many organisation-specific ones).

  Don't forget the impact too of smartphones and tablets. Many employers allow employees to bring their own device (BYOD) and use them to access company data. The boundaries between business and private are becoming blurred and smartphones may present a security risk – if only because of the list of contacts held on them. But what is your policy on their business and private use, on security procedures and who owns the data held on them? CIPD has a summary of the law. Acas also provides advice which is contained within their social media guidance and policy (for both see 'References and Further Reading' at the end of this chapter).

?   REFLECTIVE ACTIVITY 10.6

Seek out some sample social media policies from **socialmediagovernance.com/policies**; those of the BBC and Yahoo offer an interesting comparison. Read some chosen policies and make notes. Then discuss your conclusions in a group.

1   How do these policies address the particular needs and values of those organisations?

2   What can you learn for use in your own organisation?

Now let's look a little more positively at social media.

10.7.8 HOW CAN HR USE SOCIAL MEDIA TO ADVANTAGE?

There are a number of areas that might be considered here; our list is not exhaustive and applications will in any case continue to develop over the life of this book. We discuss the following areas below:

- recruitment
- communication in-house
- developing a company culture
- sharing experience with other practitioners
- other research to support you and HR initiatives
- promoting the employer brand
- social media policies.

10.7.9 RECRUITMENT

Almost all recruitment agencies use social media sites for recruitment and, if you are recruiting directly from the job marketplace, you might be losing out if you do not do so too.

The use of social media for recruitment is discussed in Chapter 5.

10.7.10 COMMUNICATION IN-HOUSE

It used to be said that if you computerised a poor business process, you would still have a poor business process: computerisation alone was not the answer to improving processes. It might be argued that this is now not entirely true. Computerisation has made for better business processes because it provides for more options and even the task of computerisation itself focuses the mind and can lead to better design. Much the same may be true of communication. Social networking in an organisation where there is suspicion, politicking or backstabbing may not lead to improvements in communication. The process may simply accelerate the negative effect and spread it more widely. In such an organisation employees are unlikely to participate in networking within the organisation. Alternatively, they may find subtle ways to use it to pursue their own agendas.

But the very openness of social networking may help counteract poor communication. Backstabbing, for example, does not usually take place entirely in the open. There is information and evidence that where social networking has been implemented, incidences of bad behaviour are remarkably low.

Furthermore, networking within an organisation offers the opportunity for organisations to communicate in ways that have not been known before. Implementing social networking, and making it work, may focus minds on how to encourage employees to communicate.

There is a strong argument for forming relaxed groups within an in-house social network based on common interests such a cycling or car-sharing so as to ease employees into your internal social network. This avoids creating the feeling that work issues need to be discussed first. These are activities that, as an HR practitioner, you may be able to encourage. There is an increasing merging of personal and work as employees are available out of work hours on smartphones and tablets. Furthermore, such devices are increasingly allowed to access company servers.

Indeed, social networking is being driven in many cases by employees themselves. Colleagues who are friends set up their own groups and can do so whether or not the organisation participates. Unlike computers, fax and mobile phones, where companies adopted the technology first, social networking has been taken up by individuals already and many businesses are still pedalling hard to catch up. Where they can, HR practitioners would benefit from being part of existing social networks in their organisations, even if there is no official network as such.

An internal social network breaks down the 'silo culture' (where employees in different departments rarely talk to each other) and spreads knowledge around the organisation. The statement, 'If Hewlett-Packard knew what HP knows we'd be three times more productive' epitomises the value that organisations will get from spreading knowledge around the organisation rather than leaving it buried in individual departments. When Tata Consultancy Services in India set up an online question-and-answer forum, they consistently found invaluable contributions from employees working outside their strict job descriptions.

Over the last decade, there has been a significant trend towards openness and less privacy. This often concerns senior managers and business owners – they fear commercial information leaking out of the organisation. Indeed, from an HR viewpoint, data-protected information could come into the wrong hands. But this can happen anyway. However, unlike conventional leaks, social media leaves an audit trail which seriously discourages such leaks. It is an HR role to ensure employees are educated as to what is commercially sensitive and confidential. Sound policies are a good protection and the evidence to date (see 'Social networking (selling to CEOs)' in References and Further Reading at the end of this chapter.) is that horror stories are few.

As an HR practitioner we hope you will be seeking to encourage your organisation to make greater use of social networks to foster better communication in your organisation. Indeed, you may be doing so already.

10.7.11 DEVELOPING A COMPANY CULTURE

Company cultures are essentially created by communication or, perhaps more accurately, *how* senior management communicates its vision and values, and how different parts of the organisation communicate (or fail to communicate) with each other. So the section above on communication in-house is relevant to creating a culture. Social media offer the opportunity to those in HR (and those in other parts of the organisation) to influence other employees and help to develop a consistent culture in your organisation. This assumes, of course, that there is a coherent culture to communicate. In the context of social media, a more pertinent question may be: what part is social media to play in company culture?

If HR practitioners analyse traffic between individuals and groups in an organisation, they may pinpoint 'exactly where organisational structures need to be better linked-up or dispersed' ('Harnessing Social Media for Organisational Effectiveness' – see References and Further Reading at the end of this chapter below). In the same publication, Jon Ingham points out that most organisations succeed or fail as a result of the way people work together rather than because of the quality of the individuals. Social media will change the way people work together. Those HR departments that grasp and influence this development will help their organisations to succeed.

Already many organisations are embedding social media in their culture. One is Dell, which was once embarrassed by an article entitled '22 Confessions of a Former Dell Sales Manager', which gave insider tips on how to get the best deal from the company. Dell subsequently formed a Social Media and Community University so its employees can learn to connect with customers in meaningful ways.

There is a possibility that if, as an employer, you don't communicate your company culture strongly through social media then others may do it for you in ways with which you and senior managers may be uncomfortable.

10.7.12 SHARING EXPERIENCE WITH OTHER PRACTITIONERS

If you are undertaking the Certificate course, you should be learning from your colleagues on the course. Perhaps you are already social networking between yourselves as many on our courses have done. But sharing can continue after the end of the course so you can continue to learn from people whom you have met and know.

And there are other groups out there from whom you can learn. For example, we often come across tricky areas of employment law such as TUPE. By posting questions on a network such as LinkedIn or in CIPD Community, we may gain invaluable guidance from top lawyers and experienced HR practitioners on quirky aspects of the law. We use TUPE as an example because one LinkedIn group is dedicated to just that topic. Groups of all kinds exist on many social media sites and they are a great way of sharing experience – that means give and take, of course.

Some of the research for this chapter, as well as for other parts of this book, has been done by such posting, yielding information from around the world. Keep in mind, though, that social networking is not always accurate. Although discussions usually 'get there in the end', the end cannot be identified in advance. See Case Study 10.1 for an example.

CASE STUDY 10.1

This is a summary of a typical exchange on a LinkedIn group (HR Professionals UK) discussion in which one of the authors participated.

An HR manager with a firm of solicitors posts the folllowing question to the group: 'Do notice periods have to be reciprocal?'

Almost immediately, an HR consultant confirms that they do not, followed quickly by two heads of employment law who also confirm this. There is some further comment that while notice periods are often reciprocal, it is a question of negotiation between employer and employee.

Then another consultant makes the suggestion that an employee cannot be required to give more notice, but can give less. She also makes helpful remarks about good practice.

However, she misquotes (see later) the statutory minimum notice periods.

A director of consulting supports these contributions and comments on how business-critical employees are often offered extended periods of notice in return for the same obligation.

The author then raises questions. He thinks that the statutory periods of notice have been misquoted and restates the legal requirements. He also questions the assertion that the employee cannot be required to give more notice than the employer and asks the contributors where they are getting their information from.

He is then supported on both counts by both a head of employment law and a consultancy director.

Finally, the original HR manager posts a big 'thank you' for the comments.

This summary illustrates several points and in particular that not everything that you read on a social networking site, even a professional one such as LinkedIn is, is necessarily correct. Nonetheless, if you doubt the answer, you can pose your own query and errors are usually corrected. Second, also note this author's question about the authority of the information (ie its source). It is easy for people to think they know the answer, but they may only be repeating something they have heard: much better if they can point to an authority such as an eminent commentator, a statute or regulation, or a court case.

Note too that a great deal of helpful information emerged around the original question and note the final 'thanks' from the person who started the discussion. The CIPD website contains much useful advice on how to participate in a discussion.

Incidentally, if they needed it to resolve a practical matter, CIPD members could have reached the answer to this question in five minutes simply by calling the CIPD legal helpline.

10.7.13 OTHER RESEARCH TO SUPPORT YOU AND HR INITIATIVES

If you wrote down everything that happened to you in your lifetime for every minute of the day, would that be of value? The information would be so unordered and critical points would be so deeply buried in detail that they would be unlikely ever to be discovered. But such detail, and more, is held on the Internet, and search engines can find pertinent information in milliseconds.

As HR practitioners, we can take few executive decisions, but at the same time are well placed to advise on strategy because of our understanding of the people aspects of our organisation. It can be frustrating to see obvious opportunities but be unable to put cogent arguments because we lack the hard facts to support our arguments. As practitioners, the authors have been in that place many times.

But today's HR practitioner has access to the Internet and someone somewhere will have not only cogently expressed arguments, but the data to support them too. For example, do you want to get the head of your organisation sold on social networking? Then check out 'Social networking (selling to CEOs)' in References and Further Reading at the end of this chapter.

Whatever initiative you would like to take, someone will almost certainly have taken it before and succeeded. Evidence of their success can support your initiative.

? REFLECTIVE ACTIVITY 10.7

Research the various ways in which you can keep updated as an HR practitioner; for example, via Twitter, LinkedIn groups, smartphone apps, and of course radio, television and newspapers.

Make a list of all the primary sources available to you and the information they could provide that would be relevant to you.

Prepare your own plan of how you will keep up to date, which groups you might join, how often you would access each source, what alerts you will accept, etc. The plan must be manageable on a daily basis because, just as you wouldn't read every daily newspaper, you cannot utilise every source that might be available.

Discuss your plan with others.

10.7.14 PROMOTING THE EMPLOYER BRAND

Finding out what working for a particular company is really like used to be quite a task; to some extent it still is. If you were lucky, you would know someone who worked for the company already. If not, you would be dependent on one of the published lists, such as the 100 best companies list. But then you might not want to work for a private sector company, or be applying for a job at one of the top 100 companies.

However, looking at it from the applicant's perspective, that applicant can now tap into social networking, find who works for your company or organisation, or read reviews from current employees. They can very quickly get a flavour of what it might be like to work for your company. They may even ask some of your employees via social media. That is aside from a wealth of other information that applicants can research on the Internet. What do people post about you? Do you have published values? Are your policies and procedures in the public domain? What is their tone? Employers increasingly need to give attention to these questions if they are to attract talent. Care needs to be taken over 'dirty linen' because it can be so easily washed in public. So that means listening in to traffic on the Internet, not just from a marketing viewpoint but from an employer viewpoint. You could be tapping into relevant communities on the web and checking out employer-review websites such as Glassdoor to be kept informed. But the positive aspect of building the brand is also to inform those communities.

A risk in participating is that social networking may help competitors to lure your best employees away. But the converse is that you may be able to find top employees yourself, including those who were not even thinking of moving – a double-edged sword.

10.8 CONFIDENTIALITY, OPENNESS, AND SOCIAL MEDIA

Confidentiality and openness are complex areas that are often ethical and philosophical in their content. It is not our intention to provide direct guidance in these matters but rather to 'air' them so that you are aware of the need to consider them and of the need to be very careful in how you proceed.

10.8.1 CONFIDENTIALITY

Personal matters

As an HR practitioner, it is inevitable that you will be party to confidential information. Some may include sensitive data of the type described above, some may contain detail about management intentions towards individual employees, and yet more may be commercially sensitive information. For example, you might become aware that someone is HIV positive, or that an individual is being tipped for promotion, or you might know something about the true market value of an employee who is key to the business. Most of us aspire to work in or create open, honest organisations whose 'mission' is one to which we relate and one which is full of people with good intentions towards each other. Reality is often different. Moods and feelings such as jealousy, envy, ambition, apathy, greed, fear, arrogance and insecurity can be found wherever groups of people come together. The extent to which they are present in any particular organisation is a matter of conjecture or opinion. Personal information about individuals is of great interest to those who seek to exploit the weaknesses of others and much of that personal information is in the hands of HR.

Senior managers are not immune to these feelings and moods and yet often have legitimate reasons for knowing personal information about individuals. The question of confidentiality is, therefore, a complex one for HR and one where the answers are not necessarily clear-cut. But your ability to keep confidential information and to keep information confidential – at least confidential to those who have legitimate reasons for having it – is a key HR skill. At times, you will have to exercise judgement.

Corporate confidentiality

Confidentiality goes beyond the personal. As an HR practitioner, you may know that restructuring of the company is being considered, whether redundancies are likely or whether the business is being sold. All these can have a disturbing effect on morale within a company, and senior managers will want to be able to deliberate on such critical matters without setting rumours running. Indeed, in some cases the law may require them to keep matters confidential. In other cases, the law runs counter to some of these deliberations. For example, consultation on redundancies should commence as soon as they are contemplated and should run for significant periods of time. However large the organisation, leaked information about potential redundancies, or other sensitive matters, could be circulated amongst your employees in minutes. You may want to think through who would also have access to confidential information; those working in the IT department, for example. Guidelines for employees generally might be worth providing too – perhaps in that social networking policy.

10.8.2 THE IMPORTANCE OF FACE-TO-FACE COMMUNICATION

IT and communication have effectively merged. But as we explained in Chapter 2, it is important to remember that only a small percentage of the communication in a face-to-face encounter is made up of the words used. Body language and intonation account for most of the rest. Remove body language (as in a telephone conversation) and less is communicated. Remove intonation (as in an email) and you are left with a fraction of what might have been communicated had your exchange been face-to-face. It is also easier for words to be misinterpreted and misunderstandings to arise. In September 2001, Prime Minister Tony Blair crossed the Atlantic when no civilian airliners were doing so. Following 9/11 he considered an immediate face-to-face meeting with President George Bush to be crucial. There are times when technology-based communication is inappropriate.

? REFLECTIVE ACTIVITY 10.8

Visit an exhibition such as the CIPD HR Software Show held in London each year and persuade exhibitors to show you their software in a free demonstration.

Agree an 'exchange' with a colleague on a college course, or an outside learning source. Spend half a day with them understanding how they manage information and spend a further half a day showing them your systems.

? REFLECTIVE ACTIVITY 10.9

'It is not the strongest of the species that survives, or the most intelligent; it is the one most capable of change,' wrote Charles Darwin.

Review the collection of thought-pieces provided by the CIPD ('Harnessing Social Media for Organisational Effectiveness'; see References and Further Reading at the end of this chapter) and consider your own experiences. We have the May 2012 publication to hand, but there may be a more recent edition. Discuss the paper with your learning sources and then respond to this quotation with reference to social networking.

Assuming those who can adapt to the opportunities of social networking will 'survive' better than those people who are simply more intelligent, how will you, or would you, change HR practices to take advantage of the new opportunities? We assume you are already engaged in social networking, so you might add your own experience in answering this question.

Write an action plan.

10.9 THE ROLE OF HR PRACTITIONERS

Information and communication systems are tools that you use to support line managers and to assist you in your other HR roles and activities. We suggest the following roles in relation to information and communication.

10.9.1 AN ADMINISTRATIVE ROLE

This involves keeping well-organised records and providing information. It is seen by some as the dull area of HR activities. However, the flow of information around an organisation is vital to effective decision-making. Providing the management of the organisation with high-quality HR information (that is, pertinent, clear, timely and accurate) represents a major contribution to the business. At the same time, it is a substantial job for HR practitioners and one that can be underestimated far too easily. It is an area where social networking (such as a private Yammer group) may ease the task of disseminating information and serving other management functions more effectively.

This assumes, of course, a willingness to share information.

10.9.2 AN INFLUENCING ROLE ENHANCED BY NEW RESEARCH OPPORTUNITIES

In this role, you are meeting the challenge of providing high-quality information that improves the credibility of the HR function in your organisation. Researching HR principles and practice in using social media will assist you in being well informed and enhancing your credibility, which leads to greater access to decision-makers. That makes your job more rewarding and may provide the opportunity to extend your role and influence into interesting areas.

10.9.3 A USER ROLE

This concerns being the user of computerised systems. Here you may become the customer of an IT department or of an external supplier. You will have a part to play in ensuring that the systems meet your needs so you can in turn provide your own 'customers' with the information they need. It is a substantial task to make sure that computers, the available software and web applications assist you.

10.9.4 AN ADVISORY ROLE TO LINE MANAGERS

It is quite possible that the issue of data protection in your organisation will fall to the HR department. In addition, the increasing use of social media means that you may be called on for advice on policy issues and the actions that will be required if there is abuse of these facilities. If so, you need to know and understand the basics of the relevant legislation, and to know where to go to find more detailed information. We have already cautioned you about the complexity of the legislation when we looked at a similar role in relation to other employment law. It is vital that you do not overestimate your understanding of the law, so if you are in any doubt, always seek further advice.

10.9.5 A GATEKEEPER BETWEEN CONFIDENTIALITY AND TRANSPARENCY

We have examined the need for confidentiality, but also highlighted the trend towards transparency and openness. Within people-focused areas, HR cannot avoid a central role. Decisions are likely to be taken at a senior level in HR, but if you are a sole practitioner, you will need to give thought to policies and procedures that guide employees and managers.

10.9.6 GUARDIAN OF THE SOCIAL MEDIA POLICY

It is highly likely that your employer will look to you for this policy, and indeed we consider that they should – although the IT department may also be a relevant participant in its evolution and maintenance. But when it comes to disciplinary processes, the role of HR in that policy will be crucial. You need to make sure it will serve its purpose if necessary.

10.9.7 A LEADER IN SOCIAL MEDIA

Many senior managers and business-owners are still bemused by social media: it is territory that is potentially dangerous. So if you can rise to the challenge there will be an opportunity to lead others and, if you are ambitious, get noticed.

If you join social networks inside and outside your organisation, you can become a central point for information on recruiting, communication, company culture and employer brand. By becoming a 'node' of many networks, you will extend and enhance your standing. Just be aware of the warnings earlier in this chapter.

10.10 SUMMARY

We have looked at the need to keep records and you should now have a broad idea of the important reasons for keeping information. Most records and information can now be managed on computer systems and there is a broad range of applications software to assist in information management and HR tasks. There is increasingly wider access to records and information and facilities to manage them, not only on company servers but on internal and external social networking sites.

In our view, social media offers a huge opportunity for HR to become more effective in an organisation through improved recruitment, communication, developing a culture, sharing new initiatives and promoting an employer brand.

Confidentiality is of crucial importance in HR and we have considered both this and the increased openness being fostered by social networking.

You must take time to keep up with the trends in software, new applications, social networking and other new approaches to communications.

EXPLORE FURTHER

References and further reading

BEE, R. and BEE, F. (2005) *Managing Information and Statistics*. London: CIPD.

SWIRES-HENNESSY, E. (2014) *Presenting Data: How to communicate your message effectively*. Chichester: Wiley.

EMC EDUCATION SERVICES. (ed). (2015) *Data Science and Big Data Analytics: Discovering, Analyzing, Visualizing and Presenting Data*. Chichester: Wiley.

HAMMONDS. (2004) *Data Protection*. 2nd edition. London: CIPD.

THE INFORMATION COMMISSIONER. *Employment Practices Data Protection Code*. Available from The Information Commissioner's Office, Wycliffe House, Water Lane, Wilmslow, Cheshire SK9 5AF. (Also online; see below.)

TAPSCOTT, D. and WILLIAMS, A.D. (2011) *Wikinomics: How Mass Collaboration Changes Everything*. London: Atlantic Books.

Web references

Acas on social media policies: www.acas.org.uk/index.aspx?articleid=3381

Best companies: appointments.thesundaytimes.co.uk/article/best100companies/

BYOD risks: employersolutions.co.uk/2014/06/could-you-be-blown-out-of-the-water

Company Facebook page building: www.facebook.com/advertising

Data Protection Code: ico.org.uk/media/for-organisations/documents/1064/the_employment_practices_code.pdf

Data protection guidance on references and subject access: ico.org.uk/media/2775/references_v1_final.pdf

Harnessing social media for organisational effectiveness: A collection of thought pieces: cipd.co.uk/NR/rdonlyres/736010C3-C752–4B9D-A501–76F04954F6D9/0/5843_SOP_Social_Media_Insight_Report_2012.pdf

How social media is changing HR jobs: www.wantedanalytics.com/analysis/posts/social-media-is-changing-human-resources-jobs

Ownership of contacts: cipd.co.uk/pm/peoplemanagement/b/weblog/archive/2014/12/01/who-owns-your-linkedin-contacts.aspx

Social media and HR in India: www.wipro.com/Documents/Social_Media_Report_Feb_2012.pdf

Social media and the organisation: cipd.co.uk/hr-resources/research/harnessing-social-media.aspx

Social media engagement: www.personneltoday.com/hr/social-media-engagement-building-collaborative-workforce

Social media (guidance): www.acas.org.uk/index.aspx?articleid=3375

Social media in HR: www.cipd.co.uk/hr-resources/social-media-hr.aspx

Social media policies database: socialmediagovernance.com/policies.php

Social networking adoption: c15056394.r94.cf2.rackcdn.com/MITSMR-Deloitte-Social-Business-What-Are-Companies-Really-Doing-Spring-2012.pdf

Social networking (selling to CEOs): sloanreview.mit.edu/article/what-sells-ceos-on-social-networking

Using personal devices at work: www.acas.org.uk/index.aspx?articleid=3982

Yammer: about.yammer.com/yammer-blog/adecco-medical-yammer-strengthen-human-resource-solutions

See also survey reports on the CIPD website: www.cipd.co.uk/hr-resources/survey-reports:

- Social technology, social business (2013)
- Focus on E-learning (June 2011)

See also Factsheets on the CIPD website: http://www.cipd.co.uk/hr-resources/factsheets:

- E-learning (September 2014)
- Employer Brand (May 2015)
- HR Analytics (July 2015)
- Retention of HR Records (July 2015)
- Using Social Media in Education: for Tutors in Centres (November 2011)

Websites

Chartered Institute of Personnel and Development: www.cipd.co.uk

Information Commissioner: www.ico.org.uk

CIPD Community: www.cipd.co.uk/community

Squire Sanders Employment Law Cloud (smartphone app) – provides alerts for employment law updates

REFLECTIVE ACTIVITIES FEEDBACK

Reflective Activity 10.9

Answers to this question are to be found in numerous discussion groups, blogs, chatrooms, and so on. Here a just a few suggestions:

- Build your own network of contacts. It used to be said that, 'It is not what you know but whom you know that counts,' and while there is a need for some substance behind your expertise, this statement is still substantially true.
- Participate in intra-organisation communication facilities – or, if there are none, set up Yammer, an employee Facebook page, etc. Take care to ensure first that any such action is consistent with your organisation's culture.
- Participate in relevant groups and communities, posting discussion questions of interest to you and making constructive contributions to the debates started by others.
- Find a career opportunity.
- Recruit new staff.
- Use the reference facility on LinkedIn to research candidates.

Change in Organisations

11.1 INTRODUCTION

Change is a constant activity in many organisations. Indeed, much research suggests that small-scale change is happening almost all the time while major change happens in organisations approximately every three years. Change may be voluntary and prompted by the organisation for positive business reasons, or forced, such as changes brought about during times of economic downturn. As such, change is a key activity for both managers and HR practitioners – who have responsibilities to achieve the desired change, build on the positive aspects of change, manage any negative impacts of change, and manage the impact on people while keeping the day-to-day business running: quite a challenge!

HR practitioners can have a variety of roles in change processes, and these will often depend on the size and nature of the change being introduced. The introduction of a new organisation-wide pay system will necessitate a very involved role for HR – from devising and leading the change to supporting individuals through it. A departmental restructuring, on the other hand, will generally be led by the departmental manager with support from HR to guide the manager through the change and to give support to the employees affected.

In this chapter we consider the context for change in organisations – why it is important and why organisations need to change. We look at approaches to managing change to achieve a successful outcome and then move on to consider the impact of change on individuals and what you can do to support individuals through change.

11.2 WHY IS MANAGING CHANGE IMPORTANT?

Change is a process of moving from one state to another state. It affects all types of organisation – public and private sector, voluntary and charitable, national and local, large and small. It can also occur in any aspect of organisational life, from large-scale change that affects a whole organisation and the core purpose of the business to much smaller change, just affecting one business process or one team or activity. Change can be driven by external factors (see Chapter 2) or by internal matters. Most commonly, change can be seen in the areas of:

- organisational structure
- technological developments
- working practices and processes
- reducing costs
- mergers and takeovers
- business relationships – increasing use of collaborative/partnering arrangements between organisations
- business location and infrastructure
- organisational culture
- workforce profile, capability and terms and conditions.

Any change, however large or small, will impact on the people working in the area where the change happens, and one aim of all change processes will be to achieve buy-in from the people affected – which is easier said than done. The type of change being introduced and the impact it will have on individual members of staff will affect the degree of this buy-in. Some change may be viewed positively and be welcomed by those affected by it – for example, introducing flexible working arrangements – whereas other change – for example, reductions in the size of the workforce – may be seen in a more negative light, leading to resistance on the part of those affected. Every individual interprets and will respond to change in a different way depending on a number of factors, such as their personal circumstances, how much the change affects them, their resilience and ability to adapt to change and their previous experience of change. Change in organisations often requires employees to change the way they work or to change their behaviour and attitudes – not something that everyone will be keen to do or have the capability to do. All of this can make change very unpredictable and difficult to manage.

A wide range of research shows that change is not always successful – over 40% of change programmes can fail to achieve their stated objectives. It is therefore very important to do everything possible to increase the chances of success.

11.3 WHY ORGANISATIONS NEED TO CHANGE

Change happens because organisations need to remain competitive in order to survive. Pressure for change may be internal – for example, because of increasing costs or a desire to enter new markets – or it may be external – for example, because of changing economic conditions or pressure from customers. To survive in a competitive business world or deliver highest quality and best value for money in publicly funded bodies, organisations need to be adaptable and agile. A wide range of factors, both internal and external, affect organisations and prompt the need for change. This can be seen by considering some well-known organisations/types of organisation and looking at some of the changes that have affected or are affecting them.

11.3.1 THE BIG SUPERMARKETS – ASDA, SAINSBURYS, TESCO

Over the last few years many changes have occurred that have had an impact on the business strategies and structures of the large supermarkets. We have seen a change in consumer habits from a large proportion of people doing a big weekly shop at out of town stores, to more people now shopping more frequently and buying less at each visit at local town centre 'express' stores. Online shopping is also changing the way in which many groceries are bought and therefore how they are stocked and distributed. We have seen the emergence and growth of new low-cost competitors – Aldi and Lidl – forcing prices down and leaving the big supermarkets struggling to compete. We have seen consumer and supplier campaigns (think of the price of milk campaign by farmers in 2015 and the sight of cows in the milk aisle) forcing supermarkets to rethink their pricing and marketing campaigns.

11.3.2 LONDON UNDERGROUND

The planned roll-out of the 'night tube' is a response to changing lifestyles, London as a 24-hour city, and a huge increase in customer demand – passenger numbers on Friday and Saturday nights are up by 70% since 2000. The introduction of this new service has been possible because of both this increased demand and the ongoing modernisation of parts of the London Underground network. However, it hasn't been trouble-free, with some significant disputes between Transport for London and its workforce and their union representatives regarding the terms and conditions of employment and the working practices of those employees who will be required to staff the new night-time services.

11.3.3 APPLE

Ongoing innovation and technological developments (for example, not only the new versions of the iPhone and iPad, but also new products such as the Apple watch) have seen Apple continue to thrive in a globally competitive market. This has also been helped by the rapid adoption of supporting technologies across the world, such as the roll-out of 4G phone networks in China, a huge marketplace. A further change adopted by Apple that has contributed to its success is the opening of market-leading retail stores designed to give the consumer a high-end experience and offer expert support from well-trained and enthusiastic staff in store.

11.3.4 BANKS

Since the global economic crisis of 2010, we've seen significant change in the way the banking system operates and is regulated. Regulatory change has led to the requirement to split investment banking and retail banking functions. From this we have seen the emergence of some new and some revisited names on the high street: Lloyds, Williams and Glyn and The Midland (the latter was suggested and later rejected in favour of HSBC UK). We have also seen the emergence of so-called 'challenger banks'. In addition, the adoption of digital technology continues to change the experience of customers from online banking to the contactless methods of paying for goods and services.

Just from these few examples it can be seen that change in organisations is affected by a multitude of factors: developments in new technology; growing, contracting and changing markets; changing legislative requirements; the economic climate; changing consumer habits; and so on. Other factors also driving change in organisations include the arrival of new competitors, government policy, customer pressure and changes in the population. With so many factors having an influence, it is clear to see why change is so common in organisations striving for success.

?   **REFLECTIVE ACTIVITY 11.1**

Consider a change that has happened in your organisation in the last 12 months. Think about why the change was necessary and what the driving forces for the change were, and note down your ideas. Then talk to some of the people involved in planning and managing the change to find out their views on why the change happened and what the driving forces were.

How close are your views to the actual reasons?

11.4 APPROACHES TO CHANGE

Change can be viewed in a number of different ways and many different models of, and approaches to, change exist. Sometimes change is deliberate and prompted by the organisation. This is often referred to as 'planned' change. Conversely, where change seems to evolve in a less structured and planned way, it is often known as 'emergent' change. Such emergent change may result from apparently unrelated decisions and actions by managers, although these might be linked to assumptions that managers make about what is happening in the environment within which the organisation operates.

As well as considering whether change is planned or emergent, the extent and scope of change is often also considered – Ackerman and Anderson (2010) distinguish between three types of change – transitional, developmental and transformational – and argue that over the last two to three decades, change has moved from being more manageable and controllable (transitional and developmental) to the majority of change now being transformational, which is significantly less so. For the purposes of this introduction to change, it is worth considering all three briefly.

The *transitional* model of change seeks to achieve a known future state that is different from the current situation. This transitional change model can be traced back to the work of Lewin (1951), who described change as a three-stage process involving:

- 'unfreezing' the existing situation
- moving to a new position
- 'refreezing' in the new state.

Developmental change is change that improves or corrects existing aspects of an organisation and often focuses on improvements to skills or processes – an improvement of an existing situation. For example, many organisations adopt processes such as 'Lean Six Sigma' or the 5S methodology (you can google these terms for more information if your company uses these methods and it would be helpful for you to know more) to review and change processes and systems to generate greater efficiency.

Transformational change requires a fundamental change in assumptions by the organisation and those who work within it. The outcome of transformational change can be an organisation that differs significantly in terms of structure, culture and strategy from the previous one. The change period is difficult to control and manage and may feel quite chaotic. The type of change many organisations have had to make in response to the online/digital world can be seen as transformational – just think of how some large retailers have had to change their whole business model to survive – and those who didn't change their model and have become victims not only of the recession but of their own failure to change.

This short section has just provided an overview of three different ways of viewing the change process – there are many more. Reading some of the further reading references at the end of this chapter will provide you with more information. We will now consider approaches to managing change.

11.5 MANAGING CHANGE

It must be considered that there is nothing more difficult to carry out nor more doubtful of success nor more dangerous to handle than to initiate a new order of things; for the reformer has enemies in all those who profit by the old order, and only lukewarm defenders in all those who would profit by the new order; this lukewarmness arising partly from the incredulity of mankind who does not truly believe in anything new until they actually have experience of it.

Niccolò Machiavelli (1469–1527)

Fortunately, there are numerous different approaches to managing change in organisations, which will hopefully produce a more successful outcome than suggested here! 'Change management' is the name usually given to a varied set of processes, tools and techniques, methods and approaches for managing the 'people' aspects of change and achieving a desired change. (The term 'project management' tends to be used to refer to managing the more technical, less people-oriented aspects of change.) Whatever tools and approaches are used in your organisation, the aim will be the same – to successfully achieve the goals of the change while minimising any negative impact of change. The CIPD tool for supporting change – 'Approaches to Change: Building capability and confidence' – identifies a seven-step flexible framework for change with a focus on seven key actions that can add value and improve the chances of success. These seven steps are:

11.5.1 SET DIRECTION

In this first part of the change project you are answering the question, 'Why must we do this?' You have to present a 'burning platform' or sense of urgency that people understand. Along with this you need to paint a clear, concrete and actionable picture of what benefits the change will bring to individuals and the organisation.

11.5.2 DESIGN AND PLAN

Successful change draws upon project management disciplines. And as with any journey, it is important to plan the route. Employee involvement must take place in the context of clearly defined milestones and rigorous project management.

11.5.3 MOBILISE

Confirm you have the resources (time, equipment, people, stakeholder support, budget, and so on) to deliver the planned change. (An overview of the various roles different people and teams within an organisation play during times of change can be seen in Table 11.1.)

11.5.4 DELIVER

Focus on getting short-term measurable and communicable results quickly.

11.5.5 TRANSITION

If you can, begin transitioning in small autonomous units where you can monitor the effects and take actions to keep things on course (essentially a pilot process).

11.5.6 CONSOLIDATE

The change will not succeed unless you align all organisational elements behind it. Continuous improvement that follows the planned project is the goal; this means looking at things such as policies, reporting relationships, rewards – and revising them to support the new world.

11.5.7 IMPROVE

If you're using a project-management approach, you'll be doing regular reviews of progress through standard monitoring and tracking methods. Use the information from these to make course corrections. If you are not using project-management approaches, take the time and make the effort to do a rigorous review.

A range of other factors will also need consideration when embarking on any change process – such as project management, training, leadership and organisational culture.

Table 11.1 Key people and their responsibilities for change

Who	Key responsibilities
Top team	Aligning change with organisational strategy. Providing leadership to make change happen. Internal and external communication. Monitoring and evaluation after implementation.
Line management	Owning their part in change. Cascading communications. Preparing teams for implementation.
HR professionals/ HR function	Championing the 'people' agenda. Redefining the roles, jobs and skills. Training and developing the staff involved. Adapting and refining HR policies – for example, careers, reward. Building learning on/knowledge of change. Communicating with and involving staff.
Programme and project managers	Establishing project capability and accountability. Communication. Management and implementation. Project planning. Engaging senior management and key stakeholders.

Source: CIPD (2010) Approaches to Change: Building capability and confidence

11.6 THE IMPACT OF CHANGE ON INDIVIDUALS

Almost any change in any organisation will impact on the people who work in that organisation because all organisations are essentially human systems – made up of the people who work within them. In any consideration of change it is therefore important to consider the impact of change on individual employees. The impact that any given change will have on employees in an organisation will depend on a number of factors, including how significant the change is for the individual employee, the individual's personal circumstances and ability to cope with change, and whether the individual views the change positively or negatively. To a large extent the views of individuals are determined by how the individuals think in relation to the change. The way in which the change is communicated to them can therefore be crucial to their reaction.

What is also important is to consider the reverse – the impact of individuals on change. Where a change is happening that has been driven by external factors rather than by the people affected and involved, it is unlikely to succeed unless some of the people affected are in favour of it. Individuals or groups in an organisation can resist and sabotage change to the extent that it either doesn't happen or fails to achieve the goals set. It is therefore helpful to think about the different individual positions people affected might take when faced with change. Peter Senge identifies the different positions individuals might take in response to change (see Table 11.2).

Table 11.2 The responses of individuals to change

Position	Response to change
Commitment	Want change to happen and will work to make it happen.
Enrolment	Want change to happen and will devote time and energy to making it happen within given frameworks.
Genuine compliance	See the virtue in what is proposed, do what is asked of them and think proactively about what is needed.

Position	Response to change
Formal compliance	Can describe the benefits of what is proposed and are not hostile to them. Do what they are asked, but no more.
Grudging compliance	Do not accept that there are benefits to what is proposed and do not go along with it. Do enough of what is asked of them not to jeopardise their position. Voice opposition and hopes for failure.
Non-compliance	Do not accept that there are benefits and have nothing to lose by opposing the proposition. Will not do what is asked of them.
Apathy	Neither in support of nor in opposition to the proposal, just serving time.

Adapted from Peter Senge (2006) *The Fifth Discipline*

For a change to succeed, not everyone needs to commit, but it can be helpful to think about the positions different individuals or groups might take and consider how support at the right level might be achieved.

? REFLECTIVE ACTIVITY 11.2

For the purposes of this activity, consider three independently owned businesses manufacturing double-glazing products. All have been affected by an economic downturn and they have decided to merge into one business to reduce costs. One is family-owned and that family will be selling up. The ownership and management teams in the other two businesses will merge and run the three separate businesses as one. Two of the businesses are in the same town, while the third is in a neighbouring town. The new management will want to centralise operations in one place.

Now try to identify the different individuals/groups of individuals that will be affected by this merger and think about what position they are likely to take in this change. What are the factors that will influence the positions taken?

Compare your responses with the feedback at the end of this chapter.

11.6.1 INDIVIDUAL RESPONSES AND REACTIONS TO CHANGE

Although the impact of change on people is subject to variation and individual reactions will be different, the first response people most often have to change is an emotional one. This will often also be a fairly self-centred reaction: 'What's the effect of this going to be on me and my job?' Depending on the nature of the change and what impact it will have for a particular individual, this emotional response may range from positive feelings such as excitement and anticipation to more negative feelings such as anger and cynicism. The emotional reaction to change is a well-researched area, many commentators using a variation on the 'change curve' to describe individual emotional responses to change. This change curve was described by Elisabeth Kübler-Ross in work she did on grieving, and it has subsequently been adapted by many people to reflect the stages an individual experiencing change goes through (see Figure 11.1). The curve looks at an individual's emotions over time as change is happening.

Using the change curve in supporting individual employees through change can be very helpful – think about the emotions at play, how they might be affecting each individual's behaviour and how you might act to support employees through each phase. The individual reactions involved can include:

- *Shock, denial and anger* – the initial reactions where people may be stunned by the news of the change and individuals may be thinking that the organisation is not really going to go through with the change or that the proposed change is a complete waste of time or money. Those who view the change negatively may have this emotion for longer than those who don't. At this stage of reaction employees often need information and communication. Although messages about change can be complex, you should think about what information is available to be shared, and when, and also how the messages can be kept as clear and simple as possible. Here employees are still absorbing the news about a change. It is helpful to communicate information as early on as possible so that employees can begin to see the need for change and the end point. At this stage, however, individuals are not yet ready to hear how things will be better for them once the change has happened. It is useful to provide opportunities for individuals to discuss their feelings – where frustration and grievances can be aired constructively, the degree of bitterness and anger can be reduced. Even when angry or in shock, what individuals have to say must still be listened to and taken seriously – they may have legitimate concerns and what they have to say might affect the success of the change initiative.

Figure 11.1 Kübler-Ross's change curve

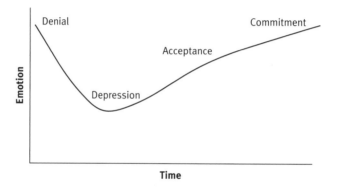

- *Frustration, fear, depression* – where individuals may start to grudgingly accept that the change is really happening but feel there is either nothing they can do about it or think about ways they might resist or frustrate the change process. During this phase employees need emotional and practical support in order for them to start thinking more positively about the change. It is important to acknowledge that emotions are important and real for people. It can be a challenge to get people to listen at this stage, so extra effort must be put into communication processes.
- *Acceptance, understanding, exploration* – where individuals start to really acknowledge that change is happening and may start to see some of the positives in the change, appreciate the need for the change and be thinking about how they will move on. Here individuals will probably be in need of support and guidance about what the future holds for them. The challenges for managers and HR practitioners during this phase can be developing and maintaining a common understanding about the future state and ensuring that everyone feels involved. This is when it is essential to generate buy-in from all those affected by the change. Additional information will be needed at this stage to support employees in developing a real understanding of what the future looks like and how it will affect them. It can be useful here to set goals for individuals both to be involved in the change process and for the future once the change has happened as a

way of taking ownership of the future state. It is during this stage that any benefits for individuals can really start to be discussed in a constructive way. Attention should be paid to any new teams that are going to be formed and facilitating them in coming together to discuss the future and working together. It can also be helpful in this phase to think about some quick wins that are achievable, and to ensure wide communication of these once they start to take place.

- *Commitment and moving on* – where individuals may really start to embrace the change and think about how they can make it work for them. The challenges here can be about keeping up momentum, starting to really make the change happen and become embedded, ensuring that the whole organisation moves at a similar pace, and making sure that any unrealistic expectations of what the change might mean are managed. It can be helpful here to find ways for individual employees to test out the changes by supporting them in being creative and taking some risks in order for them to improve performance. It can also help to identify those employees who reach this stage earlier than others and to use them as advocates for the new way of doing things – having a colleague talking about the change positively can be much more powerful than a manager or HR practitioner doing so.

Although it can be very helpful to think about individual employees moving through this journey during a change process as a way of taking action to support them, you should always bear in mind that not everyone will react in the same way and that people will move at different speeds in their reactions and responses to change. Of course, if the change is viewed as positive by employees from the outset – although reaction may still be emotional – it is likely to be positive emotion rather than the more negative and potentially damaging emotions described above.

CASE STUDY 11.1

Two separate GP practices, both of which occupied old, inadequate accommodation, agreed to move to a new purpose-built building. One GP practice would occupy the ground floor of the new building and the other would occupy the first floor. Although they would continue to operate as separate practices, there would be a shared waiting and reception area on the ground floor. The change was necessary because the old accommodation for both practices did not meet accessibility requirements for people with disabilities and could not be easily adapted. One practice was considerably bigger than the other.

Even during the earliest stages of discussion with staff in the practices about the move, there was a lot of complaint, disagreement and anxiety about what the change would mean. This started to have an impact on staff morale, sickness levels and relationships at work. Discussions with staff in both practices highlighted a range of emotions and reactions to the proposed move, including:

- fear from staff in the smaller practice that this was a 'takeover' by the bigger practice
- worries about a new IT system that would be introduced as part of the move
- concern that a shared reception and waiting area would not work and would in effect mean the two practices becoming one
- concern that the new building would not be as close to patients' homes as the old buildings, making it more difficult for them to attend
- anger that what staff perceived as two very good practices were having to change at all.

In order to deal with these responses and help the change process move more smoothly, a number of actions were taken. Staff were given the chance to discuss these reactions both individually and collectively, along with opportunities for staff from the two different practices to meet and get to know each other.

Significant work took place to communicate the reasons for the change to staff and to seek and respond to feedback. A joint working group representing both practices was established to provide a vehicle for staff to be involved in building design.

Joint training sessions for staff from both practices on the new IT system were introduced. Acknowledging the feelings of the staff affected, keeping them informed and providing opportunities for staff to discuss their feelings and get to know each other meant that staff felt listened to and much more involved in the change than they had expected to be – that they had some influence over the outcome. All of this worked well to ensure a smooth change process with staff acknowledging the benefits of the move to them and their patients.

In our experience of change processes, whatever the final outcome of change, employees more usually start with a negative than positive reaction and view the change as something undesirable and to be resisted. This is partly because negative effects are often very real and more immediate and in some cases individuals will suffer serious loss. Conversely, positive effects are invariably some way into the future and therefore less real and are not guaranteed. There are usually other factors at work too. We now move on to look at resistance to change.

11.6.2 RESISTANCE TO CHANGE

One of the common reactions you may see to change – often during the second phase of the change curve – is resistance to the change. It is a very human characteristic to resist change, generally based on the organisational culture we work in. Change can lead to people losing their jobs, having their career pathways blocked and having increased pressure to perform, to reach targets or to work longer hours. It can almost be an automatic reflex to resist change. Resistance emerges when there is a threat to something the individual values. This threat may be real or perceived; it may arise from a genuine understanding of (but disagreement with) the change or from misunderstanding what the change is really about. The resistance may stem from disagreement with the proposed change based on intellectual reasons, personal values or more deep-seated psychological reasons. Thus there are a number of reasons why people will resist change:

- loss of control or authority – the less in control people feel, the less they will be inclined to co-operate in change
- change has been imposed
- lack of understanding about the change or its implications
- fundamentally disagreeing with the proposed change
- uncertainty about what the change means or how it will be achieved
- fear about losing something they value – a way of doing things, their job, benefits or status
- worry about being able to cope with the change and learn new ways of doing things
- 'change fatigue', where change has been occurring all too frequently
- lack of trust and confidence in the managers leading the change
- lack of trust arising from past failures where positive benefits may have been 'promised' but never materialised
- experience of change that brought adverse consequences in the past, or was perceived to have done
- having to move to a new team or get to know new colleagues.

Whatever the reasons for resistance, there can be a reasonably predictable pattern to how it emerges and affects performance – using the change curve depicted above can help you to think about this.

? **REFLECTIVE ACTIVITY 11.3**

Consider your own organisation and think about any change that is in the early planning stages. How might this impact on individual employees? What sorts of resistance do you think might occur, and why? Come up with three ideas for how you might overcome resistance. Discuss these with one of your learning sources and see how appropriate and effective these ideas might be in your organisation.

11.6.3 CHANGE AND THE PSYCHOLOGICAL CONTRACT

The concept of the psychological contract has already been mentioned in previous chapters. It concerns the mutual perceptions the two parties to the employment contract (employer and employee) have about their obligations to each other. It is important because the 'health' of the psychological contract can impact on company performance. By its very nature the psychological contract is unwritten and hard to pin down, so any organisational change that affects the perceptions of employers or employees can have a significant effect, but without necessarily being clear and transparent. Traditionally, the basis of the psychological contract was an offer of stability and job security from the employer in return for commitment and loyalty from the employee. Much change in organisations affects this stability and security – from the introduction of new technology to changing market conditions to restructuring and redundancy programmes – and thus impacts on the psychological contract.

Research and surveys have shown that while not all employee responses to change will be negative, some kinds of change are more likely to have a negative impact on employees' attitudes and this can impact on the success or not of a change programme. Whereas changes in job design, new technology and products and job responsibilities can be viewed positively by employees, changes in HR policies, changes that result in redundancy programmes and large amounts of change have been found to have a negative effect. Given that employees often have an emotional reaction to change and may seek to either passively or actively resist change, this shows how important it is for the type of change and likely impact on employees to be considered carefully and plans made to specifically manage this.

11.6.4 SURVIVOR SYNDROME

This is a term you may come across if you are involved in any change that results in downsizing of the workforce or redundancy. It refers to those employees who remain with an organisation once the change has happened – the 'survivors' – and is about the attitudes, feelings and perceptions they have about what has happened. Generally, in a downsizing or redundancy situation a lot of attention will necessarily and rightly be paid to the people who will be losing their jobs. Far less attention is ordinarily paid to those who remain. In the same way that being involved in change creates a range of emotions, so being a 'survivor' of change can also lead to feelings such as fear, anger, depression, guilt and lack of trust. The impact of this in the workplace can include:

- lower levels of employee morale
- increased work pressure and stress on the survivors

- survivors feeling 'cheated' if those leaving get generous severance packages
- perceptions of fewer career development opportunities
- negative impact on the psychological contract.

11.7 SUPPORTING EMPLOYEES THROUGH CHANGE

By considering the impact change can have on individual employees as outlined above, you will be able to see how important it is for organisations to support all those affected by organisational change. There are a number of ways in which this can be done, including ensuring that communication and consultation processes are effective, putting in place employee support schemes such as employee assistance programmes and outplacement, and having effective policies for managing change in a consistent way. We will now consider each of these in turn.

11.7.1 COMMUNICATION AND CONSULTATION

There is no one right way to communicate effectively with employees during change. The effectiveness of communication will depend on the type of information to be shared, on the type of change concerned, on the individual preferences of those involved about how they hear information, and on ensuring that opportunities for employee feedback and involvement allow everyone to have a voice. It is important to know exactly what the change is trying to achieve so that this can be communicated clearly as a starting point for getting employee buy-in. Make sure you know exactly how things are changing and why, who is losing what, what is changing and what is not. It is also important to think about methods of and channels for communication during change. We have all heard stories of employees being notified of change, including redundancies, by text or email – and have seen the negative consequences that can arise. We would always recommend making communication as personal as possible during change so that every employee feels that he or she matters. In unionised workplaces it is crucial to involve the trade unions in the communication and consultation processes. In some circumstances, such as redundancy, failure to consult a trade union can have legal implications (see Chapter 3). But there are positive benefits from such consultation and involvement, as shown in Table 11.3, because this can help to stop rumours getting out of control.

Table 11.3 Communicating with and involving employees during change

Activity	Benefits
Involve employees	<ul><li>encourages ownership of the change</li><li>ensures that they hear the official information, not just the rumours, and promotes openness and transparency</li><li>provides opportunities for two-way communication and dialogue and for employees to feel they have been heard</li><li>helps you to identify those in favour of change to use as advocates/champions for change</li><li>allows employees to influence and have input to the design of the new/changed processes</li></ul>
Involve trade unions	<ul><li>encourages ownership of the change</li><li>can help to stop rumours getting out of control</li><li>can help generate greater acceptance of the change from employees</li></ul>
Interview employees	<ul><li>helps you to understand employees' feelings about the change</li></ul>

Activity	Benefits
	• gives you an insight into employee ambitions/preferences for the future • provides a confidential environment for employees to discuss their anxieties • provides a measure of how effective your communication processes are
Use those who are both negative and positive about the change	• allows you to identify informal leaders – those who influence other employees • helps you to understand and respond to objections and concerns about the change • helps to reduce resistance to change
Over-communicate Anticipate questions Have answers where you can; be honest where you haven't	• more likely that messages will be heard • makes the changes more visible and real • helps you to deal with rumours and misinformation more rapidly • fosters trust and understanding
Vary the medium	• will be effective with more employees as people like to hear things in different ways • ensures greater thought is given to what and how to communicate • reinforces key messages
Consider timeliness, consistency and, as far as possible, simultaneous communication	• people get the right messages at the right time • rumour and speculation is less likely and there is therefore less danger of distortions going through the grapevine • avoids bad news being delivered at inappropriate times (for example redundancy notices issued on Christmas Eve) • allows support processes to be put in place as news is given • ensures that key messages are not lost as they cascade through an organisation
Stay positive	• will help develop a positive climate and culture while change happens • more likely others will stay positive too

Although there is no one correct way to communicate with and involve employees during change, the ideas outlined in Table 11.3 should help.

? REFLECTIVE ACTIVITY 11.4

For the purposes of this activity, consider a restructuring and downsizing change programme in an online retail business moving from three different offices ten miles apart to one new purpose-built office building. Think about the different methods of communicating with and involving employees in change listed below:

• team meetings
• individual interviews
• blogs and social media

- newsletters
- hotlines
- online discussion groups
- focus groups
- working groups
- employee surveys.

1   What do you think the benefits of each will be?

2   Can you think of any other methods of communicating that will work in this environment with this change programme?

CASE STUDY 11.2

A large unionised organisation in the service sector was closing one of its service divisions because of technological developments that would enable it to deliver the service in a new way. The new service would be established ten miles away from the existing service and would require 30 fewer employees in total. The organisation gave a lot of thought to the communication processes that would be appropriate for communicating the change to employees and involving them in planning the new service. The organisation planned the new service over a number of months, during which time they held a number of seminars and workshops to share information about the technological development with employees, about the likely changes it would mean in working practices, and to get employee input to developing a new way of working.

Once a final decision was made about implementing the change, a meeting was held with all employees, and their union representatives, in the service division affected to let them know that the change was now moving ahead. At this meeting the director responsible shared information with employees about what was happening and when, and talked about the process that would be followed to implement the change. An opportunity was provided at the end of the meeting for any questions, to which answers were forthcoming.

Despite the previous involvement of employees in developing the plans, there was still shock that the change was now really happening and that 30 employees would lose their jobs. Later that week, individual meetings were held with every employee in the division at which the trade union representative and the HR manager were present. These allowed employees to discuss their individual position, share any concerns and talk about their aspirations for the future and indicate whether they would be interested in the voluntary redundancy package on offer. Over the next few weeks during the formal redundancy consultation period, further team and individual meetings were held, newsletters were issued and an employee assistance and outplacement service was put in place to ensure that two-way communication channels were kept open. After the changes were implemented, both those employees who were made redundant and those staying in the organisation were asked for their views on the change process.

Regardless of how the employees felt about the change and their personal outcome, they all indicated that they thought the communication and support aspects of the change had been effective, and that this had helped them cope with the change more easily.

Consultation

In certain change situations – for example, redundancy programmes – there are legal requirements to consult with trade union representatives. Information on formal consultation requirements has already been provided in Chapter 3 and you are advised to refer back to this when considering change in organisations.

11.7.2 EMPLOYEE SUPPORT

Employee assistance programmes

One way of providing practical and emotional support for employees experiencing change is to introduce an employee assistance programme (EAP). Although designed to provide support for employees with any issues – at home or at work – they can be a particularly valuable tool during times of change. EAPs generally provide a confidential counselling service, delivered by qualified specialists, who can address a range of issues from advising on personal and emotional problems to providing legal and financial advice.

Organisations will generally buy EAPs from external expert providers and the services on offer are usually accessed online or by phone, but face-to-face sessions are often also provided if needed. For employees undergoing change – particularly where there is a risk to job security – they can provide an opportunity for employees to discuss their fears and anxieties in a safe and confidential way.

Outplacement

Outplacement services were first introduced for executives and senior managers facing redundancy situations, often in larger organisations. Now, outplacement is something that many more employees expect to be provided with. Outplacement typically provides practical support for people facing being/having been made redundant and can create structure for those faced with a very big change to their daily routine. The sorts of services offered include:

- help with CVs and applications
- job search support
- interview skills practice
- guidance on making decisions about the future
- career guidance and counselling
- a review of existing skills and capabilities.

Where a company is able to take a long-term view, they may provide support and training towards qualifications to better equip employees for the 'outside world'. As well as providing individual employees with support, outplacement also offers organisations the opportunity to manage their employer brand for the future. If those leaving the organisation have as positive an experience as possible and feel that they were supported and treated well by the organisation, it becomes easier to attract people in when the organisation changes or grows in the future. Providing outplacement services can also send a positive message to employees not facing redundancy that your organisation cares about people and seeks to support them in difficult situations, which will help with the impact of any survivor syndrome.

Training

Some large organisations, who anticipate a reduced workforce, give special attention to training. A form of forward-looking outplacement, such training can give employees the skills and qualifications to move easily to new employers. Qualifications, particularly, can be important in looking for a new employer.

Change policies

An increasing number of organisations, particularly large ones, have policies for managing and dealing with change. Having such a policy can provide useful guidance for managers leading change, can increase the degree of consistency seen and experienced by those affected, and can outline any formal consultation requirements.

? **REFLECTIVE ACTIVITY 11.5**

Find out if your organisation has a policy or some written guidance on managing change. If it does, see if the policy covers everything you would expect it to in the light of this chapter. If your organisation doesn't have a policy, consider drafting one or alternatively some guidelines for managers involved in managing change. Discuss what you have found/written with one of your learning sources.

11.8 THE ROLE OF HR PRACTITIONERS

HR practitioners must adopt a range of different roles in any change process. This can include being involved in both supporting the management of change and supporting the individuals affected by change. In unionised environments there will also be a key role in liaising and communicating with relevant trade union representatives. It is likely that you will carry out some or all of the following roles.

11.8.1 AN ADVISORY ROLE

Managers may look to you for advice on handling any of the people-related aspects of change – including dealing with individual reactions and responses to change. Where the change is likely to impact on job numbers, you will be called on to provide advice on issues such as redundancy and other legal aspects of change. As well as managers seeking your advice, you may well find that individuals affected by change also seek your advice – on issues such as redundancy payments and CV-writing and applying for new positions.

11.8.2 AN ADMINISTRATIVE ROLE

When a large-scale change is happening, it can increase the chances of success to ensure that the whole change is managed in a co-ordinated way. Your skills may be called on to develop project plans or roadmaps, to monitor and keep track of the change while it is happening or to produce progress reports. In any change process there is also a great deal of work involved in making sure the personal records of any staff affected by change are up to date so that if the change affects aspects such as job descriptions and contracts of employment it is easy to check what the change means on an individual basis.

11.8.3 A SUPPORTING ROLE

You may be called upon to work with individuals to support them in coping with the change – particularly around the behavioural and emotional aspects of what is happening. This can involve being part of any individual interviews and discussions that take place with those affected to discuss the personal impact on them and their future and offering counselling and coaching for individuals about their future direction. It may also involve you in setting up more formal schemes for employee support, such as outplacement and employee assistance programmes.

11.9 SUMMARY

This chapter has examined various aspects of change – why organisations need to change, the factors to be considered in managing change through to a successful outcome, the impact of change on individuals and their reactions and responses to it, and the various options available to you and your organisation in supporting individuals affected by change. It is clear that getting individuals to change – their behaviours, work practices, and so on – is key to success. In our experience the challenge of these people elements of change are probably the most difficult to deal with. The following quick checklist summarises key issues for you to remember:

- Give maximum warning of the change to allow people time to go through the emotional responses.
- Explain the reasons for change.
- Involve people in the planning and implementation.
- Communicate, communicate, communicate.
- Introduce change gradually if possible, with activities which will show quick results.
- Give appropriate consideration to training – offer people the chance to develop new, relevant skills.
- Sell the benefits – 'what's in it for them' matters more than the organisation.
- Take the present situation and personal circumstances into account.
- Always remember the impact on individuals – think of the change curve.
- Check on how individuals are coping and remember to support them.

You should by now be clear about some of the key aspects involved in managing change and supporting individuals through the change process. You will have developed an awareness of what a complex and difficult area of work change is, but also how it is a fact of life in most organisations these days. Even if you have not yet had any experience of managing or supporting change in your organisation, it is still highly likely that you have been affected by change. Think about your reactions and how you coped with change, and about what support you got and what support you would have liked. This personal experience of change will be invaluable to you as you begin to work more in this area of HR practice.

EXPLORE FURTHER

References and further reading

ACKERMAN, L. and ANDERSON, D. (2010) *The Change Leader's Roadmap: How to Navigate Your Organization's Transformation*. 2nd edition. London: John Wiley & Sons.

CAMERON, E. and GREEN, M. (2015) *Making Sense of Change Management: A Complete Guide to the Models, Tools and Techniques of Organisational Change*. London: Kogan Page.

CIPD (2005) *HR's Role in Organising: Shaping Change*. London: CIPD.

CIPD (2010) *Approaches to Change: Building Capability and Confidence*. London: CIPD.

CIPD (2014) *Research Report: Landing Transformational Change*. London: CIPD.

CIPD (2015) *Beyond the Organisation: Realising HR's vital role in the success of partnering arrangements*. London: CIPD.

DONKIN, R. (2004) *HR and Reorganisation: Managing the Challenge of Change*. London: CIPD.

HIATT, J. and CREASEY, T. (2013) *Change Management: The People Side of Change*. Prosci Learning Centre Publications.

HUGHES, M. (2010) *Managing Change: A Critical Perspective*. London: CIPD.

HUGHES, M. (2006) *Change Management*. London: CIPD.

KOTTER, J. (2012) *Leading Change*. Boston: Harvard Business Review Press.

KÜBLER-ROSS, E. (2008) *On Death and Dying*. London: Routledge.

LEWIN, K. (1951) *Field Theory in Social Science*. New York: Harper & Row.

NEWTON, R. (2007) *Managing Change Step by Step: All You Need to Build a Plan and Make It Happen*. Harlow: Prentice Hall.

SENGE, P. (2006) *The Fifth Discipline*. New York: Random House.

Websites

Chartered Institute of Personnel and Development: www.cipd.co.uk

People Management: www.peoplemanagement.co.uk

See also factsheets on the CIPD website: www.cipd.co.uk/hr-resources/factsheets:

- Change Management (2015)
- PESTLE Analysis (2013)
- Redundancy (2015)

REFLECTIVE ACTIVITIES FEEDBACK

Reflective Activity 11.2

The different groups of individuals likely to be affected include:

- the family in the family-owned business
- the owners of the other two businesses
- managers within all three businesses
- employees within all three businesses.

The range of factors that will affect the positions they take include:

- whether they are selling up or forming part of the new ownership team
- whether there will be any opportunities for career advancement for them
- where the new business will be located
- whether their job will be at risk of redundancy
- the culture and management style of the new merged business
- whether any working practices are changing.

CHAPTER 12

Personal Effectiveness

LEARNING OUTCOMES

After reading this chapter you will:

- understand the concept of self-development and the need to take some risks in seeking to improve your own personal effectiveness
- appreciate the main concepts behind a range of skill areas that underpin much of effective HR practice – that is, those under the broad headings of communication, negotiating, handling difficult conversations and assertiveness
- understand the importance of emotional intelligence and empathy in working with people
- be willing to identify your existing strengths and development needs in these areas and plan to address the latter by proactively seeking out appropriate learning experiences
- be able to select and take appropriate actions to develop your skills
- plan to employ measures to improve your knowledge and skills continually, in compliance with the CIPD's continuing professional development requirements.

12.1 INTRODUCTION

The majority of the previous chapters contain sections on the role of the HR practitioner in, for example, recruitment and selection and in handling disciplinary matters or grievances. You may have been daunted by the multiplicity of roles performed by HR practitioners. This is not the end of the story, though, because in order to perform these roles, effective HR practitioners have to develop some broad skills that have wide-ranging applications and consider their behaviours in key areas of work – that is, both the 'what' and 'how' of what you do. One prime example is interviewing skills: we have seen that HR practitioners have to possess well-developed interviewing skills for a variety of purposes such as selection, discipline- and grievance-handling, appraisals, as well as a whole host of less formal situations.

Interviewing skills have been dealt with in the earlier chapters. In this one we shall be concentrating on the following broad skills areas:

- communication – report-writing, making presentations and making a business case for introducing change
- negotiating, influencing and persuading – in formal and informal situations
- handling difficult and sensitive conversations – in handling redundancies, early retirements, sickness absence and personal problems
- assertiveness – in work-related and personal situations.

This is not intended to be an exhaustive list, because we are sure that you can think of other useful skills that you utilise on a regular basis in your jobs as HR practitioners.

While there is some overlap between the generic skills needed and the behaviours (for example, around influence), other behaviours (as captured in the CIPD's HR Profession Map – see Figure 12.1) underpin how these generic skills might be used.

One example here would be the behaviour of 'curiosity', with an effective practitioner adding value to their organisation by bringing open-mindedness, inquisitiveness and a future focus to all that they do – be that making a business case, working to resolve some conflict or dealing with a sickness absence case.

Another example would be the behaviour of 'courage to challenge'. This is about having the courage to speak up and challenge the decisions, approach or behaviour of others when you have concerns. For example, what would you do if you were interviewing with a senior manager in your organisation and he or she said (as happened to one of the authors not too long ago), 'I know all about equal opportunities but I'm not appointing a young woman as I've had far too many people go off on maternity leave in the last couple of years'?

Although we will touch on these behaviours, the focus in this chapter will be on generic skills. Further information is available on the CIPD website, the address for which is given in the 'References and Further Reading' section at the end of this chapter.

The contents of this chapter are not intended to provide you with comprehensive reading in these areas. We do hope, however, that you will find this introductory guide a useful starting point on the road to personal effectiveness in your role as an HR practitioner, and in life in general. The important topics of self-development and continuing professional development (CPD) are also covered in this chapter.

Undoubtedly, you will have already acquired some of the skills listed above owing to your past experiences (both at work and outside work) and innate abilities. Others you will need to work hard at developing by gaining as broad a range of experience as possible.

Note that we are not suggesting that you will ever reach the stage when your skills are honed to such a degree that everything runs smoothly. Life is not like that and, in any event, life-long learning is a valuable approach that we would all be wise to adopt no matter how experienced we are. In the context of your working life, the organisational environment is in a constant state of change (and, if you think about it, without some changes occurring, life would be rather dull). Further, you may find some situations more difficult than others and feel that you will never develop the full range of skills necessary. For instance, your job might entail notifying workers whose jobs have been made redundant, dealing with members of staff who appear to doubt your credibility and authority, or visiting the spouses of employees who have died in service to discuss pension details. The first time that you are confronted with these circumstances you may feel very inadequate. You will, however, through experience, learn how to effect tasks such as these in a sensitive and professional manner.

Readers of this book who are or wish to become HR professionals will be aware (or should make themselves aware) of the CIPD Profession Map mentioned earlier in relation to behaviours. The Map provides a comprehensive view of the HR role at every level and specialism within the profession. It provides a detailed overview of what HR people do and it looks at the different areas of professional competence required and the behaviours necessary to be an effective practitioner. It also creates a clear and flexible framework for career progression, recognising both that HR roles and career progression vary. If you have not already done so, you would be well advised to look at the Map on the CIPD website and consider how it relates to your role as an HR professional. Further brief information on the Map is given later in this chapter.

12.2 WHY IS PERSONAL EFFECTIVENESS IMPORTANT?

We saw in Chapter 6 that 'effectiveness' means 'doing the right things' (whereas 'efficiency' means 'doing things right'). In the organisational context it has long been recognised that choosing 'the right things to do' at the individual level means performing those activities or attaining those targets that are in line with business or organisational goals. Thus as HR practitioners you should seek to determine which activities are the 'right' ones and then acquire the requisite knowledge and skills to perform them to a level that ensures the optimum result. Success then breeds success: a positive result will enhance your status and your credibility in the eyes of your co-workers. That is personal effectiveness.

If you are a member of the CIPD, you will find it useful to consult the CIPD Code of Professional Conduct. The Code defines the standards expected of members, in relation to professional competence and behaviour, ethical standards and integrity, stewardship and, as representatives of the profession, to ensure the maintenance of good practice within the profession. HR practitioners have a dual role in acquiring the knowledge and skills necessary to perform their tasks and activities effectively at work and to meet the exacting standards of professional behaviour laid down by their profession. We will now look at the skills areas listed above in the introduction and their importance to you.

12.3 COMMUNICATION

This is a vast subject, so here we shall be concentrating on two main topic areas: one in the field of written communications (that is, report-writing) and the other (a classic example) in the field of oral communications (that is, making presentations). These activities are both important and may often occur together, especially when, as an HR practitioner, you are engaged in project work. In fact, we should rarely rely on written reports alone if we wish to influence management decisions – the written word may be powerful, but oral communications are usually much more effective in, say, persuading others to agree to a particular course of action.

The value of good written reports is that they often gain you access to more senior managers in the organisation and hence provide the initial route to influencing them. Writing a report also forces you to think through your ideas in a logical and structured fashion, which is invaluable if you then get the opportunity to promote your ideas in a formal presentation.

Let's take an example. You are involved in issuing an attitude survey to all staff prior to your organisation's being involved in a friendly merger with a former competitor. The aim is to gauge the feelings of staff about the merger with a view to gradually bringing about a culture change that ensures as smooth a transition as possible. You present your analysis of the attitude survey results, other research evidence and your proposals for the future in a written report. Regardless of how well written and presented the report is, it is unlikely to 'sell' itself (after all, you would be dependent on senior managers' reading it thoroughly, which not all managers have the time, or inclination, to do). It would therefore be advantageous for you to make an oral presentation. This would afford you the opportunity personally to 'sell' your ideas and influence decisions, through dialogue, and will have more impact than the written report on its own. A presentation also lends itself to two-way communication, especially if you incorporate a question-and-answer session to address concerns. Brief guidelines on successful report-writing and making presentations are provided below.

12.3.1 REPORT-WRITING

Reports are written for a variety of reasons. Often, they are based on research into a particular subject and are intended to convey information and ideas and get buy-in from others. Reports may lead to action because they help managers to take decisions. There are no rigid rules governing the art of report-writing, but there are well-accepted guidelines, summarised below.

Terms of reference

Before you commence any analysis, you must be very clear about your terms of reference:

- What is the subject matter of your report (for example, sickness absenteeism in Company XYZ)?
- Why is the report necessary (that is, what is its purpose – for example, to get buy-in to a project to decrease the level of sickness absence)?
- Who will read the report, what prior knowledge do they have and what additional information do they need in order to make decisions (for example, consider the difference between writing for XYZ's senior management team and writing for a college tutor)?

Plan your report

It helps to plan your report before you start writing it so that you can be clear it will include everything it needs to and will address the target audience appropriately. Things you will want to consider include:

- how long the report should be
- the key messages
- how you will gather and collate information for the report
- what style you are going to use for the report.

Layout

Informed opinion is generally in agreement on the following sequence:

1 Title page

2 Summary (abstract or synopsis)

3 Acknowledgements

4 Contents page

5 Introduction

6 Main body of text

7 Conclusions

8 Options

9 Recommendations, including a costed implementation plan and a cost–benefit analysis

10 Appendices

11 References and bibliography

(Note: Not all these features need to appear in every report. You should select such sections as are appropriate for the length and complexity of your material and the style requirements of your organisation.)

Checklists

Two checklists are provided in the Appendix at the end of this chapter to give further assistance on the process up to and including the writing up of your report. Like most things, practice makes perfect!

? REFLECTIVE ACTIVITY 12.1

Approach your manager or one of your colleagues and ask for help in choosing an HR issue that is topical within your organisation but that has not yet been tackled. Carry out some research by studying information available internally (for example, statistical data, minutes of meetings) and externally (for example, legislation and journal articles). Write a short report to your manager or colleague and other appropriate members of management. In your report, examine the issue and put forward proposals on how the organisation could respond. Follow the guidelines provided in this chapter on effective report-writing.

12.3.2 MAKING PRESENTATIONS

However experienced you are, it is usual to be nervous at the thought of standing up in front of a group of people to make a formal presentation. There are two main ways of attempting to control your nerves:

- Never do it.
- Take a risk and have a go!

If you take the former route, you will never know how well you could have done and it might impede your career as managers and professionals are increasingly expected to be able to make effective presentations. Indeed, many recruitment processes require candidates to make a presentation as part of the selection process, so becoming more confident in this area may well help you with future job applications. If you follow the latter route, you will find that your nervousness will create adrenaline that will help you to perform and that with good preparation, the use of relaxation techniques and more experience, you will find the fear diminishes. Never expect to become completely laid-back at the thought of making a presentation: even very experienced presenters may find the prospect of presenting to an unknown audience a daunting one, but their experience helps them to keep their fears under control.

We recommend that you do take a risk and get into the habit of volunteering to make presentations. (Sometimes you will be nominated anyway by well-meaning bosses or colleagues.) Inevitably, you will improve your presentational skills in both formal and informal situations. For instance, you will become more adept at succinctly expressing your point of view in a meeting, even at short notice. You will also increase your profile within the organisation.

We shall now look in more detail at the two stages to making presentations: planning and preparation; and delivery.

Planning and preparation

1 **The approach**
  You must establish answers to the following questions:

  - Who? – the audience
  - Why? – the purpose
  - When? – the time
  - Where? – the place
  - What? – the subject
  - How? – the means

2   **The subject matter**

There are four stages:

- Do your research.
- Arrange the information logically – for example, introduction, main theme, summary and conclusion.
- Prioritise and prune to suit your:
  - **Audience**
  - **Purpose**
  - **Time**

In a word, your presentation must be APT.

- Prepare appropriate concise notes and any visual aids/supporting material.

If you use PowerPoint then do so sparingly with a minimum of slides and short bullet points. Make lots of notes around the items on a printed copy of your draft PowerPoint presentation, so you can embellish those items in your presentation and bring the talk alive.

3   **Plan delivery**

This will help you to overcome your nervousness.

- Be thoroughly prepared; carry out at least one full dress rehearsal. Imagine your audience in front of you.
- Notes are valuable, but speaking your presentation out loud during your rehearsal can be helpful too. You may find different ways of expressing the same thing then, when you actually present, you have options.
- Make sure you know how to operate any equipment you might be using – for example, laptop and projector.
- Make sure you are familiar with PowerPoint if you intend to use it.
- If possible, get feedback on your rehearsal.
- If you know that you tend to get a dry mouth, arrange to have water available.
- If you know that you get a blotchy neck, wear appropriate clothing.
- If you know that your hands tend to shake, don't hold your papers, but place them on a table in front of you.
- Adapt the content of your presentation as necessary to ensure that it will be APT.
- Practise deep breathing.
- If you can, immediately before the presentation, practice a relaxation technique such as meditation, mindfulness (see References and Further Reading at the end of this chapter) or a confidence-builder audio.

Delivery

You will have heard the maxim:

- Tell them what you are going to say. *Introduction*
- Say it. *Main theme*
- Then tell them what you have said. *Conclusion*

Depending on the length of your talk (and it is important to stick to the time allotted, including time for questions and answers), you will be able successfully to present only a limited number of key points. Pick these points carefully and deliver them effectively by:

- being enthusiastic about your subject
- being yourself, with your own style
- speaking naturally, with only minimal reference to notes
- monitoring reactions – that is, watch out for body language to gauge interest and understanding
- asking questions to keep the audience interested and on their toes.

> **? REFLECTIVE ACTIVITY 12.2**
>
> Volunteer to make a presentation to an outside body (for example, a local school or college) on, say, the work of an HR practitioner or your organisation as an attractive employer. Follow the guidelines provided in this chapter.

12.3.3 MAKING A BUSINESS CASE

It is likely that when writing reports or making presentations you are seeking to influence managers to agree to some sort of change – and your role is to make the case for this change. In the section that follows we look at the need for HR practitioners to develop the skills of negotiating, influencing and persuading. These skills are obviously critical to success if you wish to be proactive in seeking improvements or responding to the need for change.

Here we are concentrating on those factors you should consider if you wish to strengthen your business case. There is no exact science in determining which the most appropriate ones are because this will depend on the organisational culture. Your learning sources may be able to help you to select wisely from the suggested list below:

- Legislation – is the proposed change necessary to comply with existing or forthcoming legislative requirements?
- Good practice – is there a case for suggesting that the organisation goes beyond minimum legislative compliance and adopts good practices, perhaps in response to competitive pressures?
- Risk – what are the risks associated with not making the change; for example, employment tribunal claims, loss of key individuals, theft of commercial knowledge, workplace conflict, safety issues, and so on?
- Employee engagement – can you demonstrate the benefits that would result from your proposals in terms of increased attraction, retention and motivation?
- Productivity, profitability and growth – are there strong arguments to suggest that successful implementation of your plans will bring about discernible improvements in company performance? Will your proposals have a positive effect on the image or reputation of the organisation as viewed by clients, service users, potential employees, key stakeholders or the public at large?
- Customer care – can you show that the quality of customer service will improve if your proposals are adopted?

As you are no doubt aware, decision-makers are usually less interested in views and beliefs and more interested in facts. To convince them, you invariably require evidence. You first need to make it clear where your arguments are backed up by research evidence – for example, workforce profiles or employee attitude survey results.

Second, managers will not be swayed by vague promises of future benefits, so you will need to translate your proposals into credible and realisable financial benefits. Very few business decisions are taken without being backed by a clear financial case. Below are a few hints to help you to identify the relevant cost–benefit information:

- Use plausible estimates – familiarise yourself with some typical costs, such as average salaries for different grades of staff. Then take account of the fact that people are employed for more than their salary cost because in addition to direct employment costs there are indirect ones such as pension contributions, office space and the cost of providing employee benefits.
- Remember opportunity cost – when they are not engaged in normal day-to-day activities, employees will not be contributing to organisational performance in the usual

way, so there is an opportunity cost to, say, being on a training course or being absent through sickness (for example, lost sales, lower production).

● Distinguish between one-off and ongoing costs and benefits – for example, absence management policies and training may cost several thousands of pounds to prepare and implement, but this is a one-off cost, whereas the resultant benefits of reduced absenteeism should continue year after year. Further major investment is unlikely to be necessary although there will be some annual 'maintenance' costs attached to managing absence.

We hope that you find the above guidelines useful in seeking to improve your communication skills and in making a business case, both verbally and in writing. We now consider the associated skills of negotiating, influencing and persuading.

12.4 NEGOTIATING, INFLUENCING AND PERSUADING

As an HR practitioner, you are likely to find yourself in situations, formal and informal, that require you to use negotiating skills in order to reach an agreement. Further, you will find it difficult to promote your ideas, affect decisions and 'sell' changes without well-developed influencing skills. Both of these need to be backed up by powerful persuasive techniques (see 12.6 'Assertiveness').

Negotiation, in the simplest terms, is a process aimed at reaching agreement. It can be a one-off discussion between two parties or a time-consuming process that takes place over several days/weeks; for example, company pay negotiations with trade unions. The different parties to a negotiation will have their own aims, interests and positions which they will argue for, try and achieve and potentially compromise on. The process involves trying to find common ground and reach agreement in order to resolve a conflict or settle an issue that is of concern to all parties. It is important to remember that negotiation is not the end (the agreement) but the process of getting to agreement. Negotiations do not have to result in win-lose outcomes but may lead to win-win results. For example, if I have an orange that you and I both want, and we negotiate, there are various possible outcomes:

● I keep the orange. I win, you lose.
● You get the orange. You win, I lose.
● We cut the orange in half. I win, you win (compromise – where the outcome is acceptable but only partially satisfies each party's concerns).
● We divide the orange so that I keep the peel for baking a cake, and you get the fruit to decorate a drink. I win, you win (collaboration – where the outcome completely satisfies each party's concerns).

There will also be times when, as an HR practitioner, you need to influence (that is, have an impact or effect on others' thinking, actions or behaviour and to gain commitment) and persuade (win someone over or induce them to take a particular course of action or embrace a particular point of view). It is likely that you will frequently be in situations, ranging from formal meetings to chance corridor discussions with other parties, when you will need to use influence and persuasion to reach an agreed outcome. For instance, we mentioned in Chapter 8 that sometimes there is no satisfactory resolution to a grievance.

In such cases you will need to persuade the employee(s) concerned to accept that there is no point in continuing to pursue the grievance to the next stage, because the answer there will be the same. A range of factors will always be at play in any influencing situation, and it is helpful to be aware of these and any impact they may be having on how you are approaching the situation. Such factors include the respective roles you and the other party hold, the power relationship between you, any previous history between you, your respective access to relevant information, your personal styles, what you are both expecting in terms of outcomes, and issues such as race, gender, age, etc can also play a part. In any situation where you have to influence others, you should assess what the particular factors at play are and what impact they may be having on you and the other party.

Once you have carried out this analysis, you can use some of these factors to your advantage and resist the temptation to be adversely influenced by those that favour the other party – or you may positively take action to counter them. Let's now consider Case Study 12.1 in order to demonstrate this last point.

CASE STUDY 12.1

We considered above a situation in which you might wish to influence the outcome of a management decision under discussion at a meeting. This case study concerns a meeting at which the topic for discussion was the reduction of car parking spaces due to the erection of a Portakabin for contract workers. The car park was used by technical and office workers during the day and at night by shop-floor workers and a small number of technical staff who worked nights on a rotational basis.

The administrator for the technical department was due to attend a staff consultative committee meeting and saw that this item was on the agenda circulated. The topic had been the subject of considerable discussion within the department and the administrator was concerned at the effect that it would have. There was already pressure for spaces at night because the shift for the technical staff commenced after that of the shop-floor workers. He carried out an informal analysis which showed that 90% of the technical staff brought their own cars to work and all would have concerns for their safety and that of their cars if they had to park further away from the main building at night. The administrator decided on two possible solutions: to designate three spaces for the use of the technical staff at night (but he was not confident that this would be adhered to) or to relocate the Portakabin.

The administrator knew that the chairperson would normally introduce such a change as a *fait accompli*, and he realised that there were several influencing factors that acted in the chairperson's favour: he was senior in status and had more influence with important members of senior management. Further, he was known to be fairly dogmatic in outlook, but was also under a lot of work pressure at that time.

The administrator completed his research, considered alternatives and decided to put forward proposals, backed up by sound reasoning. He also decided to canvass support from one of the engineers present at the meeting (thereby discovering that the engineers' 'on call' system would provide them with similar problems).

He successfully gained some 'air time' and in making his business case the administrator highlighted those factors that would help to strengthen his arguments – for example the safety issues – as well as putting forward the cost benefits of the alternative proposals. The *pièce de résistance*, from the chairperson's point of view, is that he then offered – on the condition that the committee accepted his proposal – to talk to the chief engineer and health and safety officer to decide on an alternative location for the Portakabin.

The chairperson, faced with sound reasoning and someone prepared to take responsibility for the problem, was much more open to influence and changing his mind. The administrator, on the other hand, had not only resisted the urge to be daunted by the influencing factors that worked in favour of the chairperson, but had found a way of working around them!

Let's return to your powers of persuasion. Fowler (1998) provides an excellent self-assessment questionnaire to investigate this. Analyse the range of negotiating situations that you are currently involved in before responding honestly to the statements in Table 12.1. Think of situations that are formal and informal, and that take place inside and outside the workplace.

Table 12.1 Assess your powers of persuasion

Rarely Always 1 2 3 4 5	Rate yourself on a scale of 1 to 5
1 I adopt a positive and collaborative style.	
2 I am successful in avoiding confrontation.	
3 I assess the other person's viewpoint.	
4 I adapt my position to reflect the other person's viewpoint.	
5 I encourage a dialogue and do not set out all my case immediately.	
6 I do not interrupt the other person when they make statements I disagree with.	
7 I am a very attentive listener.	
8 I use questions, not statements, to probe or challenge the other person's case.	
9 If I need time for thought, or for emotions to cool, I seek an adjournment.	
10 I first introduce proposals for compromise or concession on a no commitment basis.	
11 I link my proposed concessions to moves by the other person.	
12 I emphasise the benefits to the other person of proposed compromise.	
13 I use summaries to ensure mutual understanding and move the discussion on.	
14 I take the initiative in bringing the discussion to a constructive close.	
15 I ensure that any agreement includes details of how it will be implemented.	
16 I ensure that any agreement is mutually understood and is not ambiguous.	
17 I observe body language for clues about attitudes and intentions.	

Obviously, you are aiming to develop your powers of persuasion so that you will eventually be able to award yourself a rating of 5 on each criterion in Table 12.1. To be realistic, this may never happen, but in the meantime the results will show which areas you should start working on.

A very common approach to considering and describing influencing style is the push–pull model. Managers and leaders are increasingly recognising that simply telling people what to do does not work, is unsustainable and many people at work, including HR practitioners, often have to influence without line authority, which requires a more sophisticated approach. Influencing is often an ongoing process rather than a one-off intervention and it is helpful to understand different styles and approaches – both your own and that of the person or people you are trying to influence.

The rationale of the 'push' style of influencing is that people will be persuaded and influenced by convincing proposals and well-researched alternatives. This style can be directive and involves persuasive reasoning and logic. It often involves the influencer making proposals, giving information, using subject expertise. Conversely, the rationale of the 'pull' style is that people will be more readily influenced when their needs, motives and concerns are understood and attempts are made to include and build on these in the influencing process. This style is collaborative and often future-focused. Someone using this style of influencing will ask questions and seek information and understanding, testing understanding and building on the ideas of others. Both these styles have a place and will be effective in different situations; for instance, the push style can be effective when you are an expert or have greater knowledge and experience, where a rapid decision is needed, or where there is a 'best' answer. On the other hand, the pull style can be effective when there is no clear answer, where genuine commitment from others is needed, or where innovative thinking and ideas are needed. One important thing to remember is that influencing is rarely a one-off action and is more usually an ongoing process that requires persistence and patience and may well allow you to try out different styles.

We have now seen how interlinked are the three areas of negotiating, influencing and persuading. Another connected behavioural style is assertion, which is dealt with later in this chapter. Let us now turn to another important communication skill – handling difficult and sensitive conversations.

12.5 HANDLING DIFFICULT CONVERSATIONS

What do we mean by a 'difficult conversation'? Such conversations can take place in any context and with any individual, but by 'difficult' we mean conversations about subjects that have all or some of the following characteristics:

- a complex or sensitive subject matter
- different (and often strongly held) views and opinions
- a high-stakes outcome
- feelings and emotions run high.

The ability to handle difficult conversations is key for both line managers and HR practitioners and is useful in a number of different situations – managing performance, dealing with redundancy, managing sickness absence, dealing with grievances, and allegations of bullying and harassment, to mention just a few. Although difficult conversations can push managers and HR practitioners outside their comfort zone, they should not be avoided – this just allows the issue to fester and develop, potentially leading to an even more difficult conversation at a future point, or worse. One of the most important things in having difficult conversations is to provide both space and opportunity for the matter to be surfaced. Considering the tips and pointers in the box below will help.

12.5.1 TIPS AND POINTERS

Think about the appropriate time and place for the conversation: when might the other person be most receptive and where will provide the most appropriate environment?

Prepare well for the conversation; make sure you've got your facts right, reflect on what you know, check any relevant policies, plan for the conversation in terms of what you're going to say and how you're going to say it.

- Think about where you can get support from.
- Think about and try to anticipate the range of responses you might get – how will you deal with these?

- Use your skills in questioning and active listening.
- Be prepared to challenge in a neutral, non-judgmental manner.
- Have a quiet word at the first sign of a problem issue and 'nip it in the bud'. This kind of early intervention can work wonders in matters such as minor performance problems.
- Acknowledge the other person's feelings and point of view and allow exploration of these.
- Look out for and assess non-verbal communication – body language, tone of voice, and so on.
- Avoid being judgemental and focus on specifics.
- Try and be future-focused, looking for a resolution or a way forward.

After the conversation, if appropriate, keep in touch with the other person – particularly useful, for example, where you have spoken with someone about their management style or approach.

? REFLECTIVE ACTIVITY 12.3

Think about a time when you have had to have a difficult conversation (outside work, if you cannot think of an example at work). Consider the following questions:

1 What made it difficult or sensitive?

2 How did you prepare (if at all) for the conversation?

3 What went well?

4 What could have gone better?

5 What was the impact/outcome of the conversation?

Think about how you might address and handle the issue differently in future.

12.5.2 THE COUNSELLING APPROACH

Depending on the nature of the difficult conversation, it can be helpful to use a counselling approach, particularly where support, help and development are the aims of the conversation. In any situation where you are being called upon to have a difficult conversation or undertake counselling, you should always consider whether it is appropriate for you as an HR professional to do so, or whether the issue would be best dealt with by an employee's line manager, or indeed whether the issue is one on which the employee should really seek more expert support. This is often a judgement call and you will become more practised in making good decisions about this as you gain more experience.

What do we mean by 'counselling'? We will begin by stating what counselling is *not*:

- giving advice
- giving opinions
- sympathising
- giving practical help – for example, taking over the problem and solving it.

Counselling is not better than these helping devices, but it is different and more suited to certain situations. In fact, in one meeting you may need to use a range of helping devices. For instance, when discussing early retirement options with an employee, you will need to:

- counsel the employee to help him or her decide whether to retire early or not
- give practical help by providing the pensions calculations.

Counselling is about – in simple terms – helping people to help themselves. It can involve acting as a sounding board for employees to explore their situation, problems, thinking and feelings; providing a safe and confidential place for employees to talk about any difficult issues; helping employees to see things from a different perspective and helping them to work out their own solutions.

Thus a professional counsellor aims to assist clients in exploring their problems, considering the range of options available to them and deciding on their chosen course of action. Professional counsellors are generally independent third parties with no vested interest in the outcome of the process. As an HR practitioner this may not be the case, because it is often the actions of the organisation that you represent that have led to the need for counselling. For instance, a potential applicant for early retirement would perhaps not have considered this option if the organisation had not recently announced a major restructuring exercise that may greatly change his or her job role in the future. Counselling is a complex subject, as is evident from the number of professionally trained specialists in the field. As an HR practitioner you will increasingly find that managers and employees expect you to be the person responsible for dealing with those problems that require counselling as the helping style. You should always question whether this is appropriate in your role and ensure that a request for such intervention from a line manager is not motivated by them wanting to abdicate their own people management responsibilities. However, there will be occasions where it is right for you to undertake such tasks, and this will to some extent depend on usual practice in your organisation and the role(s) agreed for HR professionals.

We do not wish to suggest that after a little practice you would be competent in dealing with every possible situation requiring counselling skills in the workplace. As the saying goes, a little knowledge can be a dangerous thing. You should seek to develop your counselling skills so that you are able to help some employees in some situations, even if it is only in a very limited way. If you have a tendency to try to avoid dealing with employees who you know have particular problems, your employer may be seen as unapproachable and uncaring. You may even lose good employees because you did not take the appropriate action at the time.

One story worth relating is that of a young brother and sister who lost their father. Both went straight back to work on the day after the funeral, but each had rather different experiences.

On her return to work, the sister was invited into the office of the HR officer, who expressed his sympathy (he had previously sent a note signed by the young woman's colleagues together with flowers from the company). He reassured her that if she felt she could not cope with coming back to work so soon, she should just inform him and he would make the appropriate arrangements with her manager.

On the other hand, when the woman's brother returned to work, nothing was said by his supervisor at all, although he had known why the young man had been absent. In fact, a couple of days later, when he was feeling very disheartened, his supervisor said to him within earshot of other workers, 'It's about time you pulled yourself together.'

Can you guess which employee remained longer with the employer?

There are a number of commonly occurring situations that you may be expected to deal with personally. These may include problems between an employee and his or her manager, redundancy, early retirement, sickness absence, work-related problems and some personal problems. In fact, organisations often have in place formalised counselling procedures to deal with such situations. In such cases the counselling procedure replaces, or runs in parallel with, other procedures. (See the Acas publications 'Discipline and Grievances at Work' and 'Redundancy Handling' for further details.)

12.6 ASSERTIVENESS

Assertiveness is one of the most useful skills of all. Developing it will have an immediate impact on your working and non-working life. Assertiveness is clear, honest and direct communication that pays heed to our own needs and the needs of others. It is best described by comparing it with the two extremes of submissive and aggressive styles of behaviour – see Tables 12.2 and 12.3 (both adapted from Back and Back 1986).

Table 12.2 Behaviour styles

Assertive	Submissive	Aggressive
• Communicates impression of self-respect and respect for others. • Our wants, needs and rights are viewed as equal to those of others. • Achieves own objectives by influencing, listening and negotiating. Others are able to co-operate willingly. • Behaviour is active, direct and honest.	• Communicates a message of inferiority and results in lowered self-esteem. • Allows the wants, needs and rights of others to be more important than own. • Ignores own rights and needs in an attempt to satisfy the needs of other people. • Anger towards others is directed inwards.	• Communicates impression of superiority and disrespect. • Puts own wants, needs and rights above those of other people. • Achieves own objectives by not allowing others a choice. Violates the rights of others. • Behaviour is domineering, self-centred and self-enhancing.
I'm okay…You're okay.	**I'm not okay…You are.**	**I'm okay…You're not.**

Table 12.3 What are the differences?

Assertive	Submissive	Aggressive
Verbal		
• 'I' statements that make it clear you are speaking for yourself – for example, 'I think', 'I would like', 'I feel'. • Distinctions made between fact and opinion – for example, 'As I see it…', 'My opinion is…' • Statements or questions that acknowledge disagreement and seek to resolve it – for example, 'We have a disagreement on this, so how can we move it forward?'	• Few 'I' statements, and those often qualified – for example, 'It's only my idea but…' • Opinions qualified with such words as 'maybe', 'perhaps', 'I wonder', 'possibly'. • Statements that downplay a disagreement or pretend that it does not exist – for example, 'Well, having aired that one, I think it's best if we move on.'	• 'I' statements that are boastful or too numerous, and the use of the royal 'we' when it is really 'I' – for example, 'We don't want to do that.' • Opinions expressed as facts – for example, 'The scheme's crazy.' • Statements that inflame or keep disagreements going – for example, 'Anybody with an ounce of common sense can see that won't work!'
Voice		
• Tone – steady, firm, clear.	• Tone – apologetic, wobbly, dull, monotonous.	• Tone – harsh, sarcastic, blaming, challenging.

Assertive	Submissive	Aggressive
• Volume – not overloud or quiet; may be raised to get attention.	• Volume – quiet, dropping away at the end.	• Volume – overloud, rising at the end.
Body language • Gestures – open hand movements used with firm, measured pace to emphasise or demonstrate. Arms open or lightly crossed. • Posture – upright but relaxed, moving slightly forward. • Eyes – direct, relaxed gaze.	• Gestures – covering mouth with hand, tight and nervous hand movements – for example, fiddling with pen. • Posture – shoulders hunched, huddled over papers. • Eyes – averted.	• Gestures – dismissive hand movements. • Pointing with finger/pen, thumping table, 'steepling' (that is, fingertips pressed together as sign of superiority), arms crossed high (that is, unapproachable). • Posture – head in air, chin thrust out, leaning far back, hands behind head. • Eyes – glaring, hostile.

Once you are familiar with the differences between these three behavioural styles, you should note the following three essential skills of assertive behaviour:

1 Be specific and direct about what you want/how you feel.

2 Be prepared to repeat what you have said calmly and directly, even in the face of opposition.

3 Acknowledge the other person's view and perspective, but don't let that deflect you from what you want/feel.

Successful assertive behaviour is demonstrated in Case Study 12.2.

CASE STUDY 12.2

From personal experience we have found that the approach above can work very effectively and have recommended it to others. Recently, a colleague was finding that she had taken on more than she had realised when she agreed to do some tutoring on an open learning programme. She hadn't realised that some students would require additional support from her, either face-to-face or on the telephone or via email correspondence.

The tutor was paid by the hour for running workshops and was paid a set amount for marking assignments. There was no provision for student support outside these provisions. Initially, the tutor was happy to provide the support because she was committed to the programme and wished to give the students as much assistance as possible. Gradually, however, she became more and more resentful and thought about withdrawing from the programme, even though she enjoyed the work. Luckily, she took our advice before taking this step and talked to the programme manager. She decided what she wanted and explained the position, having kept a record of her recent contacts with students. The programme manager was sympathetic to her case.

They agreed that in future the tutor would ensure that she acted assertively in seeking to limit the tendency for some students to become overly dependent on her advice. However, where the

> additional support was warranted, the tutor could make a claim for any additional hours worked.
>
> Several months on the tutor has found that setting ground rules for student contact has reduced the additional demands made on her time, and the working relationship between the tutor and programme manager continues to be a happy one.

We can see in Table 12.3 that assertive behaviour involves lots of 'I' statements. It also involves the use of the word 'no', which can be a very difficult lesson for us to learn. If, for instance, a colleague asks you to help out with some salary calculations so that she can meet a deadline for a report on anticipated workforce costs, your first inclination is likely to be to agree. This is acceptable so long as:

- your own work does not suffer
- you know that your colleague will be glad to return the favour at a later date
- you do not feel that your colleague is taking advantage of your better nature (and is only in this predicament through her own fault).

However, if any of these preconditions is unlikely to be met, you should seriously consider saying no. Remember that by saying no you are refusing the request, not rejecting the person. You will find that if you say no assertively, the person concerned will not consider that you have let him or her down or hurt his or her feelings. It will instead be clear that you simply cannot help him or her to solve this particular problem. So, in appropriate circumstances, practise saying no clearly and firmly without excessive apology or excuses and directly without lying or letting the other person down.

As an HR practitioner you will be dealing with all sorts of people in a variety of emotional states – for example, upset, nervous, under pressure, angry, dogmatic, inconsiderate. There will be occasions when you feel that submissive or aggressive behaviour is more appropriate than assertive behaviour. An example of the former situation might be when you are not as interested in the outcome of a discussion as the other party and so allow their views to override your own. An example of the latter might be when you use aggression in a controlled way to indicate that you really have come to the end of the road in a negotiating situation. The choice of behavioural styles is always open to you. However, by practising assertive behaviour you are ensuring that you do consciously choose a particular style rather than rely on whichever behavioural style is your natural tendency.

12.7 EMOTIONAL INTELLIGENCE, EMPATHY AND RESILIENCE

These can be very important characteristics in an HR professional. We have seen throughout this book how factors such as emotion, feelings, motivation and a sense of justice and fairness can impact on and affect individuals' behaviour. Having an understanding of this, and how your own feelings, emotions and motivations might also be impacting, can make a real difference to how you work, how you are perceived and your credibility as a professional.

12.7.1 EMPATHY

Empathy can be defined as the ability to identify with and understand another person's feelings, situation and motives, to understand another person's situation from their perspective. I am sure you are all familiar with the concept of standing in someone else's shoes – this is empathy. Having empathy can help you start to understand and appreciate the way another person has behaved or the decisions they have made and can help you understand people's needs and concerns. So how might you actively develop and demonstrate empathy in your activities at work?

- Listen actively and without bias.
- Probe what you see/hear to get greater clarity.
- Identify and seek to clarify the 'private' thinking of others.
- Check out what you're thinking to make sure you've understood things properly.
- Communicate understanding of the other person's perspective – summarise what you've heard.
- Start to anticipate the concerns and needs of others.

Using these approaches actively and consciously can help you make sure that your perceptions of the other person's feelings and situation are correct. If you can demonstrate empathy at work, others will see that you are taking them and their situation seriously – a big step on the way to dealing with and resolving conflict, for instance. Using empathy helps to engage people and build trust and confidence, which is important in dealing with performance issues, personality clashes, problem absence and running negotiations, for example. In demonstrating empathy, use of particular phrases such as 'I can see you feel strongly about that' or 'I understand that you are worried by this' can really help – try it out next time you are in a situation where you think empathy will be useful.

12.7.2 EMOTIONAL INTELLIGENCE

Unlike empathy, which as we've seen is about recognising and seeking to understand the emotions and feelings of others, emotional intelligence is all about understanding your own emotional responses to things – recognising your emotions, understanding what they're telling you and realising how your emotions might be impacting on others. It can help you in knowing when and how to express emotion at work and when and how to control it. It is about the impact your emotional state has on you and others with whom you work and come into contact.

Five elements that make up emotional intelligence were identified by Daniel Goleman, an American psychologist (see Table 12.4).

Table 12.4 Elements of emotional intelligence

Element	Impact
Self-awareness	Helps you understand your emotions and not be ruled by them. Promotes confidence and trust in your own intuition. Likely to know your own strengths and development needs.
Self-regulation	Able to control your emotions and impulses. Unlikely to make careless or impulsive decisions. Likely to think before you act.
Motivation	High emotional intelligence is likely to result in high levels of motivation. Likely to defer immediate results for long-term success.
Empathy	Usually good at managing relationships, listening and relating to others. Avoid judging. Usually bring an open and honest approach.
Social skills	Helps with being a team player. Usually help others to develop and shine. Effective at building and maintaining relationships.

It can be difficult for many people to express emotion at work – you may have been discouraged from expressing and dealing with (particularly negative) emotions in childhood; your organisation's culture may not encourage or value understanding the impact of emotion at work; and you may feel expressing emotion will make you seem weak or needy – yet many difficult and sensitive situations at work cannot be appropriately dealt with unless emotion is acknowledged. Strong emotions will always have a way of 'leaking out' and manifesting in other ways.

Tips to improve your emotional intelligence

- Pay attention to how you react to others – do you rush to judge other people, for example?
- Do an honest self-evaluation – what are your development needs?
- Assess how you react to stressful situations – do you get upset or angry; do you blame others?
- Take responsibility for your actions – be honest and open with yourself and others.
- Think about how your actions will affect others – assess how they will feel.
- Talk to a trusted friend or colleague about the impact you have on others – particularly when you are tired, stressed or angry.

12.7.3 RESILIENCE

Whilst looking at the subject of emotion in the workplace it is worth also considering the issue of resilience – a characteristic that can serve people very well and help us to deal with stress and adversity. A useful way of thinking about resilience is to think of it as 'bouncebackability'; that is, the ability to cope with what life and work throw at you and to keep going. We're sure you'll all have heard the phrase 'what doesn't kill you makes you stronger' and this can also be a useful analogy for resilience. It is a key component of well-being, motivation and engagement, which are mentioned elsewhere in this book – important for you at a personal level as well as for your employees. Being resilient can help us cope with stress, adapt to change, persevere through difficulty and be more open to new opportunities and challenges. As well as coping, resilience helps us with letting go, learning and growing.

So what can we do as individuals to increase our personal resilience? Some people will be naturally more resilient than others, but research shows that resilience can be developed and built by everyone. Some of the things we can do to build our resilience include:

- building and nurturing relationships of support – with family, friends, in local communities and in workplaces
- knowing when and where to ask for help and not being afraid to do so
- engaging with, rather than ignoring, problems and reframing things to see the positive and the potential benefits rather than the negatives; recognising what is in your control and doing something about it rather than spending time on things outside your control
- not shying away from challenges, but rather approaching them as opportunities to learn
- recognising when things have gone well – for you and for others – and acknowledging that success
- being flexible, recognising that things can and do change, and trying to embrace that change rather than resisting it
- treating mistakes and failure as opportunities to learn rather than beating yourself (or others) up about them
- taking care of your physical and mental health.

Many of these approaches will require us to think differently; to train our minds to have different responses. There are a lot of resources available to support us with this; possible starting points would be to read Butler and Hope's (2007) *Managing Your Mind: The Mental Fitness Guide* and Covey's (2004) *The 7 Habits of Highly Effective People.* Alternatively, there are a number of websites listed in the 'References and Further Reading' section below that could be of interest.

This has only really scratched the surface of the subject of emotion at work and we encourage you to do some further reading around the subject. This is an area where HR practitioners can really make a difference and build insight in their organisations.

It would be worth, therefore, giving some attention to your own mental fitness. It will help you with many of the skills and behaviours highlighted in this chapter and, therefore, your professional life and career. Your personal life is likely to benefit too.

We come back now to look at the issue of behaviours included in the CIPD Profession Map.

12.8 BEHAVIOURS

As stated by the CIPD, 'the HR Profession Map captures what successful and effective HR people do and deliver across every aspect and specialism of the profession, and sets out the required activities, behaviours and knowledge.' The Map is shown in diagrammatic form in Figure 12.1.

Figure 12.1 CIPD Profession Map

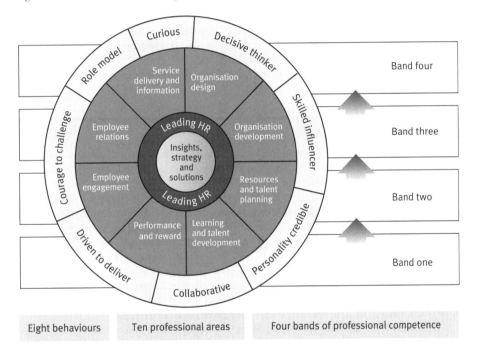

| Eight behaviours | Ten professional areas | Four bands of professional competence |

The eight behaviours included on the Map describe the behaviours an HR professional needs to carry out their activities effectively. Although specifically aimed at HR professionals, many, if not all, of the behaviours included are likely to be just as relevant and useful to any manager dealing with staff and staffing issues. Each behaviour is described at four levels of competence (recognising career progression and development of skills and experience over time) with contra-indications – indicating how the behaviours might manifest and be displayed in a negative way – also given. Readers who are also CIPD members can undertake a self-assessment of their capability against the activities, knowledge and behaviours on the CIPD website in the area on 'How CIPD's Profession Map is used... for you'. Also see the CIPD website for full information on the Map itself. The Map is refreshed and updated every couple of years and the most up-to-date version can always be found on the CIPD website.

We will now move on to look at self-development and continuous professional development.

12.9 SELF-DEVELOPMENT

Self-development is about taking personal responsibility for your own learning and development. You will make decisions (often with your manager or a mentor/coach) about where you have development needs and how you will meet these. This development may be about your performance in your current role, preparation for a new role, wider career development or the development of particular skills that you are keen to enhance. So in aiming to improve your personal effectiveness, you will inevitably have to get involved in some self-development exercises. These should include an initial analysis of your strengths and development needs in order to highlight areas that require further development (the CIPD Profession Map self-assessment tool could help here). A plan to concentrate on these development needs can then be put into effect through:

- self-assessment questionnaires
- role-playing 'difficult' situations in a safe environment and carrying out a review of performance, possibly using one or other of the last two points below
- setting up real experiences such as secondments, projects and work-shadowing
- project work requiring the production of written reports and verbal presentations
- observation and feedback from a trusted third party
- self-analysis of experiences through techniques ranging from diary entries to viewing of recordings of real or simulated situations.

In general terms, you will need to experiment with new behaviours and would be well advised to follow the simple stages of Kolb's learning cycle in order to gain maximum benefit from the learning experience (see Figure 12.2).

A general point to note is that attempting to improve skills will usually involve a change in behaviour and will often require you to take a risk (of failure). For instance, if you wish to influence the outcome of a particular management decision that is on the agenda of a meeting you are attending, you will not succeed by sitting quietly and taking no part in the discussions. You will, however, have an improved chance of success if, after carrying out some research, you are able to present your findings logically, put forward proposals that are backed up by sound reasoning and understand the viewpoints and positions of others. This could be done by way of a written report or an oral presentation. Regardless of the outcome, you should then seek honest feedback on your performance from people whose judgement you trust. (We saw earlier in the section on negotiating and influencing that, at a more advanced level, you may first decide to canvass support from other parties at the meeting to ensure that your ideas get a fair hearing.)

There are two further tips for self-development worthy of comment that will assist you in travelling down the road to enhanced personal effectiveness:

- Think about how you learn, and make use of this information to plan your learning in the future. Think about when you have learnt things in the past – at school or college, at work, whilst taking up a new hobby or interest, and so on – and how you have done this. What helps you to learn what needs to be learnt and then remember, replicate and develop further?
- Increase your personal profile inside and outside your employing organisation by being proactive. At work, 'walking the floor' helps you to get to know a large number of employees and, probably more importantly, to become known by them. Also, volunteering to take part in activities that extend your normal range of duties – such as taking notes at meetings, involvement in working parties, project work and making presentations – will have the same effect of increasing your profile. If you do not take up such opportunities, you may be respected for your work, but you will have less chance of really impressing 'onlookers'. Further, a 'backstage worker' approach may mean that someone else gets all the credit for your hard work – for example, the person whose name ends up on your report, or your boss when he or she presents your

proposals to a senior management meeting. Outside work you should set time aside for networking through, for example, getting involved in your local CIPD branch activities, and attending seminars, meetings and other events designed to facilitate networking. You never know: at the next event you could end up sitting alongside your future boss!

Figure 12.2 Kolb's learning cycle

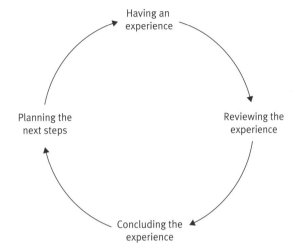

Before moving on to enlarge our understanding of the specific skills areas listed above, it is worth bringing to your attention *A Manager's Guide to Self-Development* by Pedler et al (2006). This excellent book covers a vast number of areas and provides several exercises and questionnaires aimed at an initial self-assessment. Please also take time to read *Personal Effectiveness* by Diana Winstanley (2009). This book covers many of the same topic areas as this chapter and provides a range of innovative activities and exercises to enable you to practise the skills and apply the knowledge to your own life.

12.10 CONTINUOUS PROFESSIONAL DEVELOPMENT

Two terms are commonly used when discussing personal effectiveness: 'continuous development' and 'continuing professional development' (CPD). The first term means learning from real experiences at work on a continuous basis; for example, not assuming that a two-day skills training programme will provide you with all you need to become fully competent in the skill concerned. Thus learning continues throughout our working lives through formal events such as training programmes, but also through our day-to-day experiences, planned and unplanned.

The second and connected term is often used by professional bodies such as the CIPD to reassure outside parties that members of the Institute are fully competent in today's working environment – that is, that they did not put all their books and journals away on qualifying, but take great pains to keep up to date with legislation and other developments in the field of HR management. CPD is therefore a requirement for Chartered Member status of the CIPD, and evidence of CPD will be required at the time of upgrading membership and on a random selection basis at any time.

Records should show a mix of learning activities, such as courses, seminars, conferences and self-directed or informal learning, including reading, networking, special projects or indeed anything that develops your professional abilities. Ideally, it will not all be directly work-focused and will include reference to activities that take place outside work. Most importantly, you must include a synopsis of how the learning has been used or will be used in future activities. This, for example, could be the writing of a policy or a specific change in the way in which you will do your job or approach a particular situation in the future.

Your development plan encourages you to commit to future learning by specifically focusing on areas where you wish to develop your skills and knowledge and/or achieve your goals.

The CIPD policy on CPD states a number of essential principles, including:

1   Development should be continuous in the sense that the professional should always be actively seeking improved performance.

2   Development should be owned and managed by the individual learner.

3   CPD is a personal matter and the effective learner knows best what he or she needs to learn. Development should begin from the individual's current learning state.

4   Learning objectives should be clear and wherever possible should serve organisational or client needs as well as individual goals.

5   Regular investment of time in learning should be seen as an essential part of professional life, not as an optional extra.

See the CIPD policy statement on the CIPD website for full details. The main message here is that the acquisition of skills is not a finite exercise. We can never be fully effective in all situations and are constantly thrown into new experiences that promote new learning.

Useful and comprehensive information on CPD for HR practitioners, including online records and development plans, can be found on the CIPD website at **www.cipd.co.uk/cpd/default.aspx**. This features further information on managing and recording your CPD, provides a template for use in recording CPD, gives examples and case studies, and outlines the benefits of CPD.

?   **REFLECTIVE ACTIVITY 12.4**

If you have not already done so, obtain the CIPD's information pack on CPD. Use it to set up a record of your CPD and a development plan.

Discuss your development plan with one or more of your learning sources in order to gain their support in putting some of your action plans into effect.

12.11 SUMMARY

In this chapter we have looked at a range of topics pertinent to your role as an HR practitioner. We have not tried to provide a comprehensive coverage, either in range or content, but an introductory guide to a number of skills areas. As your career progresses, you will find that you need to develop these skills in order to perform tasks and activities in as professional a manner as possible.

We chose the skills and techniques of report-writing and making presentations as prime examples of communication skills that help you to 'sell' your ideas and proposals. We also considered the connected skills of negotiating, influencing and persuading and their application in both formal and informal situations.

Next we examined the skills necessary to deal with the difficult conversations that you are likely to face throughout your career. If you cannot manage yourself, it may be difficult to convince others that you are worthy of promotion to a position in which you will also be managing others.

We proposed that assertive behaviour is appropriate in nearly every role played by the HR practitioner in the workplace (and in many other situations occurring outside it, too). It is an important skill that backs up the others necessary for you to achieve personal effectiveness. Of all the skills areas we have considered in this chapter, assertiveness is one you cannot afford to ignore. Assertive behaviour is enormously powerful and, used correctly, helps to build your credibility in the workplace. Try it at work and at home – you'll be amazed by the results.

We also briefly touched on the important issue of emotion at work – both yours and others' emotions and the importance of trying to recognise, understand and deal with these appropriately.

Finally, we briefly looked at the CIPD Profession Map in the context of personal effectiveness, signposted the wealth of resources on the CIPD website and considered self-development and the ongoing process of continuous professional development.

Completion of a number of appropriate activities, referred to throughout the chapter, will provide you with a useful starting point before you undertake some further reading into those skill areas that you decide are priorities for you. You should by now be aware of the importance of self-development and the need continually to keep up to date and seek further to improve your skills and knowledge in order to warrant the title 'HR professional'. You should aim continuously to develop yourself throughout your working life.

We wish you every success!

? REFLECTIVE ACTIVITY 12.5

Buy or download a book on one of the topics covered in this chapter – for example negotiating, handling difficult conversations, assertiveness or emotional intelligence. Apply the techniques that you learn about to any important situation that you are currently facing. Use any self-assessment exercises and questionnaires provided in the book to begin the process of increasing your self-awareness.

EXPLORE FURTHER

References and further reading

ACAS (2014) *Guide on Challenging Conversations and How to Manage Them.* Leicester: Acas.

ACAS (2014) *Advisory Booklet on Handling large scale redundancies.* Leicester: Acas.

ACAS (2015) *Discipline and Grievances at Work, The Acas Guide.* Leicester: Acas.

BACK, K. (2005) *Assertiveness at Work: A Practical Guide to Handling Awkward Situations.* Maidenhead: McGraw-Hill Professional.

BACK, K. and BACK, K. (1986) Assertiveness training for meetings. *Industrial and Commercial Training.* Vol 18, No 2. March/April. pp 26–30.

BORG, J. (2010) *Persuasion: The Art of Influencing People.* 3rd edition. Harlow: Prentice Hall.

BOWDEN, J. (2009) *Writing a Report: How to Prepare, Write and Present Really Effective Reports*. London: How To Books.

BRADBURY, A. (2006) *Successful Presentation Skills*. 3rd edition. London: Kogan Page.

BUTLER, G. and HOPE, T. (2007) *Managing Your Mind: The Mental Fitness Guide*. 2nd edition. New York: Oxford University Press.

CIPD
Profession Map. London: CIPD.

CIPD (2012) *Code of Professional Conduct*. London: CIPD.

CIPD (2012) *Fresh Thinking on CPD: The Value of What You Do*. London: CIPD.

CIPD (2014) *Learning Styles and the Psychology of Learning*. Factsheet. London: CIPD.

COVEY, S. (2004) *The 7 Habits of Highly Effective People*. New York: Free Press.

FOWLER, A. (1998) *Negotiating, Persuading and Influencing*. London: Institute of Personnel and Development.

GOLEMAN, D. (2011) *Leadership: the Power of Emotional Intelligence*. Northampton, MA: More Than Sound.

GREEN, H. and HOWE, A.P. (2011) *The Trusted Advisor Fieldbook: A Comprehensive Toolkit for Leading with Trust*. London: John Wiley & Sons.

GREENBERGER, D and PADESKY, C.A. (2015) *Mind over Mood*. New York: Guilford Press.

GRIMSLEY, A. (2010) *Vital Conversations: Making the Impossible Conversation Possible*. Princes Risborough, UK: Barnes Holland Publishing.

KABAT-ZINN, J. (2004) *Wherever you go, there you are: Mindfulness meditation for everyday life*. London: Piatkus Books Ltd.

MEGGINSON, D. and WHITAKER, V. (2007) *Continuing Professional Development*. 2nd edition. London: CIPD.

PEDLER, M., BURGOYNE, J. and BOYDELL, T. (2006) *A Manager's Guide to Self-development*. London: McGraw-Hill.

URY, W. (2007) *Getting Past No: Negotiating in Difficult Situations*. New York: Random House Publishing Group.

WINSTANLEY, D. (2009) *Personal Effectiveness*. London: CIPD.

Websites

- BBC Education: www.bbc.co.uk/education
- Chartered Institute of Personnel and Development: www.cipd.co.uk
- People Management: www.peoplemanagement.co.uk
- www.actionforhappiness.org
- www.theworkfoundation.com

APPENDIX TO CHAPTER 12

Terms of reference

- Are you clear about the purpose of your report? Have you specified its aim and objectives?
- Are you clear about who will read your report and their level of knowledge?

Collecting information

- Have you used a workable recording system?
- Have you collected information from as many sources as possible?

Organising information

- Is your report presented in clear sections?
- Are the sections logically sequenced and easy to follow?
- Do you provide signposts (subheadings, for example) for the reader?

Grammar and style

- Are your paragraphs short, clearly defined in material and easy to read?
- Have you chosen simple, unambiguous wording?
- Have you checked sentence construction, spelling and punctuation?
- Is the style appropriate to the content of the report, your organisation and the reader(s)?

Checking your work

- Have you checked structure and language?
- Have you asked for a third person's comments?
- Have you proofread your final draft?

Layout

- Have you presented your report in the accepted organisational format?
- Are the sections numbered and headings highlighted consistently?
- Are quotes, illustrations, appendices and cross-references all referred to correctly?

Final presentation

- Have you chosen the most suitable form of presentation and distribution?
- Have you allowed enough time for these final stages?

Title page

- Does the report have a short, self-explanatory title?
- Does the title page contain other appropriate identification data; for example, name of organisation, name of author, date of completion?

Summary

- Does it give the reader a framework showing the main features of each section?

- Does it include any conclusions reached?
- Is it self-contained and self-explanatory?

Acknowledgements

- Do they record a debt for help or use of facilities?

Contents page

- Are section/page numbers clear and accurate?

Introduction

- Does it refer to the terms of reference, limitations or constraints, scope, and the research method(s) you have adopted?
- Does it contain appropriate background information (depending on the needs of the reader(s))?

Body of the report

- Do you provide an analysis of the perceived problem and include the research findings?
- Does the discussion lead naturally on to the conclusions and recommendations of the report?

Conclusions

- Do you summarise your main research findings?
- Do you state clearly your interpretation of these results?
- Do they lead logically to the recommendations you are intending to make?

Options

- Have you considered the pros and cons of a number of alternatives before deciding on your final recommendations?
- Do they address the issues identified in your conclusions?

Recommendations

- Have you written clear recommendations that identify specific actions and assigned responsibility for those actions?
- Are they supported by good reasoning that is provided either here or earlier in your report?
- Have you costed them and made some assessment of the benefits?
- Have you included timescales?

Appendices

- Do they contain lengthy or technical information?
- Are they correctly referenced in the report?

References

- Has a consistent referencing system been used?
- Have you included full details: surname, initials, title of article/book/journal, date of publication, volume/issue/page numbers?

Bibliography

- Do you acknowledge other works used and those for useful further reading?

Index